Behold also
the ships
which though
they be so
great, and
are driven of
fierce winds, yet
are they turned
about with a very
Small Helm

From the Author

Think Jewish to Understand the Bible is about Christian theology from my heart to your heart.

In *Think Jewish* in conversational style, I tell of my personal interaction with the Lord in my study of his Word, and by so doing, I hope to inspire confidence in him and in his Word.

With acute awareness of my human limitations, and yet with strong conviction about my major premise—I present the case that Israel and the Jews are central to understanding the Bible.

This book is for those who want to gain a panoramic view of the biblical drama. My goal has been to present that which is complex in a clear and compelling way.

I submit my interpretation of prophecy from the premillennial and pretribulation view. In respect to redemption, I believe that scripture promises eternal salvation in Christ for those who belong to him.

THINK JEWISH

Other Books by the Author

Hidden Danger in the Classroom:
Disclosure based on ideas of W. R. Coulson

Marx or Jesus: Two men - two plans

China - The Lion and the Dragon

Dancing with the Times: What's a young adult to believe!

THINK JEWISH
to understand the Bible

Pearl Evans

Small Helm Press
San Diego

Small Helm Press
San Diego, California
smallhelm@yahoo.com

Library of Congress Cataloging in Publication Data

Evans, Pearl
    Think Jewish to understand the Bible:
    Why evangelicals love Israel and the Jewish people/ Pearl Evans
    p. cm.
    Includes bibliographical references, glossary

ISBN   978-0-938453-00-0
eISBN 978-0-938453-07-9

Library of Congress Control Number: 2019908858

This edition is printed on acid-free paper.
Printed in the United States of America.

U.S. $15 Canada $17

Small Helm Press—a business in San Diego—was established in Petaluma, CA in 1988.

Contents

Abbreviations of Bible book titles

OT

Genesis	Ge		Ecclesiastes	Ec
Exodus	Ex		Song of Songs	SS
Leviticus	Le		Isaiah	Is
Numbers	Nu		Jeremiah	Je
Deuteronomy	Dt		Lamentations	La
Joshua	Jsh		Ezekiel	Eze
Judges	Jg		Daniel	Da
Ruth	Ru		Hosea	Ho
1 Samuel	1Sa		Joel	Jl
2 Samuel	2Sa		Amos	Am
1 Kings	1Ki		Obadiah	Ob
2 Kings	2Ki		Jonah	Jon
1 Chronicles	1Ch		Micah	Mi
2 Chronicles	2Ch		Nahum	Na
Ezra	Ezr		Habakkuk	Hk
Nehemiah	Ne		Zephaniah	Zph
Esther	Es		Haggai	Hg
Job	Job		Zechariah	Zch
Psalms	Ps		Malachi	Ml
Proverbs	Pr			

NT

Matthew	Mt		1 Timothy	1Ti
Mark	Mk		2 Timothy	2Ti
Luke	Lk		Titus	Tit
John	Jn		Philemon	Phm
Acts	Ac		Hebrews	He
Romans	Ro		James	Ja
1 Corinthians	1Co		1 Peter	1Pe
2 Corinthians	2Co		2 Peter	2Pe
Galatians	Ga		1 John	1Jn
Ephesians	Eph		2 John	2Jn
Philippians	Php		3 John	3Jn
Colossians	Col		Jude	Jd
1 Thessalonians	1Th		Revelation	Re
2 Thessalonians	2Th			

References that are abbreviated in the notes:

New Testament = NT; Old Testament = OT; Strong's Exhaustive Concordance = Str;
Bible Knowledge Commentary = BKC; Jamieson, Fausset, Brown = JFB;
Expository Biblical Commentary = EBC; "cf" = Latin "confer" = English "compare."

Abbreviations of alphabetical Bible book titles: OT and NT

Acts	Ac	1 Kings	1Ki
Amos	Am	2 kings	2Ki
1 Chronicles	1Chr	Lamentations	La
2 Chronicles	2Chr	Leviticus	Le
Colossians	Col	Luke	Lk
1 Corinthians	1Co	Malachi	Ml
2 Corinthians	2Co	Mark	Mk
Daniel	Da	Matthew	Mt
Deuteronomy	Dt	Micah	Mi
Ecclesiastes	Ec	Nahum	Na
Ephesians	Eph	Nehemiah	Ne
Esther	Es	Numbers	Nu
Exodus	Ex	Obadiah	Ob
Ezekiel	Eze	1 Peter	1Pe
Ezra	Ezr	2 Peter	2Pe
Galatians	Ga	Philemon	Phm
Genesis	Ge	Philippians	Php
Habakkuk	Hk	Proverbs	Pr
Haggai	Hg	Psalms	Ps
Hebrews	He	Revelation	Re
Hosea	Ho	Romans	Ro
Isaiah	Is	Ruth	Ru
James	Ja	1 Samuel	1Sa
Jeremiah	Je	2 Samuel	2Sa
Job	Job	Song of Songs	SS
Joel	Joel	1 Thessalonians	1Th
1 John	1Jn	2 Thessalonians	2Th
2 John	2Jn	1 Timothy	1Ti
3 John	3Jn	2 Timothy	2Ti
Jonah	Jon	Titus	Tit
Joshua	Jsh	Zechariah	Zch
Jude	Jd	Zephaniah	Zph
Judges	Jg		

Abbreviations of Bible translations
NIV translation is used except when stated otherwise.

New International Version = NIV; King James Version = KJV; New King James Version = NKJV; Revised Standard Version = RSV; New English Translation = NET; English Standard Version = ESV; Holman Christian Standard Bible = HCSB; New Living Translation = NLT; Contemporary English Version = CEV; American Standard Version = ASV; Jewish Publication Society = JPS; New American Standard = NAS; Amplified Bible = Amplified; Common English Bible = CEB; Young's Literal Translation =YLT; Nestle Greek Interlinear NT = Nestle Gr Interlinear NT; NIV Hebrew-English OT= Interlinear NIV Tanakh. Also, Chapter = Ch, Page = p, Volume = Vol

For readers unfamiliar with scripture

Names of Paul, John the apostle, John the Baptist, Peter, Matthew, James, Judas, Mary, Martha, Lazarus, Nicodemus, and others are often presented in this book without identifying them as those who lived in New Testament times.

Names of Abraham, Moses, Isaiah, Jeremiah, Ezekiel, Joel, Zechariah, Malachi, Daniel, Jacob, Solomon, David and others are also presented without always referencing them as those who lived in Old Testament times.

Also, throughout this book, in order to make the most graceful, grammatical choices, the author uses male pronouns generically to refer to both male and female identities.

THINK JEWISH
to understand the Bible

A. Understanding the author
  1. Theology from my heart to your heart
      A. *A seemingly insurmountable barrier to overcome*
      B. *My three straightforward guidelines for Bible study*
      C. *My view of biblical authority challenged*
      D. *My enlightenment through miracles experienced*

1 Theology from my heart to your heart

One thing have I desired of the LORD, that will I seek after; that
I may dwell in the house of the LORD all the days of my life, to
behold the beauty of the LORD, and to inquire in his temple.
—Psalm 27.4 KJV

Some things take time… like wisdom. And since wisdom is being able to place a matter in the broadest possible context of life,
I've found the Bible to be the greatest source for that wisdom. I
learned this at a Bible study in our home, where each week a group
from our church met. There—while our family's four preschool-
ers slept upstairs—I met Carl Zimmerman, whose wisdom
impressed me, and I learned that the source of his wisdom came
from his knowledge of the Bible. Still in my twenties, I coveted
that wisdom, and so began my quest to understand the Bible.

Now in my early nineties,—with the hope that you will gain
confidence in God's Word—I'm passing along to you what has
been helpful to me.

Theology from my heart to your heart:

    A. *A seemingly insurmountable barrier to overcome*
    B. *My three straightforward guidelines for Bible study*
    C. *My view of biblical authority challenged*
    D. *My enlightenment through miracles experienced*

A. *A seemingly insurmountable barrier to overcome*

After a number of years in my quest to understand the Bible, I faced an insurmountable barrier—how to interpret biblical prophecy. The problem was not that I feared controversy, for
though the topic is controversial, Christians do not often break
fellowship over such differences. Nor was I put off by the intensity
of study the pursuit requires because prophecy is too fascinating
to dismiss on that ground. What has held me back is to see equally
intelligent, devout Christians differ so widely in their views about

biblical prophecy, and yet each expresses his view so vehemently.

With this impasse, for years I could not study prophecy whole-heartedly nor could I dismiss it either, for interpretation of proph-ecy determines a person's theology. However, one day I discov-ered how to find the path I could follow with confidence. This discovery came when I determined the point where schools of eschatology* diverge! That point stands at a fork on "the prophecy road" and therefore affects all interpretation that follows.

Here is the crucial issue that a Bible reader must face:
    What are you going to do with the Jews?
    What is their place in the future?

Roughly speaking, we could say that two broad views divide the study of prophecy. One view says the Bible is the story of the church and sees the church in our age as replacing Israel. A second view says God will always have a place in his heart for both Israel and the church as his two distinctive people groups. I chose the second view because after my study through the years, I could see that the Bible honors not only the church but also God's promises to Israel, with some already fulfilled and others pending. Once I became clear about the alternatives and eliminated the path that denies the rightful place of the Jews in scripture, I was free to go full steam ahead without fear or trepidation.

Taking this first step was a giant leap because prophecy is a major topic in scripture. As time passed, I began to "think Jewish" in all of the Bible, for in acknowledging the Jewish role in God's total plan—not just in prophecy—I realize God's dealings with Jews are central to his purposes, not peripheral. Consequently, I find enhanced meaning throughout the Bible.

B. My three straightforward guidelines for Bible study

For my first guideline, I present a prerequisite for Bible study —that you must recognize and accept how the Bible frames itself. Let's look at examples of what I mean by frame of reference. In Peter Rabbit, the frame of reference presents life from a perspec-tive that says rabbits wear clothes and talk to each other. A second

---
* This book has a glossary.   example, *The Diary of Anne Frank,* presents

life through the eyes of a Jewish teenager suffering under Naziism. In each of these books, the author sets up the frame of reference, which the reader has to accept; he cannot dictate the terms. When I explained this to an atheist—whom I met while promoting the Bible literature class that I taught in adult public education—he came to the realization that we do have to suspend disbelief, at least temporarily, in order to read the Bible, for it presents itself as of divine origin. Although he didn't come to my class, he recommended that I explain this to my students.

My second guideline for Bible study is that you read with the goal of learning whole-Bible context. This is so important because to read texts in isolation without knowing the context is to forge ahead like a horse with blinders on, with vision restricted and perception distorted. For me, I've found it helpful to read whole books of the Bible at one sitting and the whole Bible itself in a very short period of time and to keep repeating the process until I get the lay of the land. I realized that I had to know what the Bible says before I could figure out what it means. As theologian James W. Gray says, "Facts must come first and interpretation afterwards" (Gray 1906, 11). Following Gray's sequence, I compare scripture with scripture in the context of a passage, a chapter, a book of the Bible, or the whole Bible, for I, like many others, have learned that the Bible is its own best commentary.

My third guideline for Bible study is for the reader to choose an objective rather than a subjective approach. The way I seek objectivity is to note the plain and normal sense of a biblical text, except when indicated otherwise by literary clues and context or in special circumstances, such as when subjectively applying scripture to life situations. And regarding external commentary sources, be warned that though such sources are helpful, they must be weighed for reliability.

I believe an objective approach reveals the coherence and consistency of scripture and draws a person into study of and love for the biblical text itself. My observation is that those who abandon accepted literary principles tend to dismiss biblical authority and become preoccupied with authorities external to the Bible more than with the biblical text itself. Therefore, subjective interpretation tends to become dictated by shifting emotions, biases, agendas, and trends—but I'm not saying that any of us ever becomes totally free from such detractions. I've also seen that subjectivizing not only lacks consistency in method but is also less likely to be consensual with other subjective interpreters. Some interpreters seem to come to the Bible *only* as intellectual scholars, not as ones hungry to be fed and strengthened by God through his Word.

My perspective is that the Bible claims divine origin, that it presents a living story through human agency, that its message is cohesive, and that its parts fit together as a whole, all of which support the Bible's premise that God is the author. What's most important to me is that the God of the Bible is the God I love.

C. My view of biblical authority challenged

In a life span of so many years, I have seen trends away from biblical faith. In the late forties, a college professor occasionally substituted in my hometown pastor's absence. Though I was young, lacked knowledge, and had a lot of questions myself, I could tell that his sermons strayed somewhat from traditional theology, but no one seemed to care.

At first, society's sexual mores remained intact. My observation is that not until the late forties did *The Kinsey Report* on sex research begin to erode America's social compact by emphasizing how widespread immorality was at the time. Then, in the sixties and seventies, a gradual cultural shift seemed to morph into antipathy toward our Judeo-Christian culture and developed beyond that into affinity for Eastern religions, paganism, relativism, secular humanism, godless ideologies, and hybrid New Age ideas, all of which challenge God's relevance or even his existence.

In a cultural shift away from acknowledging the existence of objective truth, Professor Stanley Fish, a leading deconstructionist, is one of many who have held a worldview that seeks to displace the Judeo-Christian heritage of America. He says, "Since all principles are preferences [implying, no absolutes], they are nothing but masks for the will to power… Someone is always going to be restricted next, and it is your job to make sure that that someone is not you" (Jones 1997, 117). Such a view centers on power, and since a person can use this "will for power" for political gain, would not this "law of the jungle" destroy the foundations of civilization if totally implemented? Yes, says Peter Jones, noted theologian. "The new view of truth as power," he says, "tries to saw the legs off the throne of the universe" (Jones 1997, 118).

In the Christian world, a good example of a widespread view of biblical authority that contrasts with mine is that of Karen Armstrong, a popular author in a recent decade. In *The History of God*, she portrays a god whose nature changes, not a God who remains eternally the same. She writes, "We shall see that Yahweh [Jehovah] did not remain the cruel and violent god of the Exodus." She presents the Bible as a record of man's evolving viewpoint of god, not as God's revelation of himself to man. Her biblical view is humanity-centered, not God-centered, and—by virtue of her worldview—subjective. That's why she calls her book *The History of God* (Armstrong 1996), not *The God of History*. My belief is that the God of the Bible never changes but that human hearts open up to his revelation gradually as he sharpens human interpretation through the ages. He brings progress not through changes in himself—for he is eternal—but by the increased understanding of his people. God is eternal and unshakable. He is the Rock upon which Christians stand.

Today, even with threatening clouds overhead, I don't lose heart because through the years I've seen the gospel message shine more brightly the greater the darkness. I first observed this when our family moved from the Texas Bible belt to the Northwest.

Knowing that the gospel shines brightest in the darkness, I know I don't have to be defensive about God, his Word, or my beliefs because truth has a way of speaking for itself. An amusing incident illustrates this. When I taught Bible Literature in adult public education in Petaluma, California, the class's outspoken skeptic wanted to demonstrate that oral recollections by biblical writers could not possibly be accurately passed down to future generations. So, setting up the situation, she asked me this question: "Do you know what you were doing twenty years ago on today's date?" "Yes," I said. Taken aback, she asked, "What were you doing?" I said, "I was in the hospital giving birth to our second son on my birthday." Yes, truth does speak for itself.

D. My enlightenment through miracles experienced

Today I see that miracles together form one of the pillars upon which scripture stands, but in college, I used to wonder about miracles. I found it difficult to accept as real the parting of the Red Sea when Moses held forth his rod because I had never seen anything like that. But early in my marriage, skepticism about biblical miracles melted away when I saw how faith in the Lord Jesus so totally transformed my late husband George. To my surprise, one day while sitting at the kitchen table, he announced, "I'm going to be a preacher." That day a pastor, who was a customer at his dry-cleaning shop, had led him to the Lord. George said that he had known since childhood that he would have a calling into the ministry if he ever committed himself to the Lord. After that day of his conversion, he was still the personality I loved when I married him, but he was different in ways that made those two months of his transformation seem like heaven on earth. He carried a small New Testament around with him to read, had such good judgment, and was so thoughtful. And though shortly thereafter he discontinued his walk with the Lord, my life was profoundly changed, for after witnessing his marvelous conversion, I became open to what the Bible says about the miraculous.

I still had a lot to learn about the reality of the miraculous and of the reliability of Hebrew scripture. What has strengthened my confidence in both has been Jesus' authentication of both. In the New Testament, he accepts the most controversial of Hebrew writings about the miraculous. For example, he referred to the stories about Jonah in the big fish (Mt 12.39-41; Jonah 1-3) and Daniel in the lion's den (Mt 24.15). Jesus also commends Israelite characters like Abraham, Moses, Isaiah, and David. Over time, since I've witnessed the miraculous in my life and in the lives of others, God's miraculous acts in scripture have ceased to be a barrier to my wholehearted acceptance of biblical teachings. Since my husband's conversion—though I was already a Christian—my clarity in thinking about the Bible has gradually improved. The process could be compared to coming out of a twilight zone into ever-brighter sunlight as my confidence in the truth of God's Word has grown. That is why I have no problem with the passage about Jesus' bodily ascension into the clouds of heaven when he left this earth and the promise that he will return in the same way.

The book of Acts describes the experience of the disciples when Jesus ascended: "He was taken up before their very eyes, and a cloud hid him from their sight. They were looking intently up into the sky as he was going, when suddenly two men dressed in white stood beside them. 'Men of Galilee,' they said, 'why do you stand looking into the sky? This same Jesus, who has been taken from you into heaven, will come back in the same way you have seen him go into heaven.'" (Ac 1.9-11). These were angels talking about Jesus' return to earth to set up his messianic kingdom.

But before Jesus returns in the clouds to set up his kingdom, the church will be taken to heaven, along with those Christians who have have already died. Paul writes this about what is called "the rapture": "For the Lord himself will come down from heaven, with a loud command, with the voice of the archangel and with the trumpet call of God, and the dead in Christ will rise first. After that, we who are still alive and are left will be caught up together with them in the clouds to meet the Lord in the air. And so we will be with the Lord forever" (1Th 4.16,17).

I'm glad God communicates with us through his Word made alive by his Spirit! For when I read an easy-to-understand passage like the one above, I don't need to "spiritualize" it in order to dismiss its obvious meaning. In other words, just because scripture goes beyond the bounds of ordinary experience, I don't feel a need to distort what it says to make it fit into my sense of the natural realm. Therefore, when I look up at the clouds, I can think in unabashed wonderment and yearning: "Will today be the day?

2 Israel's past: How Jews shaped Western culture

No hypothesis... can change the fact that Israelite religion... is unique among the thought systems of the ancient world and that it is responsible for the unique values of the West.
—Thomas Cahill in *The Gifts of the Jews, 257*

Learning about the uniqueness of the Jewish people is not only fascinating. it is also important for understanding our American culture. For without an understanding of our culture, we are like fish unaware of the element in which we swim. In this book, we'll look at the influence of the Jews by beginning with this four chapter introductory unit about understanding Israel and the Jewish people—three chapters on the past, present, and future of Judaism and the other chapter on the Judaic legacy.

The Jewish heritage of Western culture
   A. Judaism, a totally new way of seeing and thinking
   B. Western culture inherited from the Jewish worldview
   C. American culture made stable by Jewish roots

A. Judaism, a totally new way of seeing and thinking

Western culture's roots began with one man and his family. In *The Gifts of the Jews*, Thomas Cahill says that when Abraham, father of the Jews, obeyed God's call to leave the city of Ur in the Chaldees, he became God's friend and entered a life with promise, and in so doing, he introduced a totally new way of thinking and feeling (Cahill 1999). The city he left was Ur, a city state within an alliance of city states called Sumer, which was located between the Tigris and Euphrates rivers in the southern part of Mesopotamia, which is now southern Iraq (Ac 7.1-4). (Ur in Sumer is on the east side of Figure 1, next page. See the arrow pointing to Ur.)

For many years, the existence of Abraham's birthplace, the city of Ur in Sumer, lacked historical verification, but archeologists finally found thousands of clay tablets there with cuneiform writ-

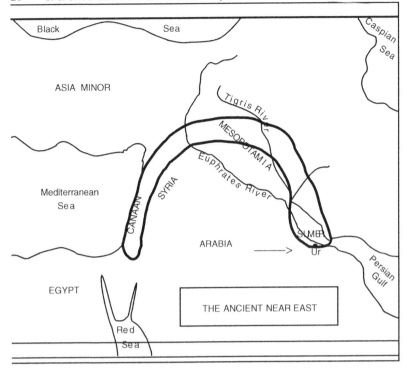

Sketch of the Fertile Crescent in the ancient near East
Figure 1: A Sketch

In the city of Ur[*] in Sumer of southeastern Mesopotamia, God called Abraham to be the Father of the Jews. Sumer, also called Chaldea, is now believed to be the earliest known civilization. Abraham probably left there at about the end of the third millennium B.C. to go to Canaan, which later became Israel. The path of his route to the land that God promised him is called the fertile crescent because of its shape like a crescent moon.

Although the land of the crescent was fertile, it was bordered by deserts and mountains unfavorable to human life and fit only for hardy nomads. Therefore, periodically, the surrounding tribal survivalists invaded southern Mesopotamia. In time, the civilization of Sumer had to give way to the Assyrian and Babylonian civilizations, and today that area is part of Iraq. On the other hand, another ancient civilization, Egypt, did not have the same problem. It was surrounded by land so barren that no one could settle in it, making Egypt isolated from invaders and able to exist continuously until this day as one people in the land of their ancestors.

The Tigris-Euphrates Valley has an interesting biblical history. In the creation story, the Tigris and Euphrates rivers are named. Later, in that valley, the tower of Babel was built. And in the latter part of Hebrew biblical history, the Babylonian empire—formerly Sumer—was the place where Israel suffered in captivity. Finally, in the anti-God end times, a religious/political/commercial system called Babylon will play a large part.

---

[*] English scholar John George Taylor was first to excavate Ur (1854) (*Jewish Virtual Library* 2013).

ing, the world's earliest writing. This discovery shows three things about that civilization. It was timeless in regard to development, pointless in thought processing, and directionless in purpose.

First, the worldview of Sumer was *timeless* in the sense that its people had no awareness of ongoing development. For them, all of life was but part of an eternal cycle. Cahill says that ancient pagans believed that "no event is unique, nothing is enacted but once… Every event has been enacted, is enacted, and will be enacted perpetually; the same individuals have appeared, appear, and will appear at every turn of the circle" (Cahill 1998, 5). Nothing was new—even that which people invented or discovered, The wheel, tools, fire, agriculture, irrigation, and writing were all part of a revolving cycle. Everything that existed had always been and would return. Theirs was a story of gods in control of recurring cycles of seasons—gods whose decisions determined their fate.

Second, the worldview of Sumer created thought processing that was *pointless*. Thomas Cahill explains: "Even their stories miss a sense of development: They begin in the middle and end in the middle. They lack the relentless necessity that we associate with storytelling, from which we demand a beginning, a middle, and an end: a shape. When reading a book or watching a movie that seems to wander without direction, we ask impatiently, 'Where is this going'" (Cahill 1998, 19)? Cahill says that all Sumerian stories are shaggy-dog stories that sound like children imitating the jokes of their elders, not realizing that there has to be a punchline.

Third, the worldview of Sumer was *directionless*; it was not goal oriented. In the physical realm, the lack of a point of reference causes a person lost in the wild to walk in a circle. When I taught a fourth/fifth/sixth grade class at a country school near Rainier, Oregon, we did an experiment that confirmed that a person walks in a circle when lost. We went to a large field close to the school and blindfolded several students, who then tried to walk in a straight line. Though the field was too small for a person to walk in a complete circle, it was big enough to see that the path those students made was a big arc. To their amazement, the blindfolded students could not walk a straight line, no matter how hard they tried.

My husband George also demonstrated the fact that a person without a point of reference walks in a circle, but unlike my students, he didn't intentionally demonstrate that fact. In about 1950 in the south Texas brushland of the Lower Rio Grande Valley, he went hunting wild javelinas with his buddies. He especially enjoyed sitting around the campfire with them, swapping stories as they roasted the javelina over the mesquite branches in the campfire. He said nothing tasted so good to him as that meal, killed and eaten in the wild. And the fact that this small, wild pig is so aggressively ferocious must have satisfied the campers' primeval instincts. However, searching for game wasn't so enjoyable for George when he got lost, because in the brushland, one mesquite bush looks like another. So, when he came upon his own footprints, he knew he had hiked back to the place where he had begun; he had come full circle. As in paganism, he had no point of reference—no path, no fence, and no creek to guide him back to the camp. Like the pagans of Sumer, he was lost.

Just as George kept walking *physically* in a circle because he had no point of reference, the pagans of Sumer, without God as an absolute reference point, kept returning *spiritually* to where they began. Their timeless, pointless, directionless worldview was circular; it was cyclical. For them, there was no future, no beginning, no end, and no hope, says Karl Lowith (Lowith 1949, 163). The pagans were lost. All they could do was resign themselves to dependency on capricious gods, who had to be coaxed or appeased—gods like themselves but more powerful. From this oppressive cycle, God rescued Abraham and us future Westerners.

B. Western culture, inherited from the Jewish worldview

"The Jews," Thomas Cahill says, "were the first people to break out of this circle to find a new way of thinking and experiencing, a new way of understanding and feeling the world, so much so that it may be said with some justice that theirs is the only new idea that human beings have ever had." But the Jewish worldview has become such a part of us in the West that it's written into our cells like a genetic code. The Jews' unique idea says there is only one supreme, unchanging, God who creates and controls all that exists.

Cahill says Judaism irrefutably differs from other ancient thought systems and is responsible for the unique values of the West. The Jewish belief system rejects the cyclical perspective of paganism—the perspective that nature is the "end-all and be-all," with the sun, moon, and earth as arbitrary ruling gods. When Abraham answered God's call to go to another land, he began to live his life in cooperation with Jehovah:[*] God led; he followed. He dared to step out of the only culture he knew by making a choice that was drastic, real, and irreversible. When he went, he "really went" is the way Cahill expresses it, for in his going, Abraham and his family forsook not only their home but the cyclical way of pagan thinking, which sees life as a never-ending, revolving Wheel with no present, past, or future.

Instead of accepting a revolving wheel as a picture of his worldview, Abraham chose to embrace what would become a new, straight-arrow way of seeing the world, an outlook that is linear and purposeful. This new way of thinking can be pictured by Abraham's journey to the promised land; his journey had a beginning, a middle, and an end. Abraham broke away from his home and its religion, embarked on the journey, and arrived at the promised destination—a goal, an action, and a mission accomplished *with God as his point of reference.* How basic yet how revolutionary!

Theologian David Wells says that in this Judeo way of thinking, human beings are above the natural world. About non-Judaic thinking, he says, "A being that is not immortal, tends to sink back into nature and in some circumstances may be regarded like any other natural reality, as a means rather than an end" (Wells 1993, 5). The idea that every individual is a unique being of a higher order began with Abraham, for through his friendship with God (Is 41.8; Ja 2.23), he developed a true consciousness of self and personal worth. Martin Buber, a Jewish philosopher, notes that by saying *Thou* (you) to God, man can at last identify self and say *I,* because

---

[*] *Jehovah or Yahweh* is the name God is called by his covenant people, the Jews. The word has only consonants; therefore, without vowels, we do not know the proper pronunciation.

(To the Jews, the name *Jehovah* was so sacred they substituted LORD (in capitals in translations).

the relationship of *Thou* (God) to *I* inspires relationships with other *thou's* (Cahill 1998, 250)—that is, relationship with other people.

Having entered into this new relationship with God and with others, Abraham as an individual could gain a sense of personal worth and could then build a personal identity with a history and a destiny. To recognize how important identity, history, and destiny are to human makeup, let's consider the consequences of their loss. An amnesiac who loses his history—memory of his past—loses his identity in the present. He doesn't know who he is, so he wanders through life disoriented and without dreams for a future; therefore, he has no sense of destiny. Basically, he loses the matchless treasure of individuality.

Actually, the absence of individuality is the hallmark of the pagan worldview, which views human beings en masse, not as individuals of worth in and of themselves, for in paganism, the life and remembrance of their lives is not valued above any other living or nonliving thing in nature. According to these assumptions of early man and the assumptions later of the more sophisticated Buddhists, the endless waves in the massive sea of humanity go nowhere; they just keep rising and falling (Cahill 1998,5).

Buddhism, although it does not include the gods of paganism, is nevertheless like paganism in that it devalues personhood by denying the reality of a permanent self. Its approach to the problem of suffering is to offer a way of escape, not a way to overcome. Kenneth Woodward writes, "For the Buddha, the real evil is existence itself, since all sentient beings are subject to suffering, death, and rebirth. In Buddha's view, these evils are ultimately rooted in our attachment to the illusion of a permanent self. In short, evil is explained as ignorance, and the only way to escape the endless cycle of death and rebirth is to realize our own emptiness through meditation techniques aimed at destroying the illusory sense of self" (*Newsweek,* May 21, 2001, 36, 37).

To get an idea of how oppressive a worldview can be if it does not recognize and treasure selfhood, look at the twentieth and twenty-first centuries with their totalitarian regimes, destructive cults, and "idealistic" social philosophies. Like pagan groups, these groups enforce conformity and discourage dissent because the worth of an individual is measured only in terms of a person's value to the larger group (Wells 1993, 18). In the individuality-destroying world—whether in primitive darkness or under modern tyranny—all that an anxious individual can do is seek to please through appeasement the hostile forces in control of his world. So for primitive peoples their only hope was to try to manipulate their impersonal gods. They saw no other option.

Abraham's new outlook changed everything. With a personal commitment to the Lord, he could gain a sense of identity and develop a personal history worth preserving. Even before Abraham had left Ur (Ac 7.2) and before he had any children, God promised him that his progeny would bless the world. Therefore, by giving up the concept of preordained fate in order to embrace the Lord's wonderful promises about the future, he could set his feet on the path toward a destiny. For when God gave Abraham a new worldview, he gave him more than just an identity, a history, and a destiny; he gave him life, meaning, and hope.

C. American culture made stable because of Jewish roots

In America, colonists found life, meaning, and hope in new opportunities. With freedom of religion, they brought to the new world a biblically grounded worldview that became the bedrock of America's culture. These pioneers united around the Judeo-Christian idea of individual worth and freedom—unlike other countries which are united by ethnicity and nationality. The homes that had any books usually had a Bible. Schools taught morality based on the Bible. Colleges came into existence for the purpose of training men for Christian ministry; therefore, until the closing decades of the eighteenth century, the colleges' "primary mandate remained that of instructing students in the classics and teaching them lessons in theology and moral philosophy" (Gross 2007).

When the nation was founded, the most convincing evidence of America's faith in God is in the Declaration of Independence. The Declaration says that people "are endowed by their Creator with certain unalienable rights." With this affirmation of God as the source of the nation's blessings, colonists were able to write the most enduring constitution in the history of the world (Blaustein 2004). Other factors that contributed to the colonists' ability to write an enduring constitution, of course, came from lessons they learned under England's tyranny and also from their experience in self-governance while far from mother England. However, the God-factor has been the greatest stabilizing influence to hold the nation steady through the years despite immigration of people of all backgrounds and despite revisionist historians, who seek to obscure and destroy memory of America's heritage. Therefore, since the Bible's worldview is the heartbeat of American culture, the continued recognition and acknowledgment of biblical integrity is crucial for what happens in America's future.

America's culture has been stable because it was built on the foundation of the integrity of scripture, which can be seen in the accuracy of current copies compared to ancient Dead Sea Scrolls and other early manuscripts. This meticulousness is a result of the value that Jewish people placed on cultural memory, which care and concern contrasts with that of other ancients, who did not value memory as the Jews did. Other peoples, instead of recalling facts about events, created myths to explain the inexplicable in nature; they created myths such as the one about recurring cycles of seasons. THe Jews, on the other hand, passed down the *memory* of their encounters with the one and only God from one generation to the next. And beginning with Moses—or earlier with the book of Job—they kept a written record of their relationship with the God of Abraham, Isaac, and Jacob.

What makes the Bible unique is that it's a book by which God makes himself known to the world in real-time history. From the time of the ancient Jews to the early Christians, it chronicles the relationship of God to his people. The Jews were not merely creating literature when they wrote about their relationship to the Lord. Cahill says that they were retelling a personal story that actually happened to them and that helped them become the people that they are. Their historical memory carries over into other Hebrew writings that are not strictly historical in the ordinary sense—poetry, wisdom literature, and the oracles of the prophets. For even though the Bible contains hyperbole, metaphors, poetic license, short illustrative stories, and other literary devices, they are nonetheless historically grounded. Scriptural writings are not imaginary creations; they were written by real people writing real thoughts on feelings, situations, and observations, which actually arose from life (*Life and Times Historical Reference Bible* 1994, ix, x).

Cahill believes biblical writings possess a "kind of specificity—a concreteness of detail, a concern to get things right—that convinces us that the writer had no doubt that each of the main events he chronicles *happened*" (Cahill 1998, 127. Italics added). In other ancient civilizations, no one ever thought to ask, did that really happen? "For ancients," Cahill says, "nothing new ever did happen except for the occasional monstrosity... One came to peace by coming to terms with the Wheel [cycle]" (Cahill 1998, 128). Therefore, pagan myths did not require verification but biblical stories do, because if Abraham and Moses never existed or did not receive their calling from God, their stories would have no point at all[*] (Cahill 1998, 127). This Hebrew zeal for accuracy and historical context also continues into the writing of the New Testament, which was also written by Jews. (Of authors in the New Testament, only Luke, a convert to Christianity, may have been a Gentile by birth (Co 4.10-14).)

The world's written record of history as we know it began with the Jews. Mircea Eliade says of Jewish thinking: "For the first time, we find affirmed and increasingly accepted, the idea that historical events have a value in themselves, insofar as they are determined by the will of God" (Eliade 1954, 104). Yet, though the case for the historicity of the Bible is convincing, history is only the framework for its message; ultimately its message is about God.

Finally, the Bible is a book from which came America's beginnings, and it is a book whose ideals continue to guide and undergird America's maintenance of stability and liberty. In fact, the

[*] Sometimes, of course, verification is not forthcoming until much later, as in the case of finding artifacts in Sumer.

Hebrew perspective is still so pervasive in America that it affects not only people of faith but also the irreligious and the atheistic, including those who reject their heritage and even those who heap scorn upon their heritage. Because of the cultural legacy to America and to Europe, believers and unbelievers alike process their thoughts in the Hebrew framework of past/present/future; they embrace the concept that time has direction; and they think about setting and seeking goals—so much so that those who turn to cyclical-based Eastern religions tend to bring their western assumptions with them by adapting their belief system into a New Age version of paganism. And, of course, regardless of their ideology, everyone enjoys the fruits of progress in Western culture.

Yet, some in the present age actually do embrace a paganistic worldview—for example, the idea that human beings are just one species among many and with no more worth than other life forms. A pagan mindset targets certain forms of human life as expendable nonpersons. In 1985, when I was traveling on a train in China where a one-child policy is enforced by abortion, a soldier in the People's Liberation Army presented the party line, which is that one does not become a person until he or she trains for and becomes a worker. In Nazi Germany, by classifying Jews as nonpersons, or as subhuman, the state could persuade people to go along with the government's plan for their extinction. In the 1800s in America, slavery sustained the economy and was justified by a distorted view of black personhood. Even today in America, since some regard the human fetus as simply physical tissue, or a nonperson, they can argue for "*the right*" of the mother to make the choice to end the life of the most vulnerable of human beings.

On public radio I heard that bioethicists now debate "postbirth choice," or infanticide. Justification for this would be that an infant does not become a person until he has a consciousness of self. In all these cases—in communist China, in Nazi Germany, in slavery, in abortion, and in infanticide—a person can be disposed of for convenience sake or to further an agenda because the one enslaved or destroyed is a means, not an end—all this because people reject the biblical belief in the sacredness of human life.

Facing the truth about America's identity

America seems unable to settle on its cultural identity, for it seeks to assimilate the endless, continuous movement of paganism, while rejecting its cyclical structure. Also, although the modern mind accepts the Judeo-Christian idea of progress, it rejects its biblical concept of creation and consummation—the concept of a beginning and an end. But Karl Lowith counters, "How can one imagine history as a continuous process within a linear progression, without presupposing a discontinuing… a beginning and an end? Modern mankind has not made up its mind whether it should be Christian or pagan…" (Lowith 1949, 207).

Elliot E. Cohen, founding editor of *Commentary* magazine was aware of the threat of forces hostile to America's Jewish legacy. He knew how necessary it is to preserve America's rootedness in Jewish thinking, not for the sake of preserving Judaism but for the sake of preserving America. Norman Podhoretz, author and former editor of *Commentary*, points out that Cohen recognized that Jewish influence "had bred special habits of mind and being that were a highly valuable, and indeed indispensable, part of the Western heritage of which America had become the main custodian… The culture of Jewishness demanded to be preserved…" for the sake of American culture (Podhoretz 2000, 145).

Christian apologist Ravi Zacharias also affirms Jewish influence on America's culture: "Let us be absolutely certain of this. It was not the Code of Hammurabi that touched America's conscience. Nor was it the intent or content of the Koran. By no stretch of imagination was it the pantheistic framework of Eastern mysticism. America's soul was indubitably formed in keeping with the basic assumptions and injunctions of this, the moral law of the Hebrews, which gave her a vision of history's linear thrust whereby she [America] was to reconcile liberty with law" (Zacharias 1997, 154).

Now, from Israel's past, let's go on to its present and future.[*]

---

[*] In this chapter, the author has woven her thoughts into the thoughts of others—Cahill's *Gifts of the Jews*, Eliade's *The Myth of the Eternal Return*, Lowith's *Meaning in History*, and *The Life and Times Historical Reference Bible*.

3   Israel's present: Why Israel is called God's miracle

> The birth of Israel was in a tousled bed, circled by enemies who wished it to die. Time has proven how hardy it is. But alas, the hate of the Arab neighbors has lasted.
> —Herbert Feis, *The Birth of Israel*

Introduction: The miraculous birth and survival of the Jews

Unlike many other displaced peoples, the Jews were able to keep their identity in tact through their long exile from Israel after A.D. 135. The nature of their supernatural survival is captured in an anecdote about Frederick the Great of Prussia. When he asked his chaplain to defend the divine inspiration of the Bible, the chaplain said simply, "The Jews, Sire."* Further confirmation of God's hand at work in Israel's survival came in 1948 when the Jews were allowed to return to their homeland as prophesied. This return to the promised land silenced the scoffers, who had said Israel would never again be a nation. In this chapter, therefore, to show that God's miraculous intervention in the life of the Jews is not over but is ongoing and eternal, I present facts about the rebirth and survival of Israel as a modern nation.

Modern Israel's population is almost 76% Jewish. In September 2012, its population was 7,933,200 (Israeli Central Bureau of Statistics), and surrounding it were roughly 150,000,000 hostile Arab Muslims, a ratio of almost nineteen to one, Arabs to Jews. Yet, though Arabs and Jews are Semites—both descended from Father Abraham—ancient hostility remains between them. Steve Herzig says, "If the Middle East were a place of serenity and peace, size and population differences would be insignificant" (Herzig 1997), but that is not the case.

Though modern Israel is numbered among world powers, its area is tiny. See land areas described in Figure 2 and compared in Figure 3.

* In another version, England's Queen Victoria, in mourning for her prince consort, asked Disraeli if he knew of any proof of the existence of a God. And all he said was, "The Jews, ma'am." (Columnist Paul Greenberg, "The Search: We Leave Egypt Tonight," 3/26/2002). There is a French version, too.

Israel, bridge between three continents
Figure 2: Map

In the Mideast: Israel connects three continents: Asia, Africa, and Europe. Can you find Israel on this map? It's the tiny, dark speck in the middle. It is north and east of Egypt, south of Lebanon, and between the Mediterranean Sea and Jordan.

This map shows that the land is long and narrow, only about 290 miles from north to south, only eighty-five miles at its widest point, and only eight or nine miles at its narrowest point (Hutchins 1996).

On the map, Israel, the little, dark speck, is slightly smaller than the state of New Jersey (Meyer 1982, 54).

Area of Israel's land compared

Figure 3

Israel now	8,131 square miles
California*	163,707 square miles
Iraq	169,190 square miles
France	212,934 square miles
Iran	630,575 square miles

California Almanac 1996. Also, *US Global Health Policy 2006* (Kaiser): *Global health facts.*

The original and ongoing animosity between Israel and the Arabs was set in motion by Abraham's wives, Sarah and Hagar, before the birth of their sons, Isaac and Ishmael respectively. At that time, wife Sarah, who was barren, suggested to Abraham that he have a child by her servant Hagar, but trouble followed, for after Ishmael was conceived, Hagar despised Sarah. Then in response, Sarah treated Hagar harshly, which caused Hagar to flee. But the angel of the Lord appeared and told Hagar to return to Sarah and submit to her, for God would give her descendants too numerous to count. He also told her that her son Ishmael, ancestor of the Arabs, would "live in hostility toward his brothers"—that is, Ishmael would live in hostility toward Isaac and his Jewish descendants (Ge 16.1-12). This was the beginning of the centuries-old Arabic-Jewish conflict. Talk about a family feud!

Six miracles marking the birth and survival of modern Israel:

A. Israel's rebirth as a modern nation in 1948, a miracle
B. Israel's first military miracle on its birth as a nation
C. Israel's second military miracle in March 1956-57
D. Israel's third military miracle in the 1967 Six Day War
E. Israel's fourth military miracle six years later in 1973-74
F. Israel's miraculous ongoing history

A. Israel's rebirth as a modern nation in 1948, a miracle

May 14, 1948. That's when modern Israel's miracle began. On that day, Israel accepted the United Nations (UN) decree for its independent statehood (Is 66.8). Arabs, however, rejected the United Nation's plan for Israel's statehood. Nevertheless, the UN decree opened the door for exiled Jews to rejoin those Jews who had lived in Israel thousands of years (Though many Jews had been exiled, some had always remained in the land and had multiplied in number.)

How did Israel's present refugee problem arise? Neighboring Arabs in Egypt, Syria, Jordan, Lebanon, and Iraq, saw an opportunity for invading Israel in order to rid their enclave of the only non-Arabic country in the region. Therefore, while the Arab coalition invaded Israel to gain all the land for themselves, Israel's recently-located Arabs fled to safety in Arabic lands to wait until their Arab brothers would route the Jews from the state of Israel. As it turned out in the end, the Arabic coalition was defeated... but the five Arab countries would not allow the displaced "Palestinians" to return to their former Arabic land; instead, they sent them back to Israel to be refugees. As a result, 750,000 Palestinians, as they are known, had to live as refugees in territories under Israel's control.

Islamic Arabs, recent immigrants

However, the original Arabic immigrants who had settled in Israel's land in an earlier generation—before Israel's revived statehood—did not flee when Arabs attacked. They now make up about twenty percent of Israel's present population, and as citizens, they enjoy legal equality with Israelis and can vote and form political parties. These original legitimate citizens are in contrast to those Arabs that live in the territories and demand the so-called "right to return" to Israel proper.

Islam differs from other major religions. What unites them is a desire for expansion of Islamic territory. This desire for territory has been Islam's political aim from its origination under Muhammad in the 600s. That could explain why Palestinians fight for

3. ISRAEL'S PRESENT: WHY ISRAEL IS CALLED GOD'S MIRACLE • 41

Israel's land. Elishua Davidson writes that in Islam, "Allah is not a father to any individual; he is the leader of the community... And the politics of the community are far more important than any considerations of personal religion. Islam is concerned not so much with the numbers of those who accept the faith as with the size of the territory under its control... The purpose has not been primarily to create individual Muslims but rather an Islamic society" (Davidson 1991, 20).

In pursuing land expansion, Arab Muslim "refugees" seek to gain credibility by calling themselves "Palestinians," for this title creates the impression that their heritage goes back to ancient Philistines, the people after whom the Roman Empire named Palestine. But not until Israel began to become a nation did Arabs take the name of Palestinians. Earlier they rejected the name because at that time, only Jews were known as Palestinians. That's why reference to Arabs as Palestinians "cannot be found in any dictionary, encyclopedia, or history book until the state of Israel started to become a reality" (Randall Price 2001, 137, 138).

In ancient Palestine, the historic residents were Philistines from the Aegean. The Philistines were non-Semitic and were not ancestors of modern Arabs. "They did not speak Arabic. They had no connection—ethnic, linguistic or historical—with Arabia or Arabs" (Palestine Facts 2006).

Israel now has the right to be an independent state because it has the backing of the world community through the agency of the United Nations. In addition, the Jews are "the sole direct survivors of the ancient Jewish population of the land. They alone have maintained an uninterrupted link with the land since the dawn of recorded history," because some Jews have always stayed in Israel during the nation's exiles (Doron 1999, 132).

In fact, virtually *no* significant number of Arabs *ever* lived in the land until its conquest by the Arabic Islamic Empire in the A.D. 600s. Furthermore, Palestinians never ruled the land even during Islamic rule. Instead, they were *subjects* in the Islamic

---

* In the 1970s in Petaluma, CA, the author talked with a rabbi from Israel, who traced his ancestry to the tribe of Benjamin. He is an example of one whose ancestors were not exiled from Israel.

caliphate—*not rulers*—for Palestine was only part of the greater Islamic Empire. Those Palestinians never had their own government, but, in contrast, the Jews ruled Israel for centuries.[*]

Compared to the thousands of years of Jewish habitation in the land, Arabs were recent arrivals; they immigrated in the past one or two hundred years (BBC News 1/6/09). And ironically, what attracted the Arabs to the land was Israel's good economy,[*] which resulted from Israel becoming a haven for Jews, as set up by the League of Nations after World War I under a 1920 British Mandate. Under that Mandate, England allowed an influx of Islamists, but limited the immigration of desperate, persecuted Jews (Medved 2001). Nevertheless, the Mandate proved to be a blessing for Israel, because the mandate gave international recognition to "establishing in Palestine a national home for the Jewish people" (Palestine Facts 2007). The Mandate paved the way for the UN in 1947 to divide the land into states: Israel and Palestine.

In the past, rulers came and changed Israel's culture, social fabric, and the identity of its inhabitants (Doron 1999, 130). John Walvoord says that since before World War I, Jerusalem's streets "have been trampled underfoot by Egyptians, Assyrians, Babylonians, Persians, Seleucids, Romans, Christian Crusaders, Saracens, Mamelukes, and Ottomans" (Walvoord 1984, 88).[†] Yet, out of suppression of the Jews came Israel's amazing birth. Prophecy in scripture asks, "Can a country be born in a day" (Is 66.8)? And the answer is yes! Miraculously, the nation Israel was born in a day—on May 14, 1948.

B. Israel's first military miracle, on its birth as a nation.[‡]

In 1948 immediately after Israel's birth, five Arab nations—Egypt, Syria, Jordan, Lebanon, and Iraq—attacked the new state of Israel, but instead of annihilating it, they met defeat. The Egyp-

---

[*] Under Islamic Ottoman rule, before Israel developed an economy under the 1920 English Mandate, the Palestinian standard of living was lower than in surrounding Arab countries. But by the 1930s after Jewish economic development, analyses show that the standard of living for Palestinians was about twice that of Arabs in surrounding countries (Mideast Web, "Population of Palestine Prior to 1948"). © MideastWeb & Ami Isseroff 2002-07.

[†] Since the Jewish commonwealth fell, "Jerusalem has been overrun about 50 different times, and no indigenous government was established there until 1948 [when Israel became a nation]." Until then, Jerusalem was always ruled from somewhere else" (LaHaye 2006, 305).

[‡] However, earlier—ever since the 1920 Mandate—armed conflicts between Jews and Arabs had already become frequent (Columbia University Press 2006),

LEBANON

SYRIA

GALILEE

Golan Heights

Israeli citizenship available

Sea of Galilee or Lake Tiberias

Mediterranean Sea

West Bank

Under Palestinian Authority

JORDAN

Jerusalem

Israeli citizen- ship avail- able

Dead Sea

Gaza Strip
Under Hamas

ISRAEL

EGYPT

THE NEGEV

Gulf of Aqaba

SAUDI ARABIA

tians, however, did take the Gaza Strip in the south, and the Jordanians took Jerusalem's Old City. The outcome was that Israel, though greatly outnumbered and not well armed, not only defended its territory, but also gained more territory. This was Israel's first military miracle.

To better comprehend modern Israel's wars, we'll look at Figure 4 on page 43 to follow Israel's wars in regard to territories gained or lost through time—in Gaza, in Golan Heights, in the West Bank,* and in East Jerusalem.

History of the Gaza Strip

Before we discuss Israel's listed wars, let's look specifically at the past history of the Gaza Strip, which was originally inhabited by ancient Philistines, who were not ancestors of Arabic Palestinians. This was before the Gaza Strip became part of Israel. In modern times, Gaza has been a bone of contention in Israel's wars with Egypt. In 1948 when Israel was first attacked, Egypt captured the Gaza Strip from Israel. In the 1956 war, Egypt attacked Israel from Gaza, and in that 1956 war, Israel regained Gaza, never to lose it since—more about Gaza later. Eventually, however, Israel would voluntarily withdraw Jewish settlements from there.

In the 1967 war—Egypt again tried to seize Gaza but failed. Those skirmishes set off the six-day war, but Egypt still didn't regain Gaza. Then again, in the 1973 war, Israel still kept Gaza as a territory. Many years later, in December 2005, Israel unilaterally withdrew settlements from Gaza, but peace did not come because the regime in Gaza continued to harass Israel. After 2005 when Israel pulled out of Gaza, BBC News reported that Arabic "militants continued to attack Israeli interests from the [Gaza] Strip" (BBC News 1/6/09). Now, this important background on Gaza prepares us to take notice of that territory as we continue to review Israel's miraculous military victories.

C. Israel's second military miracle in March 1956-57

First, let's look at Israel in the mid-century fifties. Israel was

---

* The vast West Bank, though in Israel's east, got its name under Jordan's rule because at that time, the West Bank territory lay west of Jordan—on the west bank of the Jordan River. Historically, this area where Jesus ministered was called Judea and Samaria. (He also ministered in Galilee.)

repeatedly raided by Egypt from the Gaza Strip, which Egypt had gained in the 1948 war. In this harassment, the Arabs continued to move toward their stated goal of destroying Israel. Also, on another front, since 1950, Egypt had banned Israeli ships from entry into the Suez Canal and had also blocked entry to the Gulf of Aqaba (bottom of Figure 4; and on Figure 2), Israel's only outlet to the Red Sea. Finally, the conflict came to a head when Egypt blocked access to the Gulf and seized the Suez Canal from British and French control. Under leader Moshe Dayan, Israel retaliated by invading Egypt and two days later were joined by the British and French in order to protect international access to the Suez Canal.

Again, in this second war, Israel fared better than before because they regained the Gaza strip and access to the Gulf of Aqaba, both of which were lost in 1948. In the end, the UN reopened the Suez Canal under Egyptian management, thus ending Israel's second war with another astounding victory. More significantly, the 1956 war "enhanced Israel's standing as a military power and as a viable nation." (Library of Congress, Country Studies 1998).

D. Israel's third military miracle in the 1967 Six Day War

After the 1956 war, raids into Israel came from Syria in the north and Jordan in the east. And though Egypt in the southeast was prevented by the UN from participating in the raids, it closed Israel off from the Gulf of Aqaba in the south. As stated earlier, when Egypt again tried to retake Gaza, skirmishes erupted into war, but on June 5, 1967, Israel won that war by mounting lightning attacks on airfields in Egypt, Jordan, and Syria.

In just six days against great odds, Israel gained or maintained hold on these territories from three countries: from Syria the Golan Heights; from Egypt the Gaza Strip and the Sinai Peninsula; and from Jordan the rest of Jerusalem and the West Bank. Counting the extremely vast Sinai Peninsula—which Israel later returned to Egypt in 1982—the new territories more than doubled the previous 1967 size of Israel (Library of Congress Country Studies 1988). As a side note on the Six Day War that ended June 10, 1967, Israel gained Russian arms that Arabs left behind.

E. Israel's fourth military miracle six years later in 1973-74

In 1973 on "the Day of Atonement[*] while Israelis fasted and prayed, Syria and Egypt attacked Israel. Though caught off guard, Israelis won, but "at high cost in soldiers and equipment" (Columbia University 2001). As a result, they became aware of their vulnerability and had their confidence shaken (Library of Congress Country Studies, 1988).

F. Israel's miraculous ongoing history

Closing with more recent history, in 1978, Israel and Egypt signed the Camp David Accords for peace (Jimmy Carter Library 1978). Also, by a 1981 law, Israel annexed the Golan Heights as part of Israel, primarily for security reasons (Dailey 1992, 23; Residents of Golan Committee 2002). Israel also annexed the Old City of Jerusalem and gave residents there the choice of Israeli or Jordanian citizenship. In 1982, Israel followed through on its peace agreement with Egypt by returning the Sinai Peninsula.

In December 2005, Israel unilaterally withdrew settlements from Gaza (Ghazali 2005). Yet even so, Hamas Palestinians from the south in Gaza aimed weaponry against Israel while Hezbollah terrorists from the north in Lebanon kidnapped two Israeli soldiers and launched rockets into Israel—all of this in spite of Israel's recent, voluntary withdrawal of settlements from Gaza. Thus, fighting from the north and south ensued. After cessation of hostilities, tensions remained, but a physical wall that Israel built now eliminates ninety-five percent of the past suicide bombing violence (Ham 2008); the wall, however, cannot protect against rockets. In 2007, after winning an election, Hamas, a terrorist group, took over Gaza by force and in 2008 launched rockets daily at Israel. Finally, Israel bombed and then invaded Gaza briefly to take out terrorist leaders. Though Palestinian Abbas of Fatah in the West Bank has said he desires peace between Palestinians and Israelis, some believe there can be no peace unless Palestinians in Gaza also participate.

Ongoing after December 17, 2010 - 2013, a movement called "Arab Spring" brought Mideast nations into a state of flux and

_____
[*] "Yom Kippur" in Hebrew.   turmoil, with Iran threatening war with Is-

rael. Israel continues to be the target of conflict. Arabs and Jews face the world's most volatile issue today—possession of East Jerusalem, especially Mount Moriah, which has holy sites that both peoples claim—the Islamic Dome of the Rock and the Israeli Western Wall, also called the "Wailing Wall," which is the last vestige of the Jewish temple. Israelis have had jurisdiction over both holy sites on Mount Moriah since they won the 1967 War after enemy Arabs attacked them. Nevertheless, the Israelis allow Arabic Muslims exclusive access to their holy site, the Dome of the Rock—even though under previous Arabic control, Israelis were denied access to their holy place, the Wailing Wall.

In 2011, I learned more about Israel from a visiting American-Israeli citizen. He said that over the last twenty years, the hand of God can be seen in another growing development. As a longterm Israeli citizen with knowledge about Christian life in Israel, he said that though the government still restricts proselytizing, the Israeli attitude is changing toward evangelical Christians. Behind this change is the fact that more and more Christians themselves are finding that throughout the Bible, past and future, the Jewish people play a key role. As a consequence of this enlightenment, American evangelical Christians have greater appreciation for Israel and its Jewish people. And then in turn, Israel responds to American evangelicals with gratitude for their strong support of Israel. Also, within Israel, Israelis are beginning to look with favor upon local, messianic Christian churches since Christians in those churches observe Judaic holy days and identify themselves as Jews. With the world lined up against the nation, Israel now appreciates its tie with evangelical Christians within and outside the nation.

Mark Twain's tribute to the Jewish people

In conclusion, the oft-irreverent Mark Twain was optimistic about the Jews' future, even though he didn't live to see Israel become a homeland for Jews because he died before the 1920 British Mandate. Yet, with great bravado and an uncharacteristic sense of awe, Twain wrote this about the future of the Jew: "If statistics are right, the Jews constitute but one percent of the human race.

[Twain's statistics were before the genocide of six million Jews in the holocaust and before other assaults on the population.] It [the small Jewish population] suggests a nebulous dim puff of star dust lost in the blaze of the Milky Way*... Yet his [Jewish] contributions to the world's list of great names in literature, science, art, music, finance, medicine, and abstruse learning are also... out of proportion to the weakness of his numbers. He has made a marvelous fight in this world, in all the ages; and has done it with his hands tied behind him."

Twain said this about the Jew: "He could be vain of himself, and be excused for it. The Egyptian, the Babylonian, and the Persian rose, filled the planet with sound and splendor, then faded to dream-stuff and passed away; the Greek and the Roman followed, and made a vast noise, and they are gone; other peoples have sprung up and held their torch high for a time, but it burned out, and they sit in twilight now, or have vanished... All things are mortal but the Jew; all other forces pass, but he remains. What is the secret of his immortality?"

Twain's enlightenment about the hand of God upon the Jews came to him before there was any evidence that Israel would once again become a nation. Since Twain's day, how much more apparent is the hand of God upon Israel and the Jews in restoring them to their land, Israel!

In the next chapter of this unit on understanding Israel and the Jewish people, we find the answer to Twain's question about the secret of the Jews' immortality. Their secret lies in their faith in God's plan for their destiny.

4 Israel's future: Its eternal destiny revealed to God's friends

> What a Friend we have in Jesus, all our sins and griefs to bear!
> What a privilege to carry everything to God in prayer!
> Oh what peace we often forfeit, O what needless pain we bear,
> All because we do not carry everything to God in prayer!
> —"What a Friend," by Joseph Scriven / Charles Converse

God's revelation of Israel's eternal destiny to his friends

A. Israel's eternal destiny prophesied to God's friend Abraham
B. Israel's eternal destiny prophesied to other old covenant friends
C. Israel's eternal destiny prophesied to God's new covenant friends

A. Israel's eternal destiny prophesied to God's friend Abraham

"God's friend." That's what the Bible calls Abraham (2Chr 20.7; Ja 2.23). He was a friend in whom the Lord could confide. We know this, for when God was going to destroy Sodom and Gomorrah, he said, "Shall I hide from Abraham what I am about to do?" And God didn't stop there. To Abraham, the Lord also laid out his greater plan. In this chapter, we'll seek to catch the wonder of that plan by looking beyond its dry and dull legalese to see in it the grand, eternal destiny of God's people the Jews—as described below in Genesis 12, 13, 15, and 17.

In Genesis 12, God called Abraham to come out of idolatry and into the plan he had for his people. The plan was wonderful, but the challenges were great. God told him, "Leave your country, your people and your father's household and go to the land I will show you. I will make you into a great nation and I will bless you; I will make your name great, and you will be a blessing. I will bless those who bless you, and whoever curses you I will curse; and all peoples [Gentiles] on earth will be blessed through you" (Ge 12.1-3).

Here God promises Abraham a new land, which would become a blessing to all nations. He promises that Abraham would enjoy personal stature and that from his roots would come blessing for Israel and for all his natural and spiritual descendants.

How God is fulfilling his Genesis 12 covenant with Abraham

Figure 5: Genesis 12.1-3

First in Genesis 12.1-3, God is fulfilling his promise that Gentiles would be blessed through Abraham, for today they are blessed by being part of the church, whose head is Christ/Messiah, Abraham's heir—"the anointed one," or "chosen one" in both Old Testament Hebrew and in New Testament Greek.

Second, in Genesis 12.1-3, God's promise to make Abraham into a nation is being fulfilled in Israel's present statehood.

Third, in Genesis 12.1-3 God's promise to make Jews a blessing to others is being fulfilled through their present-day contributions in fields like literature, science, art, music, finance, and medicine. About this blessedness of the Jewish people to others, Charles Murray in *Human Accomplishment* says that in the late 18th century, after the Jews were allowed to participate in the arts and sciences, their rate of contribution exploded disproportionately to population. Murray says the high IQ of Ashkenazi Jews doesn't fully account for this—but God's blessing does account for the Jewish sense of purpose, scholarliness, creativity, and diligence.

Fourth, in Genesis 12.1-3, God's promise that curses or blessings follow those who curse or bless Israel is fulfilled in history, for God has cursed enemies of Israel—from Pharaoh in ancient times, to Haman in Esther's day, and to Hitler in modern times—and has blessed America as a faithful friend to Israel. Yet, though persecution and efforts at genocide have plagued the Jews since the days of Isaac and Ishmael, still God has preserved them and has circumscribed the length of time that Israel's enemies prevail. And besides all else, the Lord promises Israel a glorious future in the messianic kingdom and beyond.

Fifth, in Genesis 12.1-3, God's promise that Abraham himself would enjoy personal status was fulfilled by his land inheritance, wealth, protection, leadership and legacy.

Figure 5, previous page, shows in what ways God continues to fulfill his Genesis 12 covenant with Abraham.

In Genesis 13, God promises Abraham and his descendants a prime piece of real estate on the Mediterranean Sea, which is to be theirs *forever (Ge 13.15)*. In fact, God told Abraham, he would give him all the land he could see in every direction. Then he used hyperbole to describe Abraham's descendants. He said, "I will make your offspring like the dust of the earth, so that if anyone could count the dust, then your offspring could be counted" (Ge 13.16). *But* Abraham had a problem. He still had no son.

In Genesis 15, when Abraham saw God in a vision, he told God his problem. He said that because he was childless, his estate would have to go to his servant Eliezer. God said, "This man will not be your heir, but a son coming from your own body will be your heir… Look up at the heavens and count the stars… So shall your offspring be" (Ge 15.4b). Then God reminded Abraham the reason he had brought him out of Ur of the Chaldeans—for the very purpose of giving the land to him and to his descendants.

But Abraham was still troubled, so he said, LORD,* how can I *know* that I will gain possession of it [the land]" (Ge 15.8. Italics added)? God delayed answering his question by asking him to bring animals for sacrifice. Then God revealed to him that the Jews would be enslaved four hundred years) but afterwards would be freed (Ge 15.13-16). In fact, that's what happened later in Egypt. To portray that period of slavery, the Lord had Abraham fall into a deep sleep in a thick and dreadful darkness (Ge 15.12). In that darkness, God promised that after the four hundred years of slavery, the Jews would return to their own land, which would one day stretch "from the river of Egypt to the great river, the Euphrates" (Ge 15.18). This is an area that some people say was fulfilled in Solomon's reign† and that others say will not be completely fulfilled until Jesus returns to earth as the Lion of Judah.

Also in Genesis 15, to reassure Abraham, God himself ratified this historic covenant through a ritual that is strange to us today,

* In the OT, *LORD* in small capitals represents a substitute name for the sacred name of *Jehovah*.
† The river of Egypt was probably the Wady el Arish on the border of Egypt. In the days of Solomon the promise was fulfilled" (Dummelow 1936, 25 on Ge 12.18; 1Ki 4.21, 24).

but which was common between treaty partners in that ancient time. What's unusual about this covenant is that God revealed himself to Abraham as a smoking firepot and a flaming torch, and in that form, he passed between the pieces of the sacrifice, and in that way ratified the covenant. Something else was also different about this covenant. Ordinarily both parties involved would pass through the pieces of the sacrifice to confirm their agreement to a covenant's obligations, but in God's covenant with Abraham, God alone passed through the sacrificial pieces, thus signifying that he alone guarantees the covenant's fulfillment and that he alone makes a promise to Israel that is unconditional. Through this ritual, Abraham received the reassurance he had asked for, and because he had faith to believe God, he was then accepted as righteous in God's eyes (Ge 15.6 and Ja 2.23). Faith is always the key for being accepted by God.

In Genesis 17, the Lord said, "I will make nations of you, and kings will come from you... No longer will you be called Abram [father of one nation]; your name will be Abraham [father of many nations]" (Ge 17.6b-.7a). In this way, the Lord reaffirmed the divine nature of the covenant.

By this time, ninety-nine year old Abraham had given up on Sarah bearing him a son, but he clung to the hope that thirteen-year-old Ishmael, his son by Sarah's servant, would fulfill the prophecy (Ge 17.25). So, when God told Abraham he would give him the promised son through Sarah, he laughed and thought, "Will a son be born to a man a hundred years old? Will Sarah bear a child at the age of ninety?" (Ge 17.17).

But when Abraham spoke, his words came from his heart: "'If only Ishmael might live under your blessing!' Then God said, 'Yes, but your wife Sarah will bear you a son, and you will call him Isaac... And as for Ishmael, I have heard you: I will surely bless him... But my *covenant* I will establish with Isaac, whom Sarah will bear to you by this time next year'" (Ge 17.19-21. Italics added). At last, Abraham's covenant-son Isaac was to be born!*

Also in Genesis 17, God told Abraham that he and his male

---

* A reminder: Isaac's descendants would be Jewish, and Ishmael's descendants would be Arabic.

descendants were to be circumcised, and this circumcision would be the sign of the covenant between him and God. He said, "My covenant in your flesh is to be an everlasting covenant" (Ge 17.13b). He had already commended Abraham for his faith, but now he gave Abraham and his male heirs a chance to express acceptance of the covenant by becoming circumcised as an act of obedience.[*]

To the Jews, this physical circumcision of the Abrahamic covenant was to be a constant reminder of Israel's eternal destiny. Nevertheless, many modern Jews view the rite as a cultural indicator, not a faith indicator. For as Elliott Abrams writes, American Jews have fled from their traditional faith identity, "fearing precisely the 'apartness' that Judaism demands" (Abrams 1997). Many of them accept only the cultural identity of being Jewish.

B. Israel's eternal destiny prophesied to other old covenant friends:

To friends David and Daniel, Israel's destiny prophesied

This is how God describes *King David*—"a man after my own heart" (Ac 13.23 mid)! A person cannot get a higher commendation than that! When David asked if he could build a house for the Lord, God's response was that instead, *he, God,* would build a house for David—a permanent "house," a dynasty for David *forever.* God says, "I will provide a place for my people Israel and will plant them so that they can have a home of their own and no longer be disturbed… Your house and your kingdom will endure *forever* before me" (2Sa 7.10-16. Italics added). Here God tells his friend David that Israel has an eternal destiny under Christ/Messiah.

Daniel, "highly esteemed" *(Da 9.23),* also received a prophecy from God that he had not sought. It was a 490 year prophecy that predicted Israel's future to the time of the thousand-year messianic kingdom, which will be Israel's link to its eternal destiny.

To Isaiah, prophecy of Messiah's trial and crucifixion (Is. 53) given

Isaiah the prophet was God's friend. To him, God gave graphic details about Messiah as a suffering servant (Is 52.13 - 53.1-2 OT).

---

[*] Earlier, Egyptians practiced circumcision, but God gave meaning to the Hebrew practice (Dummelow 1936, 26).

Although many prophets foretold the coming of Messiah, the Jews failed to see that he would have to die. Some say that since the bulk of Hebrew prophecy speaks of him coming as a conquering king, the people overlooked prophecies about his first coming as a suffering servant. They failed to see prophecies about his death, resurrection, and return, for the Bible says the Jews of that day were blinded to the truth. The Bible also says that this God-given blindness will continue until the times of the Gentiles is fulfilled—until Gentile world dominance comes to an end (Lk 21.24b). Again, the Bible says "God hath given them [the Jewish people] the spirit of slumber, eyes that they should not see, and ears that they should not hear unto this day" (Ro 11.8 KJV; cf Dt 29.4; and Is 29.10).

This blindness and deafness speaks of *Jews as a people*, not as individuals, for today some Jewish individuals have had their eyes opened to recognize Christ as their Messiah and Savior. Ever since the birth of the church on Israel's day of Pentecost, many *Jewish individuals* have come to recognize Jesus as their Messiah and have entered into a close relationship with God through Christ under the new covenant. Indeed in all eras, the only way for reconciliation with the Father is through the Son. In the Old Testament, all sacrifices pointed forward to Jesus' sacrifice, and in the New Testament, Jesus' sacrifice is also central but is viewed looking back.

That individuals in the present age are capable of comprehending such prophecies can be seen in scripture—for example, in Acts 8.26-28. In this New Testament passage about the earliest days of the present church age, Philip, a Christian disciple, was led by the Spirit to ask an Ethiopian foreigner in a chariot if he understood what he was reading in Isaiah 53 about the suffering servant. The man said no and asked who Isaiah was talking about. Philip said Isaiah spoke of Messiah, and he told the man "the good news about Jesus" (Ac 8.35b). Then, because Isaiah 53 (OT) so accurately tells about the crucified Christ, the Ethiopian understood, believed, and asked Philip to baptize him in water.

Isaiah predicted Jesus' crucifixion. In the first half of Isaiah 53, he writes, "His appearance was so disfigured beyond that of any man..."

Isaiah also says that rhe Messiah " had* no beauty or majesty to attract us to him, nothing in his appearance that we should desire him. He was despised and rejected by men, a man of sorrows, and familiar with suffering. Like one from whom men hide their faces, he was despised, and we esteemed him not. Surely he took up our infirmities and carried our sorrows, yet we considered him stricken by God, smitten by him, and afflicted. But he was pierced for our transgressions, he was crushed for our iniquities; the punishment that brought us peace was upon him, and by his wounds we are healed. We all, like sheep, have gone astray, each of us has turned to his own way; and the Lord has laid on him the iniquity of us all" (Is 52.14 mid - 53.6. Italics added).

Not only is this passage in Isaiah 53 the gospel of salvation for all believing individuals, it is also the gospel message that pictures Christ as Lamb of God for Israel. The passage opens the way for the Jewish people to enter the new covenant, which was promised the Jews in the writings of the prophets—the same new covenant to which Christians enter in the new birth as the bride of Christ.

Hundreds of years before Christ, Isaiah prophesied about Christ's crucifixion (Is 53.9): "He [Messiah] was oppressed and afflicted, yet he did not open his mouth; he was led like a lamb to the slaughter, and as a sheep before her shearers is silent, so he did not open his mouth… For he was cut off from the land of the living; for the transgression of my people he was stricken. He was assigned a grave with the wicked, and with the rich† in his death though he had done no violence, nor was any deceit in his mouth. Yet it was the Lord's will to crush him and cause him to suffer… My righteous servant will justify many, and he will bear their iniquities. Therefore I will give him a portion among the great, and he will divide the spoils with the strong, because he poured out his life unto death and was numbered with the transgressors, for he bore the sin of many and made intercession for the transgressors" (Is 53.7-12. Italics added). The Savior bore the iniquities of those willing to receive his salvation…. (Only the sinless Christ qualifies to be that sin-bearer.)

---

* From an eternal view, the Bible often uses the past tense in prophetic passages about the future..
† Jesus was crucified with two *wicked* thieves and was buried in a *rich* man's tomb, as prophesied.

To David, Isaiah, and Zechariah, Christ's piercing prophesied

To dear Hebrew friends—David, Isaiah, and Zechariah—scripture tells about the *piercing* of Messiah's body on the cross, which was fulfilled by the nails in Jesus' hands and feet and by the Roman spear thrust in his side (Jn 19.34). This piercing prophesied that blood would be shed, sinners would be saved, and that Israel would be redeemed and exalted in God's eternal program.

David—who lived hundreds of years before Isaiah or Zechariah and about a thousand years before Christ—predicted such piercing and spoke in the voice of Messiah when he said, "They have *pierced* my hands and my feet [with nails]" (Ps 22.16b. Italics added).

Isaiah—in Isaiah 53—tells why Messiah's body must be pierced: "*He was pierced for our transgressions*" (Is 53.5a). In this statement, Isaiah says to the Jews of his day that the coming Messiah would be pierced because of their sins, which would be laid upon him, but when the crucifixion became reality, the Jews as a people did not believe in Jesus' sacrifice and *as a people* still do not believe. Individual Jews, of course, do understand and believe.

Zechariah—another friend of God who predicted Messiah's piercing—prophesied that the Jews would not repent until the last days when they'll look back at the cross and see clearly: "They will look on me, the one they have *pierced* and they will mourn for him as one mourns for an only child…" (Zch 12.10 b. Italics added).

What makes these predictions extraordinary is that for the Israelites, capital punishment had always been by stoning, not by the piercing of crucifixion. From this we can conclude that only God's supernatural prophecy could have predicted hundreds of years earlier that Jerusalem would later be under Roman rule, during which executions would be carried out by piercings on a cross.

C. Israel's eternal destiny revealed to God's new covenant friends

Why discuss at length the first coming of Messiah when this chapter is about Israel's destiny? The reason is that Israel's future depends on Jesus' past sacrifice. If there had been no redemption accomplished by him at his first coming, there would be no second coming because sinners' cleansing must be by Jesus' blood.

The testimony of the risen Christ to new covenant friends

After Jesus' crucifixion, he appeared incognito to two persons walking on the road from Jerusalem to Emmaus. They told Jesus they'd lost all hope because the one they thought to be Israel's Messiah had been crucified (Lk 24.13-35). In response, Jesus pulled no punches: "He said, to them, 'How foolish you are, and how slow of heart to believe all that the prophets have spoken! Did not the Christ have to suffer these things and then enter his glory?' And beginning with Moses and all the prophets, he explained to them what was said in all the scriptures concerning himself" (Lk 24.25-27).

Thus, by interpreting Israel's history and destiny in relation to himself, Jesus opened the eyes of the understanding of these grieving friends. He probably told them that Christ fulfills Hebrew typology, for as prophet, priest, and king, Christ fulfills the roles that Israelite prophets, priests, and kings simply typified.

As Israel's high priest, Messiah ascended to heaven to present his own blood to the Father in heaven's Most Holy Place. To Jewish Christians, the book of Hebrews (NT) explains Christ's present priesthood by saying, "For Christ [Messiah] did not enter a man-made sanctuary that was only a copy of the true one; he entered heaven itself, now to appear for us in God's presence [as high priest]…" (He 9.24), In the past, Jesus came to die for people's sins but in his future return, he will come to set up his kingdom and will bring joyous fulfillment to those waiting for him (He 9.28).

Then after the two strangers invited the resurrected Jesus to stay with them, they had another surprise. The Bible says, "He [Jesus] took bread, gave thanks, broke it and began to give it to them. Then their eyes were opened and they recognized him, and he disappeared from their sight. They asked each other, 'Were not our hearts burning within us while he talked with us on the road [to Emmaus] and opened the scriptures to us'" (Lk 24.32)?

The Lord also warms *our* hearts, when we look at his plan for his people the Jews. The more we see his intervention in their lives, the better we understand his plan for the rest of us believers.

My testimony of friendship with God

I, too, testify to God's friendship with me through the years. In 1954, I faced a serious crisis when our daughter was born prematurely. Our young doctor in Longview, Washington was Dr. Stanley Norquist, who had a crew cut in those days, was still in his late twenties and was not much older than I was. When he came into the hospital room after the birth, he looked serious when he told me I shouldn't get my hopes up because our baby, who weighed only three pounds ten ounces at birth, had only a fifty-fifty chance of surviving. (Odds were lower in those days.) But I said, "You're too late, Doctor. I already have my hopes up."

I had to stay in the hospital a while, for I'd had five blood transfusions before the delivery. Fortunately, this extended hospital stay gave me an opportunity to go often to the window of the "preemies" ward to see our tiny infant girl in an isolette and to pray for her. Other babies in the ward had tubes in their noses for feeding, but our little one immediately drank right from the bottle, which a nurse held for her as she drank. It had the breast milk that I expressed daily for that purpose. Having been born on the Monday before Thanksgiving, our child reached the requisite five pounds and was able to come home by Christmas and has lived a normal life ever since. How special for the Lord to spare this precious girl in our family! Also, in other incidents, *regardless of outcome,* what a blessing it is to know that my friend God is in control of every situation I meet!

And God is in control of Israel's destiny, too. He promises that Christ/Messiah will reign over the world as the King of Israel. His kingdom will fulfill the covenant the Lord made with Abraham.

The messianic kingdom will be the earth's grand finale (Da 2.44), —a fitting thousand-year transition into eternity. At that time, Israel will recognize Jesus as their Messiah and Israel will be exalted among nations and will have an eternal destiny, for God *will* fulfill his promises about Israel to Abraham.

Next, in this unit on Israel, we'll, learn about its legacy.

5 Israel's legacy, friendship with God

The truth is that men and women were made to be friends and lovers of God! We were made with no other purpose. Until we realize this we will live lives of turmoil, confusion and despair.
—Dwight L. Moody

Friendship was something I pondered early in life. When I was about seven, our retired pastor asked me who my friends were, and I remember being hesitant to name any, for I felt I'd be leaving out some people I knew. In sixth grade, however, I knew I had two special friends. We'd draw a tiny picture on the upper corner of our school papers, which showed three flies on flypaper. That was supposed to show that we stuck together. Then in my high school health class, I learned more about friendship, for I found out that classmates thought I wasn't friendly. In that class, each of us had to stand in front of the room while classmates wrote anonymous comments about us. Mostly, the notes about me said, "Not friendly enough." Though this routine sounds barbaric, it was helpful to me because I didn't know I wasn't friendly.

Later in college in a small, Episcopal dormitory, I loved the opportunity to get to know others in an open-door atmosphere. Then, after marriage, when our family of four lived a few months in Birmingham, Alabama as newcomers there, I chose a neighbor that I wanted to get to know better, but that didn't work out. Instead, I met a young woman at the laundromat who *needed* a friend and from that, I learned about the giving side of friendship. All this is to make us think about Israel's legacy of friendship with God.

A. *Friendship with God made possible*
B. *Faith, the Biblical Foundation for friendship with God*
C. *The blessedness of friendship with God*
D. *The place for individual Jews in Abraham's heritage today*

A. Friendship with God made possible

The blood sacrifice on Mount Calvary has made close ship with God possible. Let's look back at that awesome crucifixion scene. Scripture says that at Jesus' death, there was a thunderbolt clash between heaven and hell. The earth convulsed, the rocks split, and tombs broke open. The centurion and the guards of Jesus' tomb "were terrified, and exclaimed, 'Surely he was the Son of God!'" For on that day at noon, the God who is holy had to turn his back on the Lamb who bore the sins of the world upon himself. It was at that moment that darkness shrouded the earth. Then, finally, after three full hours of unfathomable darkness, Jesus gave his last, loud, heart-wrenching cry, "My God, my God, why have you forsaken me (Mt 27.51)?" That's when the hand of God, which could be stayed no longer, came down and ripped from top to bottom the curtain that separated mankind from the Most Holy Place in God's temple in Jerusalem (Mt 27.51).

When that curtain ripped open, the barrier to man's fellowship with God under the *temporary old covenant* was removed. On the cross, the sin-debt was paid in full to satisfy the justice of the Father who is holy. Since then, by Christ's death, resurrection, ascension, and presentation of his blood to the Father, he has opened the way for man to enter the peace and joy of his *eternal new covenant*—a covenant that is for Jewish and Gentile Chris-tians today and for Jews in the future when *as a people* they accept Christ as their Messiah. Under this new covenant, believers pray to the Father in the name of the Son and in the power of the Holy Spirit, and they enjoy intimate friendship with this three-in-one God—Father, Son, and Holy Spirit.

B. Faith, the biblical foundation for friendship with God

When God looked for faith upon which to build Israel and his church, he found it in the faith of his friends.

In the Old Testament, God found faith in his friend Abraham (Is 41.8), who believed God's promise and followed him to an unknown land (Ja 2.23). On that faith, God would build his nation.

In the New Testament, the Lord again found faith, this time in his friend Peter, who said to Jesus, "You are the Christ, the Son of the living God" (Mt 16.17b). And on that declaration of faith in Christ's deity, God would build his church. Both Israel and the church enter Abraham's legacy to become friends with his God.

Christ, the sacrificial Lamb of God

The God of the Bible is a three-in-one being—Father, Son, and Holy Spirit—yet he is one God. This triunity of God is the foundation of the true Christian church. If a group that claims to be a Christian church builds on any other foundation, that group is a cult. The necessity for standing on the foundational truth of the triunity of God came to me after a discussion I had with a former member of a Christian cult.* This man defended the position of his former cult, which was built on the false foundation that Jesus is a created being, not God in the flesh. The man agreed that Jesus existed before the world was created. However, he was misinformed when he said Jesus *did* have a beginning and therefore could not have existed forever and could not be God incarnate. He claimed also that though Jesus is a created being, he could nevertheless do all that the Bible says that Jesus could do.

Let's consider the premise of that man's cult. to see what difference his reasoning makes. Let's say that Jesus was a created being and had a beginning, just as the cult man said. If that created being did what the Bible says Jesus did—if he took part in the creation of the world, sought out the lost, did miraculous works, spoke life-giving words, died on the cross, rose again, and will return one day as King of Kings—then what does it matter whether he is considered to be God or if he is considered to be a created being?

The difference may appear inconsequential, but it isn't—because to deny the eternal existence of Christ is to attack the very heart of what makes the Christian faith what it is—the scriptural fact that God himself came to earth as a man to be the Savior of sinful human beings (John 1.1,2)—"Through him were al things made." God had to enter the world as a human being in order to

---

* There are few Christian cults but a multitude of Christian denominations that present historic Christianity. For more on cults, see footnote, in ch 6, p 85. On true Christianity, See Fig 7, p 84,

become the substitute Lamb that bears man's sin, and he had to be sinless—hence divine—to shed blood that reconciles sinners to the Father, who is altogether holy.

For any person to deny the deity of Jesus is also to deny what Jesus says about himself, for he says, "I tell you the truth, before Abraham was born, *I am*" (Jn 8.58. Italics added)! This statement is significant because *"I am"—translated Yahweh or Jehovah* in Hebrew—is the name of God that Moses invoked to identify the God who sent him to the Egyptian Pharaoh to request the release of the Jews from slavery. Therefore, when Jesus came to earth and called himself by the name, *"I am" (Jehovah)*, he was claiming to be Jehovah, God in the flesh.

We know the Jewish leaders understood what Jesus was claiming because of their violent reaction to him (Jn 8. 25-30). The Bible says that at one point, "they [the Jewish leaders] picked up stones to stone him, but Jesus hid himself, slipping away from the temple grounds" (Jn 8.58 b-59. Italics added). Later, because of his *I am* statement and his other claims to deity, the Jews handed him over to the Romans to have him crucified for blasphemy.

Roman law, however, didn't outlaw blasphemy, so the Jewish crowd had to convince Pilate to act on their behalf. They cried,, "Crucify him! Crucify him!" Pilate asked, "Shall I crucify your king?" But the crowd became even more vociferous in their shouting for his crucifixion. Therefore, Pilate surrendered to the crowd's demand and posted a sign on the cross that said "Jesus of Nazareth, the King of the Jews" (Jn 19.19).

Today Jews, Gentiles, Muslims, Buddhists and all others are confronted with the issue that those first century Jews faced: Is Jesus a blasphemer or is he God incarnate? Is he a deranged man making wild assertions, or is he God in the flesh as he said? Today, Jesus invites whosoever will to become his friend, for he makes this promise: "All that the Father gives me will come to me, and whoever comes to me I will never drive away" (Jn 6.37). "He [Jesus] came unto his own [people], and his own received him not. But as many as received him, to them gave he power to become the sons of God, even to them that believe on his name" (Jn 1.11-12. KJV).

Quid-pro-quo friendship in the Near East and Far East

So let's look at what Jesus' offer of friendship meant to his followers in their Mideastern culture. I've learned that in the Mideast, friendship is not as casual as in America.

I learned what I know about the Far East when I taught students and professors of English in a college in China in the 1984/85 school year.* Since friendship there is more formal; it seems more like setting up an alliance under an unwritten covenant that includes a binding pledge of loyalty. I found out that if a friend does something for you or gives you something, you are obligated to express appreciation, not with thank-you's but with an equivalent deed or gift. In fact, in the Mideast and far East culture, to express thanks verbally without responding in kind is a sign of insincerity. The Chinese laughed at me for saying "thank you" all the time, as most Americans are in the habit of doing to express appreciation.

In the Chinese environment, a person's world consists of ties to family, friends, and those with whom a person interacts in personal and communist-party affairs. That person is obligated to those in his circle, but he has no obligation to others because all others are outsiders. As an example of this mindset, I saw the Chinese unapologetically crowd into lines or shove others to make their way in crowds. I think they behaved this way because outsiders are not part of their personal world. Countless times in China, when I was bumped or brushed against—though I was not the guilty party—I instinctively said, "I'm sorry," as most of us Americans do in such a situation—but the Chinese in their dense population are used to pushing and shoving. They do not see such behavior against "outsiders" as a big deal, so they just go blithely on their way pushing their way through a crowd. As for myself, I finally learned that when accidentally brushing against someone, I should not say anything. I learned to react as the Chinese do—by *not* reacting and by going blithely on my way... but I didn't shove.

I found a similar description of Eastern friendship in an entry

---

* The author wrote *China, the Lion and the Dragon* after teaching in China for a school year.

on a blog about the Mideast. The entry was called Echo Depiction. It was written by Arianna A., a young daughter of an Arab and an American. She grew up in Saudi Arabia but has lived in America since she was sixteen. She describes what friendship is like in Mideastern culture by saying, "Westerners, especially Americans, tend to think of a friend as someone they can enjoy being around and who is there for a favor or help if necessary, but the focus of American friendship is not primarily on what can be gained from the other person or from his or her privileged status. In Arab culture, a friend is more than just someone whose company a person enjoys. Equally or even more important in the Arab relationship is the benefit of favors and help." Though Arianna wrote about friendship in the Mideast *today*, that concept of friendship is not new. I'd guess that what she describes about friendship in the Mideast today is similar to friendship in biblical times in Jesus' day.

The gospel in the context of Israel's culture

Now, with our knowledge of the *quid pro quo* concept of mutual benefit in mid-East friendship, let's see how Jesus' listeners might understand the friendship that he offered. Then, by applying that Eastern principle to Jesus' message, we find out what Jesus expects from his followers. If the Lord had offered us *his works* by creating a lesser being than himself to save us, then wouldn't he reason-ably expect us to respond in like kind by expecting us to offer *our works* to him—that is, by offering deeds and gifts commensurate with his deeds and gifts? God, however, did not offer us his works for that would not accomplish his purpose, because the purpose of Christ sacrificing his life for us was to express his love (1Jn 4.8,16). He wants us to respond to his love with our love. He has given us *himself*, and what he wants from us is for us to give *ourselves* to him. "We love because he first loved us" (1Jn 4.19).

I'm saying that God cannot reconcile man to himself by "the work" of creating a being to send to earth as a Savior. He didn't make a creature to fling to earth. His goal in creation was to express his love *for* people and to express his love *through* them.

Coming to earth was the only way he could express his love and thereby bridge the chasm between himself and sinners. He didn't just give his creative works; he gave himself without restraint, even to death. He came to us, the human race, and we rejected him, but now by his love, he inspires us to express our love for him, not by our works but by giving ourselves to him without restraint.

How to distinguish the false from the true

After my encounter with the man of the cult, I reviewed my thoughts about God. What I already knew was what all true Christians know from scripture—that man cannot save himself by his good works because God's standard to enter his presence is holy perfection, which no one can attain in himself. That's why a person needs a Savior, a substitute, to die in his place to redeem him. After my experience with the cult man, I came to the realization of a related truth—that just as man cannot save himself by his works, neither can God save man by *his* works, divine though they be. God had to come to earth as a human being and give himself as the Savior in order to be a blood sacrifice for sinners.*

All that the Lord expects of his friends is that they have faith like the faith of Abraham—that is, that they have faith that trusts in God, believes what he says, and follows him, just as Abraham did. Note that it was because Abraham believed God that he was able to serve God without restraint. That's why he was willing to risk going to a land that God would show him. When he believed, he became the friend of God, and today that friendship is the privilege God offers all who are willing to *believe* that God is the One who came to earth as the man Jesus to be Israel's Messiah.

Here's the bottom line for distinguishing that which is true Christianity from that which is not: If a belief system is not built on Jesus as God in the flesh, it is not Christian. And if it is not

---

* "The Jews called Psalm 136 'the great hallel' Other hallels are Psalms 113-118 and 135. They are Psalms that praise the Lord. The chorus in Psalm 136 says his kind love always continues. 'Kind love' is a very special Bible word. The Hebrew word translated 'kind love' is 'hesed.' Really, there is no English word to translate 'hesed.' 'Kind love' is the best we can do. It comes from the old English Bible that translated it as 'lovingkindness.' People have written a lot about 'hesed.' But we must remember that it means these two things: God does not have to love us but he does love us. And God will always love us." (1999-2002. Wycliffe Associates [UK]). God's kind love is for forever.

Christian, it is a system for earning favor with God by good works because that is the basis for all non-Christian belief systems. Salvation by God's grace alone is Christian. Only Jesus as God is Christian, and only Christianity builds on that true foundation.

Building upon a false foundation results in a salvation based on what sinners *do* to earn God's favor, in contrast to the position of historic Christianity, which says that salvation depends on what God has *already done* on the cross for sinners. There on that cross as the embodiment of both God and man, Jesus was suspended between heaven and earth and between God and man. His outstretched, nail-pierced hands are open to sinners, the ones he loves, yet at the same time, his Father's perfect justice is also satisfied at the cross, for the God who is holy cannot accept sinners in their sinful state. Only the blood of the cross redeems sinners and satisfies the Father's justice.

The blood of the cross brings friendship with the Father and changes the very essence of life, for response to God's love brings divine motivation. When one becomes a Christian, his dead spirit becomes alive to God. He is born from above. He is born again.

Though I consider what I'm saying to be basic and important, nevertheless, with all my perambulations through the whys and wherefores of Christian doctrine, a person can get hung up on trying to understand it all. To illustrate that possibility and to show how to resolve such a problem, let me cite an incident.

In a small community church on a hill in Penngrove, California just outside where I lived so many years—in Petaluma—a young band teacher began playing the guitar on our community church's worship team. This was the church his Christian wife had been attending. Since the gospel was new to him, he had a hard time grasping what it's all about, so finally one day he sought out our pastor, Al Colton, to tell him his problem—to tell him that he didn't seem to be able to understand enough about Christianity to become a Christian. In telling his story, the young man said that when he told the pastor his plight, Pastor Colton actually laughed at him… but then the pastor went on to explain to him that he never would fully understand. The pastor explained that all he had to do was to receive what God offered. The young man did receive and did begin a new life in Christ. The gospel is so simple that even a child can become a Christian and have the life of God living in his spirit—for even a child can ask Jesus to come into his heart as his Savior.

C. The blessedness of friendship with God

An Old Testament example of friendship with God

The meaning of having God as a friend is best described by a story about Jehoshaphat, one of the early kings of Judah. King Jehoshaphat—like all of us human beings at some time or other—faced a situation too big for him to handle. In his despair, he stood on God's promise to Abraham with this reasoning: "O our God, did you not drive out the inhabitants of this land before your people Israel and give it forever to the descendants of *Abraham, your friend?*" (2Chr. 20:7. Italics added) Then he cried out to God: "We have no power to face this vast army that is attacking us. We do not know what to do, but our eyes are upon you" (2Chr 20.12.). God answered Jehoshaphat's plea for Israel through a Levite, who told him, "'Do not be afraid or discouraged… for the battle is not yours, but God's… You will not have to fight this battle. Take up your positions; stand firm and see the deliverance the LORD will give you, O Judah and Jerusalem'"(2Chr 20.15b).

Therefore, like Abraham, the friend of God, Jehoshaphat believed the LORD. Then in expression of that faith, he appointed a group of men to march in front of the army singing, *"Give thanks to the LORD, for his love [mercy] endures forever"* ((2Chr 20.21. Italics added). The Bible says, that when the men began to sing and praise as they marched, the LORD set ambushes against the invaders and defeated them (2Chr 20.22). The God of Abraham prevailed.

A New Testament example of friendship with God

In an incident in my life as a Gentile friend of God, I called on the God of Abraham through the Lord Jesus Christ, and God gave me victory over a two year ordeal. This was while our family was living on Fern Hill Road in Oregon. The victory was similar to what God gave Jehoshaphat—that is, the Lord sent me against the Enemy with a song. I called on the same God of Abraham that he called on, and I stood on the same truth upon which he had stood.

In this two year ordeal, one of our children at the age of two began to have seizures from grand mal epilepsy. When a seizure began to take control, I'd hold the child close and rock while singing the following simple, little chorus about God's love and about the glorious future of Christians. Singing that chorus was an expression of my faith in God and a comfort to our tiny child.

> For God so loved the world he gave his only Son
> To die on Calvary's tree, from sin to set me free.
> Some day he's coming back, what glory that will be,
> Wonderful his love to me.*
> —Alfred B. Smith and Frances Townsend·

Early in the two years of the ordeal, a Christian friend, Rose Fidler, had laid hands on the toddler and prayed for healing. However, faith for healing for our child did not rise in my heart until I became able to look at the child without dread for what lay ahead. However, that feeling of dread did not leave me until after I took a stand on the verse that I felt God had given me—*"Oh, give thanks to the LORD, for he is good! For his mercy endures forever"* (Ps 136.1 NKJV, Italics added; 2Chr 20.20).

With faith in God's goodness, thanksgiving began to replace the dread in my heart. Also, as time went by without medication for the child, the seizures did not recur, (Previously, medication hadn't stopped the seizures.) The rest of the story is that after three years without medication, the child began school in first grade with a clean bill of health given by our Longivew, Washington physician, Dr. Stanley Norquist. And that clean record has stood the test of time. What a joy to know Abraham's God!

My story concerning God's mercy and grace is about the healing of that child who grew up to live a long, fruitful life. It's a story

---

* The above chorus and its history were on *You Tube* at the time of the writing of *Think Jewish*.

about life free from lifelong medication and its sedative and addictive side effects on physical and mental health. Some may say the child outgrew the epilepsy, as evidently happens in rare cases. But when I pray and God answers, I praise and thank the Lord regardless of the circumstances that surround the answer.

D. The place for individual Jews in Abraham's heritage today

For the church, the present age is the church age of grace. For the Jews as a people, the present age is an interim when God is not dealing with them *as a people*. In fact, at the present time, the Jews have no temple and no place to offer their atoning sacrifice, for their temple was destroyed in A.D. 70. And since Mount Moriah is the only legitimate site for their temple, and since building the temple there is impossible for Jews in the current, political situation, the Jews today say prayers at "the Wailing Wall," their most ancient holy site,

Therefore, without a temple for atoning sacrifice, the question becomes, what is the place of Jewish individuals today in Abraham's heritage? Though God is not dealing with *Jews as a people*, he is dealing with them as individual sinners in need of Christ as Savior, just as he deals with all individual sinners today. In our present church age, God opens the door of salvation to *all* who repent and become willing to believe in Jesus as Savior. In God's eyes, the question today is not whether a person is a Jew or a Gentile but whether a person accepts God's terms for redemption. Therefore, individual Jews face the same issue before God as any other sinner in this age—whether to accept or reject his Son.

The Bible calls Abraham, *God's friend*, and it calls his Old Testament descendants under the law of Moses, *God's servants*. But today God calls *all* individual Jews and Gentiles to become *God's friends* by becoming Abraham's spiritual heirs through Christ, who is the genealogical descendant of Abraham, Isaac, and Jacob. (See Figure 8, page 86) to see that Jesus is the bridge to Abraham's covenant of grace.

Jesus as servant demonstrates God's friendship

At the last supper before his crucifixion, Jesus prepared his followers for a future transition into an intimate relationship with himself. He said he would send the Holy Spirit to live *within* them, and this prophecy was fulfilled when, as the resurrected Christ, he appeared and said to them, "Receive the Holy Spirit" (Jn 20.21-23).

Earlier that evening, Jesus had told his disciples they were coming out of the servanthood of the old covenant of the law and into the spiritual friendship of the new covenant. He said, "You are my *friends* if you do what I command. I no longer call you servants, because a servant does not know his master's business. Instead, I have called you friends, for everything... I learned from my Father I have made known to you" (Jn 15.14-15.). With those last words, Jesus prepared his Jewish disciples for the future when he'd go to heaven. He prepared them to continue as his friends.

In the present age, while individual Jews are gaining greater understanding about the Jewish factor in God's plan, they are beginning to realize that when Jews become Christians, they are not forsaking their heritage. Rather, they are entering into the fullness of their heritage. When Jews as individuals answer God's call to be regrafted into Abraham's tree of faith through Christ, they leave the temporary, death-dealing letter of the law (2Co 3.6) to accept God's eternal life under *God's new covenant*. By faith, they enter personal friendship with the Christ who fulfills the law.

For one Jew, however, the faith hurdle seemed to be too high to leap over. That is how the situation seemed to Richard Harvey after he heard Keith De Berry speak about Christ at his school in England. Keith wanted to really know God in a personal way. In a series of meetings, de Berry told the students that although some like to think that God does not exist, they still have a sneaking suspicion that he does. Therefore, for those who are wavering on the brink, De Berry said, God is like "the man who wasn't there," which he describes in this couplet:

> "As I was going down the stair, I met a man who wasn't there.
> He wasn't there again today. I wish that man would go away."

DeBerry showed the students historical evidence about Jesus' life, death, and resurrection and also presented what Jesus said about himself. He invited students to test the truth of Jesus' claims by going ahead and accepting his invitation to receive him because, he said, as sinners, we cannot find or reach God without his help. Fortunately, we can ask for that help because, as Jesus explained, he never drives away anyone who comes to him (Jn 6.37). DeBerry concluded his talk by spelling out how to become a Christian— REPENT of sin, RECEIVE Jesus, RELY on him!

After DeBerry's talk, Richard, a Jewish youth, was attracted to the invitation to get to really know God, but he was unsure and did not want to commit himself. So he went to DeBerry and asked him, "How can I possibly put my faith in something I have not already proved true? That would be compromising my integrity." DeBerry replied, "Are you sure that it's not just your pride that is speaking?" Telling about the incident, Richard said, "I had to admit it was true: I was too proud to be open to God. I felt an utter fool. It pierced me like an arrow shot deep into my heart."

That night Richard knelt by his bed and in tears asked Jesus to forgive his sins and come into his life. He says, he felt for the first time that he was letting go of himself and reaching out to someone or something outside of himself. He thought, "If God really is there, he will have to help me now. Somehow I knew he would… I knew I could trust God, although I did not understand how or why… Slowly [after accepting Jesus], I began to see that a difference had been made in my life, and my behavior changed" (Matt Sieger, editor of *Stories of Jews for Jesus* 2010, 347-349). The reason evangelical Christians now express such love for Israel and the Jewish people is that more Christians are beginning to recognize the centrality in scripture of God's promises to the Jews. These Christians know that in a future generation, Jews as a people will accept Christ and enter the thousand year messianic kingdom. As for Jews and Gentiles today, those who receive Christ not only receive new life now but also receive a place in the messianic kingdom. And then, as Christians, the church will be bride of Christ when he reigns as King over the nations of the earth.

Next, we'll see how necessary it is to understand Israel's Torah in order to be able to understand the rest of the Bible.

THINK JEWISH
to understand the Bible

C. UNDERSTANDING THE OLD COVENANT IN ISRAEL'S TORAH

   6. Israel's Torah: The DNA of sacred scripture
     A. *Spiritual DNA of the entire creation story* (Ge 1-3).
     B. *Spiritual DNA of the first verse of the creation story* (Ge 1.1)
     C. *Spiritual DNA of the first three verses of the creation story* (Ge 1.1-3)

   7. Israel's Torah: What the law is and is not
     A. *Israel's history under Moses' covenant of law*
     B. *Defining God's covenant of law*
     C. *The faith of intermediaries under the covenant of law*
     D. *The temporary law compared to the eternal covenant of grace*
     E. *Grace versus legalism in the parable of the prodigal son*
     F. *The rest of the story of Israel*

6 Israel's Torah: The DNA of sacred scripture

> Torah is the essence of our unique faith and lifestyle, the material
> which must be transmitted from generation to generation if we
> are to remain an eternal nation.
> —Rabbi Shlomo Riskin (Scott 1997)

As the earliest written, historical record of its kind, the Torah differs from all other written records of that day, for it is the personal
history of an ordinary man and his descendants, a man who was
neither king nor warrior. Abraham is that man, and the Jews are
his descendants. The Torah is important because everything in the
Bible relates to it in some way, including the church. In reference
to the church, we can assume that God was speaking of it when he
made a sweeping promise to Abraham saying, "All peoples [Jews
and Gentiles] on earth will be blessed through you" (Ge 12.3).

In this chapter and the next, we'll look at the Torah—Genesis,
Exodus, Leviticus, Numbers, and Deuteronomy. These first five
books of the Bible give the story of the Jews from Abraham to
Moses and give details of Judaism's old covenant of the law.

To the Jews, this Torah is the most sacred portion of the Hebrew Bible. As the introduction to the rest of the Bible, it is the
basic building block of the whole Bible and is therefore the guar-
antor of the Bible's unity and cohesiveness. The Torah is the bedrock on which both Judaism and Christianity stand, for it is the
starting point of God's biblical revelation to man and serves as a
benchmark for determining the legitimacy of later writings.

The Torah is more than a blueprint and more than a master
plan, for it is like DNA information—predictive, not just descrip-
tive. This predictive element in the Torah reveals that the New
Testament is a continuation of the truth presented in the Torah,
for indeed, if the New Testament's concepts had not grown out of
the Torah, the earliest Christians—all Jews—would not have accepted those teachings. Scholar Paul Tan states it well: "The doc-

trine of progressive revelation, demands that newer revelations…
must never supplant, annul, or superimpose on prior revelations"
(Tan 1974, 229).

This predictive and unifying quality of the Torah is what leads
us to think of the Torah as the spiritual DNA of the Bible. To
understand spiritual DNA, therefore, let's compare it with physical DNA. *Physical DNA* identifies inherited genetic information that
can be found in the organism's past ancestry and present makeup,
and, in addition, predicts future development. Likewise, *spiritual
DNA* in scripture reveals truth in its past and present, and predicts future expectations. To state another way, the DNA of early
scripture identifies truth and reveals what to expect in its unfold-
ing, while the DNA of later scripture establishes connection and
confirms the truth earlier identified. What is fascinating is that
in both physical and spiritual DNA, every part stores information
identical to the whole and to all of its parts.[*] This means that
minute bits of hair, tissue, fingernails, skin, or saliva can disclose
physical DNA information. And by analogy, this means that tiny
fragments of scripture can yield a treasure trove of spiritual DNA
information, as will be shown in this chapter.

The first chapter of *Think Jewish* emphasizes the necessity for
studying the whole Bible in order to understand a given part. This
chapter will now take the parts and show how meaningful they become in the context of the whole Bible. In this chapter we take the
DNA of the creation story in its totality and in its parts to see if they
correspond to the DNA of later writings in the Bible. If they do, this
helps us see the hand of God in the writing of scripture over so many
centuries by so many authors.

Israel's Torah is the DNA of sacred scripture:
   A. Spiritual *DNA of the entire creation story* (Ge 1-3).
   B. Spiritual *DNA of the first verse of the creation story* (Ge 1.1)
   C. Spiritual *DNA of the first three verses of the creation story* (Ge 1.1-3)

---

[*] In a similar analogy, fragments of a holograph also disclose information about the whole because
each of its cut-up parts stores information which, when exposed to light, reproduces the three
dimensional image of the original whole (Susan R. Sheridan 1997, *Holographs* in its Appendix).

A. Spiritual DNA *of the entire creation story* (Ge 1-3).

"Someone has said the first three chapters of Genesis determine everything else that one will say about theology" (Jones 1997, 93). These three chapters show us that the Torah is the spiritual DNA of the Bible, for the Torah's DNA is found in all of the Bible's parts as well as in its whole. Therefore, we look at the DNA of the creation story to gain an understanding of what later scripture will reveal.

Read Genesis 1-3 to look for the Bible's major themes in the story of creation and its parts: who God is, his holiness and justice, the triune relationship within the godhead, God's creative acts, his relationship to his creation, the fall of man, evidence of God's grace and truth, man's awareness of good and evil, blessings and curses as related to issues of life and death, the free will of man, God's sovereignty, the role of Satan, the reality of temptation, the necessity for blood atonement. These issues in microcosm in the creation story are fully developed as the Bible's story progresses.

The pointed message of this three-chapter creation story is the kernel of the whole Bible—man's sinfulness—his willful separation from God, and hence the necessity for atonement and for final judgment. Put yourself in the scenario. Imagine how you'd feel if, like Adam and Eve, suddenly you were to become aware of real guilt in your life as you prepare to stand before God. What would you do? In such a moment of conviction of sin, Adam and Eve tried to cover their nakedness with fig leaves to no avail, and they tried to hide, but that didn't work either. There was nothing they could do about the shame of their disobedience. Their plight was hopeless.

Since in the story, the Lord is the offended party, Adam and Eve could do nothing themselves to bring reconciliation; only the Lord could frame the terms for their redemption. This he did when he clothed them with the skin of an animal and revealed just how offensive sin is to him—offensive enough to require the shedding of blood, an act that foreshadows the death of the Lord Jesus Christ, the Savior who is without sin, the only one qualified to reconcile a sinner with his Maker. Only the sinless Son's blood meets the standard of his Father's perfect justice and fulfills man's need. Only the royal robe of Jesus' righteousness can replace the fig leaf of self-righteousness. Only Jesus can save. And only he can save another person, for all other persons must die for their own sins; they cannot save anyone else.

Finally, when God spoke to the serpent (Satan), he addressed mankind's future: God told Satan that he would put enmity between Satan's people and God's people. Therefore, from that time to this, unbelievers have been at enmity with believers.

God also told Satan he'd crush Satan's head and Satan would strike Messiah's heel (Ge 3.15). Looking back today, the message is clear: Satan did strike Jesus' heel when he incited man to crucify the One whom God had sent—Jesus, the human child of Mary, descendant of Eve. Also, God the Son did crush Satan's head when he conquered sin and death by paying the penalty for man's sin. This is the gospel's good news—that faith in Christ delivers from Satan's rule and reconciles with God, even though during this lifetime, man still has to deal with the world, the flesh, and the devil (1Jn 2.16).

B. Spiritual DNA *of the first verse of the creation story* (Ge 1.1)

Hebrew scripture though unadorned is profound. The first verse does not try to convince a person that God is Creator, for that is a given; it is an axiom that a creation has a creator. In this axiom we have a starting point from which to reason. The first verse says, *"In the beginning, God created the heavens and the earth"* *(Ge 1.1)*. This statement implies three truths. First, if God existed before that which he created, *he lives outside of space*, for though he works within creation, he exists apart from it and rules over it. Second, the verse shows that *he lives outside of time*, because he existed before the beginning of earth's creation. Third, because a beginning has an ending, the phrase "in the beginning," implies that *the earthly creation progresses toward an end*.

The worldview of Genesis 1.1 introduces a brand new way of seeing the world. This worldview rejects pagan gods, who were viewed as "not essentially different from humanity" but who "were more powerful and were immortal" (Armstrong 1996). This first verse stands in opposition to pagan belief systems that say the universe has always existed and will always exist and that history repeats itself in never ending, never changing cycles. With nature as its center, paganism blends everything together while forever moving toward universal oneness with no beginning, no end, and no Creator. Paganism also does not distinguish right from wrong nor sin from holiness and does not recognize a Creator as distinct from creation because in pagan thinking all is one—gods, human beings, worms, flowers, animals, dirt, fish, stars.

In contrast to paganism, Genesis 1.1 sets God apart from his universe. Its biblical worldview acknowledges differences, separateness, and individuality within an interrelated whole and recognizes linear progress in terms of past, present, and future. The Creator God of the Bible not only recognizes distinctions; he revels in them; he specializes in making things new. He makes the pattern of every snowflake different from all the flakes that have ever fallen (Engber 2006).[*] He creates no two identical persons, for even identical twins have different fingerprints and personalities. Above all, "if anyone is in Christ, he is a new creation; the old has gone, the new has come" (2Co 5.17). Praise God for that!

The Lord himself is most different of all, for he stands alone as the all powerful yet personal Lord over creation. That he is above and superior to his creation means that he is "set apart," which is actually the definition of *holiness* and the distinguishing feature of biblical truth. And because the Lord is holy, he calls for his people to be holy. He calls for them to be set apart to himself—willing to be different from the world. In the Torah, God says, "Be holy because I, the LORD your God, am holy" (Le 19.2b).

C. Spiritual DNA of the first three verses of the creation story (Ge 1.1-3)

Right out of the gate, Hebrew scripture presents the defining doctrine of the Christian faith, the *triunity* of God—that is, the *trinity* and *unity* of Father, Son, and Holy Spirit (Ge 1.1-3). In these first three verses, Christians see that though all three persons of the godhead took active part in creation, they acted as one being, yet at the same time each remains distinct from the other. Figure 6 shows that the Bible's first three verses are about God's triunity.

---

[*] Kenneth Libbrecht verifies that since ice crystals are made up of water molecules, they aren't exactly the same. He says, "symmetrical snowflake forms (like the stellar crystals) never repeat themselves" (Engber & Stoddardt 2006).

The triunity of God in creation
Figure 6

Genesis 1.1 "In the beginning, God created the heavens and the earth."
God the Father, first person of the godhead, created all.

Genesis 1.2. "Now the earth was formless and empty; darkness was over the surface of the deep, and the Spirit of God was hovering over the waters."
God the Holy Spirit, third person of the godhead, took part in creation.

Genesis 1.3. "God said, 'Let there be light,' and there was light…"
The first verse of the book of John says Christ is the creative Word: "In the beginning was the Word [Christ], and the Word was with God, and the Word was God… Through him all things were made; without him nothing was made that has been made"(Jn.1.1-3). Scripture also says, "For by him [Christ the Word] all things were created: things in heaven and on earth, visible and invisible, whether thrones or powers or rulers or authorities; all things were created by him and for him. He is before all things, and in him all things hold together" (Col 1.16-17).
God the Son, second person of the godhead, created all.

It is difficult for us to comprehend the concept of Jesus' incarnation, for he is not just God and not just human, nor is he partly divine and partly human. Rather, he is totally God and totally human. As God, Christ gave up his glory to inhabit a human body. As a human being, he laid down his life. He did so because he was called by his Father to do so. He didn't blame the Jews for his death, and he didn't blame the Romans who caved to Jewish pressure; Jesus was not a victim. He was a victor, who by free will chose the path of obedience unto death. Jesus' obedience was to the Father who sent him to die. Jesus lay down his life because he knew that since his Father is the one who sent him to be cruci-

fied,, he knew that the Father would raise him up again by his
Spirit. He said, "I lay down my life—only to take it up again" (Jn
10.17). The triune God also took part in resurrection. (Figure 7,
next page.)

Now let's seek to understand Jesus the Son in his relationship
within the trinity, including his human relationship to the Father
and Holy Spirit so that we can understand our own human relationship to God. Jesus as man lived for the glory of his Father,
who sent him. He says, "If I glorify myself, my glory means nothing. My Father… is the one who glorifies me" (Jn 8.54).

For though Jesus was without sin, he did not glory in his perfection. Instead, when he became a human being at the behest
of his Father, he lived for his Father's glory (Jn 8.54). Jesus says this
about his relationship to his Father: "The Son can do nothing by
himself; he can do only what he sees his Father doing, because
whatever the Father does the Son also does" (Jn 5.19). Jesus divested
himself of his heavenly glory in order to glorify his Father on earth
by his sacrifice. Facing the cross, he said, "Now, Father, glorify me
in your presence with the glory I had with you before the world
began" (Jn 17.1,5).

Jesus as a human being leads us in such a way that we too are
able to follow. He made this possible because he did not operate
from his perfection but instead chose a role of dependence on
the Father. He lived for his Father's glory, and he showed us that
therefore we too can live for our Father's glory. For though we
cannot operate from perfection, we can surrender ourselves to the
Father just as Jesus in his ministry surrendered himself to the Father. We can follow the Son's path because through the indwelling ministry of the Holy Spirit, we too are able to depend upon
the Father, according to the measure of our desire to please him.

Smith Wigglesworth is a shining example of one who learned
from Jesus' example to put the full weight of his dependence
upon the Lord. Whereas Jesus did not operate from his perfection, Wigglesworth did not operate from his imperfection either.
In England, he was born to a poor family in 1859 and early in life
became a plumber. He did not learn to read until his wife Polly

taught him. During the twenty-five years that he and Polly ministered in a mission that they started, she did the preaching because he could not preach more than a few minutes before breaking down in tears and turning the meeting over to someone else. However, after his Holy Spirit baptism in 1907 at the age of forty-seven, he had forty more years of anointed ministry in England and far beyond in other countries. His book, *Ever Increasing Faith* describes a multitude of miraculous healings, deliverances, and of people saved and filled with the Holy Spirit under his ministry.

David W. Dorries makes this over-the-top tribute about Wigglesworth: "Smith Wigglesworth operated consistently at a level of faith and power that is unique and almost without rival in the annals of Christian history" (Dorries, Fall 1992, 4). From my view, I can at least say that Wigglesworth had an extraordinary ministry.

We looked at how the three-in-one God has operated as one being. In the first three chapters of Genesis, we saw the triunity of God at work in creation (Figure 6, page 80). In addition, we see the triunity of God at work in the New Testament, as shown in Figure 7 below.

The trinity of God in the resurrection of Jesus in the New Testament

Figure 7

The Father: "God raised him [Jesus] from the dead" (Ac 2.24).

The Son: Jesus before his crucifixion said, "I lay down my life— only to take it up again" (Jn 10.17b).

The Holy Spirit: "The Spirit of him who raised Jesus from the dead is living in you" (Ro 8.11b).

In Christianity, the triunity doctrine is so important that it is actually a litmus test for distinguishing authentic Christianity from its counterfeit, for the identifying mark of a "Christian cult" is its denial or distortion of the foundational truth of either the trinity or the unity of God, or of both. This denial and distortion of the truth of God's triunity causes a cult to miss what Christianity is all about; therefore, no matter how beautiful that cult's superstructure or how great its respectability in society, its foundation is false, so that makes all its other teachings irrelevant. The god of the cult is not the God of the Bible, for the God of the Bible is a three-in-one being who acts as the one God that he is.*

The best way to understand God's triunity is to recognize that *human personhood is also triune.* Just as God is a three-in-one unity of Father, Son, and Holy Spirit; a human being is a three-in-one unity of body, soul, and spirit (1Th 5.23b). The general consensus is that the *body* is physical, that the *soul* involves the will, emotions, and intellect, and that the *spirit* is where God dwells within a believer, yet the fact remains that this triune human being of body, soul, and spirit is only one person, for no part of a person acts independently. Nevertheless, although for both God and for human personhood, the three parts are distinct from each other (He 4.12), yet together they constitute only one entity. This could be one indication that we are made in the image of God (Ge 1.27; 9.6).

To recognize the unity and the distinctiveness of body, soul, and spirit, consider the act of reading. When your eyes read a page, *you* are the one reading, not just the eyes of your body. When reading results in your thinking, feeling, or choosing, *you* are the one who thinks, feels, or chooses, not just your soul, which is the vehicle for your thinking, feeling, and choosing. When you worship the Lord in song, *you* are the one so engaged, not just your spirit and not just your voice. No part of you acts independently. Whatever part of you—body, soul, or spirit—acts, thinks, feels, chooses, or worships; that is *you* acting or reacting. You function as one being, even as God functions as one being.

Going further into the doctrine of the trinity because it is so important for biblical faith, the Bible also presents the trinity through grammar. In Genesis 1.1, "Elohim," a Hebrew name

---

* A few well-known "Christian" cults: *Jehovah's Witnesses* say Jesus is Michael the archangel, a created being. *Mormons* say that the Father, Son, and Holy Spirit are three gods. *Christian Science* and *Unity* say Jesus is just a good man, "the way-shower"—not *the* way and not God. Some cults say Jesus had a beginning and did not exist forever. Some cults say God is "Jesus Only."

for God in plural form, is paired with a singular verb. This Hebrew use of a *plural noun* with a *singular verb* fits the concept that this three-in-one God acts as one being. J. R. Dummelow's *One Volume Bible Commentary* says, "The Hebrew word [Elohim] is plural in form, but as a rule, it is significantly followed by verbs in the singular, except when used of heathen gods" (Dummelow 1936, Genesis 1.2 note). Dummelow says that for heathen gods, Elohim is followed by a plural Hebrew verb—but for the triune God of the Bible, the verb is singular. This grammatical construction makes sense: The authentic God is not three gods; He is One.

Again, to reveal the plurality of the godhead through Hebrew grammar, God uses *plural pronouns* in reference to himself. He says, "Let *us* make man in *our* image, in *our* likeness…" (Ge 1.26). About the fall of man, he says, "The man has now become like one of *us*" (Ge 3.22). Again, in the story of the tower of Babel, God also uses a plural pronoun for himself: "Come, let *us* go down and confuse their language so they will not understand each other" (Ge 11.6-7) (Morey 1996, 94-96).

As interesting as these examples are, the most astounding example of the grammar of the Bible upholding the triunity of God is in Judaism's own central tenet, *the Shema*: "Hear, O Israel: The Lord our God, the Lord is *one*" (Dt 6.4. Italics added). Note this! Steve Herzig, director of North American Ministries for *Friends of Israel* writes in the magazine *Israel My Glory* that God's triunity "is upheld in the Shema by using the word *echad* for 'one God' because *echad* denotes plurality within unity" (Herzig, Jan/Feb 2009).

The Bible opens with "In the beginning, God created…" and ends with Jesus saying, "Behold, I come quickly" (Re 22.12a). These truths—*God created* and *Messiah will come*—are truths that constitute the central message of the Torah and of all the Bible (Ge 1-3). The New Testament of the Bible ends with this open invitation to both Jews and Gentiles: "The Spirit and the bride say, 'Come.' And let him that heareth say, 'Come.' And let him that is athirst come. And whosoever will, let him take the water of life freely" (Re 22.17, KJV).

Next, to become thoroughly grounded in Jewish thinking let's now look at the Torah to see "what it is and what it is not."

7 Israel's Torah: What the law is and is not

"On that day, tell your son, 'I do this because of what the LORD did for me when I came out of Egypt.' This observance will be for you like a sign on your hand and a reminder on your forehead that the law of the LORD is to be on your lips. For the LORD brought you out of Egypt with his mighty hand. "
—Exodus 13.8, 9

An author cannot "find his voice"—the full and free expression of his individual identity—until he masters writing's fundamentals. And a Christian cannot find his voice unless he first masters the fundamentals of the faith. As a Christian matures and enters into his calling from God, he learns to express his unique identity.

So too, Jews as a people find their identity by building on basic truths in the Torah—the law of Moses—as God has led and trained them. Now, in this chapter, we'll look at the Torah in order to become grounded in the Jewish way of thinking.

Israel's Torah: What the old covenant of law is and is not:
A. Israel's history under Moses' covenant of law
B. Defining God's covenant of law
C. The faith of intermediaries under the covenant of law
D. The temporary law compared to the eternal covenant of grace
E. Grace versus legalism in the parable of the prodigal son
F. The rest of the story of Israel

A. Israel's history under Moses' covenant of law

Figure 8, next page, shows two parallel paths symbolically progressing along two parallel vertical lines. The paths show Abraham's eternal covenant of grace and Moses' temporary covenant of law. In the covenant with Abraham, God told him that the Jews would become slaves in a foreign land, would multiply there, and after four hundred years would return to the land of Israel (Ge 15.13-14), where they would become a great nation (Ge 12.2). Remarkable!

Figure 8 shows how the prophecy has unfolded: Christ's cross is the bridge for Jews to pass over to Abraham's eternal covenant of grace. Today, through the blood of Jesus, God calls all Jews into Abraham's covenant of grace. And according to the New Testament, Gentiles are also called by God "for *all* have sinned and fall short of the glory of God" (Ro 3.23. Italics added.). All are in need of the cross to be their bridge to grace.

Figure 8 below shows how the prophecy unfolds from the bottom up. There, we see that under the law, Jews as a people failed to acknowledge Christ as Messiah. (Read from bottom up.)

Israel trained by the law to follow God

Figure 8

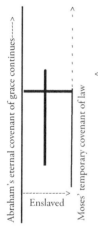

A.D. 135: The Jews as a people were exiled from their land.

A.D. 70: Sacrifices ceased after the Judaic temple was destroyed.

<-- About A.D. 33 :At Jesus' death, Jewish people were offered *the bridge to Abraham's eternal covenenat of grace.*

The cross is the bridge from Moses' temporary covenant of law to Abraham's eternal covenant of grace.

About 1500 B.C.: Moses received God's covenant of the law.

About 1930 B.C.: The Jews were enslaved in Egypt 400+ years.

About 2100 B.C.: Abraham received God's eternal covenant.*

*Grun, *Timetables*, 1991.

Though the law was given to train Israelites for the messianic kingdom, when the time came to enter Abraham's grace covenant, they rejected Christ, the only bridge to that grace covenant. They clung to the law and plotted Christ's crucifixion. After Christ's ascension, Jewish leaders in A.D. 135 again failed to recognize the church as God-given and therefore persecuted those Christian Jews even though Christianity had actually begun as a sect within Judaism (Baughman 1972, 102, 107).

Figure 8 shows that in A.D. 70, God allowed the Jewish temple to be destroyed. Then, later in A.D. 135, the Jews lost their land to the Gentiles and had to live in exile—until A.D. 1948 when the nation of Israel was miraculously reinstated as a nation. Yet, remember, since the time of the wilderness exodus, some Jews have always lived in that promised land.

Consider this. Since the temple is the only legitimate place for Jews to offer blood sacrifice, and since the legitimate site for building their temple is occupied by the Muslim's religious shrine, "Dome of the Rock," Jews presently have no legitimate place to offer blood sacrifice. Therefore, rabbis teach their people to repent, pray, and perform acts of charity. The Torah, however, says that God's forgiveness can come only through blood sacrifice (Rosen, June 2007). Therefore, since God requires blood sacrifice for forgiveness of sin (He 9.22b), he gives all present-day sinners the option of receiving Christ's blood sacrifice. Though *Jews as a people* do not yet acknowledge the legitimacy of Christ's sacrifice, individual Jews today do find salvation in his sacrifice. My devoted pastor is one example.

B. Defining God's covenant of law

God didn't intend for the old covenant of the law to be a system for earning his favor, nor did he intend for the law to be an end in itself. He intended for the law to expose the sinfulness of man and thereby reveal the need for blood sacrifice to atone for sin. And though blood sacrifice is central in Judaic and Christian doctrine, yet nevertheless, the offerer's attitude also determines whether God accepts or rejects a sacrifice. God rejects offerings not motivated by sincere devotion, as shown below when Isaiah spoke for God in a plea to the Israelites:

> "Stop bringing meaningless offerings! …
> Your appointed feasts my soul hates…
> Your hands are full of blood;
>   wash and make yourselves clean.
> Take your evil deeds out of my sight!
> Stop doing wrong, learn to do right!
> Seek justice, encourage the oppressed.
> Defend the cause of the fatherless,
> Plead the cause of the widow" (Is 1.13-17).

Here's how my understanding of God's covenants of law and grace developed over time. In early, superficial reading of the Bible, I saw the Old Testament as being about how people under Moses' law worked to earn God's favor. I saw the law as a severe taskmaster, conditional and demanding—a "works" system with requirements impossible for an ordinary human being to comply with fully. I came to this conclusion because I saw that from the giving of the law until the destruction of the temple in A.D. 70, Israel under the law of the old covenant continually failed to measure up. But I was wrong to think that under the law, salvation had to be earned. William S. LaSor correcrly states that there's no place in the Old Testament that teaches that man fulfills the law by doing works (LaSor 1976, 90). I now know that to be saved, a person must offer the prescribed blood sacrifice with faith in God's mercy, for this is the message of the Torah and of the rest of the Bible—animal sacrifice in past Judaism and in future Judaism (Eze 40-48), both of which point to Christ's sacrifice in the present era.

About the severity of the law, I was right—the law *is* severe—but I had more to learn about the Torah. Further pondering clarified my thinking, for I learned in Genesis that Abraham, Isaac, Jacob, and the twelve patriarchs did not live under the law, for they lived *before* the law. They lived under God's covenant with Abraham, which is the rock-solid foundation upon which both Judaism and Christianity stand. This guaranteed foundation is unshakable because the eternal God is unshakeable. He alone ratified his covenant with Abraham, for God alone appeared and walked between the sacrificed pieces. (Ge 15). The covenant foundation is strong and its fulfillment certain. God's eternal promise in scripture is that Gentile and Jewish Christians would one day enter God's grace covenant—and also that *Jews as a people* woud enter God's grace covenant under the future thousand year messianic reign of Christ/Messiah.

In contrast to God's eternal covenant with Abraham, God's later covenant of the law with Moses was temporary and conditional. Moses' covenant offered blessing, but only *if* the Jews obeyed its law, for if they rebelled, they would forfeit God's blessings. If they continued to rebel, they would suffer judgment. Unfortunately, theirs was a life of recurring rebellion, which would bring down God's judgment. Then after suffering the consequences of disobedience, they would repent and again receive restoration and blessing. This became a cycle that was repeated over and over in Hebrew scripture—rebellion, judgment, repentance, restoration, blessing… rebellion, judgment, repentance, restoration, blessing—cycle after cycle. The Israelites failed because the law could only instruct; it could not impart life, for "if a law had been given that could impart life, then righteousness would certainly have come by the law" (Ga 3.21b). Indeed, the law *cannot* produce righteousness; all it can do is expose sin. Again I say that God gave the law to reveal people's need for blood sacrifice.

To think Jewish is to see that in spite of Jewish failure under the law, God's covenant with Abraham is unconditional and cannot be abrogated. He says, "I will establish my covenant as an everlasting covenant between me and you and your descendants" (Ge 17.7a). Other prophets have expanded God's promises, but like the constancy of a north-pointing compass, God's plan for Israel, as given to Abraham, has remained a constant (Lowith 1949, 18).

C. The faith of intermediaries under the covenant of law

Israel's old covenant of the law is the building block of the Bible, so let's consider its purpose. I became puzzled about that purpose, for I reasoned that if faith has always been the coin of God's realm and the measure of what's important to God—as most agree—then why does Paul say the law is not based on faith? Paul says, "Clearly no one is justified before God by the law, because, 'The righteous will live by faith.' The law is not based on faith; on the contrary, 'the man who does these things will live by them'" (Ga 3.11,12). This seems to say that he who lives by the law lives by the merit of his own deeds, not by faith in God (cf Php 3.8b, 9).

Here's why I was puzzled. Faith connects to God, but Paul says the law of the Torah is not of faith; therefore, if the Israelites under Moses' law could not connect with God through the law, how could they relate to him at all? This puzzle gave me pause until I realized that the faith of the Israelites was based on the faith of

The roles of Israel's intermediaries

Figure 9

Prophets spoke for God to the people.
Priests spoke for the people to God.
Kings in Israel's theocracy led the nation under God's guidance.

These God-appointed and God-anointed intermediaries connected the Jewish people to God but only *indirectly*. We know this because we see that intermediariares acted as go-betweens.

1) *The role of the prophets was to speak for God to the people* to bring them to repentance, to proclaim a word from God for specific circumstances, to perform miracles, to review Israel's scriptural history, to anoint future leaders, to advise those in authority, to instruct in God's ways, to give people hope or warnings about the future, and generally to speak for God—to encourage, upbraid, or advise the people and their leaders.

2) *The role of the priests was to present atoning sacrifices to God for the people.* This served as a firewall to protect the Israelites from the destruction that would otherwise be theirs as sinners. The priests also presented offerings of praise and adoration for God on behalf of the people.

3) *The role of kings, under God, was to rule over Israel.*

Christ is the fulfillment of the roles of Israel's intermediaries.

their *intermediaries* as described by the law. These intermediaries were set up by God as anointed ones. The faith of intermediaries—prophets, priests, kings—connected the Israelites to God.

To learn about the faith role of intermediaries, see Figure 9.

Besides through intermediaries, scripture set up other ways for the Israelites to connect with God *indirectly*. One way they connected with God was that in the exodus journey under Moses, they saw God's presence over the tabernacle guiding them in the cloud by day and in the fire by night. Also, they knew that God's presence dwelt above the ark of the covenant. Then again, in the rebuilt temple after captivity in Babylon, the Israelites recognized God's presence when his glory filled the temple. And lastly, they knew of God's presence when he accepted the blood sacrifice that the priests offered to cover the nation's past sins each year.[*] Under the old covenant of the law—in the exodus tabernacle and later in the Jerusalem temple—the Israelites received the training they needed, and yet in all of this, they were linked to God only indirectly.

The Israelites were connected to God *indirectly* by faith, but in contrast, Christians today and Jews as a people in the future messianic kingdom (millennium) are connected to God *directly* by faith through his indwelling Spirit in believers. Before the first Jews became Christians, they had God's presence when Christ walked *with* them on earth, but after they became Christians, they had his Spirit living *within* them.

The lesson I've learned is that faith is the connecting link to God, whether directly now under the new covenant or indirectly under the old covenant in ancient times. The faith chapter in Hebrews 11 bears this out: "Without faith it is impossible to please God, because anyone who comes to him must believe that he exists and that he rewards those who earnestly seek him" (He 11.6). Through the faith of the intermediaries and through the Israelites' own faith in the God who set up the intermediaries, the Israelites were able to connect indirectly to God by faith.

---

[*] On the day of Atonement, if God did not strike the high priest dead during his ministry in the Most Holy Place, the Israelites knew that God had forgiven Israel's sins of the past year.

Moses, who led the Israelites out of Egypt, was a man of faith who faced difficult choices. Figure 10 describes his expression of faith as described in Hebrews 11: "By faith Moses, when he had grown up, refused to be known as the son of Pharaoh's daughter. He chose to be mistreated along with the people of God rather than to enjoy the pleasures of sin for a short time. He regarded disgrace for the sake of Christ as of greater value than the treasures of Egypt, because he was looking ahead to his future reward. By faith he left Egypt, not fearing the king's anger; and he persevered because he saw him who is invisible. By faith he kept the first Passover and applied the sprinkling of blood on the doorposts so that the destroyer of the firstborn would not touch the firstborn of Israel" (He 11.25-28 NT).

Moses expressing his faith by making difficult choices
Figure 10
Hebrews 11.25-28

1) *by his will,* choosing God and rejecting the pleasures of sin
2) *by wisdom,* not by expediency, but by seeing his reward
3) *by obedience* to God, without fear of Pharaoh's anger
4) *by vision,* seeing the invisible God
5) *by trust,* in offering God's prescribed blood sacrifice

Hebrews 11 in Figure 10 reveals the proactive side of Moses' faith. This is how Moses intentionally expressed his faith. His motivation led him to fulfill God's will. Figure 10 describes in discrete terms Moses' active expression of faith by his will, wisdom, obedience, vision, and trust. These traits play a key role in the expression of faith by believers who live in any era.

In short, Moses persevered by faith in spite of mistreatment, disgrace, and having to face the king's wrath. In the first **Passover**, Moses could persevere because he believed in the God who would save Israel's firstborn by the blood of the lamb placed on the top and sides of the doorway like a cross to turn away the angel of death. (This blood symbolizes the blood of Christ, Lamb of God.)

However, Moses, great prophet though he was, did not always express faith through obedience. In the isolation of his desert exile, he failed to circumcise his son according to the dictate of God's covenant with Abraham (Ge 17.10b). Scripture says that on Moses' journey from his desert exile to the land of Egypt to answer God's call to liberate his enslaved people there, Moses faced God's hand of judgment for he did not obey the circumcision requirement for his son, but just as the Lord was about to kill him, his wife took a flint knife, cut off her son's foreskin, cast it at Moses' feet, and said, "Surely you are a bridegroom of blood to me" (Ex 4.25b). The Lord in his mercy used this Gentile woman with a bad attitude to intervene in order to bring Moses to repentance and to the restoration of his life and his ministry.

God gave Moses the vision to recognize the *spiritual* significance of the physical circumcision of the Jews. God revealed to Moses that the Lord himself would one day spiritually circumcise the hearts of his people, the Jews. Moses understood this, for at the end of the exodus, Moses said, "The Lord your God will circumcise your hearts and the hearts of your descendants, so that you may love him with all your heart and with all your soul, and live" (Dt 30.6). Here Moses uses the analogy of physical circumcision to illustrate spiritual circumcision of the heart. God's surgery will give each of the *Jews as a people* a new heart and spirit under the new covenant of the messianic kingdom, just as he now does for J*ews as individuals in* the church under the new covenant

In the Torah, Moses' analogy of physical and spiritual circumcision is the earliest biblical reference to the regeneration of believers under the new covenant. In the future, Jews as a people will enter into the new covenant of the messianic kingdom, and now in the present age, both Jewish and Gentile Christians enter the new covenant individually through the shed blood of Jesus.

Also, hundreds of years after Abraham, the promise of a new-covenant was spelled out by Hebrew prophets Ezekiel and Jeremiah (Je Je 31.31-34; Eze 36.26). Ezekiel spseaks for God when he says, "I will give you a new heart and put a new spirit in you; I will remove from you your heart of stone and give you a heart of flesh. And I will put my Spirit in you and move you to follow my decrees and be careful to keep my laws." Today, the new covenant is for the church. and in the future generation of the messianic kingdom (the millennium), the new covenant is for Jews *as a people* and for their sympathizers.

D. The temporary law compared to the eternal covenant of grace

Looking at Figure 8, page 86, we see that God's covenant *with Abraham is an eternal covenant of grace*, with blessings extended unilaterally to mankind by God himself. On the other hand, God's covenant *with Moses was a temporary covenant of law* and was for Israel specifically. So let's look at how these covenants differ. Let's begin by saying that man's natural inclination is not toward the self-denial that Jesus teaches but instead toward the self-righteousness of obedience to the old covenant of the law—in other words toward legalism. In Paul's day, because of Jewish persecution, Galatian Christians were tempted to return to Judaism, but Paul warned that if they yielded to the temptation to forsake Christ and return to the law, they would return to the curse of the law (Ga 3.10). He writes that "it is for freedom that Christ has set us free. Stand firm, then, and do not let yourselves be burdened again by a yoke of slavery" under the law (Ga 5.1).

Though Christians today are nor tempted to be yoked to Moses' law, they are tempted to fall into the bondage of a rule-driven life by which *self*, in the pursuit of its own glory, seeks to satisfy "self" according to its own plans and its own agenda. A legalistic mindset ensnares those who forget that new life in Christ is about a personal relationship with the Lord, not about a relationship to rules and not about the approval of others.

A focus on the world's "do's and dont's" brings death, not life, for legalism is man-created, self-centered, morality-driven, and ego-building. In contrast, new covenant fulfillment of Abraham's covenant of grace is God-centered, love-motivated, and Spirit-led.

And yet, though the gospel of grace offers liberty, this liberty doesn't give license for immorality, for the gospel doesn't promote abandonment of all restraint. No, it says "everything is permissible, but not everything is beneficial…" (1Co 10.23). The book of Galatians says, "You, my brothers, were called to be free. But do not use your freedom to indulge the sinful [self-seeking] nature; rather, serve one another in love… Since we live by the Spirit, let us keep in step with the Spirit" (Ga 5.13,25). Also, "Whether you eat or drink or whatever you do, do it all for the glory of God" (1Co 10.31). God's new covenant offers the new life that results from a personal relationship with the heavenly Father.

Finally, the letter of the law can be compared to written instructions left by parents for a baby sitter. Their written instructions are not in effect after the parents return, for upon their arrival, the authority of the actual presence of the parents supersedes the authority of their temporary, written instructions. In the same way, since the law has been fulfilled by Christ sending the Holy Spirit to live within the believer, that believer begins to live under the grace of God's inner guidance and love, not under the bondage of the written covenant of law. The book of Romans speaks to Christians with this: "Now, by dying to what once bound us, we have been released from the law so that we serve in the new way of the Spirit, and not in the old way of the written code" (Ro 7.6).

E. Grace versus legalism in the parable of the prodigal son

People have different views on Jesus' parables. One way I see Jesus' parable of the prodigal son (Lk. 15:11–32) is as an illustration of a comparison between grace and legalism. The prodigal son in the parable rebelled and asked for and received an early inheritance from his living father. Then after he had wasted that inheritance, he survived by taking a job feeding husks to pigs, which was a job of the lowest degradation, according to the sensibilities of Jesus' Jewish audience.

But when the prodigal son came to himself, he headed home, intending to say, "Father, I have sinned against heaven and against you. I am no longer worthy to be called your son; make me like one of your hired men" (Lk 15.18b-19). How humbled he must have felt when his father ran out to greet him, showered him with gifts, and gave a feast in his honor for their family and friends!

That was a night of great celebration for everyone except for the elder son, whose envy was like that of the Jewish leaders in Jesus' day (Mt 27:18; Mk 15). In the parable, the elder son complained that as firstborn son he had worked faithfully for his father all those years and had received no celebration, yet his younger Johnny-come-lately brother—who had wasted his father's inheritance and disgraced his father's name—returned home and received a hero's welcome. The angry son refused to take part in the festivities even though his father pleaded with him to do so. As head of the estate, the father told his elder son, "Everything I have is yours" (Lk 15.31b). The father told the elder son he had not been deprived of anything, for he had been blessed all those years in the father's house.

This parable contrasts grace and legalism. Jewish leaders in Jesus' day, God's insiders, were like the elder son who never left home and felt "entitled" to his father's blessings. Those leaders in Jesus' day were envious of God opening the door to Jesus' followers. To the Jewish leaders, Jesus said, "Woe to you, teachers of the law and Pharisees, you hypocrites! You shut the kingdom of heaven in men's faces. You yourselves do not enter, nor will you let those enter who are trying to" (Mt 23.13). That was only the beginning of Jesus' discourse against the self-righteous enemies of God.

Because those ancient leaders were without faith, they shut their hearts to the Father and his blessings in Christ under the new covenant. On the other hand, today for believing Jewish and Gentile individuals, the new covenant in Christ is open to all sinners who repent and believe. As with the prodigal son, sinners without God and without hope can now become reconciled with the Father. Incidentally, if God had chosen another people as his own instead of the Jews, that people group would have rejected Jesus just as the ancient Jews did, because human beings all have this in common: "All have sinned and fall short of the glory of God" (Ro 3.23) and can be saved only by God's grace. Jesus' divine purity would have offended any people group into which he might have been born.

F. The rest of the story of Israel
The Bible tells the rest of the story of Israel—that Jews as a

people in a future generation will recognize Jesus as their Messiah. Today, however, God invites all Jewish and Gentile individuals of the present generation to be delivered from the bondage of sin and death and to begin to find their "voice," for as they walk with him, they become more truly who they were meant to be. Their entry into the kingdom of heaven today will be only a foretaste of the fulfillment experienced when Jewish and Gentile Christians return from heaven to earth as the bride of Christ.

This ends the unit on understanding God's old covenant in Israel's Torah. The next unit reveals God's new covenant as presented by Israel's seven feasts.

THINK JEWISH
to understand the Bible:
Christ/Messiah as past prophet, present priest, and future king

D. UNDERSTANDING THE NEW COVENANT IN ISRAEL'S SEVEN FEASTS*

8. Christ/Messiah as past prophet
First pilgrimage: Fufilled by past wilderness exodus to promised land
   1.Passover
   2.Feast of unleavened bread
   3.Feast of firstfruits

9. Christ/Messiah as present priest
Second pilgrimage: Fulfilled by present interim between exoduses
   4. Pentecost - Feast of weeks

10. Christ/Messiah as future king
Third pilgrimage: fulfilled by future messianic-kingdom exodus to eternity
   5. Feast of Trumpets
   6. Day of Atonement
   7. Feast of Tabernacles

---

*In ancient times, all adult male Israelites had to make three pilgrimages a year to Jerusalem.

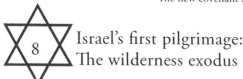

8 Israel's first pilgrimage: The wilderness exodus

> In the past God spoke to our forefathers through the prophets…but in these last days he has spoken to us by his Son, whom he appointed heir of all things, and through whom he made the universe.
> —Hebrews 1.1-2 NT

The story of Israel *is* the story of the Bible. With this recognition we can see that the story of the Bible is told in Israel's seven feasts, which are set up as three mandatory pilgrimages to Jerusalem each year. The first pilgrimage is about Israel's past exodus through the wilderness, and the third pilgrimage is about Israel's future exodus through the thousand-year messianic kingdom. Between the first and third pilgrimages is the second pilgrimage—fulfilled in the present church age, which for Israel is the present interim age between Israel's past and Israel's future. To think Jewish is to see that the Bible is organized according to Israel's history, as symbolized by Israel's three pilgrimages.

> First pilgrimage: three feasts—Israel's wilderness exodus
> Second pilgrimage: one feast—Israel's interim
> Third pilgrimage: three feasts—Israel's kingdom exodus

Israel's story has a beginning that progresses toward a conclusion: "The Bible tells its story, not with the past in mind, but with the future clearly in view. Even the purely historical portions are written as if the historian were stating the past and viewing all events in the light of the future" (Bloomfield 1961).

This forward-moving story of Israel has two covenants—the old covenant of Israel's past wilderness exodus and the new covenant of Israel's future messianic kingdom exodus. In Jeremiah 31.31, God tells how the new covenant differs from the old covenant of law: "I will make a new covenant with the house of Israel and with the house of Judah.* It will not be like the [old] covenant I made with their forefathers when I took them by the hand

---
* At one point, Israel divided into two kingdoms, northern and southern—Israel and Judah.

to lead them out of Egypt... I will put my law in their minds and write it on their hearts. I will be their God, and they will be my people" (Je 31.31b-33).

This biblical narrative moves forward by means of a literary device called Type-Antitype. This device presents parallels. In Figure 11 below, Israel's past exodus (Type) under the old covenant points to Israel's future exodus (Antitype) under the new covenant.

Israel's parallel exodus events

Type	Figure 11	Antitype
Past Exodus	Present Interim Age	Future Exodus
The wilderness exodus		Messianic kingdom exodus
1. Slavery under Pharaoh		1. Tribulation under Antichrist
2. Shaking of the earth		2. Shaking of earth and heaven
3. Israelites led by Moses		3. Jews & supporters led by Christ
under the old covenant		*under the new covenant*
of the law		*of the kingdom*
to the promised land		to eternity

Israel's story, two dramatic crises

Before the wilderness exodus, God displayed his power by shaking the earth, but in the future exodus, he'll shake earth *and* heaven.

Before the past wilderness exodus began, God displayed his power by shaking the earth. At that time, the Jews as slaves in Egypt had no identity, unity, or purpose. Therefore, at the outset, God had to express his sovereignty powerfully to unify them as his people, to authenticate Moses as their leader, and to establish Jewish identity.

At Mt. Sinai, God displayed his great power to Moses and the Israelites: "There was thunder and lightning, with a thick cloud over the mountain, and a very loud trumpet blast. Everyone in the camp trembled... the Lord descended on it [the mount] in fire. The smoke billowed up from it like smoke from a furnace, the whole mountain trembled...and the sound of the trumpet grew louder and louder" (Ex 19.16-19a), and everyone waited in fear. *Before the future messianic kingdom exodus begins,* God will, display his power to establish his sovereignty—by shaking both earth *and* heaven. At Jesus' return, he will display supernatural signs to authenticate his role as King of Kings. He will express his sovereignty not only over Israel but over all creation. "There will be signs in the sun, moon and stars… Nations will be in anguish… Men will faint from terror… for the heavenly bodies will be shaken. They will see the Son of Man coming in a cloud with power and great glory" (Lk 21.25-27)! This cosmic display will announce Christ's return to earth to lead Israel's exodus through a thousand-year messianic kingdom exodus on the way to eternity (Jl 3.15-16; Hg 2.6,7; Is 13.13; 24.18-19 OT).

Israel's story, the sustainer of Jewish heritage

Figure 12, next page, gives an overview of how Israel's seven feasts are fulfilled in Christ's three roles—as past prophet, present high priest, and future King of Kings. About these feasts, I have real-life confirmation that knowledge of them has helped preserve Jewish heritage. Here's what I learned. An elderly Jewish friend from Ukraine told me that until the time when she left Ukraine as a wife and mother, she'd lived under Stalin's atheistic communism and that growing up, she and her friends would laugh at people who said they believed in God. Nevertheless, she got a glimpse into her Jewish heritage because of her family's celebration of Judaism's feast of Passover.

That glimpse came each year when her mother-in-law would pull down all the shades in their home to avoid detection by Soviet authorities, and then the family would celebrate Passover with a special dinner. My friend said they didn't know any of the prayers, had no matzo, no script, no Bible, and no Jewish calendar, but her mother-in-law, who grew up before the rule of communism, remembered enough to honor God by preparing a special dinner for Passover each year. She had the courage to act on what she knew about God, even at great risk to her family.

---

* Judaism's three branches—Orthodox, Conservative, and Reformed—differ on biblical interpretation.

Seven feasts fulfilled in Christ in three pilgrimages of Israel

Christ/Messiah as prophet, priest and king
in chapters 8, 9, 10 of this book

Figure 12

I. Christ as past PROPHET

Chapter 8 - Israel's first pilgrimage - **Israel's past wilderness exodus**

As prophet, Christ was sent to be God's Word to the Jews. Christ says, "I was sent only to the lost sheep of Israel" (Mt 15.24).

I. THREE FEASTS:

A. Passover: Deliverance in Christ's death (Jn 1.29)

B. Unleavened Bread: Fellowship in Christ's holy life (1Co 5.8)

C. Firstfruits: Future bodily resurrection and newness of life (1Co 15.22)

II. Christ as present PRIEST (He 6.19-20)

Chapter 9 - Israel's second pilgrimage - **Israel's present interim, during the present church age**

Today, Christ is high priest in the order of Melchizedek. In heaven, he has already presented his blood to the Father on behalf of all sinners, but since *the Jews as a people* have not yet acknowledged his sacrifice, the messianic kingdom is held in abeyance. For the Jews, the present age is an interim.

II. ONE FEAST:

A. Pentecost, one feast: the church's birth and empowerment (Ac 1.8)

III, Christ as future KING OF KINGS in messianic kingdom exodus

Chapter 10 - Israel's future pilgrimage - **messianic kingdom exodus**

In that future kingdom with Christ as king, there will be a wedding celebration for Christ as groom, the church as bride, and Israel as exalted among nations.

III. THREE FEASTS:

A. Trumpets: Return of Christ (Mt 24.31)

B. Atonement: Redemption of Israel in Christ (Eze 37.12)

C. Tabernacles: Reign of Christ (Is 11.1-9)

In America, though my friend's family joined a Conservative[*] synagogue, she still didn't know what to think about God. In fact, when I first met her, she said, she was an atheist—"that all we have is ink on paper in a Bible written so long ago." So I pointed out to her that what we have in Israel's seven feasts is a *living* drama that reached her in the atheistic Soviet Union thousands of years later through her mother-in-law's memory of the celebration of Israel's Passover. (Today, my friend *does* acknowledge God.)

Jewish survival is unique, for no other ethnic group has been able to maintain its identity in exile for so many centuries. This in itself is a miracle of God, for by celebrating Israel's God-given feasts in three pilgrimages each year, the Jewish people pass on to each new generation the knowledge they need to appreciate God's care of them throughout their miraculous past. This creates in them the faith to believe scripture about their future.[*]

Israel's story in three pilgrimages in this book's chapters 8, 9, 10
(See Figure 12, page 104.)

*Ch. 8. In the past, Jews **under the old covenant of the law of Moses**.*

*Ch. 9. Today, Jews **in an interim** between two exoduses.*

*Ch. 10. In the future kingdom, Jews as a people **under the new covenant**.*

This **Chapter 8 in this book is about** Israel's first pilgrimage. which began with a cry. Abraham's grandson Jacob with seventy persons in his extended family (Ex 1.5) left Israel to go to Egypt because of famine. Yet four hundred thirty years later (Ex 12.40), Jacob's household had become Pharaoh's slaves, two million strong.[†] When the Israelites cried out, God told Moses, "I have heard them crying out because of their slave drivers, and I am concerned about their suffering. So I have come down to rescue them from the hand of the Egyptians and to bring them up out… of that land into a good and spacious land…" (Ex 3.7-8). From this we see that the first pilgrimage celebrates Israel's deliverance from slavery and their escape to a new land by their wilderness exodus.

---

[*] The Bible is also confirmed by archeology. Recently, Tom Levy, the author's son John's neighbor, an archeologist at the University of California, San Diego, led an excavation of Solomon's mines, dated in the 10th century B.C. (1Ki 1-12; Lk 12.27). This was filmed by National Geographic.

[†] "Two million" is based on scripture that says 601,730 men (Nu 26.51). With women and children, that extrapolates to an estimated two million (Expositor's Bible Commentary [Ex 38.21 - 39.1]).

Chapter 9 in this book: Israel's second pilgrimage has only one feast, Pentecost, which illustrates Israel's interim between the nation's two exoduses. Timewise, this interim for Jews as a people lies between their past exodus through the wilderness on the way to the promised land and their future exodus through the messianic kingdom on the way to eternity. In Israel's present interim, God doesn't deal with Jews as a people but instead deals with them as he deals with everyone else in the present age—as individuals in need of the Christ/Savior.

Chapter 10 in this book: Israel's third pilgrimage is about Israel's future exodus through the thousand-year messianic kingdom under the new covenant. Just as in the first pilgrimage, this pilgrimage will also begin with a cry, for prophecy tells us that Jews as a people will suffer greatly in the future tribulation period under Antichrist. In the end, God will rescue them. This rescue will be more spectacular than the first, for in the exodus under the old covenant, the Jews escaped only iron chains and slave masters, but in the future exodus under the new covenant of the messianic kingdom, Jews as a people will not only escape persecution but will also be exalted among the world's nations. This third pilgrimage under Christ/Messiah is about Israel's exodus through the thousand-year messianic kingdom on the way to eternity.

Celebrating the seven feasts keeps alive in Jewish memory God's plan for them, for the feasts are still celebrated annually in Jewish homes just as they have been through the ages, sometimes in far-flung places and often under desperate circumstances.

Fulfillment of Israel's first pilgrimage: The wilderness exodus

This chapter eight in this book is about Christ as new-covenant prophet in the Feasts of Passover, Unleavened Bread, and Firstfruits, which symbolize Christ's supernatural work in the hearts and minds of believing Jews and Genties today under God's new covenant.

Israel's first pilgrimage, fulfilled in Christ's regeneration of believers:

A. *Passover: Deliverance from sin through Christ's death* (Jn 1.29)
B. *Unleavened Bread: Fellowship through Christ's holy life* (1Co 5.8)
C. *Firstfruits: Newness of life & resurrection by Christ's resurrection*

A. Passover: Deliverance from sin through Christ's death (Jn 1.29)"

If we walk in the light as he is in the light, we have fellowship with one another, and the blood of Jesus… purifies us from every sin" (1Jn 1.7). This blessed fellowship is possible only as believers walk in the light together in oneness of spirit.

Figure 13, below, shows that the purity and fellowship of the feast of Unleavened Bread overlaps timewise with the feast of Passover and the feast of Firstfruits (Scott 1997). For me, this overlap of the feast of Unleavened Bread suggests that the purity and fellowship symbolized by Unleavened Bread permeates all three feasts of the first pilgrimage, as shown below.

First pilgrimage: Man's regeneration fulfilled in Christ

Figure 13

The feast of Unleavened Bread, in its timing, permeates the other feasts:

Passover (14th)	**Unleavened Bread**	Firstfruits
1st - 8th day	2nd - 8th day	3rd day only
Jesus' crucifixion	His godly, sin-free life	His resurrection

The feasts of Passover and Unleavened Bread

This chapter on Israel's first pilgrimage is fulfilled in the new covenant regeneration of sinners, which brings deliverance from sin.

In Israel's initial Passover feast, each Jewish home was to kill a lamb in the first month, fourteenth day,[*] of Israel's religious calendar. This feast, memorializes a crisis when Jews were slaves in Egypt (Scott 1997, 38). In that crisis, Passover marks the beginning of their deliverance by God from the bondage of that slavery.

Before the initial Passover, God gave the Jews this message: "I will pass through Egypt and strike down every firstborn" (Ex

---

[*] Christian fulfillment of Israel's feasts corresponds only to the *initial* dates of Israel's feasts because since then, Gregorian dates differ from dates on the Jewish calendar, which is based on moon phases.

12.12). He instructed the Israelites to apply the blood of a lamb on the door frames of their homes. He said, "When the Lord goes through the land to strike down the Egyptians, he will see the blood [like the sign of the cross] on the top and sides of the door frame and will *pass over* that doorway, and he will not permit the destroyer to enter your houses and strike you down" (Ex 12.23. Italics added). So, God promised the Israelites that the death angel would spare their blood-redeemed homes, but he'd slay Egypt's firstborn.

The symbolism: Christ's crucifixion fulfills the Jewish Passover, for the blood of the Israelite's lamb symbolizes the blood of the Lamb of God, who delivers sinners from the bondage of sin, saves them from the second death in the fiery lake (Re 20.14b), and promises them life forever with Christ.

B. Unleavened Bread: Fellowship through Christ 's holy life (1 Co 5.8)

The initial feast of Unleavened Bread, was celebrated in the first month, fifteenth day of Israel's religious calendar (Le 23.6). This feast lasts seven days—from the second day of Passover to the eighth day of Passover (Scott 1997, 58-59).

In the feast of unleavened bread, leaven is prohibited in baked bread and is totally cleansed from homes, for in both Old and New Testaments, leaven symbolizes evil (Spangler 2009, 106; Vine 1940, 327). One reference to leaven as evil is stated by Paul to Christians: "Purge out… the old leaven that ye may be a new lump, as ye are unleavened. For even Christ our Passover is sacrificed for us" (1Co 5.7 KJV). For believers, Christ is the Lamb of God without the leaven of sin. He is Passover's sacrifice.

New life, as symbolized by the wilderness exodus

Ruth Winegar, a late friend at Penngrove Community Church near Petaluma, California, entered the new life symbolized by the three feasts of Israel's first pilgrimage, by learning from God's Word about salvation, by believing what the Word says, and by receiving what God offers.

First, she prayed the sinner's prayer—"God, have mercy on me, a sinner"—and asked Jesus to come into her heart to make her a new person in Christ (Lk 18.13b). Then, though she waited on God, assurance of her salvation did not come even though people around her tried to encourage her.

Finally, someone prompted her to thank the Lord for the *promise* of salvation for those who believe. When Ruth gave thanks, the floodgates opened, assurance came, and *fulfillment* engulfed her soul. God's new life entered her, and she served him the rest of her life in resurrection power. She learned that fulfillment comes after believing and receiving.

Ruth's experience of entering God's new covenant in Christ illustrates the sequence in Figure 14 below—first, learning biblical facts, then believing them, and finally, thanking God for fulfill-ment of his promises.

The sequence for receiving from God:
Fact, Faith, Fulfillment
Figure 14

1. FACT: By seeking God in his Word, a believer learns facts about who God is and what he promises.
2. FAITH: A person believes God's promise in his Word.
3. FULFILLMENT: He receives fulfillment of the promise.

Scripture provides facts about God's character and his promises so that believers can stand on the facts. By faith believers appropriate in the present what they know to be promised in God's Word, without having to see or feel any evidence. Such God-inspired faith believes now before fulfillment. Evangelist Smith Wigglesworth said the same thing, for he "knew that as he moved toward God in faith, God would move toward him in power (Stormont 1989, 83).

C. Firstfruits: Bodily resurrection and newness of life (1Co 15.20)

On Israel's calendar, *Firstfruits* comes in the first month on the sixteenth day, which is the third day after Passover. In the Christian interpretation of feast days for redeemed people, resurrection

The time sequence of "The First Resurrection"

Three stages of the first resurrection for redeemed people
1Corinthians 15.20-24

Figure 15

A. Firstfruits—Jesus
1. Jesus Christ, Redeemer—first one in the first resurrection

Three days after crucifixion (Passover), **Christ** became the first[*] resurrected forerunner (Firstfruits) (1Co 15.20).

B. Harvest—Christians
2. Christians—second in the first resurrection of the redeemed:

Before the tribulation period begins, all living and dead Gentile and Jewish Christians will be resurrected and caught up to meet Christ in the air to go to heaven in the rapture (1Th 4.13-18). This means the church will not go through the tribulation on earth that follows.

C. Gleanings—Jews and sympathizers
3. Jews as a people—third in the first resurrection of the redeemed:

After the tribulation period and before the kingdom begins, **deceased Israelite believers and tribulation martyrs** will be resurrected to serve in the administration of King Jesus. Their residence will be in the heavenly New Jerusalem during Christ's reign in his world-wide kingdom on earth (Pentecost 1958, 541) (He 11.16; Je 2.3; Da 12.1,2).

After the messianic kingdom begins, resurrected people will live in the heavenly New Jerusalem, and the living survivors of the tribulation— believing Jews—will live on earth as redeemed human beings, yet the two groups will interact with each other in fellowship (Re 21.24-27).

---

[*] Earlier, Lazarus was brought back to life but in a mortal, human body, not in a resurrected body.

is in just one stage just before eternity begins. At that time, all the unredeemed will stand for judgment before God at the great white throne (Re 20.11). And since they will stand there without a Savior to pay for their sins, they will be sentenced according to their unforgiven sins and will suffer "the second death," which takes place in the lake of fire (Re 20.15).

In Figure 15, previous page, the three resurrected stages represent the ingathering of a single crop of redeemed people. Figure 15 shows the firstfruits of the crop (Christ), the harvest of the crop (the church), and the gleanings of the crop (Jews as a people and their supporters).

9 Pentecost in Israel's second pilgrimage: An interim between two exoduses

> Because Jesus lives forever, he has a permanent [high] priesthood.
> Therefore he is able to save completely those who come to God
> through him, because he always lives to intercede for them.
> --Hebrews 7.24, 25

On the day of Pentecost, Christ as new covenant high priest in heaven poured out the Holy Spirit to give birth to the church. On that day, the apostle Peter quoted two prophecies by the Hebrew prophet, Joel.

Joel's first prophecy foretells birth of the church.

Joel's second prophecy foretells Christ's return to earth.

Between these two events lies the present age, Israel's interim.

Two OT Prophecies by Hebrew prophet Joel (Jl 2.28--32)

1) Joel's Old Testament prophecy on the the birth of the church: In Acts 2, Peter interprets Joel 2.28-29 as a Hebrew prophecy that points ahead to an outpouring of the Holy Spirit which happened on Pentecost at the birth of the church. Peter paraphrases Joel's prophecy: "In the last days, God says, I will pour out my Spirit on all people. Your sons and daughters will prophesy, your young men will see visions, your old men will dream dreams. Even on my servants, both men and women, I will pour out my Spirit in those days, and they will prophesy"(Act 2.17-18). This prophecy of Christ's outpouring of the Spirit was fulfilled after Christ's ascension to heaven and continues to be fulfilled in the church today.

(Between Joel's OT prophecies,Israel's interim the present church age)

2) Joel's Prophecy on Christ's return: Peter interprets Joel 2.30-32 as a prophecy to be fulfilled when Christ returns as King of Kings —when the church will be his bride ,and Israel will be exalted. This prophecy tells of a cosmic display. About Christ's return: "I will show wonders in the heaven above and signs on the earth below, blood and fire and billows of smoke. The sun will be turned to darkness and the moon to blood before the coming of the great and glorious day of the Lord" (Ac 2.19-20).

Review of Israel's three annual pilgrimages to celebrate seven feasts

A. First pilgrimage: Three feasts in Israel's wilderness exodus
B. Second pilgrimage: One feast in Israel's present interim
C. Third pilgrimage: Three feasts in Israel's kingdom exodus

A.Pentecost, a single feast for Israel's second pilgrimage:
   Christ's church, created and empowered (Ac 2)

B. Only a single feast for Israel's second pilgrimage—Pentecost
   1) Christ's role as baptizer in the Holy Spirit (Ac 2)
   2) Christ's role as present priest under the new covenant (Je 31.33)
   3) Christ's role as priest in revivals of the present day

1) Christ's role as baptizer in the Holy Spirit (Ac 1.8, and 2)

For the church, Pentecost* is celebrated as the day of receiving the baptism in the Holy Spirit (Ac 1.8;;2). In the Old Testament, the Torah says Israel was to celebrate Pentecost fifty days after the feast of Firstfruits (Le 23.15) (Scott 1997, 59). Each family was to bring to the priest "two loaves made of fine wheat flour, baked with yeast [leaven]," which the priest was to present as a wave offering of firstfruits to the Lord" (Le 23.15-21). Besides bread, the priest was to wave two lambs.

On Pentecost in New Testament times, Christ in heaven poured out the Holy Spirit to unite Jewish believers on earth as one body, the church, and to empower them for ministry. This feast is a transition from Moses' old covenant of law to Abraham's prophesied new covenant of grace. After the outpouring, Peter gave an invitation to his fellow Jews: "Repent… and you will receive the gift of the Holy Spirit. The promise is for you and your children and for all who are far off—for all whom the Lord our God will call" (Ac 2.38, 39; Jl 2.28,29).

Acts 2: "When the day of Pentecost came, they [Jesus' fol-

---

* *Pentecost* in New Testament Greek means "the fiftieth"— 50 days after Firstfruits, or 50 days after Christ's resurrection. Pentecost is also known as the Feast of Weeks, for it is celebrated seven weeks and a sabbath after Firstfruits.

lowers] were all together in one place. Suddenly a sound like the blowing of a violent wind came from heaven and filled the whole house where they were sitting. They saw what seemed to be separated tongues of fire that came to rest on each of them. All of them were filled with the Holy Spirit and began to speak in other tongues as the Spirit enabled them. Now there were staying in Jerusalem God-fearing Jews from every nation under heaven. When they heard this sound, a crowd came together in bewilderment, because each one heard them speaking in his own language. Utterly amazed, they asked: 'Are not all these men who are speaking Galileans? Then how is it that each of us hears them in his own native language'" (Ac 2.1-8, 11b-13)? On Pentecost, the church was born.

End of the old covenant

Let's backtrack now to look at events that made possible this present age when Christ has become priest in heaven under the new covenant. Let's begin at Christ's crucifixion, the day when God opened the way for ordinary believers to become his priests, so that now they can enter the Most Holy Place of his presence. On the day of the crucifixion at high noon, when Jesus hung on the cross, the earth suddenly became shrouded in a darkness that lasted until three P.M. Then, when Jesus cried out with his last breath, that's when the heavy, knit curtain in front of the Most Holy Place of the temple (Mt 27.5) was ripped from top to bottom as though torn apart by the hand of God from on high (Mt 27.45-54)!

At that moment, the temple curtain ceased to be a barrier to man's fellowship with God. Under the old covenant, it was a barrier, for at that time, only the high priest could enter the Most Holy Place to offer the blood of the lamb once a year, but now under the new covenant, all Christians can enter directly into the Lord's presence and can have continual fellowship with him.

2) Christ's role as priest under the new covenant (Je 31.33)

The new birth experience of the new covenant

After Jesus' resurrection, he appeared to his followers for forty days. On the first evening of Jesus' resurrection, he appeared, to his disciples, breathed on them, and said, "Receive the Spirit." That's when those Jews became Christians under the new covenant. After ten more days, Jesus ascended to heaven and as high priest presented his blood to the Father to seal the salvation of Israel and the church under the new covenant.

In Jeremiah 31.33, the Lord describes that spiritual new covenant: "I will put my law in their minds and write it on their hearts. I will be their God, and they will be my people." This verse describes the believer's rebirth under the new covenant. Ezekiel also speaks for the Lord when he refers to the new birth of the new covenant: "I will give you a new heart and put a new spirit in you; I will remove from you your heart of stone and give you a heart of flesh" (Exe 3626). This is the miracle of the Christian life!

Israel and the church: Their times of entry into the new covenant

As individual Jews in need of a Savior, those disciples above were born again under the new covenant, but Jews *as a people* will not enter the new covenant until they recognize Jesus as their promised Messiah. In the present age, nevertheless, Jews *as individuals continue to* enter God's new covenant spiritually here and now by the new birth of the indwelling Spirit of the risen Christ, the Lamb of God.

We see that both the church and Israel enter into the new birth of the new covenant, but in different periods. Today, Gentiles and Jews *as individuals* enter the new covenant when they become born-again Christians (Lk 22.20), but not until a future generation will *Jews as a people* enter the new covenant of the messianic kingdom; this will be in the end times after the tribulation period.

A contrast of responses to Holy Spirit-anointed ministry

Two Jews, Peter and Stephen, were empowered to preach after their Holy Spirit baptism, but responses to their witness differed.

When we look at Peter's life, we see that as a Christian, he became empowered to witness for God after his Holy Spirit bap-

---

* The disciples were born again by their faith in Jesus' death and resurrection. This happened after Jesus' resurrection but before he ascended to present his blood to the Father in heaven and also before he poured out the Holy Spirit on the Day of Pentecost..

tism. So, let's see what Peter was like before that Holy Spirit baptism. Earlier, on the day of Jesus' arrest, while Peter was waiting to see what the outcome of Jesus' trial would be, he warmed himself by a fire in the courtyard outside the place of the trial. There, in three incidents, individuals accused Peter of being a follower of Jesus, but each time he denied he even knew Jesus, and he swore that he was speaking the truth. Later, however, after his baptism in the Holy Spirit, this man, who had been ashamed to admit that he knew Jesus became bold and full of power. And after this Holy Spirit empowerment on the day of Pentecost, Peter preached to the crowd with this charge about the Jews' role in Jesus' crucifixion: "Let all Israel be assured of this: God has made this Jesus, whom you crucified, both Lord and Christ." (Ac 2.36). "When the people heard this, they were cut to the heart and asked Peter and the other apostles, 'Brothers, what shall we do?'" And because of Peter's sermon, about three thousand Jews were "cut to the heart," turned to the Lord, and were redeemed (Ac 2.36-38). Description of this incident ends by saying that these new born Christians enjoyed the favor of all the people (Ac 2.47).

Later, under Stephen's anointed preaching, other Jewish leaders responded differently: They became fiercely maniacal. "They were furious and gnashed their teeth at him" (Ac 7.54b). Here's what happened after Stephen preached: "… Stephen, full of the Holy Spirit, looked up to heaven and saw the glory of God, and Jesus standing at the right hand of God. 'Look,' he said, 'I see heaven open and the Son of Man standing at the right hand of God.' At this, they [the Jewish leaders] covered their ears and, yelling at the top of their voices, they all rushed at him, dragged him out of the city and began to stone him… While they were stoning him, Stephen prayed, 'Lord Jesus, receive my spirit.' Then he fell on his knees and cried out, 'Lord, do not hold this sin against them.' When Stephen had said this, he fell asleep" (Ac 7.55-60).

The violent reaction of those who stoned Stephen is in sharp contrast to those who reacted to Peter's sermon on the day of Pentecost. Under Peter's preaching, people were convicted of sin, repented, and became redeemed.

The fact remains that though both Peter and Stephen were anointed by the Holy Spirit, they received opposite responses from their audiences. The lesson we take away from this is that regardless of the response a person faces as a result of his testimony for the Lord, that Christian can go forth rejoicing in the knowledge that Christ is the anchor of his soul and the master of his future.

Important points about Pentecost

A point to note here is that even though the anointing of the Spirit can be ongoing in life, that blessing's continuance does not happen automatically. So the question becomes, how can a Christian maintain that Spirit-anointing on his life? Smith Wigglesworth, a British evangelist in the twentieth century's early Pentecostal movement, had great fruitfulness in ministry, yet he confessed that he had experienced times of dullness of spirit and ineffectiveness in witness. He said that to regain purity of heart and intimacy with God, he had to humble himself before God and in so doing, he would allow himself to be broken in God's presence and thereby to be renewed in spirit: "The LORD is close to the brokenhearted and saves those who are crushed in spirit" (Ps 34.18).

Another important point about Pentecost is that its sacrificial offering differs from other Judaic offerings, for it includes leaven (yeast), which in scripture always symbolizes the presence of evil (Vine 1940, 327; Spangler 2009). In this Hebrew offering, leaven is prescribed, but in other offerings, it is prohibited, for those other feasts point to Christ, in whom there is no evil.

Israel's Pentecost points ahead to the presence of leaven in the church, which was born on Pentecost. The Torah's Levitical prescription for leaven in the Pentecostal wave offering points ahead to imperfect Christians, who would celebrate a future celebration of Pentecost. And since leaven is a symbol of evil, the message of the feast of Pentecost is that perfection—the absence of all evil—is not the standard by which Christians are to judge other Christians or themselves. We are to accept the human condition. Indeed our job is not to judge others' faults but to encourage, forgive, and support each other and ourselves, for by such acceptance, Christians are able to allow the Holy Spirit to do the work of uniting and empowering us to be his people.

Also, Peter, in his sermon on Pentecost, revealed that God would now include Gentiles in his plan. Peter confirmed that fact by quoting the prophet Joel, who says that in the last days, God would pour out his Spirit on *all people* so that everyone who calls on the name of the Lord would be saved (Ac 2.17, 21. Italics added). In quoting Joel that "all people" would be saved, Peter was saying that God would include Gentiles in his plan.

In explaining this inclusion of Gentiles, Peter paraphrased God's promise in Isaiah 44.3, which says, "The promise is for you and your children and for *all* who are far off—for all whom the Lord our God will call" (Ac 2.39; cf. Isaiah 44.3b, Italics added). This "calling" indicates that God would call out individual Jews and Gentiles from the general population in order to reconcile them with himself and with other members of the body of Christ in the church. The word "church" actually means "called out ones," which is the literal definition of the Greek word for *church*.

As for the timing, Gentiles did not become a significant part of the church until about ten years after the church's origin, according to David du Plessis's conclusion (du Plessis, 1970, 45).

Reconciliation of Jews and Gentiles within the church

Finally, since we know that Joel's prophecy says that Gentiles would become God's people, we can understand the symbolism of Pentecost concerning the two wheat loaves, which were to be presented to the Lord on behalf of the offerers. In this Judaic ritual, the two loaves were presented to the Lord as one offering (Wight 1956, 107). From what we understand about Jews and Gentiles in other scripture (e.g., Ro 9-11), we can say that the Pentecostal presentation of two loaves as one offering signifies the unity of Jews and Gentiles in one body of believers, the church (Eph 4.15-16).

The basis for reconciliation between Jews and Gentiles in the church is in the New Testament: "He [Christ] himself is our peace, who has made the two one [Jews and Gentiles in the church] and has destroyed the barrier, the dividing wall of hostility, by abolishing in his flesh the law with its commandments and regulations" (Eph 2..11-22). His purpose was to create in himself one new man out of the two, thus making peace between the two"—between Jew and Gentile.

3) Christ's role as priest in Christian revivals today

My introduction to the Pentecostal world

In the 1950s, David du Plessis was the pastor that God raised up to minister to mainstream pastors in the early days of the World Council of Churches. As a Pentecostal pastor from South Africa, he prepared the way for America's charismatic revival. His involvement with the World Council, however, was much to the consternation of his Pentecostal brethren, who at the time frowned upon his fellowship with those "modernists." Nevertheless, by his vision and by his ministry, du Plessis paved the way for the mainstream charismatic revival of the 1960s and 1970s. I learned about du Plessis's encounters with the World Council from *The Spirit Bade Me Go* (du Plessis 1970). That book tells how the Lord used him to prepare the Christian world for what would later become known as the charismatic movement—a movement that overcame denominational differences in its sweep through the country.

I was introduced to the Pentecostal world in about 1956. Though years earlier, I had been interested in the work of the Holy Spirit, I still lacked knowledge. Therefore, in practical terms for me, the world of Pentecostalism didn't exist... until I became acquainted with my neighbor, Rose Fidler.

As already explained, Pastor Fidler, a retired but active Pentecostal evangelist. lived across Fern Hill Road from out family in Rainier, Oregon, where we lived when our first three children were small and our fourth child was born. (Our fifth child was born later after we moved across the Columbia River to Kelso, Washington.) Mrs. Fidler was one of the few people who had the experience necessary to answer my questions about present-day miracles. Though I believed that God heals today, I had this question: "If God heals miraculously today, why are there not people being raised from the dead?" Mrs. Fidler had the answer, for in two cases, she had prayed for babies that were raised from the dead. And since then, I've heard of other such accounts.

Over the years, through many visits in my friend's home, through observation of her ministry and through hearing her preach, I could confirm that she had a scriptural basis for her views, and I could assess the integrity of her ministry. My acquaintance with her came before the charismatic revival took hold in America. And during that period my hunger for God continued to increase.

Now in my nineties, I treasure my memory of Evangelist Fidler's experiences and her memory of the experience of others in the days of the Pentecostal revival in the early 1900s. By the hour, I would listen to her tell of miracles of those days. When I add her memories to my own memories of the charismatic revival in the sixties and seventies, I gain perspective on the two main American revivals of the twentieth century—the early Pentecostal revival and the later charismatic revival. What I see as most notable about the revivals is their exaltation of Jesus Christ, for that's the purpose of the ministry of the Holy Spirit. The Holy Spirit exalts Christ to draw people into love for him and into love for each other. The Holy Spirit also makes the Word of God come alive in order to bring spiritual growth to Christians.

The Pentecostal revival in the early decades of the 1900s

I encountered firsthand the charismatic revival of the fifties to the seventies. I also learned about the earlier surge of the Spirit in the first decade of the twentieth century by reading about that revival. This Pentecostal movement first began on Azusa Street in Los Angeles in a building that had been a church and more recently had been a place to store construction supplies. In fact, at one time the place had been used as a stable.

William J. Seymour, an African American with one eye, was the humble servant that God used for his glory at the start of the Pentecostal revival in 1905. Seymour had learned about the baptism of the Holy Spirit at a Texas Bible school. Other pioneers before Seymour laid the groundwork for the Pentecostal revival, but the revival at Azusa Street became the spark that lit the con-flagration that spread far and wide. Also, earlier, the 1904 revival in Wales inspired hunger for God and paved the way for the Pentecostal revival in America (Bartleman 1962).

In 1906, after Seymour answered a call to preach in Los Angeles, California, he began the now-famous ministry on Azusa Street, and the rest is history, as the saying goes. Frank Bartleman in *Another Wave Rolls In!* writes that though Seymour was rec-ognized as the nominal leader in that mission, the ministry was spontaneous and continuous, night and day (Bartleman 1925, 1962). L. Thomas Holdcroft, theology professor, writes that the mission "operated in that capacity for only three years" but "it was the center at which many future Pentecostal leaders received their personal Pentecost" (Holdcroft 1999, 86).

During that revival, Seymour himself spent his time at the Azusa Street church mostly in prayer with his head behind an improvised pulpit made from a couple of crates. However, he was not baptized in the Spirit until after those meetings began. From that ministry, word spread that God was doing a special work, and so people kept flocking to the little place, which could not hold the crowds that sought entrance. In that humble setting, black and white people mingled freely, and from there, Christians carried the stream of blessing to other places, near and far.

God's work often begins in unlikely places. God chose a man-ger—a feeding trough in a stable—as the place of birth for him to break into this world as a human being. The spiritual darkness of the culture of the West Coast during my adult years was different from the culture of the Bible belt where I grew up in Edinburg in the southernmost tip of Texas in the Rio Grande Valley. And yet, God chose the darkness of the West Coast to bring revival.

Joy in the charismatic revival of the sixties and seventies

God probably chose the darkness of the West Coast for the charismatic revival because there it would have the greatest im-pact. In my childhood, I saw what a difference a lit match could make in the pitch black darkness in Carlsbad Cavern.[*] Similarly, in the spiritual darkness of the West Coast, the light of the gospel was able to shine brighter there. In fact, that's where both twentieth century Pentecostal revivals broke out most fully.

In the charismatic revival of the sixties and seventies, people were redeemed, were baptized in the Spirit with the biblical evidence of speaking in tongues. Also, there were physical healings and other manifestations of power in ministry. But for me, the outstanding characteristic of the movement was the pure joy that prevailed.

That joy was expressed in worship and in daily life. The book, *Nine O'Clock in the Morning,* describes the spontaneity of that joy. One example is that when author Dennis Bennett, an Episcopalian priest, called his secretary about a routine matter, they were so overflowing with Christian joy that they ended up verbally praising the Lord for some time before they could settle down to discuss business. This joy was expressed everywhere through prayer and praise. My church at that time had a spacious prayer room, and after the evening service, it would be filled with people kneeling, looking up to heaven, and praying in the Spirit.

Let me give a small example of the spontaneity of joy in a serendipitous encounter in about 1970, after my husband's death. After a charismatic gathering, the Lord brought to our family in Kelso, Washington—a young, Spirit-baptized Roman Catholic priest, Father Joseph Manning to visit our family. With his guitar and his three young volunteer troubadours, he stayed for a few days in our family's third-floor guest apartment,‡ fasting.

I remember the joy of that God-ordained visit.

A sermon's rallying cry for today—"Jesus is alive!"

Today, more than half a century later, one sermon about joy stands out in my memory. An Eastern Catholic priest spoke to Christians of all theological persuasions at a Full Gospel Business Men's Fellowship (FGBMF)* meeting in a local hotel banquet room in Longview, Washington—Kelso's twin city. In that re-

* Carlsbad Cavern had to discontinue the blackout demonstration because some people panicked.
† Father Bennett was greatly used in the charismatic revival worldwide, and especially in the states.
‡ The Evanses weren't wealthy; they paid the price of $18,500 for a former banker's 17 room home,

vival, the leaders and the audience had in common one thing, a love for the Savior that transcended denominational ties. In his talk, the priest exalted the Lord Jesus when he preached about the ringing of joy bells in the days of the ancient Israelites. And what were those joy bells? They were the tiny golden bells sewn between embroidered pomegranates on the hem of the robe that the high priest of Israel wore when he ministered in the Most Holy Place of the temple (Ex 28.33). As the high priest moved about, the Jews outside could hear those bells on the priest's robe ringing out, and they would know that since he was was still alive in God's pres-ence, this meant Israel's sins for the year were forgiven.

"Jesus is alive!" was the rallying cry of the Eastern Catholic priest's sermon. He explained that under the old covenant on the annual day of Atonement, the high priest entered the Most Holy Place of the temple to apply the blood of the sacrifice on the mercy seat of the ark of the Testimony in order to atone for the sins of Israel for the past year. And while the priest moved about ministering in the Most Holy Place, those tiny golden bells on the hem of the priest's garment would ring out, signaling to the Israelites outside the temple that their high priest was *still alive,* even though he was in the very presence of the God who is holy. The survival of the Israelite priest meant that the blood sacrifice of the lamb offered for Israel's sins was accepted by the Lord, and those sins were therefore forgiven for yet another year. Then, a year later and every year thereafter, the Israelites would go through the same ritual on the day of Atonement. Each year, the ringing bells signaled the joyous message of forgiveness for the past year.

"Jesus is alive!" With that cry, the Eastern Catholic priest pro-claimed that when Jesus as high priest poured out the Holy Spirit ten days after he ascended to heaven, he signaled to Jesus' follow-ers below that they were forgiven. This Holy Spirit outpouring on Pentecost signaled that sins confessed had been forgiven by the blood of Jesus' sacrifice, not just for a year as in Judaism. How glorious the cleansing of Jesus' blood, which cleanses **forever!**

---

* The FGBMF, made up of Christian businessmen, was greatly used of God in the charismatic revival. Their ministry was often held in hotel banquet rooms.

Understanding revival and the role of the Holy Spirit

My account gives a glimpse into what I became personally aware of about past revivals. The elements of praise and worship that characterized the charismatic revival continues in some congregations, but in the charismatic movement today, the greatest spiritual influence can be seen in new converts and new churches overseas—especially among Muslims in the Middle East (Rosenberg 1960, 1995).

From my view of the scene, the charismatic revival kept its momentum until the time that some prominent people on the national stage—people not on the West Coast—sought to control what was happening. They began pushing a "shepherding" agenda with lines of authority in a new hierarchical structure, and in so doing, they overstepped people's boundaries in personal and church life. I think that's why the charismatic movement began to subside., for God does not honor human dictates. At that point, Christians began to turn away from universal meetings and focus on incorporating their experience into their own churches through small groups or in the larger realm for some whole congregations, as in my church.

Now for a word about the person of the Holy Spirit! What we need to remember is that though the work of the Spirit in revival is often dramatic, the Spirit himself remains out of the spotlight, for as a member of the trinity, his role is always one of deference. He seeks to honor the Father by exalting the Son. The Spirit does not call attention to himself but instead unites people in Christ so that they can have intimate communion with the Father and with each other. Christians pray to the Father in the name of the Lord Jesus Christ, and they minister through the empowering of the Holy Spirit. What happens is that when Christ is exalted, the Spirit is released to bring glorious freedom and a oneness of spirit that is beyond comparison to anything else in this life.

The church in the present age and in the future

First, let's look at the church in the present age: The church age began on Pentecost, and the church age will end when the church is raptured to heaven. Then after a seven-year tribulation on earth, the church as Christ's bride will return with Christ from heaven to earth to reign with him in the messianic kingdom for a thousand years.

Jews as a people in their present interim age

Now let's look at *Jews as a people.* For the Jews, this present age is an interim between Israel's past and Israel's future. During this age, Jews as a people will continue to cling to the law of the old covenant even though they have no temple, no priesthood, and no sacrifice to implement the old covenant of the law in God's prescribed way. Scripture says that *as a people,* Jews will not repent until their eyes are opened during the seven-year trials of the tribulation during the rule of the future Antichrist. Then after Jewish repentance, Christ will return to earth to pardon them, to deliver them from their enemies, to exonerate them as his people, and finally to rule over all the earth from Jerusalem for a thousand years. Christ will be King of Kings in this messianic kingdom exodus on the way to eternity.

Meanwhile, *individual Jews* are called by God to enter his new covenant spiritually through the new birth (Lk 22.20). In fact, for everyone living in the present era, the Lord offers no other way for reconciliation with himself except through the blood of the Savior. Jesus himself says, "I am the way and the truth and the life. No one comes to the Father except through me" (Jn 14.6).

The Spirit is released to bring glorious freedom and a wonderful oneness of spirit. I long to see the Holy Spirit sweep across America with the purifying winds of revival, which will bring a greater love for God's Word. How we need for *purity* and *faith* to be our watchwords!

Next let's look at Israel's thousand-year messianic kingdom exodus.

10   Israel's third pilgrimage: The messianic kingdom exodus

Even the neglect of Bible prophecy itself
represents one view of prophecy.
—Paul Lee Tan, *The Interpretation of Prophecy*

Third pilgrimage: Israel's messianic kingdom exodus to eternity

    A. Trumpets (Rosh Hashanah), Christ's return and judgment (Mt 25.31)

    B. Atonement (Yom Kippur), Christ's redemption of Israel (Eze 37.12)

    C. Tabernacles (Sukkot), Christ's future reign in glory (Is 11.1-9)

The messianic-kingdom exodus blast-off to eternity *begins:*

    A. Ready—the feast of Trumpets—Christ's Return & Judgment

    B. Set—the feast of Atonement—Christ's Redemption of Israel

    C. Go—the feast of Tabernacles—Christ's Reign in glory

Each feast in this third pilgrimage has a message about Christ as the future new covenant king: The feast of Trumpets proclaims the New Year on Israel's religious calendar:* Its message is, "The king is coming!" The message of the day of Atonement is about judgment: "Prepare to meet your king!" The message of the feast of Tabernacles is about Christ's reign as King of Kings: "Rejoice in the king's reign over his people!"

A. Feast of Trumpets, Christ's return and judgment (Mt 25.31)

In this feast, Israelites were not to work the first two days of the Jewish year and were to present an offering made by fire (Le 23.25). This feast of Trumpets will be fulfilled at Christ's return. At his return, some will be prepared for his coming, and some will not be prepared. Jews as a people and Christians will be ready, but unbelievers will not be ready.

In the end time, God interacts with three people groups—Christians, Jews as a people, and unbelievers (Figure 16, next page).

---

* Israel's civil calendar begins with Trumpets on Tishri (seventh month on Israel's religious calendar).

Overview of three people groups in the end time

a) Christ Returns. b) Christ Gathers. c) Christ Tests or Judges.

Figure 16

(COMPARE ALL THE A'S, ALL THE B'S, AND ALL THE C'S)

---

1. The church

a) With a trumpet call *before the tribulation*, Christ returns for the rapture to meet Jewish and Gentile Christians in the air.

b) Before the tribulation, Christ gathers up the living and the resurrected Christians to rapture them to heaven (1Th 4.13-18).

c) In heaven, to prepare the church to be Christ's bride, God tests the works of Christians by fire and gives out rewards.

---

2. Jews as a people

a) With a trumpet call *after the tribulation*, Christ returns to earth to bring his persecuted, repentant Jewish brethren to himself.

b) When Christ returns, he gathers Jews as a people to Israel by sending angels to bring them "from the four winds" (Mt 24.31).

c) Earlier, during the tribulation, Christ will have tested the Jews as a people to bring them to repentance before they enter his kingdom.

---

3. Unbelievers

a) Without a warning *after the tribulation,* Christ returns to appear to unbelievers "like a thief in the night" (1Th 5.2; 2Pe 3.10). He comes in power, glory, and great seismic upheaval.

b) When Christ returns, he gathers his army to defeat the rebel uprising. He kills by his words—the sword in his mouth. He throws Antichrist and the false prophet into the lake of fire.

c) After the kingdom, rebels attack God's people but are demol-ished by fire from heaven. Satan is thrown into the fiery lake. At the great white throne, unbelievers are sentenced to the lake of fire.

Jews as a people ready for the return of Christ

During the seven-year tribulation period, Jews as a people will repent and serve God. What brings them to repentance in the tribulation is their discovery that the Antichrist, whom they had trusted, was a counterfeit messiah. This discovery will come after he breaks his treaty with them and demands that they worship his idol, which he'll set up in their temple (Mt 24.15). At that point, their eyes will be opened to see that he could not be their Messiah, for they know God hates idolatry. In fact, Israel has been delivered from idolatry since the end of their Babylonian captivity. Therefore, after the future unmasking of Antichrist, Jews as a people will turn away from Antichrist and will turn to Christ as their true Messiah.

After the tribulation, what a happy scene there will be in the earthly messianic kingdom, for Israel will enter a thousand years of exaltation as a nation and will celebrate the wedding feast for Christ and the church. About that wedding feast, John the Baptist spoke metaphorically when he said, "The bride [the church] belongs to the bridegroom [Christ]. The friend who attends the bridegroom [John the Baptist] waits and listens for him, and is full of joy when he hears the bridegroom's voice" (Jn 3.29). I've learned that John the Baptist is saying that the Jews, representing "the friends who attend the bridegroom" (Jn 3.29), will be present at the millennial wedding feast to rejoice with their Messiah and his bride, the church.

Unbelievers: Not ready for the return of Christ

Scripture says unbelievers will not be prepared for Christ's return. For them, the Lord will come unexpectedly like "a thief in the

---

* The word "rapture" does not appear in scripture, but its meaning is "caught up."
† Below, scripture says Christians escape *God's wrath*, which he will pour out in the tribulation era:
  Peter says Christians will never suffer *God's wrath*, for on the cross Christ has already borne their sins, the righteous for the unrighteous, to bring sinners to God (1Pe 3:18. Italics added).
  Paul repeats the same truth: "Since we [Christians] have now been justified by his blood, how much more shall we be saved from *God's wrath* through him" (Ro 5.9. Italics added)! And again, Paul says, the church will be rescued from "*the coming wrath*" (1Th 1.10. Italics added).
  Paul adds this : "For God did *not* appoint us [Christians] to suffer *wrath* but to receive salvation through our Lord Jesus Christ" (1Th 5.9. Italics added). "The wrath of God referred to here clearly refers to the tribulation," (Walvoord and Zuck, eds. 2004, 707 in *Bible Knowledge…*).
  The apostle John says, "Whoever believes in the Son has eternal life, but whoever rejects the Son will not see life, for *God's wrath* remains on him" (Jn 3.36. Italics added).

night" (1Th 5.2; Mt 24.43). The unbelievers of that future kingdom generation will be destroyed in the battle of Armageddon but will be resurrected for judgment at the great white throne, where they, along with unbelievers of all eras, will be sentenced to the lake of fire for eternity. They will be charged with unbelief, by which they will have condemned themselves to a life without God's mercy and without end (Re 20.11-15).

The prophet Zechariah describes what everyone on earth will face when Christ returns. How fearsome the earthly upheaval will be! Zechariah says, "On that day his [Messiah's] feet will stand on the Mount of Olives, east of Jerusalem, and the Mount of Olives will be split in two from east to west, forming a great valley, with half of the mountain moving north and half moving south" (Zch 14.4). This shake-up forces unbelievers to panic, but by that time its too late for them to repent, for the die will have already been cast.

The impact of such an earthly upheaval is graphically described by the website of the United States Geological Survey (USGS). So let's put the findings of the Bible and of USGS in juxtaposition: The Bible explains that the Mount of Olives will be split in two from east to west, forming a great valley—new land—with half the mountain moving north and half moving south. The USGS explains that when tectonic plates pull away from each other horizontally, east to west, and slide past each other vertically, going north and south, new land is generated ("Understanding plate motions," May 5, 1999, the U.S. Geological Survey).* This could be the new land for the grand staging ground on Christ's day of judgment.

That seismic upheaval begins as soon as Christ sets foot on earth—at which time, he is accompanied by his bride the church. At that moment, the trumpet will sound for people to assemble for judgment to determine who will enter the messianic kingdom. In his Mount Olivet sermon—to describe that time of judgment. Jesus uses the imagery that the Old Testament Hebrew prophet Ezekiel used. In Matthew 24 and 25, Jesus, like Ezekiel, calls believers *sheep*, unbelievers *goats,* and himself *a shepherd*, who sorts

---

* The U.S. Geological Survey (USGS): "Understanding Plate Motions" describes divergent boundaries, "where new crust is generated as the plates pull away from each other… New crust is created by magma pushing up from the mantle." These facts were established by the 1960s.

.

goats from sheep for judgment (Mt 25.31-46, Cf. Eze 34.1-31).

Scripture says when Jesus returns, "all the nations will be gathered before him, and he will separate the people one from another as a shepherd separates the sheep [believers] from the goats [unbelievers]" (Mt 25.32). This judgment fulfills the feast of Trumpets.

Of Jewish tribulation survivors, only believers enter Christ's earthly kingdom. About Gentile tribulation survivors, Jesus says, "I tell you the truth, whatever you [Gentiles] did for one of the least of *these brothers of mine* [the Jews], *you did for me"* (Mt 25.40. Italics added). Of that future generation, Gentiles who befriend the persecuted Jews will also be the sheep who will enter the kingdom.

On the other hand, the goats, who are unbelievers, will be sentenced to hell at the great white throne, where the judgment for unbelievers of all eras will take place before eternity begins. To them, Jesus says, "Depart from me, you who are cursed, into the eternal fire prepared for the devil and his angels" (Mt 25.41).[*]

B. Feast of Atonement, Christ's redemption of Israel (Eze 37.12)

The day of Atonement (Yom Kippur) is the holiest day of the Israelite year. On the civil calendar, the initial day of Atonement comes on the tenth day in the seventh month of Nisan. Since then on the Israeli calendar, dates are determined by moon phases, unlike on today's calendar. This day is the only day of the year that the high priest would enter the Most Holy Place. There, because of the sacredness of the place, the high priest would enter with holy fear to present blood from the sacrifices—the blood of a bull for his own sins and the blood of a male goat for the people's sins. He applied this blood to the ark's mercy seat,[†] above which God dwelt, for if the priest failed in this, the ark's mercy seat would become a judgment sea (Le 16) (Bosworth 2000, 27).

To show what care had to be taken in this ritual, let's follow the high priest as he offered the bull and the goat at the altar to atone for the sins of the nation. At that time, before the priest presented the blood of the sacrifices in the Most Holy Place, he carried a censer full of hot, burning coals and two handfuls of

---

[*] Jesus spoke of hell more frequently and more strongly than anyone else in scripture.
[†] Most translations say "the mercy seat," but the NIV translation says "the atonement cover."

incense from the altar of incense into the Holy Place. Within the Most Holy Place, he cast incense on the censer's live coals for the fragrant smoke to cover the mercy seat, God's dwelling place. This covering made by the smoking incense allowed the priest to stay alive in God's presence as he presented the blood offerings (Le 16.13).

For Israel on the day of Atonement, the blood of a bull was chosen to pay for the high priest's sins of the past year, and a goat as one of two, was chosen by lot to be the blood sacrifice on the altar for the people's sins of the past year (Le 16).

You know about Jesus' blood sacrifice for sinners, but did you know that Jesus is also the live scapegoat for sinners? On the day of Atonement, the high priest laid his hands on the second goat and confessed the people's sins before dispatching it away from domestic care to be released into the harsh and barren wilderness. I see this as a picture of Jesus leaving the glories of heaven to come to save sinners in this harsh, sin-defiled world. He came specifically for the Jews. In fact, he himself says, "I was sent *only* to the lost sheep of Israel" (Mt 15.24. Italics added). "He came unto his own, and his own received him not" (Jn 1.11 KJV).

Jews were Jesus' kinfolk, the ones with closest ties to his life, the ones who could administer the greatest pain by their rejection of him; nevertheless, Jesus chose to accept their rejection as from the Father's hand. The Bible says, "He [Jesus] came unto his own, and his own received him not. But as many as received him, to them gave he power to become the sons of God" (Jn 1.11, 12 KJV). This was Jesus' mission; he came to die that believers might live.

For me, the most meaningful part of the celebration of the day of Atonement was **the grand finale,** *the offering of the whole burnt sacrifice*, which came after the Father had accepted the nation's annual atoning blood sacrifice for sin. I'll say more about the burnt sacrifice after we finish looking at Israel's last feast, the feast of Tabernacles. I'm saving discussion of the burnt offering until last because I want to end on a message that is uplifting, a message that shows a believer's surrender of his will to God.

C. Feast of Tabernacles, Christ's future reign in glory (Is 11.1-9)

In the first month, fifteen day came the initial feast of Tabernacles, which lasted seven days. On each day, offerings by fire were made to the Lord. On the eighth day, Jews were to have a sacred assembly and a day of rest from their work.

Today, to reenact the Israelite wilderness exodus, some Jews observe the feast of Tabernacles by living seven days in temporary booths, just as the Israelites did during their first exodus. By tem-porarily staying in makeshift booths. as in their wilderness exodus, this feast reminds the Jews of God's care of them in their exodus through the wilderness on their way back to the land promised by God to Abraham and his progeny. Fast forward now, to the feast of Tabernacles, a future exodus. It will be fulfilled by the messianic kingdom during which Christ leads his people through a joyous thousand-year kingdom exodus on the way to eternity.

About the feast's spiritual significance, Bruce Scott writes, "In both biblical and rabbinical teachings, the feast of Tabernacles typifies the days of the [future] Messiah" (Scott 1997, 111). About the symbolism of the feast of Tabernacles, Zechariah says, "THe Lord will be king over the whole earth. On that day there will be one Lord, and his name the only name" (Zch 14.9). Both the Old and the New Testaments—as well as Judaic and Christian teachers—agree that the kingship of Messiah will be universal (Re 19.15a; Ps 2.1-6). Revelation says Jesus will be King of Kings and will rule with "an iron scepter (Re 15. 15 and 16)."

God is faithful to the Jews his people and will vindicate them in the eyes of their enemies. In the messianic kingdom, represen-tatives of Gentile nations will be required to make the pilgrimage to Jerusalem each year to celebrate the feast of Tabernacles (Zch 14.16). Whereas in the past, Jews were persecuted by those nations, in the future, Jews will be honored by them (Eze 37.28). THis exaltation is not because of God's favoritism but because of *his faithfulness*. Scripture says, "THe Lord did not set his affection on you [Israel] and choose you because you were more numerous than other peoples... But it was because the Lord loved you and *kept the oath* he swore to your forefathers"

The burnt sacrifice after the day of Atonement as illustrated by the story of Abraham and Isaac

A burnt sacrifice at the end of the day of Atonement deserves our attention as we examine our own lives. Not until after cleansing by the blood in the feast of Atonement could the burnt sacrifice be offered. One burnt sacrifice was for the high priest and the other one for the people. These offerings, which express the offerer's devotion to the Lord, symbolize the Son's future delight in doing the Father's will. Therefore, the offering creates "an aroma pleasing to the Lord" (Le 1.9b). Unlike other offerings, this burnt offering was totally consumed by fire and was not eaten by priests or people. It was for the Lord's glory alone.

The Hebrew burnt sacrifice is a prototype of a Christian's dedication to the will of God. The Bible says Christians are to offer their bodies as living sacrifices. They are not to conform to the world's ways but are to be transformed by the renewing of their minds (Ro 12.1, 2). Jesus surrendered to God's will by accepting the cross, and Christians do the same when they surrender to God's will and take up the cross to follow him. For Christians, the burnt sacrifice is a picture of the cost and the reward of surrender to God's will. Let's look at two illustrations of such surrender—first, this Bible story of Abraham and Isaac and second, an incident in my life.

The story of Abraham and Isaac presents the relationship of God the Father and God the Son as an analogy of God and the believer. In the story, God gave Abraham a test of faithfulness: Would he surrender (sacrifice) the son God had promised him as the seed of a great nation? From this story, we learn that Abraham's commitment was not based simply on a strong resolve to please God. Rather, it was based on the fact that *he believed God and his promises*. From Abraham's believing faith, the nation Israel was born.

In the story, when Abraham and son Isaac walked up the mountain, Isaac was puzzled. "The fire and wood are here," he said, "but where is the lamb for the burnt offering?" Abraham replied,

"God himself will provide the lamb for the burnt offering." Then Abraham built an altar, arranged the wood, bound his son, and presented him on the altar. Although youthful Isaac was strong enough to overpower his aged father, he chose to submit (Ge 22:1-18), just as later, Jesus at the cross would submit to the Father and would say, "Not my will, but thine, be done" (Lk 22.42. KJV).

As Abraham took the knife to slay his son, the angel of the Lord cried, "'Abraham! Abraham!…* Do not lay a hand on the boy… Now I know that you fear God, because you have not withheld from me your son, your only [promised] son.'* Abraham looked up and there in a thicket he saw a ram caught by its horns… He took the ram and sacrificed it as *a burnt offering* instead of his son" (Ge 22.11b-12). What a beautiful picture of Jesus as the substitute lamb in a Christian's "burnt offering!"

There are two things to note here. First, God was the initiator from the beginning; He's the one who called Abraham, and he's the one who promised Abraham that his descendants would be a great nation. And second, Abraham knew that his faithfulness to God would be rewarded, for he knew that just as he was committed to the Lord, so too was the Lord committed to him.

The Old Testament story of Abraham reveals God's trustworthiness, and the New Testament book of Hebrews gives the full significance of the story by saying this: "By faith Abraham… offered Isaac as a sacrifice. He who had received the promises was about to sacrifice his one and only son, even though God had said to him, 'It is through Isaac that your offspring will be reckoned.' Abraham reasoned that God could raise the dead, and figuratively speaking, he did receive Isaac back from death" (He 11.17b-19 NT).

Abraham *believed* God. That's why Abraham earlier said to Isaac that God would provide the lamb, and that's why Abraham told the servants, "*We* [Abraham and Isaac} will come back to you" (Ge 22.5b). In saying this, Abraham was saying that Isaac's life would be spared and that Isaac would return with him. Abraham did his part by *believing* that God would keep his promise about Isaac's future. God did his part by providing a substitute ram to die as Isaac's redeeming sacrifice. This story about Abraham and

Isaac so beautifully presents Christ as the Redeemer Lamb of God.

The story of Abraham illustrates Jesus' confident submission to the Father. The Bible says that Jesus, "for the *joy* that was set before him endured the cross, despising the shame" (He 12.2b. Italics added. KJV). On the cross he suffered separation from the Father, who had to turn his back on him because of the sins he bore for others. Nevertheless, approaching the cross, Jesus rejoiced that his sacrifice would bring salvation to sinners, whom he loves. Jesus 'for the joy set before him endured the cross,"(He 12,2(. On the cross, he bore the sinners' shame so that they would have his joy when they also take up the cross to follow him.

"Then the end will come, when he [Christ] hands over the kingdom to God the Father after he has destroyed all dominion, authority, and power. For on earth, Christ must reign until eternity when he will have put all his enemies under his feet. The last enemy to be destroyed is death" (1Co 15.24-26).

My opportunity to offer a burnt sacrifice

In the greatest crisis I ever faced, the Lord gave me an opportunity to express my wholehearted devotion to him, as in a burnt offering, but first I have to refer to another incident at an earlier time when God lit a flame in my heart that has never died.

In the first chapter of this book, I told of an experience early in our marriage in Texas in 1951. I told how stunned I was when my husband George told me, "I'm going to be a preacher." I was astonished because I didn't have a clue that the Lord had been dealing with him. He told me that since childhood, he'd known that if he ever committed his life to God, he had a calling to serve in the ministry. The way it came about was that a pastor came into his dry cleaning shop and talked to him about giving his heart to the Lord. And when George seemed unsure, the pastor told him, "You'll never learn to swim unless you get in the water."

George's supernatural transformation was total, yet the love I had for him did not waver before, during, or after his backsliding. The most surprising part was that he seemed to be instantly wise, and he always carried a New Testament in his pocket. It was a new beginning... until less than two months later when he turned away from God's call. However, the flame of wholehearted devotion that God planted in my heart the day of George's conversion consumed me while I waited for the time that George would answer the calling of God for him to be a preacher. And as I waited, the joy of the Lord was my strength—even to the time of my husband's untimely death in his early forties.

We benefit from the testimony of others. As a youth, I benefited from the testimony of Catherine Marshall about God's ministry to her at the death of her husband, Peter Marshall, who was pastor of a Presbyterian church, chaplain of the U.S. Senate, and father of their six year old son. In her book, *A Man Called Peter*, Mrs. Marshall tells how the Lord worked miraculously in her life during the funeral and in the period immediately afterwards. God lifted her into the heavens during that period of the funeral crisis. At the time I was reading the book, I remember believing in my heart that the Lord would be willing to continue the joy of that intimacy beyond the immediate future and on into the everyday events throughout the life of a widow if that Christian would look to him for that. I never forgot that inspiration from my youth; it was like a seed of faith planted in my heart in 1945 for me to be-lieve in 1969 at the time of my husband's death. That day after a visit with my husband—along with two of my children—I got a phone call at home in Kelso, Washington—from someone at the hospital in Seattle. telling me that George had died. This was too big for me to handle. That's why I knew I had to turn the whole matter over to the Lord, and so I did.

My husband died of cancer of the esophagus twelve days before his forty-fourth birthday. After twenty years of marriage, we had four teens and a six-year-old. In the fall, the oldest would enter the second year of college, the next three would be in high school, and the six year old would enter first grade.

As a person who is no one special, let me tell you what God did for me. He enabled me to surrender to him because I knew that I could trust him. What we know is that in physical healing, he ordinarily heals over a period of time, but sometimes he heals rapidly. So too with his healing of the heart. In my case, he healed my heart instantaneously. What was so unusual is that after my surrender, the Lord gave me his joy in the same measure as the depth of sorrow would have been in my loss. In that crisis, the spark that had been lit in my heart earlier at my husband's conversion burst into full flame. And ever since then, the Lord has continued to be my joy and my strength in every situation I have had to face as a widow with five children.

After my husband's death, although I shed many tears, they were the satisfying tears of a tenderized heart, for never had the Lord been so precious to me as at that time and ever since. For many years, the Lord had been teaching me to "count it all joy" when facing trials, so on the day of George's death, I was able to surrender to God's will as if offering a whole burnt offering for God's glory alone. All he asked was that I look up and not look back (He 12.2). Then, as the Lord drew me to himself, what I noticed most of all was how many troubles everyone else had.

Since that crisis, I've had the Lord as my joy, as the father of my four sons and my one daughter, and as my provider, my protector, my consultant in business matters, and most of all, as my guide and companion. My dependence and my joy have continued and the Lord has met our family's every need. Of my children, all five have college degrees—two master's degrees, two doctorates, and one Bachelor of Science—and they have all had jobs for which they are suited and for which they are well recompensed. They are kind, wise, and considerate, and they are good to me. All the glory goes to our merciful heavenly Father who has blessed our family.

The rest of the story is that after the funeral, when visitors had left, God was still with our family. That's when we discovered that because of a washing machine overflow, water was standing in our huge basement. So, with buckets, rags, and mops, my five children and I pitched in and took care of the situation. And the joy did not diminish (Ro 12.1). A Christian can say, whatever the circumstances… "yet will I be joyful in God my Savior" (He 3.17-18).

Jews as a people suffered under slavery in Egypt and will endure greater trials in the endtime under Antichrist. And they will continue to suffer in the last half of the tribulation when God will pour out his wrath on earth. But in the end, Jews as a people will come to faith in their true Messiah. And note this: Although Israel's seven feasts began with the cry of Jewish slaves in bondage, it will end under Christ with Israel's triumphant shout of victory!

Figure 17, next page, reviews Christ's fulfillment of Israel's seven feasts in the three pilgrimages. This unit has been on understanding the new covenant in Israel's seven feasts as seen in three pilgrimages. The next unit will be about understanding God's new covenant people.

Unit Review of Israel's three Pilgrimages
The new covenant fulfilled in Christ—
Israel's past prophet, present priest, and future king
The seven Feasts presented in Leviticus 23
as three harvests

Figure 17

FIRST THREE FEASTS FULFILLED AT CHRIST'S FIRST COMING
Christ as prophet when he lived on earth

In the first month of Israel's religious calendar, the Israelites' first mandatory pilgrimage to Jerusalem commemorates God's deliverance of the Israelites.

1. Christ redeems sinners and fulfills the *Jewish Passover.*

2. Christ fellowships with his own and fulfills *Unleavened Bread.*

3. Christ arises in resurrection as the first to fulfill *Firstfruits.*

Wave-sheaf of firstfruits,
Barley harvest

PENTECOST FULFILLED DURING THE PRESENT CHURCH AGE
Christ as high priest while he is in heaven today

Fifty days after Firstfruits, the Israelites' second mandatory pilgrimage to Jerusalem, commemorates God's provision for them in the wilderness.

4. Christ unites and empowers the church and fulfills *Pentecost.*

Two wave-loaves of wheat firstfruits,
Wheat harvest

LAST THREE FEASTS FULFILLED AFTER CHRIST'S RETURN—
Christ as king when he returns to rule the earth

In the seventh month, the Israelites' third mandatory pilgrimage to Jerusalem, celebrates the marriage of the Lamb and the exaltation of Israel in his kingdom.

5. Christ returns, regathers Israel, and fulfills *Trumpets.*

6. Christ pardons repentant Israel and fulfills the day of *Atonement.* for Israel's redemption

7. Christ celebrates his wedding to the church as welll as Israel's exaltation in *Tabernacles* (Da 12.1 OT).

Grapes, figs, olives,, Future endtime harvest!

THINK JEWISH
to understand the Bible

E. UNDERSTANDING GOD'S NEW COVENANT PEOPLE

11. God's new covenant people: Present church and future Israel
    A. *The church and Israel: Their stories intertwined*
    B. *The relationship of the church to the new covenant*
    C. *The relationship of Israel to the new covenant*
    D. *Truths about God's new covenant people*
    E. *An electrical circuit, an analogy of new covenant oneness*

12. God's new covenant people: Their Pentecostal experience
    A. *New covenant people: Their identity and destiny*
    B. *New covenant people: Their Pentecostal experience, a testimony*
    C. *New covenant people: The Pentecostal experience examined*
    D. *New covenant charismatic revival of the twentieth century*
    E. *New covenant people: Their vision of future revival*

13. God's new covenant people: Their spiritual growth
    A. *Godliness for new covenant people*
    B. *The daily walk for new covenant people*
    C. *The testimony of new covenant people*
    D. *Earthly and spiritual conflict for new covenant people*

11 God's new covenant people: The present church and future Israel

> It is through Israel—and, I believe, only through Israel—that God makes known what he has been doing and what he plans to do with this world."
> —William Sanford LaSor, Fuller theologian

In Israel's story, the present church age is important as a link between Israel's past and Israel's future. Yet, immersed as we are in the present church age, we fail to see that this age is only part of God's story, which in its entirety centers on Israel and the Jewish people. A statement by Fuller theologian William Sanford LaSor affirms the major premise of this book—that the story of Israel *is* the story line of God's plan. LaSor writes, "It is through Israel—and, I believe, only through Israel—that God makes known what he has been doing and what he plans to do with this world" (LaSor, 1976, 31).

Sometimes after absorbing what others say about a Bible passage, I'm still left with questions. One question I have pondered is about how Israel and the church could both relate to the new covenant. I was puzzled because I was convinced that God will definitely keep his eternal promise to Israel, in which he said, "The time is coming… when I will make *a new covenant*… This is the covenant I will make with the house of Israel… I will put my law in their minds and write it on their hearts. I will be their God, and they will be my people" (Je 31.31, 33. Cf Eze 11.19; 18.31; 36.26. Italics added). Here, God's promise says that Jews *as a people* will enter the new covenant; that is, each person will be born again with a new mind and a new hearts

In my pondering, I could also see that Jesus himself also speaks of the new covenant in reference to the church. To his disciples, he referred to the church's communion service when he said, "This cup is *the new covenant* in my blood…" (Lk 22.20. Italics added).

Therefore, since scripture shows that Israel and the church both relate to God under the new covenant and since my view and that of many others is that neither the church nor Israel replaces the other in history, I've had to conclude that the question to be asked is, in what way do the church and Israel each relate to the new covenant?

New covenant people—the present church and future Israel:

- A. *The church and Israel: Their stories intertwined*
- B. *The relationship of the church to the new covenant*
- C. *The relationship of Israel to the new covenant*
- D. *Truths about God's new covenant people*
- E. *An electrical circuit analogy of new covenant oneness*

A. The church and Israel: Their stories intertwined

This present church age, which is woven into Israel's story, is unique, for in this age God invites *all* sinners,—Jews and Gentiles—to enter his new covenant through the Jewish Messiah, the Lord Jesus Christ (Ac 2.17; cf Jl. 2.28). Today, God excludes no one except those who reject his invitation. He even synchronizes the Jewish and Christian calendars so that timewise, the seasons of fulfillment in Christ of the church's celebrations have a correlation with the initial dates of Israel's feasts—the initial dates *only,* for Israel's calendar ever since that time is moon-cycle based.

Figure 18 shows that God is in charge of all that happens to his people. He weaves together the stories of Israel and the church and brings both into the future kingdom under the Christ/Messiah. The relationship of Israel and the church is interdependent.

Two questions on the interdependence of God's two peoples:

First, what would the church be if there were no Old Testament history and prophecy to validate Jesus as the prophesied Jewish Messiah and to disclose God's eternal plan for the salvation of Gentile and Jewish Christians?

Second, what would Israel's Judaic feasts, blood sacrifices, and rituals be if there were no crucified and risen Christ of the New Testament to fulfill them and give them meaning?

Prerequisites in Christ for new covenant fulfillment of Israel's seven feasts

(Names of the seven feasts are numbered and in bold letters within parentheses.)

Figure 18

In the feasts, nothing is by happenstance! Look first at the prerequisite for the disciples' *entry into the church's new covenant.* Their entry into the new covenant could not happen until after Christ's crucifixion (1-**Passover**), for without the shedding of blood there can be no forgiveness of sin, according to the Old and New Testaments of the Bible (Le 17.11 OT; He 9.22b NT).

Before a person can become alive to God *under the new covenant,* he has to receive Jesus into his spirit; otherwise he is dead to God. When the Holy Spirit enters a person's spirit, that one becomes alive to God, just as a glove becomes alive when a hand enters it. That person is born again.

Before Jesus could impart this *spiritual life* to his disciples, he, himself as a human being, first had to die and be resurrected by divine power. This meant that not until after Jesus' own resurrection could he appear to the disciples and impart the Holy Spirit to them by breathing on them, and saying, "Receive the Holy Spirit" (Jn 20.22). At that moment, they received the Holy Spirit within so that they could become Christians and choose to walk with God in purity of life (2-**Unleavened Bread**). God's people could not have this present newness of life and a future resurrection unless Jesus had been resurrected (3-**Firstfruits**).

Just as God had his timing for the disciples' regeneration and sanctified walk, he had his timing for *baptizing them in the Holy Spirit* (4-**Pentecost**). Christ couldn't pour out his Spirit from heaven until after Jesus' requisite departure from earth and his ascension to heaven to become the present high priest there.

Today, by his ascension and his heavenly ministry, Christ has become freed from human limitations in his present high priestly relationship with his people. First, the Jewish disciples by the new birth received the Holy Spirit within to make them alive to God (Jn 20). Then later, at the Pentecostal outpouring, they were filled to overflowing with the Holy Spirit. This Holy Spirit baptism united them as one body, the church, and empowered them for ministry.

Not until after Jesus returns will the scattered Jews be *regathered to Israel* (5-**Trumpets**). But Christ will not regather and pardon them until after their repentance during the tribulation, even though he will have already presented to the Father his blood on their behalf. Before God's kingdom can begin, Jesus must return, pardon the *Jews as a people* (6-**Atonement**), transform them, and usher them into the messianic kingdom under the new covenant (7-**Tabernacles**).

The relationship of Israel and the church to God's new covenant and to each other is vital for understanding the Bible, so let's see how the two intertwine in the new covenant under Christ (Fig. 18).

B. The relationship of the church to the new covenant

Under the new covenant, Christ first ministered as Israel's sacrificial Lamb of Passover, now as Israel's priest during the present church age, and finally as Israel's king in the future messianic kingdom. Christ is past Lamb of God, present priest, and future King of Kings.

The book of Hebrews (NT) tells how much greater Christ's new covenant blood sacrifice is than the old covenant animal sacrifice: "How much more shall the blood of Christ... purge your conscience from *dead works* to serve the living God" (He 9.14. KJV. Italics added). The late radio Bible preacher, J. Vernon McGee defined "dead works" this way: "*Dead works* have to do with works that you do thinking they will save you" (McGee 1983, Vol. V, 568. Italics added.). In contrast, *live works* spring from a different motivation. Live works spring from love for Christ, who has already paid the price on the cross to save us sinners and to give meaning to our lives.

In the present church age, Christ became priest under the new covenant after he ascended to heaven and presented the blood of his sacrifice to the Father and thereby sealed the ending of Israel's *old covenant priesthood in the order of Aaron*. Then, on the day of Pentecost, according to the book of Hebrews (NT), God launched the church under *a new covenant priesthood*—a priesthood under Christ, who serves in *the eternal order of Melchizedek*.

So what does scripture mean when it says that Christ is now a priest in the order of Melchizedek? For the answer, look at the Hebrew scripture of the Old Testament, which makes only two brief mentions about Melchizedek[*] (Ge 14.18-20 and Ps 110.4).

Let's begin with the Old Testament reference in Genesis 14.18-20. This passage says that when Abraham returned from the battlefield, he met Melchizedek, king of Salem and priest of God who blessed him. In this meeting, Abraham gave Melchizedek a tenth of everything he'd gained in battle, thus acknowledging that Melchizedek was his priest. This Hebrew Scripture was centuries before Israel's wilderness exodus when Aaron's family would become the family from which Israel's high priest would come.

Then let's look at the only other Old Testament reference to Melchizedek* in Psalm 110.4: "The Lord has sworn and will not change his mind: You [Christ] are a priest forever, in the order of Melchizedek" (Cf. He 5.6. Italics added). This new covenant replaces the temporary priesthood of the old covenant of law, whose high priest could serve only for a lifetime. So, for God's new covenant people, Christ will forever be high priest in the order of Melchizedek. With this comparison, the New Testament presents Melchizedek as a type of Christ by saying, "Without father or mother, without genealogy, without beginning of days or end of life, like the Son of God, *he (Christ) remains a priest forever*" (He 7.3. Italics added). Here, the New Testament book of Hebrews says that Christ has become the new covenant believer's high priest forever.

Testimony of a sinner saved under God's new covenant

This new covenant is about "good tidings of great joy" (Lk 2.10-11 KJV). That's the message the angel proclaimed at the birth of Jesus. In fact, the word *gospel* means "good news." My good friend Laurie Case heard "the good tidings of great joy," and with her acceptance of Jesus as her Savior, she became "a new creature" in Christ under God's new covenant (2Co 5.17).

Growing up Catholic, she said she was always looking for "something else." She thought maybe she needed to go to church more or to confession or… something else.

Then, at last, she found the answer! That moment of truth came through a young man, a friend of the family, not a boyfriend. He would sometimes tap on her bedroom window at night and talk with her about this and that. He had done that ever since the two

---

* Melchizedek lived before the old covenant of law. (The law would later establish the high priest as from the family of Aaron.). Ezekiel 40-48 prophesies about Israel's priesthood in the future messianic kingdom, which differs from earlier priesthoods. Ezekiel does not mention a high priest, but we know from the NT book of Hebrews that Christ is "the mediator of the new covenant" in that future kingdom (He 9 NT), for his death saves sinners and his ministry as high priest in heaven ministers to and through believers. Some say Melchizedek represents a theophany—the appearance of Christ before incarnation.

of them were young children. One night, this Mormon friend, who was now a young man, came with exciting news. He'd found what he had been looking for. He told Laurie that he got *saved!* He had gone to a Christian evangelical outreach at a Los Angeles landmark, Knott's Berry Farm, and had asked Jesus to come into his heart, and he couldn't wait to tell her.

Laurie says that at twenty-one, as soon as she heard the good news, she knew that what he described was what she'd been longing for. This was "the something else" that she needed. And ever since that moment, Laurie's been grateful that she heard the good news of the new covenant and responded to it by seeking out those who had told her friend "the good tidings of great joy." Her burden of sin was lifted when she received the life that never ends.

From this we see that the new covenant is more than just a theological concept. Entering the new covenant brings *new life in Christ.* Everyone needs the Savior, no matter what the background—whether Catholic or Protestant, cultish or Christian, atheistic or evangelical, Jewish or Gentile. Everyone needs to be born from above "for *all* have sinned and fall short of the glory of God" (Ro 3.23 Italics added).

C. The relationship of Jews to the new covenant

Under the new covenant, "Jews as individuals" now become Christians, but in a future generation, "Jews as a people" will enter the messianic kingdom. So let's look at Jews entering the new covenant: first, "as individuals" and in the future, "as a people."

First, "Jews as individuals" in the church
enter the new covenant of the present generation

The first to enter God's *new covenant* were Jesus' eleven Jewish disciples. (Judas Iscariot was not with them that resurrection night because he'd hanged himself after he betrayed Jesus.) The disciples entered the new covenant by the new birth (Cf Jn 3.5-8), which was made possible by the blood sacrifice of Christ as Lamb of God.

On the eve of Jesus' crucifixion, he prepared his disciples for his future earthly departure by telling them they would receive the Holy Spirit into their hearts and minds: "You know him [the Holy

Spirit], for he lives **with** you and will be **in** you" (Jn 14.17b. Italics added). This would be the new birth transformation promised in Jeremiah 31—centuries after Israel's wilderness exodus: "The time is coming… when I will make *a new covenant*… This is the covenant I will make with the house of Israel… I will put my law in their minds and write it on their hearts. I will be their God, and they will be my people" (Jer 31,31-33. Italics added).

Three days after Jesus' crucifixion—when the dreams of Jesus' Jewish disciples had been shattered and their future was uncertain—they must have been seized with fear, for as Jesus' followers, they knew that they too would be targeted by religious authorities for persecution or death. That's probably why they huddled together behind locked doors. How startled they must have been on that evening when behind those locked doors, the resurrected Jesus appeared!

The disciples knew of Jeremiah's promise from God to future Israel about their entry into the new covenant by being born again (Je 31.31, 32). What they did not yet understand was that in their current era, they would enter the church. They couldn't comprehend this because there are no specific Old Testament prophecies about the future church, as such. Jesus was the first to refer to the church (ecclesia) as "called out ones," (Mt 16.18). And yet, in Hebrew scripture, countless prophecies are about the Messiah and his relationship to God's new covenant.*

On the first night of Jesus' resurrection mentioned above, the disciples entered the new covenant, for that's when the resurrected Jesus appeared and said, "Receive the Holy Spirit" (Jn 20.21-22). In that moment, they were born again and entered the new covenant as the first Christians. Since then Jesus would no longer just be *with* his Jewish disciples as a human being. He would ever after live *within* their hearts, even as he had told them before his death.

Not until Pentecost fifty days later would the church be born as a new reality. That's when Christ as high priest in heaven poured out the Holy Spirit on the disciples on earth to fill them to overflowing in order to unite

---

* "The church" is called a scriptural "mystery"—i.e.,, it is a truth concealed in the OT but revealed in the NT. However, W. W. Wiersbe's *The Essential Everyday Bible Commentary* lists over forty Old Testament prophecies about Christ as Messiah, and the list is not exhaustive (Wiersbe 1993).

Parallel tracks for Jews in God's new-covenant plan

Figure 19

Jews in present church age:
Christ is high priest.
Jews enter as individual
Christians in the church—
under the new covenant,
as human beings on earth.

Jews in future messianic age:
Zadok will be high priest.
Jews enter as a people
into the earthly temple,
under the new covenant,
as human beings on earth.

Jews in present day & forever:
Some Jews as individuals
presently enter the church
before the tribulation begins.
They will live in
redeemed bodies.
and as Christians, they'll
be raptured to heaven
   to receive rewards
and will return to earth as the
   bride of Christ to reign in
the worldwide kingdom.

Jews in the kingdom:
Jews as a people will be
gathered to Israel before the
messianic kingdom (Mt 24.31).
They'll live in redeemed
   bodies, and
In eternity they will eat
from the tree of life
while they reside on
 the new earth
throughout eternity
as God's earthlly people.

Summary
Before the tribulation, Jews and Gentiles in the church
will be raptured to heaven to be with Christ forever.
Before eternity, Jews as a people on earth
will eat from the tree of life and live forever.

In eternity, people in heaven and on earth interact (Re 21.24).

them as the church and to empower them for ministry. The church is the instrument God uses today to proclaim the gospel to Jews and Gentiles.

Second, "Jews as a people" enter the new covenant of the messianic kingdom at a future date.

Under the old covenant of law, Israelites related to God through leaders, who had special anointing. In the timing of the Jewish people's entry into the new covenant (Figure 19), we see that future Jews enter the new covenant through faith in Christ. *Jews as individuals* enter the new covenant in the present church and *Jews as a people* enter the new covenant when Christ returns to earth to set up his kingdom.

In Figure 19, *Jews as individuals* in the present age enter the new covenant only spiritually by becoming born again Christians, but a future generation of *Jews as a people* will enter the messianic kingdom both spiritually and as God's redeemed earthly nation under the new covenant. Scripture says that when Christ returns, Jews on earth, "the elect," will be gathered to Israel from "the four winds" (Mt 24.31). Also at that time, under the worldwide rule of Christ/Messiah, Israel will be exalted as a nation.

D. Truths about God's new covenant people

Since scripture shows that Christians in the church and Jews as a people enter the new covenant in different generations, we know that they are distinct entities, each with its own identity and destiny. We know that neither is superior to the other and that their roles differ. God created Jews as a people to be his earthly people, and he created the church to be his spiritual people.

Truths about God's new covenant people

Figure 20

Israel and the church enter the new covenant by his promise to Abraham, which includes an implication for Gentiles.

When Israel and the church become redeemed, each people group lives on earth as human beings, but in different eras. Israel and the church will always remain separate entities with distinct identities and destinies. Neither Israel nor the church will replace the other.

E. An electrical-circuit analogy of new covenant oneness

Looking at how new covenant people relate to Christ as high-priest , we see that new covenant people relate to Christ in a way that is analogous to an electrical circuit. The fact is that God's circuit begins and ends in God. In this analogy, Holy Spirit power flows from Christ as high priest to Christians in the present age or to new covenant Israelis in the future messianic age. Then, from these new covenant people, power flows back to Christ as they pray to the Father in the power of the Spirit and in the name of Jesus. Thus, power flows back and forth between God and his people.

In God's circuit, new covenant Christians make up "a royal priesthood" with Christ as high priest (1Pe 2.9). They are united not only to Christ but also to fellow believers. And in a sense, they even relate to unbelievers—by identifying with them and by interceding in prayer for them. And sometimes this intercessory prayer for saints or sinners becomes intense. Paul writes, "The Spirit helps us in our weakness. We do not know what we ought to pray for, but the Spirit himself intercedes for us with groans that words cannot express. And he who searches our hearts knows the mind of the Spirit, because the Spirit intercedes for the saints in accordance with God's will" (Ro 8.26b,27). In brief, God the Son as high priest intercedes by the power of God the Holy Spirit, who works through Christians in their prayers to God the Father.

At Jesus' Last Supper (Jn 13-17), he spoke of the circuit-like inter-connectedness of Christians with God and each other. In his prayer to the Father just before he was arrested, tried, and crucified, Jesus prayed this prayer for his people: "May they [Christians] also be in us [the triune God] so that the world may believe that you have sent me. I have given them the glory that you gave me, that they may be one as we are one: I in them and you in me. May they be brought to complete unity to let the world know that you sent me and have loved them even as you have loved me" (Jn 17.21b-23). God's circuit gives Christians a sense of oneness with the Lord and with each other.

For God's power to flow through this circuit, the Bible says that

Christians are to live in *love*, *brokenness*, and *humility*. Apostle John says this about love: "By this all men will know that you are my disciples, if you *love* one another" (Jn 13.35 NT. Italics added.). And Isaiah says this about being broken and humble: "For this is what the high and lofty One says—he who lives forever, whose name is holy: 'I live in a high and holy place, but also with him who is contrite [broken] and lowly in spirit [humble], to revive the spirit of the lowly and to revive the heart of the contrite'" (Is 57.15. OT. Italics added).

The truth is that the magnitude of the power of God and of electricity requires that they not be dealt with carelessly, as can be seen in the following story about Ananias and Sapphira in the earliest days of the church (Ac 5.1-11). This story, shows that God's circuitry operates not only as blessing but also as deadly danger.

The breaking of God's circuitry by Ananias and Sapphira

In the earliest days of the church, Ananias and Sapphira, after selling some property, went before Peter and the whole congregation to claim that they were giving to God's work all the money from the sale of their property, but the truth was that they were giving only a part. However, they had not been required to give all the proceeds of their property to the church, as the giving was supposed to be voluntary. They could have declared the true percentage, and all would have gone well. Instead, by their deception they put the Holy Spirit to the test (Ac 5.1-16).

They must have thought they could get away with their subterfuge but they couldn't. Judgment fell! Peter told Ananias, "You have not lied to men but to God," and Ananias fell dead instantly. Later, when Sapphira told the same lie, "Peter said, 'How could you agree to test the Spirit of the Lord? Look! The feet of the men who buried your husband are at the door, and they will carry you out also.'" At that moment she fell down and died (Ac 5.9, 10).

God's judgment, swift and strong, warned others not to impugn God's character, because his holiness—his unique "otherness"—is his highest attribute. When Ananias and Sapphira relegated Christ to human status alone, they created a break in God's spiritual circuitry, for Christ came not just as a human being but also as God incarnate. Ananias and Sapphira lied because they wanted approval from others. They loved the world's approval; therefore, the love of God was not in them" (1Jn 2.15). They thought they could relate to God deceitfully without fear of judgment.

Though the New Testament portrays Christ as a merciful high priest who reaches out to sinners, this story reveals that believers nonetheless need to face the truth of Christ's deity and the reality of the greatness of his power and authority.

The story of Ananias and Sapphira in the New Testament reveals what can happen to "Sinners in the Hands of an Angry God."* Because of this incident in the earliest days of the church, "great fear seized the whole church and all who heard about these things" (Ac 5.11). The lesson is that people are to honor the magnitude of God's power just as electricians honor the power in electrical circuits—by the care they take in their handling of circuits.

The significance of God's circuitry in Christian living

I believe that in God's circuitry, respecting his omnipotence extends to honoring those whom God puts in authority over others. In our family, my brothers and I learned in childhood about the principle of honoring the God-given authority of our parents.

In the 1930s, some parents not only spanked children but at times switched or whipped them. I remember that in our school, the boys' physical education coaches paddled Edinburg Junior High and High School boys that got out of line in their behavior. I also remember that a second grade teacher in the school where I taught would ask another teacher to be present if she paddled a student. So even that recently, paddling was acceptable at times.

My parents used none of those methods, but they had one exception—whipping with a horse whip to punish disrespect. My mother would alert our father about such insubordination. Then, the whip, as used judiciously by my father, stung but didn't injure. However, this happened only one time to one of my brothers. I can remember seeing my six-foot-two father running in the yard as he chased my brother, who at the time was a skinny little

---

* In the 1700s, Jonathan Edwards used this title in what is known as *the* most famous sermon ever.

kid. Knowing my father, I can say that though he hated having to carry out the punishment, he did so since he felt that it was necessary. As for the method, I am neither condemning nor condoning it, but I am commending the lesson taught. That one incident was all that was needed for us kids to learn to be respectful. So too, the incident about Ananias and Sapphira was all that was needed to inspire the early church to express respect for God and his teachings.

The author of Hebrews tells us what is significant about Christ as high priest. He says, "Jesus has become the guarantee of a better covenant. Now there have been many of those priests [Israelite priests], because death prevented them from continuing in office; but because Jesus lives forever, he has a permanent priesthood. Therefore he is able to save completely those who come to God through him, because he always lives to intercede for them" as their high priest in heaven (He 7.22-25).

As that passage continues, it contrasts Jesus as high priest of the new covenant to a high priest of the old covenant: "Such a high priest [Christ] meets our need—one who is holy, blameless, pure, set apart from sinners, exalted above the heavens. Unlike the other high priests [under the old covenant], Jesus does not need to offer sacrifices day after day, first for his own sins, and then for the sins of the people. As one without sin, he sacrificed for their sins once for all when he gave himself " (He 7.26, 27) as the offering.

Hebrews (NT) also says, "Therefore, since we have a great high priest who has gone through the heavens, Jesus the Son of God, let us hold firmly to the faith we profess. For we do not have a high priest who is unable to sympathize with our weaknesses, but we have one who has been tempted in every way, just as we are— yet was without sin. Let us then approach the throne of grace with confidence, so that we may receive mercy and find grace to help us in our time of need" (He 4.16-18). What joy Christians find in knowing that their all-powerful high priest is also approachable! God's circuitry offers blessed oneness with him and with other believers.

Next in this unit on understanding new covenant people, we'll look at the Pentecostal experience of God's new covenant people.

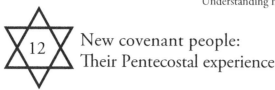

12 New covenant people: Their Pentecostal experience

> Smith Wigglesworth believed it possible... to begin in the natural and by faith rise to the spiritual... He knew that as he moved toward God in faith, God would move toward him in power.
> —George Stormont in A *Man Who Walked with God*, 107

New covenant people: Their Pentecostal experience:

A. New covenant people: Their identity and destiny
B. New covenant people: Their Pentecostal experience, a testimony
C. New covenant people, Their Pentecostal experience examined
D.New covenant charismatic revival of the twentieth century
E New covenant people: A vision of future revival

A. New covenant people: Their identity and destiny

To see clearly the identity and destiny of the church, let's compare and contrast it with the identity and destiny of Israel.

Jews as a people are God's earthly people, and Christians are his spiritual people. Jews are "children of promise" (Ga 4.28)) because they are the promised *physical descendants* of Abraham. Christians, on the other hand are the *spiritual descendants* of Abraham, for the church is built on the foundation of faith in Christ (Mt 16.18), who is the prophesied king; his genealogy can be traced back to Abraham and King David. This parallel of God's new covenant people—Israel as God's earthly people and the church as God's spiritual people—is evident in the biblical narrative.

Jewish and Gentile Christians in this present age enter the new covenant spiritually. In the future, however, after Christians have been raptured to heaven, the church will return to earth as Christ's bride and will enter the messianic kingdom fully, not just spiritually. That is, they'll return as resurrected Christians to enter the time-and-space reality of Christ's messianic kingdom.

However, Jews as a people in the present age are now caught betwixt and between their old and new covenants. They have no temple, no priesthood, no animal sacrifice, and no legitimate place to offer a blood sacrifice to God (2Cor 3.1), all of which are required in Judaism. Today, *as a people,* Jews don't accept Christ's sacrifice, but some Jews as *individuals* enter God's new covenant by receiving Christ as Savior/Messiah. As individuals, they become Hebrew believers in Christ/Messiah.

When Christ returns after the tribulation, he will commission angels to gather the "elect" (Jews) on earth to Israel to enter the thousand-year messianic kingdom (Mt 24.30-31); that is, he will gather all believing Jews and their Gentile sympathizers from all over the earth to enter the messianic kingdom. In the kingdom, they will become redeemed new covenant human beings on earth, who at a future time will have fellowship with Abraham, Isaac, Jacob, and other resurrected Hebrew saints (Mt 8.1), and with the church—for in the messianic kingdom, God's earthly human beings and his resurrected people will interact and rejoice together in the new heaven and the new earth (Re 21.26). In that messianic kingdom, people will celebrate the wedding feast of the Lamb and the church, and they will celebrate the exaltation of God's nation, Israel (Mt 26.29).

Figure 21, next page, gives a summary of what we've learned about God's new covenant people—Israel and the church.

B. New covenant people: Their Pentecostal experience, a testimony

The spiritual gift of the baptism in the Holy Spirit is for believers today. That's what I learned long before I actually had the faith to receive that gift. Though already a Christian, I had a great thirst for God. In the meantime, our family had moved from our home in Rainier, Oregon to the other side of the beautiful, broad Columbia River to Kelso, Washington.

In Kelso in about 1963, Father Dennis Bennett, an Episcopalian priest, greatly used by God in the charismatic movement of the twentieth century, came from Seattle to Kelso, Washington where our family lived at the time. That year, at a city-wide meeting sponsored by a number of local churches in the Longview/Kelso area, Father Bennett gave his testimony about his baptism in the Holy Spirit. On that day, I learned what I needed to know.

More truths about
God's new covenant people

Figure 21

In the present church and in the future messianic kingdom, people live under the eternal *new* covenant. Today, God deals with all Jewish and Gentile individuals to bring them to repentance and regeneration.

A parallel of the identities of Israel as God's earthly people and the church as God's spiritual people is revealed and confirmed throughout scripture.

When believers enter the new covenant, they are born again. The church enters the new covenant in the present age, and Israel and other future beievers enter the new covenant in the messianic age.

In the present age, God isn't dealing with *Jews as a people;* they're now in limbo. Instead, he is dealing with *Jews as individuals*—as ones to be saved by entering the new covenant spiritually as individual believers within the church.

In the future seven-year tribulation period, God will again deal with the Jews *as a people* to bring them to repentance. But meanwhile, during the time of tribulation on earth, the church—made up of raptured Jewish and Gentile Christians—will be in heaven where their works will be tested by fire to purify their hearts in order to prepare them to be the bride of Christ to reign with him.

During the thousand-year messianic kingdom, the church as bride of Christ will reign with him in his worldwide reign, and Israel will be exalted among nations.

So when the invitation was given to go forward to receive the baptism in the Holy Spirit, God gave me the faith to believe that this would be my day. Sure enough, after years of seeking—before I understood the simplicity of receiving—the desire of my heart was to be fulfilled.

In his testimony that night, Father Bennett told the crowd that it's not surprising that in Holy Spirit baptism, God chooses to take control of the tongue. As explanation, he cited two biblical quotations giving facts facts about the tongue. First, "No man can tame the tongue. It is a restless evil, full of deadly poison" (Ja 3.8b KJV). Secondly, "Behold also the ships, which though they be so great, and are driven of fierce winds, yet are they turned about with a very small helm"—an analogy about the importance of the tongue's function (Ja 3.4 KJV). From these quotations, Father Bennett pointed out that when a Christian yields control of his tongue to God, he surrenders himself to God.

Until that night, I had gone forward in meetings, had read books on the subject, had been prayed for, and had prayed alone, but I had not received the outward evidence of the baptism in the Holy Spirit—the speaking in tongues. I'd been waiting for God to "zap" me in a spectacular way, as others had testified about in their experience. But that was not what the Lord wanted in my case. He wanted me to take the gift by faith. So that night I walked forward in response to Father Bennett's call for those who wanted to be baptized in the Holy Spirit. I went forward in "cold-blooded faith" based on God's Word, as opposed to "feeling-centered faith" based on emotion. Though I had a headache, I knew I was going to receive from the Lord because Father Bennett had described my need and its remedy so clearly.

Here's a paraphrase of what Father Bennett told those of us seeking to receive the baptism in the Holy Spirit. He presented this scenario: "You're at point A, and you want to receive what God has for you at point B, but you sense that danger lurks on the path to point B. Nevertheless, the fact remains that you will never get to Point B unless you start moving in that direction. Therefore, it's necessary for you by faith to believe that God will enable you to plant your feet only on the safe spots as you begin to walk toward your destination." In this way, Father Bennett explained that in faith, a Christian cooperates with God. He said the Spirit takes over after a Christian begins to speak in faith, while at the same time believing that God will speak through him. Let me add, however, that many have been Spirit-baptized without previous knowledge about the gift. Out of their desperation to touch God, their faith brings forth the tongues speaking in the Spirit.

Before the night of Father Bennett's ministry, the Lord had already begun to prepare my heart to receive what he had for me, so when Pastor Bob Giles, Sr., a local, sponsoring pastor from Longiew, Washington, prayed for me, I began to speak and the Lord took over; I spoke readily in tongues. At the same time across the aisle, a young man from my congregation was praying freely in tongues, but on a later date I learned that he didn't accept the reality of his experience and was thereby robbed of it. He had only to continue to exercise that gift, but instead, he denied what he had received.

In my case, however, I'd been prepared by a dream that showed me that I should accept a "so what" experience as scriptural and real. In my dream, my husband began speaking in tongues and when I rejoiced in the fact that he'd been baptized in the Holy Spirit, he responded to me by saying, "So what?" In that dream, by seeing my husband's response, I was later able to see myself from the perspective of a third person. So, later when I received the gift, I did indeed have a so-what Spirit baptismal experience that was unemotional. And because God had prepared me earlier by the dream, I imderstood that he wanted me to believe that the experience that night was truly from him.

I had also been prepared for the experience earlier by a warning from my neighbor, Rose Fidler, the Rainier pastor and neighbor I mentioned earlier. Mrs. Fidler said that Satan hates the empowerment that God gives and will seek to destroy a person's faith in the God who empowers. So that night when I went forward to receive the baptism in the Holy Spirit, I was prepared for my faith to be tested. I knew that I had to go forward by faith, I had to speak in tongues by faith, and finally afterwards, I had to rejoice by faith. And sure enough, although my faith was tested, the Lord gave me victory by giving me a new dimension in my walk with God.

Let me add a note about that night. In spite of how "unemotional" I felt, I was never happier *in my spirit* than on that day when the Lord satisfied my deepest longing! And I continued to rejoice. As time went by, I began to see that my prayer life and my walk with God were changed. I used to obey the Lord "by sheer guts," so to speak, but since my baptism in the Spirit, I've learned what it's like to flow in sync with God and at times to know his presence in a new way, even emotionally and physically.

That's not all. I received another blessing, for not only was I baptized in the Holy Spirit, I also received a lifelong lesson about standing by faith on God's promises in his Word. I spoke of this in Figure 14 (ch. 8, p. 109) when I explained the sequence of "Fact, Faith, and Fulfillment" in a Christian's walk. On the night of my baptism in the Spirit, I learned that by my believing God's promises as *Facts* and by acting on those promises in *Faith*, I could see *Fulfillment* of those promises. From this Spirit-baptism experience, I learned that thereafter this sequence can be applied for receiving whatever God prompts me to seek. What a discovery!

Also, I found that because of this supernatural experience, I was empowered for witnessing, just as promised by the Lord (Ac 1.8). Beyond that, there's been a difference in my speaking to an audience as well as in my piano playing, but most of all, my prayer life was transformed. In other words, God through the baptism of the Holy Spirit has added a new dimension to my life. Indeed, I had always felt I had more potential to be fulfilled in Christ than what I knew, so when I finally received the baptism in the Spirit, I began to realize more of that potential.

C. New covenant people: Their Pentecostal experience examined

For greater clarity, let's look at the baptism of the Holy Spirit first, by comparing it to the fruit of the Spirit and then, by comparing holy Spirit baptism to water baptism.

---

* There is also a spiritual gift known as a gift of tongues. And, there is a gift of interpretation.

Holy Spirit baptism and fruit of the Spirit

In the twentieth century, there were two American revivals—the Pentecostal movement of the early twentieth century and the later charismatic movement of the 1960s and 1970s. Here's how they differ. The blessedness of Spirit baptism is that power comes to Christians in the receiving of a new prayer language, the speaking in tongues. The tongues speaking is biblical evidence of the reality of the experience of the baptism in the Holy Spirit. This Spirit baptism builds up Christians spiritually by equipping them for witness and by empowering them for ministry.

Fruit of the Spirit, on the other hand, refers to evidence of God's presence in the personal character of Christians as expressed over time. This fruit of the Spirit is seen in a person's life through his expression of love, joy peace, patience, kindness, goodness, faithfulness, gentleness, and self-control (Ga 5.22)—the Bible's listing of the fruit of the Spirit. Both the Pentecostal experience and the fruit of the Spirit play a part in effective ministry for God and for personal fulfillment.

To understand the role of each, let's look at an analogy of earthly and spiritual warfare. When duty calls an earthly soldier to face the enemy, he must have character—courage and self-control—but that alone is not enough to prepare him for battle; he also needs to be trained and equipped for warfare. Likewise, a Christian's personal character is nurtured by the Word and produces the fruit of the Spirit (Ga 5.22), but a Christian also needs to be equipped by the baptism in the Holy Spirit in order to be better prepared to serve God as his prayer warrior and as his witness (Ac 1.8). And the reverse is also true. The person who has been baptized in the Spirit needs the character that the fruit of the Spirit yields in a Christian's walk.

Holy Spirit baptism and water baptism

Let's compare two kinds of baptism in scripture—water baptism and Holy Spirit baptism. This comparison helps us understand better the baptism in the Holy Spirit. What I see is that water is the element for water baptism, and the Holy Spirit is the element for Holy Spirit baptism. When pastors baptize Christians in the element of water, candidates get wet, and when Christ as high priest in heaven baptizes Christians in the Holy Spirit, those candidates speak in tongues.* This logical perspective on understanding this manifestation of God's presence takes away the fear of receiving the prayer language of the baptism in the Spirit. Here's what to keep in mind. Getting wet is not the purpose of water baptism, and speaking in tongues is not the purpose of Spirit baptism. Instead, in both cases, the getting wet and the speaking in tongues are side effects, not the goal. The purpose of baptism in water is to glorify God by a believer's public declaration of faith, and the purpose of the baptism in the Holy Spirit is to glorify God by the candidate becoming spiritually edified and better equipped for service.

Everyone agrees that no one presents himself for water baptism because he wants to get wet and have his hair flattened out and his clothes dripping. Nevertheless, though no one seeks to get wet, still that wetness is necessary for fulfillment of water baptism, whether it's by immersion, sprinkling, or pouring. By the same token, a Christian who is willing to yield himself to God through the baptism in the Holy Spirit must also be willing to accept the collateral "foolish" effect of tongues as part of the package since speaking in tongues is the evidence that the Bible presents as evidence for the baptism in the Holy Spirit. This tongues phenomenon is found in these verses in the book of Acts: 2.4, 11; 10.46, and 19.6 and in parts of 1Corinthians 12 to 14.

Though I see this Pentecostal experience as scriptural, I recognize that the subject is considered by some to be controversial, but God does not present the baptism of the Holy Spirit to divide but rather to unify the body of Christ. Keep in mind that the first Christian Pentecost was the day God *united* Christians to become one body, the church.

There are passages about tongues other than those listed above. For example, there's a passage that speaks about tongues by inference. For example, in Acts 8.18, 19, speaking in tongues must have been the evidence that Simon the sorcerer witnessed, When Samaritan believers received the Holy Spirit, Simon offered to buy the gift of imparting the gift of the Holy Spirit to others. (But, of course, Simon was rebuked for his offer to buy the gift!)

What prompted Simon to make that request must have been that he witnessed the speaking in tongues of Spirit baptism. (There is also what's called the "gift of tongues and interpretation.") The inference of Simon's response is that the Samaritan believer must have spoken in tongues.

D. New covenant charismatic revival in the twentieth century

Now let me tell you my story as a participant in the charismatic revival in the latter half of the twentieth century. In 1963, I was baptized in the Spirit with the evidence of speaking in tongues. Then, in 1972, about two and a half years after my husband died, our three oldest children had left home to go to college and another would soon finish high school and leave for college. At that time, my youngest son, David, and I left Kelso, Washington where I had taught at Wallace Elementary, and we moved to Petaluma, California.

Because of unusual circumstances, the second year after our move to Petaluma and for a period of several years, I went to church, but I had no church home. Instead, my nine year old son and I began rotating visits to Sunday services and weekday Bible studies. Also, I met with pastors and I prayed for them and their churches. This arrangement was temporary and was not of my own choosing. It was a calling to encourage pastors and is not to be recommended as a way of life because every Christian should have a church home. During that time, I taught Bible Literature in public adult education. Before and after those five years or so, I was anchored in a church home.

Within those years, I finished reading the book *Nine O'Clock in the Morning* by Dennis Bennett. At the moment I finished the book, I heard that the Rev. Mr. Bennet was going to minister at a seminar in Vallejo, California not far from Petaluma. (When our family lived in Kelso, we'd visited his church in Seattle several times, and also I had attended one of his seminars in the San

Francisco Bay area.) On that day when I learned about his Vallejo seminar, I received what I considered to be an assignment from the Lord. What I knew was that I had to talk with Father Bennett. Then, with that realization, suddenly I became seized with a joy that could not be contained, for I knew I had a word for him at that meeting.

So I went to Vallejo. There, before the main session, Father Bennett gave a short talk to a small group, which I attended. Before that talk, I handed Father Bennett a note telling him that I would like to speak with him some time that evening. However, he didn't contact me after that meeting; he didn't contact me before the main session; nor did he contact me afterwards either. So there I sat in the main auditorium, wondering what I should expect. It seemed as if I wasn't going to have the opportunity to carry through on what I had anticipated. Finally, however, Father Bennett did show up, and he apologized for being late. He said he stuck my note in his pocket—a note that said I would like to speak with him—and then he forgot about it and had just then realized he was to meet with me. What I remember about my word for him is that it hit home, for he recognized that what I had to say was from the Lord. After that, we began to correspond for a while about spiritual issues. It's such a blessing when we see the hand of God at work in our lives.

Testimony about a revival event in the charismatic revival

During the years of my ministry to pastors in Petaluma, California, I taught Bible literature in public adult education. In the process, I came to appreciate those churches and pastors for whom I had a ministry of prayer and encouragement, including those with whom I disagreed on key points. In fact, when I taught the evening Bible literature class, the most liberal of the preachers, Herb Bauck, not only visited my class but also invited me to take part in the town's ministerial association.

During that period when I was visiting churches, I became acquainted with Father Timothy West, pastor of the Petaluma Episcopal church. I suggested to him that he invite Episcopalian

Father Dennis Bennett to Petaluma to speak and he did—but not until after he himself sought and received the baptism of the Holy Spirit at a district charismatic gathering for Episcopalian pastors.

In planning for Father Bennett's meeting in Petaluma, since a large crowd was expected, Father West arranged for it to take place in the largest sanctuary in town, a Catholic church. By this time, the Roman Catholic hierarchy had recognized and accepted the reality of the charismatic revival and had begun encouraging the personal Bible study and prayer that accompanied the movement. In fact, for some time, I had been meeting with a prayer group of devoted Catholic women."

On the night of the big event, what a delight to ride with Dennis and Rita Bennett from the local Episcopalian parsonage to the church and to find that huge church packed to overflowing with people from the surrounding area—people who were hungry for more of God. To accommodate the crowd, sliding doors to an adjoining room were opened! The Spirit of God was present in a wonderful way, and from that night's ministry came small charismatic groups in two churches in Petaluma—Episcopalian and Presbyterian—both of which groups I attended. At Father Bennett's meeting, many prayed at the altar, and I'm sure that many lives were touched that night.

From my vantage point on the West Coast, I heard about the charismatic movement spreading across the nation. People were uniting in worship across denominational lines, prayers were being answered, and large crowds were meeting for prayer and praise meetings—in homes, in conferences, and in other gatherings. The ministry of the Full Gospel Business Men's Fellowship (FGBMF) played a major part in this charismatic revival. Nationwide, the FGBMF had an effective interdenominational impact.

Charismatic youth revival in the latter half of the 20th century

During the charismatic movement, revival fire broke out among youth on the streets. Up and down the West coast and without central leadership, youths led other youths to God until finally, mature Christians did minister to them—Pastor Chuck Smith in southern California, the most notable among them. These young converts were called "Jesus people" and "Jesus freaks," names that they accepted from critics. I had contact with such groups—first at Kelso and Longview in Washington and then at Petaluma in California. Many had been delivered from substance abuse and other dead-end lifestyles. I had the privilege of attending some of their large meetings as the only older adult visitor.

Those meetings were led by young converts, both in Kelso and later in Petaluma. In both places, their meetings were crowded with exuberant, long-haired youth. What a joy to see them lifting their hands and their voices in song and in praise and worship! They were on fire for God, searching scripture and reporting on what God was doing in their lives. Also, they had a positive influ-ence on churches they visited. In Petaluma, young converts lived in a country commune, later formed a congregation and finally became a church at a prime location in downtown Petaluma—the Open Door Christian church, a church that still ministers there.

E. New covenant people: Their vision of future revival

Let's close with a thought about two revivals that evangelist

Smith Wigglesworth envisioned a week before his death in 1947. He said, "The first [revival] would bring the restoration of the gifts of the Spirit." (That prophecy was fulfilled in the charismatic revival of the sixties and seventies.) and he added that the second revival, would focus on the Word of God. (The second has not yet been fulfilled.) Wigglesworth said, 'When these two moves of the Spirit combine, we shall see the greatest move the Church of Jesus Christ has ever seen" (Stormont 1989, 123).

That's what I'm praying for—revival that has lasting influence on the culture and that brings consistent purity of life, unity of Spirit, and depth of commitment to God.

13   New covenant people: Their spiritual growth in godliness

There are many of us that are willing to do great things
for the Lord; but few of us are willing to do little things.
—D. L. Moody

Spiritual growth for God's new covenant people:

A. Godliness for new covenant people
B. The daily walk for new covenant people
C. The testimony of new covenant people
D. Spiritual and earthly conflict for new covenant people

A. Godliness for new covenant people

Hebrew prophet Isaiah, speaking in God's voice, spells out man's status with God: "As the heavens are higher than the earth, so are my ways higher than your ways and my thoughts than your thoughts" (Is 55.9). Isaiah also speaks of God's purpose for his people—that just as earthly rain and snow falling from heaven yield seed for the sower and bread for the eater, so too the Spirit's living water will not fail to accomplish God's purpose, which is to bring godliness and fruitfulness to believers (Is 55.9-.13).

Since God's ways are higher than man's ways, how can new covenant people accomplish God's purpose for them to be godly? Let's look at the seven phrases of 1 Timothy 3.16, which are amplified in Figure 22, page 173. Those seven phrases show that the Father worked supernaturally in the human life of the Son because the Son depended totally on the Father. Jesus didn't depend on his human perfection, his human striving, nor his human capability. This is the secret: Jesus as a human being depended on the Father, and in his dependence, that's how he could be both human and divine. Jesus led by example to show believers they are capable of following his example of dependence on the Father—even like little children: "Unless you change and become like little children, you will never enter the kingdom of heaven" (Mt 18.3).

Seven elements of Godliness as shown in Figure 22, page 173

The mystery of godliness is about the Son's dependence on the Father.

> 1) "Beyond all question, the mystery of godliness is great.
> 2) He appeared in a body,
> 3) was vindicated by the Spirit,
> 4) was seen by angels,
> 5) was preached among the nations,
> 6) was believed on in the world,
> 7) was taken up in glory" (!Ti 3.16) .

In the New Testament, the apostle Paul refers to godliness when he writes, "Physical training is of some value, but *godliness* has value for all things, holding promise for both the present life and the life to come" (1Ti 4.8. Italics added). Peter says, "His [God's] divine power has given us [Christians] everything we need for life and *godliness...*" (2Pe 1.3. Italics added). Jesus himself declared, "I do nothing on my own but speak just what the Father has taught me" (Jn 8.28b).

The path Jesus chose is one that all believers are capable of following. It's in the realm of possibility, for this path is not about sinless perfection, nor is it about self-condemning introspection. It's about a person keeping his eyes fixed on the one he loves, Jesus. So, for Christians, pleasing God is not a matter of trying harder but of loving more. Love *draws* a person to the Good Shepherd, and love *binds* that person to the Good Shepherd.

Godliness, a choice

Of the disciples, Peter, James, and John were closest to Jesus, but it wasn't because Jesus had favorites. I think it was because they had the deepest desire to please him and to be close to him. Happily, Jesus always satisfies that desire. But after the disciples were born again, *all* of them enjoyed a spiritual closeness with him under God's new covenant, which exceeded the communion any of them had had with him under God's old covenant while he walked with them on earth. That's why Jesus said, "Among those born of women there is no one greater than John the Baptist: yet

1 Timothy 3.16: The mystery of godliness:

Figure 22

To grow spiritually, Christians must follow Jesus' example of depending on the supernatural work of the Father

1) "The mystery of godliness is great." In the New Testament, godliness is called a "mystery" because it could not be fully understood until Jesus came in a human body. He says, "*I* am the Way…" The mystery of Jesus' incarnation is that in his life on earth, he embodied godliness. His dependence was on the Father.

2) Jesus "appeared in a body." His godliness can be seen in his miraculous virgin birth as Son of the heavenly Father and as son of an earthly mother. Jesus was totally God and totally human.

3) Jesus "was vindicated by the Spirit" in two ways. His godliness was vindicated by the undeniable purity of his Spirit-controlled life, for no one could accuse him of sin (Jn 8.46). Also, by the Spirit, godliness was vindicated in Jesus' supernatural resurrection.

4) Jesus "was seen by angels." His godliness was testified to by angels when they announced his birth, Later before his death on the cross, angels strengthened him in the garden of Gethsemane (Lk 22.43) Finally, angels reassured the women at Jesus' tomb.

5) Jesus "was preached among the nations." The supernatural power of his godliness is attested to by the speed and power of the wildfire-like spread of his message to the world, even to Gentiles.

6) , Jesus "was believed on in the world." His godliness is demonstrated to the world through born again believers.

7) , Jesus "was taken up in glory." His godliness is validated by the supernatural wonder of his visible ascension to heaven.

the one who is least in the kingdom of God is greater than he," (Lk 7.28).Jesus makes this statement because John the Baptist lived under the old covenant of the law, not under the fulness of the new covenant. For today, under the new covenant, intimacy for believers brings a capacity for them to understand who God is and creates a deep love for him, which then brings great transformation in the lives of believing Christians.

However, even though Christians today are new covenant people, the fact is that they do become sidetracked from devotion to the Lord. Nonetheless, such lapses do not negate the fact that in the present age and in the messianic age, all those believers are indwelt by the Holy Spirit. This means that sustained walking with God's guidance is at least possible when a believer keeps short accounts with the Lord by quickly confessing and repenting. Taking up the cross, such a believer keeps his eyes on Jesus and confesses when he becomes distracted or when he falls. One who walks in constant confessing-and-cleansing power is like a person in a car in the rain with windshield wipers keeping his vision clear, stroke by stroke (Nicky Gumbel in "The Alpha Course").

This continual cleansing is beautifully presented in a tiny book, *The Practice of the Presence*, which is about Brother Lawrence, a seventeenth century monk who was a lay cook in a monastery. He said that after he would acknowledge a lapse in his walk with the Lord, he would immediately confess and find forgiveness. Then he continued on his way with the Lord as if he had never stumbled. The latter statement is what most impresses me: "*Then he continued on his way with the Lord as if he had never stumbled.* Reading that little booklet greatly influenced my life.

In short, godliness is not about what a human being does in his own strength. It's about what God does through a person to accomplish what only God can do. It's about a person yielding his will to God's will. Life with God is a cooperative venture.

Spiritual growth in the story of Jacob and Esau

To understand how new covenant Christians are to live in a way that is pleasing to God, let's look at an incident in the Old

Testament story of Abraham's grandson, Jacob. The story illustrates that godliness begins at the point of abandonment of self-confidence and is manifested at the receiving of God-confidence.

In the story, when Jacob was returning after exile from his father's home, he faced the greatest crisis of his life. On his journey home, he was about to encounter his brother Esau, who had long wanted to kill him—for Jacob had wrested from Esau his firstborn birthright and had also "stolen" from him their father's blessing. The time had now come for Jacob to face the music; He had to meet Esau face to face, and this time he couldn't connive his way out of his dilemma as he used to do in the past.

Therefore, Jacob did what he could to protect his family from Esau's anger. About to meet Esau, he sent gifts to him, ahead of his caravan. Then when Jacob's messengers returned after delivering the gifts, they told him that Esau was coming with four hundred of his men. At that point, Jacob "in great fear and distress" divided his wives and children into two groups because he thought, "If Esau comes and attacks one group, the group that is left may escape"—yet nevertheless, he envisioned disaster for himself unless God intervened. He was at the end of himself. The text says, "So Jacob was left alone, and a man wrestled with him till daybreak" (Ge 32.24). And who was this man with whom he wrestled? Other scripture suggests that Jacob wrestled with God. This was the one who often appeared in Israelite times as the preincarnate Christ and was often referred to as "the angel of the Lord."* Such appearances are called theophanies. In this incident, Jacob did grow spiritually, and blessings did follow (Ge 32-33).

The New Testament gives God's pronouncement about the brothers: "Jacob I loved, but Esau I hated" (Ro 9.13). The gist of this startling statement is that God is sovereign and that whatever blessing he provides, he does so only out of his great mercy. However, I see something beyond that important truth, for I see a contrast between Isaac's sons. I see that which is spiritual represented by Jacob and that which is of the flesh represented by Isaac's firstborn son, Esau. In the story of Jacob, I think God looked at Jacob's motivation, for

*In Hebrew scripture, *angel* literally means *messenger*.

underneath his misguided scheming and manipulation during his lifetime, Jacob had a deep desire for that which is spiritual. He had an appreciation for God's blessings—in contrast to Esau, who yielded to his desire for fleshly indulgence and thus expressed contempt for his spiritual inheritance. In fact, Esau assessed his inheritance of the firstborn birthright to be of less worth than a bowl of "bread and lentil stew," for that was the price for which Esau sold his firstborn birthright to Jacob (Ge 25-27).

Hebrew scripture draws this conclusion about Esau's self-indulgence: "He ate and drank, and then got up and left. So Esau despised his birthright" (Ge 25.34). An expanded version could say, "Esau ate and drank, then got up and left, with nary a thought about the spiritual ramification of what he had chosen."

After Jacob wrestled with the angel of the Lord in this preincarnate appearance of Christ, that heavenly messenger changed Jacob's name from Jacob to Israel; that is, from "cheater" to "prince with God." Yet, though Jacob was victor, he was left with a hip injury to remind him of God's merciful intervention when Jacob could not help himself. When Jacob wrestled with God, he prevailed, not because of cleverness or effort but because of his spiritual bankruptcy. He had become "poor in spirit" (Mt 5.3a), for he had no place to go except to God. And in becoming dependent upon God, he learned to put his whole weight upon him.

My experience of wrestling with God before a looming crisis

One time, like Jacob, I faced a looming crisis. And though it may seem trivial, it nevertheless demanded a timely response.

This was after my husband's death—when I was still teaching remedial reading at Wallace Elementary in Kelso, Washington. I had several run-ins with kids on my walks to school. On one occasion, I had broken up a fight between two older elementary students in the front yard of the school and had gotten blood on my jacket. Another time, I confronted teen-age boys loitering on a street corner across from the grade school where they openly gambled, flipping coins, and set a bad example for elementary kids.

Now, later at the same corner, I faced a greater challenge with the same teens. In an earlier incident, I made them put out their cigarettes. (This was before a time when schools in another state, California, condoned smoking by setting up smoking areas for students.)

Continuing the story, on the night before the day that I was to encounter the boys again, I knew I had painted myself into a corner. I didn't know what I would do if I encountered the boys smoking again. This was going to be a Dodge City showdown. So far, I'd felt confident, but at this point, I feared that the teens would try to get the final upper hand, and I didn't have an authority figure to back me up because the boys were not from our school. Yet, I couldn't ignore the problem.

Finally, on the night before the expected confrontation, out of a long struggle came clear guidance. I received the faith to believe that love was the answer. Up to this time, the battle had been a conflict of wills, but now I became rejuvenated, for I knew this was more than a conflict of wills. I knew that no matter what happened, the motivation of love would be my guide, and I would know what to do when confronted. So I walked those few blocks to that corner with God-confidence, not with self-confidence. And what happened? No one was on that corner! The Lord had gone ahead of me. And no one was there on the days afterwards either. Though this crisis doesn't compare to what Jacob faced, it helped me understand in a small measure how intense the need for an answer can become when a crisis is pending and the deadline is approaching. This incident illustrates what it means to abandon self-confidence and receive God-confidence. That day I also learned about the part that love and compassion for others plays in spiritual warfare. That's also important to remember.

B. The daily walk for new covenant people

Learning how to deal with worrisome blunders

The following incident in San Diego illustrates the saying that it's "the little foxes that ruin the vineyards" (SS 2.15). This is to say that little worries disrupt a Christian's victory in his walk with God.

This "little-worries problem" arose in a discussion at a Christian women's gathering at our church. At our table we were discussing our insecurities and how we beat up on ourselves in dealing with them. I wanted to say something, but I didn't want to come on too strong. Yet in spite of the restraint I had placed upon myself, I found myself proclaiming, loudly, "I have a solution!" That caught everyone's attention. So, with the din of women's voices in the poor acoustics of our fellowship hall, I projected my voice to explain what I'd learned. I said, "After I've blundered and said ot done something that didn't convey what I meant to say or do, I pray, 'Father, bless my blunder and communicate to the other person the intent of my heart.'" And the women at our table kept asking me to repeat what I'd said, so I did keep repeating it. They found "the blunder blessing" helpful.

Let me say what praying this "blunder blessing" does for me. It sets me at ease, puts the matter to rest, and frees me in my walk with the Lord. What I'm referring to is a situation which an apology will not help or will make matters worse, or more likely, a situation too insignificant to deserve magnification by an apology. After such a bungle—a problem that persists in my thoughts—instead of bemoaning my blunder, I remind myself to look to the Lord. I ask him to bless the blunder and to communicate to that other person what was really the intent of my heart. This removes the worrisome static in my mind, blesses the other party, and restores peace in my walk with God.

As we bungle our way through life, let's remember this: Had we not blundered, the other person involved would not have received the heartfelt prayer of blessing that such an incident evokes—for such prayer doesn't take place unless there is a mishap that leads to praying "the blunder blessing."

Sweet fellowship with the Lord, moment by moment

Let's summarize what we know about God's new covenant people. New covenant people can renew their sweet fellowship with the beloved Shepherd by expressing faith through right choices. In trials, they can also be strengthened through God's written Word, which is the bread of life and through the refreshing that comes from the Spirit who gives the water of life. By this spiritual infusion into the vexations of daily life and in times of trial, the Lord brings his people into intimate fellowship with himself, and this intimacy results in godliness and spiritual growth.

This sustained personal fellowship with the Lord is about ongoing transformation and is called sanctification, a lifelong process that brings spiritual growth. It is a process that is marked by various crises and points of surrender along the way.

Let me tell you one very small way that this has been helpful to me in learning how to stay in a place of pleasing the Lord. I've found I am most vulnerable to yielding to Satan's tactics when I am either elated (prideful) or dejected (lacking faith). At such times, the emotion I feel is not the barometer that truly assesses the situation. In fact, the emotion of elation or dejection can make me lose my focus on the Lord.

Therefore, to stay on track, I pray, "Hide me, Lord! Hide me behind the cross!" I pray "Hide me" when others speak well of me, and I pray "Hide me" when others speak critically of me. This helps me avoid becoming either prideful or despondent.

I have to confess, however, that one time, this guaranteed application didn't work. That time, I experienced days of unrest after receiving "a high compliment" that I couldn't laugh off and that I couldn't ignore either. I didn't find peace until I took the compliment and received it not as a compliment but as a calling from God. And finally, with that revised outlook, I found peace.

The prophet Isaiah describes the satisfying fulfillment that is found in living a life pleasing to God: "The LORD will guide you always; he will satisfy your needs in a sun-scorched land and will strengthen your frame. You will be like a well-watered garden, like a spring whose waters never fail" (Is 58.11).

In the present age and in the future messianic kingdom, God's invitation is to all: "Whoever is thirsty, let him come; and whoever wishes, let him take the free gift of the water of life" (Re 22.17b). In responding to that invitation, a person can be satisfied continuously, moment by moment, for that source never runs dry.

How satisfying the fulfillment that God brings!

C. The testimony of new covenant Christians

New covenant Christians are lights in a dark world. To be such a light bearer, a person must allow the Lord to work through his life. God is the one who gives us the desire to win souls for his glory, and he is the one who fulfills the desire to win others for God.

Those with an outstanding conversion find it easy to attract others to the Lord just by giving their testimony of the change brought about in their lives by their becoming Christians. However, Christians who grow up in the church may not have a dramatic conversion and must rely on telling the message of the gospel in order to bring others into this new life in Christ.

Since I grew up in the church, my conversion was not outwardly dramatic, so I was so glad to learn I could present the gospel to win others to the Lord. In Sunday School, my brothers and I received gold perfect-attendance bars each year. Yet, in those days, I didn't have an understanding of "the gospel—the good news of salvation." Now, since gaining that understanding, my life has been blessed, as well as the lives of those touched by the gospel when I present it to them.

My early thoughts on soul winning

I remember when I first gave serious thought to what it means to be "saved," not a word commonly used in the Presbyterian church of my childhood. One summer during my college days, I visited my great Aunt Anna Crawford in Oregon. She was a feisty, elderly redhead, who was active in the church, who kept up with baseball news, who drove like a teenager, and who did water witching with a forked stick to locate water on the church grounds—a strange mixture of the divine and the not-so-divine. She attended a small, country church at Deer Island, Oregon. There I learned that people spoke of being *saved*. So when I made a return visit to that church years later after our family moved to the countryside outside Rainier, Oregon, I was able to visit her. I determined ahead of time that if anyone at that church asked me if I was saved, I would say, "Define your terms." Well, no one asked.

Years later, I found a little red gospel of John that had belonged to my mother. It had a place for a person to sign his name after receiving the Lord. So, I signed it and dated it—maybe in 1954—but that signature was not significant to me because since childhood, I'd had an intimate relationship with God. My earliest memory is of sitting on the curb with a little neighbor friend, Rose Mary Brasher, and talking with her about God.

Training for soul winning

Training for soul winning came later—after my husband died and after four of our five children either left for college or would soon leave. My youngest son, David, and I moved to Petaluma, California, where Jean Maston and I became friends. Each year, she organized a gospel outreach at the annual Sonoma County Fair by enlisting Christians from various denominations to serve in the booth. She taught us how to use "the wordless book" to present the gospel. (It is published by Child Evangelism Fellowship International.) We ministered primarily to children but in that ministry, we found that we could also engage youth and adults.

One year, after the fair ended, Jean and I decided to "take the show on the road," so to speak. Since at the fair, we got immediate response from children and teens who accepted the Lord, that experience gave us the courage to go out on the sidewalks after school was dismissed and tell young people the good news. As students walked home, we talked to them in groups, in pairs, or as individuals. Many listened, and many accepted and asked Jesus into their hearts, but some did not. Sometimes only one in a group would receive the Lord; sometimes everyone in a group would receive. Afterwards, we encouraged them to find a church home. Many of them knew someone in a church—a family member or a friend. Then at home after our adventures, we prayed for each of the ones we had talked with. The experience of those days gave me incentive to begin using the wordless book to spread the gospel, when opportunity arises.

The spiritual and earthly fulfilled in Christ forever
Figure 23

PRESENT ERA	FUTURE KINGDOM ERA	ETERNITY
Church, spiritual	**Messianic Kingdom, earthly**	**Believers with Christ forever**
1) The church, God's redeemed **spiritual** people	Israelis and supporters, God's redeemed **earthly** people	A new heaven. A new earth. The spiritual and earthly in perfect accord
2) New covenant blessings begun with regeneration	New covenant blessings begun with regeneration	Eternity, begun when the Son yields the kingdom to the Father who reigns
3) Spiritual priesthood, Christ as high priest	Earthly priesthood Zadok as high priest	No sin and no death so No need for temple or priests.
4) The believer's body, the temple of God	Jerusalem's physical temple, the temple of God	God's presence, all in all.

Expanded presentation of the above:

God's people, their blessings, the high priest, and the temple

1) *God's people:* The church is made up of God's redeemed *spiritual* people. The Jews as a people are made up of his redeemed *earthly* people, but in eternity, the earthly and spiritual of the new heavens and new earth will continue forever in perfect accord.

2) *The blessings* of the church and Israel come through regeneration. Both groups enter the new covenant by being born again, but that happens to them in different eras. Eternity begins after the Son destroys all opposing powers, hands the kingdom to the Father (1Co 15.24), and sits down beside him on his throne (Re 3.21).

3) *The high priest* in the present church age is Christ and the high priest in the messianic kingdom age is Zadok. The priesthood over whom each serves is different. For the church in the present age, Christians are a spiritual priesthood under Christ as high priest. And for Israel in the messianic kingdom age, those believers are an earthly priesthood under Zadok. But during God's reign in eternity, since there will be no sin or death, there will be no need for a priesthood or a temple.

4) *The temple* of a Christian today is his body. The temple of Jews in the messianic kingdom will be a physical temple in Jerusalem as well as Christ in their hearts. In eternity, however, there is no temple, for the Father and the Son are all in all (Re 21.22).

D. Spiritual and earthly conflict for new covenant people

God looked at creation and declared it to be good (Ge 1.31). In contrast, we mortals—locked into time and space as we are—look at creation and see sin and death and its consequent grief and misery. In essence, the story of the Bible, which is the story of mankind, is about conflict between the spiritual and natural—that is, between the heavenly and the earthly. We find examples of this earthly/spiritual conflict between Jacob and Esau, between Isaac and Ishmael, and between Israel and Judah.

Eternity—end of conflict between the spiritual and natural

Figure 23, page 182 compares the heavenly and the earthly in three eras—present era, future kingdom era, and eternity.

Eternity marks the end of the conflict of the spiritual and the natural because sin and death will be no more, for in eternity, God will express his grace and truth fully through the church and Israel, and he will bring the spiritual and the earthly into perfect accord in the new heavens and new earth (Is 65.17; cf. Re 21.1).

The Bible says that out of the present conflict between the natural and spiritual comes "a harvest of righteousness and peace" (He 12.11 NT), for out of this conflict comes spiritual growth for God's new covenant people. And for that reason, the author of the book of James says that Christians are to be joyful even when facing difficult trials. He writes, "Consider it pure joy, my brothers, when you face trials of many kinds" (Ja 1.2). James saw these times of testing as an opportunity for a person to express his love for the Redeemer, as well as to grow in grace. And since that's what Christians desire—spiritual growth—then, doesn't it stand to reason that when Christians face trials, they can be joyful (He 12.11 NT)?

Under the new covenant, Christian identity is ongoing, but continuance of new covenant blessing and power does not happen automatically. Therefore, when a Christian becomes dull of spirit or ineffective in witness, he must humble himself, seek God's face, and allow himself to be broken anew to regain intimacy with God so that he can be usable in God's hands. Charles Finney, early American evangelist, testified that such brokenness is necessary to regain and maintain tenderness of heart and power in ministry. And the Psalmist confirms this truth: "The LORD is close to the brokenhearted and saves those who are crushed in spirit" (Ps 34.18).

The next unit is on the theme of the natural and the spiritual.

THINK JEWISH
to understand the Bible

F.   UNDERSTANDING THE THEMES OF THE NATURAL AND SPIRITUAL

14. The call of God's natural and spiritual people groups
   A. *Abraham, called to be God's person in a fallen world*
   B. *Israel and the church, called to distinct but related roles*
   C. *God's call, not completely understood until fulfillment*
   D. *Israel and the church, called into God's tree of faith*
   E. *Israel and the church, called to walk in the Spirit*

15. The identity and destiny of God's natural and spiritual people
   A. *Identity in Christ for each of God's two people groups*
   B. *Identity of God's spiritual people revealed in spiritual warfare*
   C. *Identity of God's earthly people revealed in earthly warfare*
   D. *An eternal destiny for God's earthly and spiritual peoples*

16. Seeing as God sees from his higher spiritual perspective
   A. *God's precedence for favoring the spiritual over the natural*
   B. *God's sovereignty, the basis for spiritual precedence*
   C. *Times of conflict between the natural and spiritual*
   D. *Applying God's higher spiritual perspective to life*

14 The call of God's natural and spiritual people groups

The faith that binds Jews and Gentiles into an eternal destiny with Christ is the glue that holds the universe together, for "he is before all things, and in him all things hold together" (Colossians 1.17).

The two were unlikely soul mates—the young Rabbi Yechiel Eckstein and an elderly black Baptist minister—but as roommates in Israel, they experienced an unforgettable kinship. One day during their stay, the rabbi went out on the balcony, put on his prayer shawl and phylacteries, and recited prayers, as was his custom, but this was no ordinary day. He was so touched that he began to weep and to thank God for his return "home." Afterwards, when he went back to the room, he found his Baptist friend in prayer, arms lifted, crying and saying over and over, "I'm luckier than Moses." Through his tears, the Christian pastor said that Moses only got to see the promised land, but he was able to enter into it and to walk "on its holy soil." At that moment, Rabbi Eckstein realized what a profound link existed between him and this elderly Christian, and he remembered the words of the ancient rabbis who said that after the destruction of the Jerusalem temple, all the gates to heaven were closed except those of tears (Eckstein 1990, 179).

But a day is coming when God's earthly people, the Jews, and his spiritual people, Christians, will live in even greater accord (Is 2.2).

Earthly Israel and the spiritual church have distinct but related calls:

A. *Abraham, called to be God's person in a fallen world*
B. *Israel and the church, called to distinct but related roles*
C. *God's call, not completely understood until fulfillment*
D *Israel and the church, called into God's tree of faith*
E. *Israel and the church, called to walk in the Spirit*

A. Abraham, called to be God's person in a fallen world
Through the years, how has the God who is holy dealt with evil? First, after Adam and Eve disobeyed, he had to cast them

185

out of the garden of Eden. Later, he had to send a flood to cleanse the earth, but that didn't stem the tide of evil. Finally, evil people couldn't stand the discord and upheaval that evil produces, and so they assembled to create a grand plan that would unite their world in harmony and peace without God. That's why they began to build a tower called Babel to be their headquarters and by which they would centralize their power and become united as one world at peace. They said, "Come let us build ourselves a city, with a tower that reaches to the heavens, so that we may make a name for ourselves and not be scattered over the face of the whole earth" (Ge 11.1-9). Theirs was a utopian dream that has never died.

But God was not taken by surprise. He had a plan. At Babel, he disrupted the anti-God project by confounding their language so that they couldn't understand each other and would have to scatter. This dispersion was necessary since it was God's plan that Satan and his forces of evil be held in abeyance until the endtime tribulation, at which time God will allow Satan to make a full-blown bid for worldwide dominion through his man, Antichrist.

Fast forward now from Babel to the present church age. Here again, God uses language to play an important role, but this time language is the unifier of his people, not the divider, as the case had been for the ungodly who chose to be God's enemies at Babel. There, God disrupted the people's self-glorifying plan by confounding their earthly language and scattering them abroad (Ge 11).

But to God's redeemed ones on Pentecost, God gave a heavenly prayer language through the baptism in the Holy Spirit in order to unify believers as one body, the church (Ac 2). About Pentecost, Thomas Holdcroft says, "By the miracle of tongues, the effects of Babel were reversed and every linguistic group heard a testimony of the wonders of God" (Ac 2). (Holdcroft 1962, 94).

Like Holdcroft, I see Babel and Pentecost as important turning points in the history of mankind but with opposite results. From languages changed at Babel came division and scattering, but from the prayer language of the baptism in the Holy Spirit at Pentecost came the unifying of Christians as the church (Ac 2).

B. Israel and the church, called to distinct but related roles

What we learn from the biblical record is that God accomplishes his goals by placing his representatives in the fallen world. In Genesis 11, he raised up righteous Noah to continue man's natural line. Then finally, after a long conflict of the natural and the spiritual, God called Abraham to begin the godly line of Christ/Messiah.

In Genesis 12, God called Abraham, through whom, he would carry forward two ancestral lines of his people—the Jews, his natural people, and the then-future church, his spiritual people. The Old Testament presents the story of God's Jewish representatives, and the New Testament presents the story of his Christian representatives. Although their stories are recorded in separate testaments, they intertwine to tell God's whole story of the Bible.

Ronald B. Allen, a former professor at Dallas Seminary, says both biblical testaments are essential in Bible study. In a 1996 publication, he writes, "Lest I be misunderstood, let me say that were I obliged to choose whether students should be required to master the Old Testament or the New, I should without hesitation opt for the New. But the choice is a false one. I am confronted with no such choice, any more, I should say, than on sallying forth in the morning I am obliged to choose between wearing my trousers or my shirt; the decently dressed man requires both. Just so, the well-prepared minister must know both testaments."

Bible scholar Paul Lee Tan makes an even stronger statement. He says, "To value one testament above the other is to disparage both." He says critics attack Hebrew scripture because they know that "if the Old Testament falls, the New Testament topples" (Tan 1974, 230). Believers need God's whole Bible—the story line of natural Israel and the story line of the spiritual church.

Although the church is distinct and separate from Israel, the two are related. In fact, the church could not have come into being apart from the Lord's revelation of himself in Hebrew scripture, for without knowledge of God's creation and of his promises about the Messiah, no one would know who Jehovah God is or what he is like, and the gospel would hold no meaning.

In fact, for a decade after the church's beginning, *all* the earliest

Christians were Jewish (du Plessis 1970). Therefore, they needed credentials about Christ from the Old Testament to show them that he is truly the Promised One, the Lamb of God, the one for whom they were waiting. They had to have the history of Jesus' Jewish forebears, the royal lineage of his ancestry, and detailed scriptural prophecy outlining his life and ministry. Those Hebrew prophecies tell of Messiah's miraculous birth (Is 7.14; Mi 5.2; Ps 2.7), the place of his birth (Mi 5.2), his divine life (Is 53.3), his crucifixion (Is 53.12), his resurrection (Ps 16.10), his ascension to heaven (Ps 68.18), and his priesthood in heaven (Ps 110..4)—and also, his return (Zch 14.4) and his future reign as King of Kings (Ge 49.10). The reader can look up these references, which are only a few of the countless Hebrew prophecies about future Israel's Messiah and Savior.

From the above, we see that the church is related to Israel's history, and the reverse is also true—that historically speaking, Israel's future is related to the church. Scripture shows that the Jews will not be redeemed *as a people* until after the church has been completed and has been raptured to heaven. This rapture will happen before the tribulation period begins. Hebrews 11 (NT) says, "These [Israelites] were all commended for their faith, yet none of them received what had been promised. God had planned something better for us [Christians], so that only together with us would they [the Jews] be made perfect" (He 11.39-40 NT).

What ties Israel and the church together is the overarching theme of the natural and the spiritual. In the Torah, very early in Israel's history, we find an analogy—that the *natural* physical rite of circumcision under the old covenant has *spiritual* connotations pointing to God's new covenant. Moses understood this. He says, "The LORD your God will circumcise your hearts and the hearts of your descendants, so that you may love him with all your heart and with all your soul, and live (Dt 30.6 NIV 1984). Here we see that as early as the time of Moses, God presented the vision of *a spiritual new covenant*—a future new birth for Israel and for the church—though in different periods. This new spiritual covenant would contrast with the natural old covenant of Israel's ancient history.

Hundreds of years later, Jeremiah and Ezekiel, who are categorized as the writing prophets, added details to describe the future-spiritual new covenant. They said that one day God would work from the inside out by changing people's minds and hearts because God is interested in more than just people's outward actions. Jeremiah prophesied that "the time is coming... when I [God] will make a new covenant with the house of Israel and with the house of Judah.* I will put my law in their minds and write it on their hearts" (Je 31.31-33 mid). Ezekiel had a similar message: "I will give you a new heart and put a new spirit in you; I will remove from you your heart of stone and give you a heart of flesh. And I will put my Spirit in you and move you to follow my decrees and be careful to keep my laws" (Eze 36.26-27 OT). This is *the new covenant.*

C. God's call, not completely understood until fulfillment

Yet even though the spiritual new covenant of the church was prophesied, it was not completely understood until its fulfilment. This is what Bible scholars call "a mystery." A mystery in scripture is defined as knowledge that is concealed in the Old Testament and that cannot be fully understood until its meaning is revealed in the New Testament. For example, Jesus' disciples didn't understand that their own destiny under the new covenant could only be realized if Christ redeemed them by his death. For though Hebrew scripture in Isaiah 53 prophesies in detail about Christ/Messiah's sacrifice as the Lamb of God, the Jews didn't understand.

During Jesus' lifetime, his disciples didn't know that he would be testator† of his last will and testament and that only after his death and resurrection could he become the mediator‡ of the promised new covenant (He 9.15). In fact, Jews as a people still don't realize that all their past and future Judaic blood sacrifices typify Christ, who is their true blood sacrifice. Note that when Christ warned his disciples about his death and resurrection, they rejected what he said, for they didn't associate their redemption with his death. In fact, when Jesus predicted his own death, Peter corrected

---

* Note that at one time, Israel was divided in two—Judah in the south and Israel in the north.
† A testament is in force after someone dies (He 9.17), but a covenant refers to relationship. *Diatheke* in Greek means a testament *and* a covenant. No English word compares (Gaebelein 1999, He 9.17).
‡ Christ is mediator of a new covenant (He 9.15a). *Mediator* in Greek is not about dealing with compromise. Rather, Jesus, as mediator for God and man, establishes a new covenant on God's terms alone. (NET Notes 2005, note 19, He 9.15).

him by saying, "This shall never happen to you!" (Mt 16.22), and Jesus had to rebuke him, for Jesus *would* die! And because he died and rose again, sinners can now be redeemed under the new covenant.

Even at the Last Supper just before Jesus was crucified, the disciples still didn't understand that Jesus had to die even though earlier, he had told them three times. Therefore, at this last hour, he once again had to prepare them for his death and for the delay of his messianic kingdom. He told them, "You will grieve, but your grief will turn to joy. A woman giving birth to a child has pain because her time has come; but when her baby is born she forgets the anguish because of her joy that a child is born into the world. So with you: Now is your time of grief, but I will see you again and you will rejoice…" (Jn 16.20b-22). Not until after Jesus' resurrection did his disciples understand what he had told them earlier.

That last night of his life, Jesus actually spoke specifically of "the new covenant" when he introduced the church's communion ritual of bread and wine. About the communion ritual, he said, "This [bread] is my body, which is for you; do this in remembrance of me. This cup [of wine] is *the new covenant* in my blood…" (1Co 11.24b-26, Italics added). Under this new covenant, the disciples were going to enter into a new, intimate relationship with God himself. Until then, all they knew about the new covenant was that it would belong to Israel and the Jewish people because God had definitely promised the new covenant to the nation of Israel, but this will not come to pass for them *as a people* until Jesus returns.

The disciples didn't understand anything about the church. They didn't know they would be "called out[*]" to be charter members of the church. They didn't know that as Christians, they would enter the kingdom of heaven under the new covenant during their lifetime—but only spiritually in this present age. Not until Jesus returns to earth with the church as his bride will the church and Israel experience the total fulfillment of God's plan for each of them in the new heavens and the new earth.

Let's look now at Israel and the church in God's tree of faith to

---

[*] Reminder: "Ecclesia," the Latin word for church, means "called out ones.."

learn more about God's new covenant for Israel and the church.

D. *Israel and the church, called into God's faith tree (Fig. 24, p 190).*
Now let's compare Israel and the church in their relationship to the new covenant. What's the same for both Israel and the church is that they enter the new covenant as human beings on earth. What's also the same for both is that their entry into the new covenant is made possible through the blood sacrifice of Christ.

As stated earlier what differs for Israel and the church is the timing of their entry into the new covenant. In the present age, *Jews as individuals* enter the new covenant when they become Christian believers, but for Jews during the thousand year messianic kingdom, that generation of Jews *as a people* will enter the new covenant when they enter the messianic kingdom.

In that messianic kingdom, Israel will again become God's theocratic nation under his direct rule, for Christ will be King of Kings over Israel and the earth. And like present day Christians under the new covenant, Israeli believers in the messianic kingdom will have new minds and new hearts (Je 31-34). This future wave of believing Jews will be miraculously gathered to Israel from "the four winds" (Mt 24.31), and [they] will enter the messianic kingdom with those Gentiles who were their sympathizers during the tribulation.

What I once conjectured was that the new birth of the new covenant is the same for Jews and Christians but in different eras, so I was glad to find confirmation from the noted Bible scholar, Dwight Pentecost about end times. He also concludes that Jews in future Israel enter the new covenant by the new birth, the same way Christians enter the new covenant today. He says, "All believers will be indwelt by the Holy Spirit in the future millennium,[*] even as Christians are in the present [church] age" (Pentecost 1958, 486).

God's Tree of Faith (Figure 24, next page)

Scripture reveals that in the present day, *Jews as a people* have stumbled over Christ, the Rock, for they have sought God through good works of the law, not through faith in his Son (Ro 9.32 NT; Is 8.14b OT).

_____
* *The millennium* is another name for the thousand-year messianic kingdom.

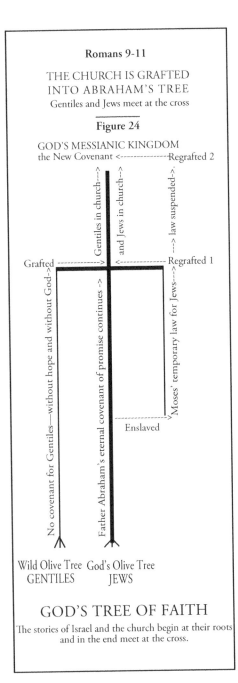

Romans 9-11

THE CHURCH IS GRAFTED
INTO ABRAHAM'S TREE
Gentiles and Jews meet at the cross

Figure 24

GOD'S MESSIANIC KINGDOM
the New Covenant <------------Regrafted 2

Gentiles in church---> | and Jews in church--> | ---> law suspended->.

Grafted -------------> <------------- Regrafted 1

No covenant for Gentiles—without hope and without God->

Father Abraham's eternal covenant of promise continues ->

Moses' temporary law for Jews--->

Enslaved

Wild Olive Tree God's Olive Tree
   GENTILES   JEWS

GOD'S TREE OF FAITH
The stories of Israel and the church begin at their roots
and in the end meet at the cross.

Yet, though they stumbled under the law, they did not "fall beyond recovery" (Ro 11.11), for Paul writes "All Israel will be saved," as it is written [in Hebrew scripture]: 'The deliverer will come from Zion; he will turn godlessness away from Jacob [Israel]. And this is my covenant with them when I take away their sins'" (Ro 11.26-27). Here scripture speaks about the Jews' future repentance and entrance into God's new covenant of grace given to Abraham.

Beeginning at the bottom, Figure 24 shows the progress of the Jewish people from their origin to the present time and beyond to their entry into God's future messianic kingdom. In text below, semibold words in quotation marks correspond to labels in Figure 24. The diagram's sequence begins at the tree's roots and progresses upward to "**God's messianic kingdom,**" where paths of Israel and the church meet under the new covenant of God's kingdom.

The roots of the two trees are "**Jews**" as "**God's Olive Tree**" and "**Gentiles**" as a "**Wild Olive Tree.**" Gentiles were a people with no covenant and "**without hope and without God**" (Eph 2.12). Jews, on the other hand, were raised up to be God's witness to the world, but alas, they became sidetracked from their mission when they were "**Enslaved**" in Egypt for 430 years (Ge 11.17; Ex 12.40; Ga 3.17). Then after their enslavement, "**Moses' temporary law for Jews,**" was given by God as a schoolmaster in order to guide them and bring them to the point of recognizing that they, like all sinners, "fall short of the glory of God" (Ro 3.23) and need the Savior (Ga 3.24, 25).

Figure 24 illustrates the grafting of Gentiles and the regrafting of Jews into "**GOD'S TREE OF FAITH.**" The diagram shows that Jewish regrafting takes place in two waves. The first wave, "**Regrafted 1,**" is about present-day Jewish *individuals* who come out from under the old law covenant as their schoolmaster (Ga 3.24, 25 KJV). Today, those Jews who have faith in the sacrifice of Jesus as the Lamb of God, are regrafted into God's new covenant as individuals in Abraham's eternal new covenant of promise. There in the church, Christians and Jews meet in Abraham's new covenant of promise. There, at the cross under the new covenant of the Messianic kingdom, Gentiles and Jews become one.

The second wave, "**Regrafted 2,**" will take place after the future tribulation period when Jesus returns to earth with his bride, the church, which was purified in heaven after the rapture of the church. At that time, that future generation of believing Jews on earth will be regrafted as a people, Israel, into "GOD'S TREE OF FAITH," for at that future time (**Regrafted 2**), Jews will recognize Christ as their Messiah. By regeneration through the blood of Jesus' sacrifice, Jews as a people will be pardoned, will be regrafted into "GOD'S TREE OF FAITH," and will enter the new covenant as born again citizens of "GOD'S MESSIANIC KINGDOM."

At the top of Figure 24, we see "**Gentiles in church**" and "**Jews in church.**" There today, as brothers and sisters in Christ, the barrier between Jews and Gentiles is broken down (Eph 2.14), for in the church under God's new covenant, Jewish and Gentile Christians are one in Christ (Eph 2). The book of Ephesians says this: "For he himself [Christ] is our peace, who has made the two one and has destroyed the barrier, the dividing wall of hostility… His purpose was to create in himself one new man out of the two, thus making peace, and in this one body to reconcile both of them [Israel and the church] to God" (Eph 2.14-15).

What "**Regrafted 2**" shows is that a future generation of *Jews as a people* will be regrafted into "GOD'S TREE OF FAITH" and will enter the new covenant of the messianic kingdom as the distinct people group of Israel. Both people groups, Israel and the church, will retain their distinctiveness as God's people, but they will have different roles in the messianic kingdom. The church will be the future metaphorical bride of Christ, Israel will be exalted among nations, and Jerusalem will be the world's capital under Christ.

During this thousand-year kingdom, Satan will be bound, and everyone will live in harmony under Christ/Messiah, yet even so, according to Hebrew prophet Isaiah, sin and death will still be present (Is 65.20)—therefore, Christ will have to rule with an "iron scepter" (Re 19.15).* This kingdom under the new covenant will be the fulfillment of the Lord's plan for his earthly people, the Jews.

After the thousand year kingdom, Satan will be loosed and will lead unbelievers into battle against Jerusalem (Re 20.9). But when

*Though unbelievers are present during the messianic kingdom, their evil deeds will be suppressed.

unbelievers surround the city, fire will come down from heaven and devour them (Re 20.9b). Afterwards, before eternity begins, un-believers of all eras will be resurrected and judged at the great white throne and will then be sentenced to "the fiery lake." As for regenerated human believing survivors still on earth, (Jews and sympathizers)— they enter eternity under the reign of God forever. Then for eternity, God the Son, reigns at the right hand of God the Father.

The Bible urges Gentile Christians in the present age to remain humble and patient toward unbelieving Jews. For Paul says, that those Jews who do not continue to persist in unbelief "will be regrafted into God's natural tree, for he is able to graft them in again." Scripture also says, "After all, if you [Gentile Christians] were cut out of an olive tree that is wild by nature, and contrary to nature were grafted into a cultivated olive tree, how much more readily will these, the natural branches [the Jews], be grafted into their own olive tree" (Ro 11.23-24) when Christ returns.

E. Israel and the church, called to walk in the Spirit

God's new covenant people in the church today and in the future messianic kingdom are called to choose moment by moment whether to walk in the Spirit or to walk in the flesh. Watchman Nee illustrates this choice between walking in the Spirit or walking in the flesh when he comments on Jesus' refusal of "the wine and the gall" offered to him to assuage his pain when he was on the cross. Nee says that some people react to trials with anger and resentment, some yield to self-pity, and others repress their emotions into a state of passivity, but he says that Jesus did not respond in any of those ways.

Watchman Nee asks, "What then is the cross of Christ? It is the will of God joyfully accepted." He says for the believer, the cross is God's will, 'recognized and received with thanksgiving" as "good and acceptable and perfect." Nee also says that "when Christ was on the cross, he refused the wine and gall for the simple reason that he did not need it; the Father's will was his delight. His followers who accept the cross do so on the same ground—that the Father's will is their deepest joy (Nee 1966, 93-95). Hebrews says that Jesus, "who for the *joy* that was set before him endured the cross, despising the shame, and is set down at the right hand of the throne of God" (He 12.2 NT). He accepted the cross with joy, for he knew that his death redeems sinners and reconciles them to the Father.

Followers of Jesus can respond as he responded on the cross—by rejoicing that God's hand is on their lives, especially in times of trial. James—author of the book of James and traditionally identified as the brother of Jesus—says, "Consider it pure joy, my brothers, whenever you face trials of many kinds" (Ja 1.2). This joy is not negative resignation; it is a positive virtue that comes from God as a fruit of the Spirit. This joy abides in a Christian's heart for Jesus always abides there; that joy simply needs to find expression through a person's life.

God's call for the church has been for it to be *grafted* into his tree of faith, and his call for Israel will be for the Jews as a people one day to be *regrafted* into his tree of faith. The church and Israel are God's representatives in a fallen world, but their roles differ.

My good friend Anne Elliott sent me an email written by her daughter Sarah Overbey about her husband Anson's experience. It illustrates how God sets up situations for his glory when Christians walk in the Spirit, ready for opportunities to serve God.

Sarah Overbey wrote this about the incident.

> "We have had an amazing day. We were on Balboa Island and went into a shell shop. An older man owned it and Anson and he got to chatting. It was taking too long so I took the kids to get a bagel at Starbucks. When I came back I looked in the shop and Anson was behind the counter with his arm around his new friend, praying, as the man wept. I waited outside and not one customer went in while they were together (about forty-five minutes total). The man's daughter died ten years ago and now his son has cancer. He told Anson he doesn't have the strength to lose another child. Anson asked if he could pray for him and the man began to cry. Anson shared the Lord with him and he was so receptive. His name is John; please pray for him. Anson has his phone number and told him he will be praying and will follow up."

Next, we'll compare identities and destinies in Christ for God's people—for his earthly Jews and for his spiritual church.

15 The identity and destiny of God's natural and spiritual peoples

Jesus weaves the destiny of the church and nations
around the destiny of the nation Israel.
—Walter K. Price

In this chapter we will discuss the identity and destiny of God's two people groups, Israel and the church, as presented in scripture.

The identities and destinies of Israel and the church:

A. *Identity in Christ revealed for Israel and the church*
B. *Identity of God's peoples revealed in their warfare*
C. *Incidents illustrating spiritual warfare*
D. *Eternal destiny for God's natural and spiritual peoples*

A. Identity in Christ revealed for Israel and the church

Thinking Jewish, we see that Israel and the church are identified as God's people groups in two prophetic incidents—one at the birth of Jesus and the other after his death.

Identity in Christ for Israel and the church
revealed at Christ's birth

Eight days after Jesus' birth, Joseph and Mary presented him for the Judaic rite of circumcision. By inference, this event reveals the identity and destiny of each of God's two people groups, Israel and the church.

Luke (NT) writes, "Now there was a man in Jerusalem called Simeon, who was righteous and devout. He was waiting for the consolation of Israel, and the Holy Spirit was upon him. It had been revealed to him by the Holy Spirit that he would not die before he had seen the Lord's Christ [Messiah]." Righteous Simeon, moved by the Spirit, went into the temple courts (Lk 2.25-28a), took the infant Jesus in his arms, and said,

"Sovereign Lord, as you have promised,
you now dismiss your servant in peace.

which you have prepared in the sight of all people,
 a light for the revelation to the Gentiles
and for glory to your people Israel."

Here we see that Simeon refers to Israel and the church when he says, "a light for the revelation to the Gentiles [the church]"- and "for glory to your people Israel [the nation]

Identity in Christ for Israel and the church
revealed again after Jesus' death

After Jesus' crucifixion, another prophetic incident identifies both Israel and the church as God's people groups in Christ. Joseph of Arimathea, a righteous man and wealthy member of the Jews' ruling Sanhedrin, asked Pilate for the body of Christ to bury him in a tomb among the tombs of the wealthy. Joseph's offer to bury Jesus in a rich man's tomb fulfilled the Old Testament Hebrew prophecy about the Messiah, which says that he would make his grave "with the rich in his death" (Is 53.9 KJV).

This request for the body of Jesus reveals that Joseph of Arimathea had dual identity first as a Jew of Israel and second as a follower of Jesus.

First, Luke writes that Joseph of Arimathea was a Jew "waiting for the kingdom of God" (Lk 23.51), and so his request identifies him with the Jews who wait for the Messiah to come to earth to set up a future worldwide kingdom with Israel foremost (Lk 23.51).

Second, Joseph, by his request for the body of Jesus, identified himself as a follower of Christ and thus identified himself with persecuted believers who would become the church. Therefore. in Joseph's request for Jesus' body, he acted as a representative Jew and as a representative Christian, both of whom look forward to Christ's reign in the messianic kingdom under the new covenant.

B. *Identity of God's peoples revealed in their warfare*

The identity of natural Israelites revealed in natural warfare

To understand the natural and spiritual identities of Israel and the church respectively, let's examine their warfare. In ancient times, the naturally descended Israelites engaged in natural *earthly warfare* as the Father's theocratic nation under his direct rule, whereas spiritual Christians today engage in *spiritual warfare* in the heavenlies, under Christ and against Satan and his demons.

Before we talk about warfare, we must address perplexing questions about biblical warfare. What must be faced is, how could God who is holy lead the Israelites to war? Even more troubling, how could he at times require his people to wipe out whole villages, within which were men, women, children, animals, and possessions of value? Rational people react against this instinctively.

As for Israel's wars, those who are not willing to wait for an answer from the Lord may reject the biblical account of those wars. Their reaction would be like Peter's spontaneous reaction after Jesus said he had to die. Peter said "Never!" and Jesus had to rebuke Peter by addressing his exclamation as though from Satan: "Out of my sight, Satan! You are a stumbling block to me; you do not have in mind the things of God, but the things of men" (Mt 16.22,23).

Peter's "Never!" evokes sympathy from us human beings because of Peter's seeming compassion and rationality in the way he addressed the subject of Jesus' death, but he received no sympathy from Jesus. In that incident, Satan was challenging the necessity and the reality of Jesus' future sacrifice as Lamb of God; therefore, Jesus had to rebuke Peter as a tool of Satan. Satan's goal was to sidetrack Jesus from his mission to redeem the Jews and mankind.

In our present age, to understand the Israelites' view toward war, let's look at what the Hebrew Bible says. In that ancient time, Jehovah God's presence actually dwelt among the Israelites on earth, because as a nation, Israel was God's witness to the world. In those days, God's dwelling place was above the ark of the covenant in the Most Holy Place of the Jewish temple (Le 9.24). God told the Jews, "There, above the cover between the two cherubim that are over the ark of the Testimony, I will meet with you and give you all my commands for the Israelites" (Ex 25.22). Also, by the movement of a cloud by day and a pillar of fire by night (Ex 13.21), God led the Israelites in their travel to the promised land.

Here's God's perspective on Israelite warfare. Since Israel was a theocracy under the direct rule of the Father, whoever challenged the Israelite armies challenged God himself. Consequently, when God faced defiance from Israel's enemies, he had to stand in judgment against them, for he is holy. Nevertheless, God's goal was not the destruction of unbelievers through war. His goal was to reveal himself to the people of the world through his Jewish people, who were to be his witness in the world.

In the New Testament, after Israel rejected their Messiah, Christ became the cornerstone (Zch 10.4; Is 28.16) of the church. And now, therefore, the church as God's spiritual people has become God's present witness to the world. But a day is coming when Jews *as a people* will repent and enter into God's blessings (Ro 9-11).

God doesn't like war, for he is "the God of peace" (Php 4.9), but since he is also the God of righteousness, he has used war in judgment against enemies that rise up against him or his people. And he has used war in the correction of his own people, the Israelites. Scripture says God had to discipline King David because he sinned against Uriah by plotting Uriah's death and then taking his widow to be his wife. So, in discipline, God allowed David's kingdom to be in continual warfare (2Sa 12.10). And because David was a man of war, God would not allow him to build the temple (1K 5.3). He gave that task to his son Solomon, "a man of peace" (1Chr 22.9).

Yet, remember that contrary to present-day sensibilities, God *did* use Israel as his instrument of war—against nations who refused to allow Israelites to pass peacefully through the land and against any who defied the Lord's authority. And in reverse, God used nations to discipline the Israelites when they went astray.

Christians continue to deal with the issue of earthly warfare, for conflict continues between nations. From scripture, Christians conclude that lasting world peace cannot come until Christ, Prince of Peace, returns to reign in the world. Meanwhile, Christians as citizens engage in war to overcome the spread of tyranny and to protect the legitimate self-interest of their nations.

Identity of God's spiritual people revealed in spiritual warfare

God's high calling for Christians today is to engage in *spiritual warfare*—in contrast to God's calling for the ancient earthly Israelites to engage in *earthly warfare*. The spiritual warfare of Christians today requires them to trust in God and to overcome the devil in his accusations, temptations, and delusions.

The weapons of Christian warfare are spiritual and have power to demolish evil strongholds (2Co 10.4). Paul writes that for Christians, "our struggle is not against flesh and blood, but against the rulers, against the authorities, against the powers of this dark world and against the spiritual forces of evil in the heavenly realms" (Eph 6.12). And since spiritual warfare is not against flesh and blood, victory comes to Christians by faith and obedience. This spiritual struggle is necessary, for even though Jesus at the cross destroyed Satan's authority over Christians, Satan is still the great deceiver and impostor, the "god of this age" (1Co 4.4). He "prowls around like a roaring lion looking for someone to devour" (1Pe 5.8). This means Christians have to call Satan's bluffs, rebuke him, resist him, and deny him ground (1Pe 5.9). This also means that believers can be called into spiritual warfare by God to deliver others from Satan's bondage.

Christian warriors are clothed in the whole armor of God with…

> the belt of truth,
> the breastplate of righteousness,
> the readiness that comes from the gospel of peace,
> the shield of faith to extinguish Satan's fiery darts,
> the helmet of salvation,
> and the sword of the Spirit, the Word of God (Eph 6.10-18).

The power of faith and prayer in spiritual warfare is best communicated by illustration, so let me give three examples—two illustrations from my life and one illustration from a friend's life.

C. Examples illustrating spiritual warfare in my life

First incident

I'll tell you first about my spiritual warfare, soon after our family moved from my homestate Texas to picturesque Rainier, Oregon, the little town where my husband matured into his teens after his childhood in Kentucky; it was from Rainier at age seventeen, he'd joined the Navy to serve in World War II. And it was in Rainier that our first four children spent their early years, from about 1950 to 1960, I had little knowledge, if any, about spiritual warfare, but I understood the blessedness of faith and obedience.

Soon after we arrived in Oregon, the five in our family lived for a brief time in a tiny house in Roxy Park in Rainier where we had one tiny bedroom, a tiny living room, a tiny kitchen, and a very tiny nursery. Our third son, born in 1953 while we lived there, slept in a bassinet in our tiny bedroom. The two toddlers slept in the very tiny nursery, a sort of lean-to enclosure off the kitchen where we had two baby beds, which left only enough room for four stacked, apple crates, which served as a chest of drawers with curtains that I made and strung up to brighten the room.

The circumstances were unforgettable. At that time, automatic washers and driers had not yet taken over the market. and the wringer on our washing machine was broken, so the diapers and clothes would be dripping wet when I hung them on a line in the carport to keep them out of Oregon's continual rain (We didn't need to use the carport for a car because since we had moved from south Texas, we had no car and no money to buy one.) Laundry was a problem because all three children wore diapers at night and the younger two in the daytime as well.

As a South Texan, I had several "new experiences"in that house. Lighting an oil heater with a match was a new experience for me. If I let too much oil flow in, it was scary to watch the heater dance around after it was lit. Fortunately it didn't explode. Another "new experience" was that we had only a "cooling closet" for a refrigerator. so it's not surprising that the children got worms while we lived there. Incidentally, a cooling closet is a closet with holes in the outside wall to allow cool air to come in.

A third "new experience" was that we had a wood-burning cook stove. And because of the continual rain of the Northwest, we had only wet, green wood. To start a fire, I had to pour oil on the wet, green wood, and again I managed not to blow up the house—but I did almost burn the house down—when I made the mistake of putting ashes removed from the wood stove into a container close to the house and which was evidentlly inflammable. The house and our lives were spared because George—who was home asleep—awoke and saved the day by putting out the flames on the outside wall of our house.

On Sundays, going to church more than a half mile away, I pulled our young infant in a wagon and pushed the other child in a stroller. Then after the third son was born, two rode and the oldest walked with me. This too was a new experience.

All of the above is a backdrop for telling something that happened during that period. Let me remind you that ever since I had experienced the astounding miracle of my husband's conversion—brief though it was—the Lord had lit a flame in my heart that has never died. That's what made it possible for me to deal with what was about to happen in that tiny house.

One evening, home alone with the children, I was fasting and praying for my husband. I happened to be in the kitchen when I heard a loud crash from the nursery. As I entered the room, the worst stench imaginable overtook me and a great fear seized me, for I faced a rat unlike any other wild creature, for ordinarily wild animals flee from humans. This one was bold and aggressive. The crash must have come from the rat crashing through the wall.

I knew the Lord was in charge of the situation; so when I became aware that he wanted me to bring our infant to the nursery, I obeyed. On my own, I never would have made that choice. Then there, with the infant asleep in my arms and my two toddlers asleep in their beds, I faced the threatening situation. And this is the strangest part of all; the Lord made me know that this bold, demonized rat was a creature that he had created and that I was not to fear but that I was to allow God's love to flow through me and toward this animal of his creation. I knew God was in charge.

We know from Ephesians 6 that Christians are not against flesh and blood but against principalities and powers (Eph 6.12). That was the situation I faced; that is, I was not against this flesh-and-blood rat but against the demonic spirit controlling it. Scripture says that "our struggle is not against flesh and blood, but against the rulers, against the authorities, against the powers of this dark world and against the spiritual forces of evil in the heavenly realms" (Eph 6.12).

As I remained in the room with the baby in my arms and with the toddlers in their beds, I allowed God's presence to fill me with his love, and when I did that, the aggressive rat retreated into the hole in the wall that he'd made earlier, but when I would begin to fear again, I could see a blue light at the hole as though the rat was about to return, which instantly alerted me to once again enter into the love that comes with God's presence. I remained there for a long time, calling on God's presence and guarding my children—until I was sure it was okay for me to leave and go to bed.

What better illustration could there be for me to learn how Christians are to respond to flesh and blood people whom God created! I often think of this incident when faced by hostility in any form from any person. I'm reminded that I am not against flesh and blood but against principalities and powers, and therefore I know that God's loving presence is to fill me and be my guide. Satan disrupts human relationships by exploiting self-centered desires. Those Christians that resist Satan—when they recognize that he is at work—can then allow the Lord's love for the other person(s) to flow through them and God's presence to fill them. Remember, since Satan has no legitimate authority over Christians, his strongholds can be broken.

I might not be telling this story if I hadn't had proof that the above incident actually happened. The proof was that the next morning, I saw a hole in the wall that hadn't been there the day before. This gave me visible proof of the reality of my experience, which, incidentally, I didn't doubt anyway, but this knowledge does validate to you the reader that the experience was not just a figment of my imagination.

Here's the rest of the story. Besides learning about the power of God's presence, something else happened that night. At some point in the incident, I heard a rattling sound like an amplified, hollow rattling of dice in a container, as used in a board game or in gambling. I didn't know what that was about until afterwards when my husband George gave me the clue I needed to understand what those sounds signified. He told me that he had been delivered from gambling, and he described his liberation as a moment of truth. He said it was like an awakening that opened his eyes and made him to know that he didn't want to continue down that road. I hadn't even known that he had been gambling. I believe that his deliverance was the result of the victory God gave me in the spiritual encounter I described.

I'm telling you all this to show that God has blessed my life—not in spite of obstacles but because of those obstacles.

I was happy when we left that house. We bought a car—a model A Ford if you can believe it—an antique even at that time. (It was in good condition. Even the pull shade for the back window was in perfect shape. We moved out in the country and had an ideal place to begin raising what would become the first four of our five children.

Another incident illustrating spiritual warfare in my life

Another spiritual battle also happened in Rainier in a year when our family lived with my husband's mother at her home. This was in 1960, the summer before the last school year of our time in Oregon. There, I had another first experience—putting up wall paper. This was about a year before we moved across the bridge from Rainier, Oregon to Kelso, Washington on the other side of the magnificent Columbia River. That summer in Oregon, we had four children, and three of them in the fall would be entering second, third, and fifth grades in Rainier Elementary, and our youngest would enter first grade in the school where I would teach a combination fourth-fifth-sixth grade class at Hudson Elementary, a two-room country school in Orregon.

It was daytime and my husband and I were at home—he in one room, and I in another. I was on my knees praying for him because I was concerned about his aberrant behavior that day.

While I was praying, George, Sr. in another room, was trying to hear a voice—one of several voices that he felt he needed to hear but was having difficulty hearing clearly. After a while, he came to me and asked me to stop praying because he said he had been told by the voices that the cause of his inability to hear clearly was that

I was praying and that he should tell me to stop. So I tested what the voices told him and found it to be true. What I learned was that George would begin to hear the Adversary's message when I stopped praying and he couldn't receive the message when I was praying. So, of course, I kept praying on my knees.

That night, George was taken to the state hospital involuntarily. What finally delivered him were the prayers of some Christians in a little, country church at Alston's Corner near Rainier, Oregon. The church was Pentecostal, a generic term, and the folks there were in the habit of everyone praying and praising God aloud at the same time, and when the need for prayer was great, they prayed LOUDLY.

Up until the evening when they prayed for my husband, I would ask myself in regard to their loud praying in unison, "Is all this noise really necessary?" But when those high-volume prayers went up for George after he had gone to the state hospital, the sound of their amplified voices was music to my ears. As they pleaded with the Lord, they meant it and were not timid about expressing themselves.

The next day when I saw George at the hospital, he was more peaceful than I'd ever seen him in all the time I had known him— even though he was not allowed access to cigarettes to calm him. In fact, he remained rational and normal, working in the kitchen throughout his mandatory six weeks stay at the hospital.

From my experience and my observations, the Lord has shown me that the Lord, who is real and hears our prayers, also equips us for spiritual warfare when we seek him wholeheartedly. However, we need to remember what Jesus says: "Do not rejoice that the spirits submit to you, but rejoice that your names are written in heaven" (Lk 10.20). So since then, I remind myself to put my supernatural experiences in perspective by rejoicing in the knowledge that my name is written in heaven. What a miracle that is!

A third illlustration of spiritual warfare

An incident illustrating spiritual warfare in a friend's home

This next incident is from the testimony of a good friend. Not all spiritual battles are so short-lived nor so dramatic as the one just cited. The real test of Christian warfare is in the long term.

While I was writing this chapter, I heard a touching story from my good friend Kim, who grew up with a mother who was addicted to narcotics and who also had seizures. That's why Kim's grandmother had to step in to care for Kim as an infant, and that's why later, Kim fell heir to caring for her younger siblings.

As an adult, Kim asked her father if he ever felt like leaving her mother, who by that time had died. He said he didn't consider that to be an option, even though it did cross his mind. He said that as a child, his father had to be away from home a lot and because of that, Kim's father grew up thinking his father didn't love him. He found out later about the necessity for the living arrangement, but no one had explained anything to him. That's why he was determined not to break up the home. He didn't want his children to grow up thinking the absent parent didn't love them.

Although the family attended church, Al-Anon was the instrument God chose to help Kim's father in his day-to-day life. Beginning with Step One of Al-Anon, he turned his problem and his life over to God ("higher power") because he knew he was unable within his own strength to overcome his difficulties. And because he chose to depend on the Lord, he and his family were blessed as they matured in the Lord.

With that daily dependence on God and with moral support from empathetic believers in Al-Anon, Kim's father won his spiritual battle, even though it might not appear that way. It does not appear that way because his wife continued on her self-destructive path... until death separated her from her family.

C. Identity of God's natural people revealed in natural warfare

In a future generation, Israel and the church will rejoice together before the God of mercy, and yet they will continue to be distinct as God's people groups. Meanwhile, the door is presently open for all sinners—whether Jewish or Gentile—to be reconciled to God by the blood sacrifice of Israel's Messiah, the Lord Jesus Christ.

Bear in mind that today Israel's temple site is not available to the Jews. This means they cannot put into practice Moses' temporary law based on animal sacrifice. Today, however, God offers them reconciliation with God as individuals if they are willing to recognize Christ/Messiah as their Savior. For when individual Jews accept Christ as the sacrificial Lamb of God, they become regrafted into Abraham's tree of faith and become individuals in the church (See Fig. 24 in chapter 14, p. 192). About God's salvation for all his people today, the Bible says, God has bound all men [Jews and Gentiles] over to disobedience, so that he may have mercy on them all. Oh, the depth of the riches of the wisdom and knowledge of God" (Ro 11.32-33a)! How striking is God's mercy!

Yet, though it's true that salvation is available for all Jews and Gentiles today, sometimes for a Jew, the hurdle seems too high to leap over to reach God. That is how it seemed to a Jewish student named Richard Harvey after he heard Keith DeBerry speak about Christ at his school in England. (*Stories of Jews for Jesus*, 347-349).

In a series of meetings, DeBerry warned that reaching out to God may seem daunting. He told students that though some like to think that God does not exist, they probably still have a sneaking suspicion that he does exist. So, DeBerry said that for those who waver on the brink, God is like "the man who wasn't there."

This couplet describes the feeling an unbeliever might have if convicted of sin when he is not ready to surrender his life to God:

"As I was going down the stair, I met a man who wasn't there.
He wasn't there again today. I wish that man would go away."

DeBerry showed the students historical evidence about Jesus' life, death, and resurrection, and he also presented what Jesus said about himself. He invited students to test the truth of Jesus' claims by going ahead and accepting his invitation to receive him because, he said, as sinners, we cannot reach God without his help. And fortunately, we can ask for that help because, as DeBerry said, Jesus never drives away anyone who comes to him (Jn 6.37). DeBerry concluded his presentation of the gospel to the British boys by spelling out how to become a Christian in three steps:

1. Repent of sin. 2. Receive Jesus. 3. Rely on him.

Repent, Receive, Rely

After DeBerry's talk, Richard was attracted to the invitation to really know God, but he was unsure, so he went to DeBerry and asked him, "How can I possibly put my faith in something I have not already proved true for myself? That would be compromising my integrity." DeBerry replied, "Are you sure that it's not just your pride that is speaking?" Richard says, "I had to admit it was true: I was too proud to be open to God. I felt like an utter fool. It pierced me like an arrow shot deep into my heart."

That night Richard knelt by his bed and in tears asked Jesus to forgive his sins and come into his heart. He says, he felt for the first time that he was letting go of himself and reaching out to someone or something outside of himself. He thought, "If God really is there, he will have to help me now. Somehow I knew he would… I knew I could trust God, although I did not understand how or why…] Then] slowly… I began to see that a difference had been made in my life, and my behavior changed."

Other Jews like Richard are finding Jesus as their Messiah and Savior, and their paths intertwine with the lives of Gentile Christians because they are knit together in the church by the Holy Spirit. Paul writes, "For he himself [Christ/Messiah] is our peace, who has made the two one [Jew and Gentile] and has destroyed the barrier, the dividing wall of hostility" (Eph 2.14). This faith that binds Jews and Gentiles into an eternal destiny with Christ is the glue that holds the universe together: The Bible says, "He [Christ] is before all things, and in him all things hold together" (Col 1.17).

D. An eternal destiny for God's natural and spiritual people

Having determined the scriptural identities of God's peoples—Israel as God's natural earthly people and the church as his spiritual heavenly people—we can recognize their destiny and inheritance. That is, from what we know in scripture, we can say that believers in earthly Israel under the new covenant will receive an *earthly destiny* in the thousand year earthly messianic kingdom. This is an inheritance promised by God to Abraham—a land, a king, and a kingdom on earth forever, and earthly heirs (Ex 12.1-3; 13.14-17; 15.18-19;

17.7-8). We can also say that Jewish and Gentile Christians enjoy present spiritual blessings under the same new covenant given to Abraham, and they receive *a spiritual inheritance* (2Ti 4.18) in the kingdom and in eternity, because the church as bride of Christ will reign with him when he rules over the earth and beyond (Re 19.7; 21.2,9; 22.17). From this, we see that the present identity of God's peoples shines light on their future destiny—an eternal earthly inheritance for God's natural people, Israel, and an eternal heavenly inheritance for God's spiriual heritage for the church. Christians are part of a living, spiritual organism—for the church is not a nation, an ethnic group, nor an earthbound organization. Christians in the church worldwide find their common identity and their unity only in the Lord through his Spirit. The spiritual identity of the church and the natural earthly identity of Israel will continue through the messianic kingdom. Those Jews and Gentiles in the church willl reign with Christ as his bride and Israel as a people and as a nation will enjoy exaltation.

Though Israel and the church will always be God's distinct people groups, God doesn't deal with them as a people today. Instead, in the present age, he deals with everyone as individuals.

Today he calls individual Jews and Gentiles to himself through the sacrifice of Christ on the cross. He offers a choice—whether to accept or reject that sacrifice. Those who accept Christ become "completed Jews." And today God also calls Gentiles to himself.

In conclusion, Israel and the church will continue to be distinct as God's people groups. Israel as God's ethnic nation has *a natural earthly inheritance*, for the Jews as a people have a religious, racial, cultural, and historical heritage. And for all those Jews who receive Christ, they will belong to him in eternity as well.

This unit on the theme of the natural and spiritual will end with the next chapter, which is about seeing life from God's perspective—that is, from a higher spiritual perspective.

16 Seeing as God sees from his higher spiritual perspective

"You are the ones who justify yourselves in the eyes of men, but God knows your hearts. What is highly valued among men is detestable in God's sight."
—Jesus in Luke 16.15

From a higher perspective, the Lord crafts his creation to express himself both in the natural and in the spiritual.

Seeing as God sees from his higher spiritual perspective:

A. *God's precedence for favoring the spiritual over the natural*
B. *God's sovereignty, the basis for spiritual precedence*
C. *Times of conflict between the natural and spiritual*
D. *Applying God's higher spiritual perspective to life*

A. *God's precedence for favoring the spiritual over the natural*

John's gospel says that Nicodemus sought a meeting with Jesus in the darkness of night, because of his fear of criticism from the Pharisees, who considered Jesus to be heretical and dangerous. In that meeting, Nicodemus gained a higher perspective when he learned he couldn't save himself by his own righteousness. He learned he had to be born spiritually to enter God's kingdom (Jn 3.3).

Like Nicodemus, my father was a noble man. He was a highly respected businessman. In the 1920s, when my parents settled in the Rio Grande Valley in the southern tip of Texas, it was just beginning to be populated. As pioneers, so to speak, they gathered several other couples to call a pastor to found the Presbyterian* church there. As a founding elder in our church, my father was a pleasant, loving family man,—conscientious and self-controlled, and he thought a lot about what life is about.

A short time before he died, I visited him in a veterans' hospital in the Texas hill country hundreds of miles from my Texas hometown and about 2400 miles from my teens and my eight year old in the Northwest. It was Thanksgiving 1971. My husband had

---

* In about 2011 or so, this Presbyterian church disbanded and sold the building to the Eastern Catholic church.

died in 1969, and I was on Thanksgiving break from teaching at Wallace Elementary in Kelso, Washington. Somehow, I envisioned this trip as a rescue mission behind enemy lines. At least, that's how it seemed to me, but I didn't know why. All I knew for sure was that this trip to a hospital near Kerrville was important.

My dad was overjoyed to see me, and we had a pleasant time chatting as we sat in the late fall sunshine outdoors, where I took him in his wheelchair. Back in the hospital room again, he said, "I've been thinking a lot about religion lately." "Oh, is that right?" I replied, expecting one of our philosophical discussions to ensue, but as he talked, I could tell he was disturbed. Finally I realized that this man—who had attended church and Sunday School every Sunday of his life and had ushered at a Billy Graham evangelistic crusade—was wanting me to tell him the gospel. He said yes, that was what he wanted, so I told him how to be redeemed, and he listened as though he'd never heard the message before.

Then in the deathly silence of that deserted hospital—with few employees on the job on Thanksgiving—I led him in the sinner's prayer to receive Christ as his Savior. His response was immediate and desperate. He cried out to God in an outburst that echoed down the empty halls. This was startling, for my father seldom raised his voice; he was the epitome of a Texan—tall, strong, and not given to small talk. I was surprised no one came running to see what was going on. With the prospect of death, my dad's *natural* nobility couldn't help him. He had to have a *spiritual* rebirth.

Then, after finding peace with God, my father referred to what he'd said earlier when he'd said that he might move to a hospital near me after my impending move to California. Now, with his newfound peace, he said, "I'm all right now. I'll be okay if I stay here." Soon he was dismissed from the hospital's isolation to live his last few months in our hometown, Edinburg, under the kind oversight of my brother and his wife. Though my Thanksgiving dinner that day was a sandwich from a vending machine—the cafeteria was closed—I rejoiced in the miracle I had witnessed. Like Nicodemus my father learned he had to be born again. Surely, God turns the natural wisdom of the world on its head.

Jesus' disciples learned about God's higher spiritual perspective when James and John with their mother approached Jesus to ask for places of honor in his messianic kingdom (Mt 20.20-28; Mk 10.35-45). Possibly, since they were Jesus' confidants, they may have had a sense of entitlement for a place of honor. This angered the other disciples. so Jesus had to explain that true greatness comes from commitment to servanthood, not from seeking prestige and power. He said, "For even the Son of Man did not come to be served, but to serve, and to give his life as a ransom for many" (Mk 10.45). With that guideline, we Christians today have to choose daily whose wisdom we'll follow—the world's wisdom or God's.

B. God's sovereignty, the basis for spiritual precedence (Is 55.9)

In Jesus' parable of the vineyard, the early vineyard workers agreed to a denarius for a day's work, yet, at the end of the day, each of the early and late workers received the same wage. The early workers, who expected to be paid more than the later ones, complained: "You have made them equal to us who have borne the burden of the work and the heat of the day." The owner replied, "Friend, I am not being unfair to you. Didn't you agree to work for a denarius?… Don't I have the right to do what I want with my own money? Or are you envious because I am generous?"

Different illustrations can be drawn from this parable, One would be to illustrate God's sovereignty as administered from his higher spiritual perspective, for he's the one who sets up the terms of his relationship with his people by saying "My ways are higher than your ways" (Is 55.9). Therefore, if today by his grace, God wants to bring his spiritual people, Christians, into his new covenant before he brings his natural people, the Jews, into his new covenant, isn't that his sovereign prerogative? For didn't Jesus say that "the last will be first and the first will be last"?

Along the same line of thinking, though God presents biblical seniority for descendants in chronological order, he gives precedence to the spiritual over the natural (1Co 15.46, 47). Significantly, through the first Adam came humanity's downfall, and through the last Adam, Christ, comes humanity's restoration, "for as in Adam all die, so in Christ all will be made alive" (1Co 15.22).

Figure 25: God's precedence for the spiritual over the natural

1) God offers man a spiritual option—heaven instead of hell. Without this offer, hell would be the inevitable consequence of sin.
"Just as we have borne the likeness of the earthly man [Adam], so shall we bear the likeness of the man from heaven [Christ]" (1Co 15.49). After Christians are caught up in the rapture, they'll have glorified bodies like Jesus' resurrected body and will be liberated from sin and death (1Co 15.20-28).

2) God gives spiritual meaning to man's present earthly life.
"Though outwardly |naturally] we are wasting away, yet inwardly [spiritually], we [believers] are being renewed day by day. For our light and momentary troubles are achieving for us an eternal glory that far outweighs them all. So we fix our eyes not on what is seen [natural], but on what is unseen [spiritual]" (2Co 4.16,17).

3) God does not judge by the natural outward appearance.
In the Old Testament, when God sent Samuel to anoint the next king, he told him not to be misled by a person's natural, outward appearance (1Sa 16.7). So, when Samuel met Jesse's eight sons, David, the youngest, seemed to be the least noteworthy, but he's the one God chose for Samuel to anoint as Israel's second king. And this pattern of precedence for the spiritual over the natural has continued.

4) God transforms people so they can live on a higher spiritual plane.
Paul describes his own unworthiness to be called by God (Ro 11.13). He writes, "Last of all, as to one untimely born, he [Jesus] appeared also to me. For I am the least of the apostles, unworthy to be called an apostle, because I persecuted the church of God" (1Co 15.8,9 ESV). Paul and the young shepherd boy David, seemed to be unlikely candidates for a high calling, yet, by God's sovereign choice, Paul became the church's greatest leader, and David became Israel's greatest king. God places the spiritual above the natural.

5) God sets up a genealogical pattern for Israel's patriarchs by giving precedence to spiritual status over natural seniority.

The spiritual over the natural in Israel's lineage

The last point on the previous page is about God giving precedence to the spiritual over the natural in Israel's genealogy.

God's precedence for the spiritual, which began with the story of the sons of Adam and Eve, will continue through the story of God's people in the messianic kingdom, and will finally come to full fruition in the new heavens and new earth of eternity.

In scripture, the natural order of inheritance passes from father to oldest son, yet, beginning with the genealogy of Israel's patriarchs, God gives precedence to spiritual over natural in assigning status. He chose Adam's third son Seth to be in the godly line of the Messiah—not firstborn Cain. Later, even Father Abraham was not the oldest son (Jamieson, Fausset, and Brown [JFB, Vol 1, Pt 1, 127]). Of Abraham's sons, God chose Isaac over firstborn Ishmael. And of Isaac's sons, God chose Jacob over the natural firstborn twin, Esau. About these twins, scripture says, "Before the twins were born or had done anything good or bad… he [Isaac] was told, 'The older [Esau] will serve the younger [Jacob]'" (Ro 9.10-12).

Now let's follow the ancestral line of Jacob, Abraham's grandson. From Jacob came Israel's twelve tribes. Of Jacob's sons, God chose Joseph, the eleventh son, to be the natural firstborn heir; he would receive a double inheritance of land. However, when God set up an arrangement for that double inheritance, he did so in an unconventional way. He doubled Joseph's land inheritance by making his sons Ephraim and Manasseh to be leaders of two of the twelve tribes that descended from the line of Jacob.

When Jacob chose Joseph's sons Ephraim and Manasseh to be leaders of two Issraeli tribes, they would be counted as if they were Jacob's two sons instead of by their natural status as Jacob's grandsons, for they would be leaders of the Israelites alongside Jacob's ten sons. Jacob made this clear when he said to his son Joseph, "Now then, your two sons born to you in Egypt before I came to you here [in Egypt] will be reckoned as mine [as Jacob's sons]. Ephraim and Manasseh will be mine just as Reuben and

Simeon are mine." In this way, through Joseph's two sons. Joseph received a double-land inheritance of the firstborn, even though Joseph himself was also not the firstborn son.

Note this! By God's precedence for the spiritual over the natural, the birthright status of Joseph's two sons also became reversed. Genesis tells how that came about. In the story, Jacob's eyes were failing because of old age. Therefore, Joseph brought his two sons close to Jacob (Ge 48.10) and placed Manasseh, the older son, at Jacob's right and Ephraim, the younger son, at his left, but Jacob reversed his hands on the ones to be blessed and in so doing, he gave senior status to Ephraim, the younger. The Bible says, "When Joseph saw his father placing his right hand on Ephraim's head he was displeased; so he took hold of his father's hand to move it from Ephraim's head to Manasseh's head... But his father refused and said, 'I know, my son, I know. He too will become a people, and he too will become great. Nevertheless, his younger brother will be greater than he'" (Ge 48.17-19).

God changed Jacob's name to Israel (from Cheater to Prince), and from Jacob's lineage came the twelve tribes of Israel.[*] Then through these twelve tribes, God continued his patriarchal pattern of setting up the natural and the spiritual with precedence given to the spiritual. This explains why God divided the birthright itself into two parts—a natural birthright and a spiritual birthright, with precedence given for the spiritual.

Accordingly, in the ancestral line of royalty, Judah's kingly lineage continued this reversal of the natural and spiritual. For Judah and Tamar, whose twins were born out of wedlock, God chose Perez, the younger son, for the firstborn title.

Division of the birthright in the future messianic kingdom

God's reversal of the birthrights is not an aberration; instead, it is highly significant. I noticed that God divided the firstborn birthrights between Joseph and Judah—giving the earthly inheritance of land to Joseph and the spiritual inheritance of kingly authority

---

[*] Jacob had twelve sons. Son Joseph's inheritance was doubled for two sons, but Israel still had only twelve tribes. (Levi's tribe had priesthood status and was not counted as one of the twelve.

to Judah and his heirs. I found this to be interesting but strange. Not until decades after pondering these things did I recognize the full significance of the division of the birthright for Jacob's sons. What I discovered is that this division foreshadows the future division of the birthright by Christ in his messianic kingdom. I was dumbfounded when I saw that just as Jacob's inheritance was divided into two parts—a natural birthright for Joseph and a spiritual and royal birthright for Judah—so too in the future messianic kingdom, God will again divide that future birthright between his natural people, Israel, and his spiritual people, the church.

In that kingdom, we see the foreshadowing fulfilled this way: To his *natural firstborn*, Israel, God gives an earthly inheritance of double land (Is 61.7) and exaltation among the nations, To his *spiritual firstborn*, the church, he gives spiritual authority to reign with Christ as his bride (Re 21.9b).

For the nation of Israel, its birthright is divided into natural and spiritual:

1) *For a natural birthright* of land, God gave Jacob's eleventh son, Joseph, a double land inheritance, which was accomplished by making Joseph's two sons, Ephraim and Manasseh, to be heads of *two* of the twelve tribes of Israel.

2) *For a spiritual birthright,* God gave Jacob's fourth son, Judah, spiritual authority as head of the household after his father's death. Judah's authority would pass on to future generations of kings in Christ/Messiah's line, as prophesied by Jacob who said, "The scepter will not depart from Judah" (Ge 49.10a).

Therefore, since Israel came into being before the church, we see that "indeed there are those who are last who will be first, and first who will be last" (Lk 13.30). For though God will bless natural Israel and the spiritual church, he calls the latecomer church to become the bride of Christ/Messiah. But the church's honor in the present age is not exclusive, for it is open to all willing present-age believers to receive. Christ will not turn away anyone who comes to him, whether Gentile or Jew. The Bible says, "Whoever wishes, let him take the free gift of the water of life" (Re 22.17b).

Now we come to the grand finale of the creation story. Above the whole order of things, Christ as God's only Son is called "the firstborn." He's the *"firstborn over all creation... the firstborn from among the dead"* (Co 1.15-18b). That is, Christ became the first to be resurrected—before any human believers.[*] He will dwell in the heavenly New Jerusalem with resurrected believers of all eras— with resurrected-and-raptured Christians, resurrected Israelites, and resurrected tribulation martyrs. At the same time, all surviving *human* Jewish believers and their sympathizers will dwell in peace on the new earth, where they will eat of the tree of life and live forever. This biblical interpretation supports the role of Israel as God's natural earthly people and the role of the church as God's spiritual heavenly people.

C. Times of conflict between the natural and spiritual

Conflict of the natural and spiritual through the ages

In Old Testament times, conflict between the natural and spiritual flared up between Israel's north and Israel's south when the nation's king began to reign with a heavy hand. This brought division of the nation into two kingdoms—Judah and Israel. Judah became the *heir* of the nation's *spiritual heritage*, because Judah had within its boundaries the sacred temple site, and it also had the promised line of kings and priests. This conflict within the nation between the natural and the spiritual arose during the reign of David's son Solomon—at the time when natural Israel's king, Jeroboam, led a faction against spiritual Judah's king.

In New Testament times, the natural and spiritual conflict has continued. In fact, centuries after the Old Testament was canonized, conflict between the natural and spiritual peaked when natural Jews in Judah demanded of the Roman ruler Pilate that their spiritual Christ/Messiah be crucified.

Mark writes this about the Jews: "'Crucify him!' they shouted. 'Why? What crime has he committed?' asked Pilate. But they shouted all the louder, 'Crucify him!' Wanting to satisfy the crowd, Pilate released prisoner Barabbas. Then he had Jesus

---

[*] When Lazarus was restored to life after his death, he had a mortal body, not a resurrected body.

flogged and handed him over to be crucified" (Mark 15.13-15).

Today, conflict between the natural and spiritual continues. Peter warns Christians to be prepared for *outer conflict* with the world. He writes, "Do not be surprised at the painful trial you [Christians] are suffering, as though something strange were happening to you" (1Pe 4.12). And Paul also warns of *inner conflict* between the natural and spiritual within Christians. He writes, "For in my inner being I delight in God's law [spiritual], but I see another law at work in the members of my body [natural], waging war against the law of my mind [spiritual]" (Ro 7.22,23).

Whether in the church today or in the future messianic kingdom, believers enter the new covenant spiritually. Yet even so, after Christ returns, he will have to suppress evil with an "iron scepter in the messianic kingdom." During that kingdom, the church— Christ's bride—will reign with Christ, Israel will be exalted, and God will be glorified. Not until eternity will the natural and spiritual conflict end altogether. Yet in spite of conflict, believers in the church today and in the future messianic kingdom enjoy "the peace of God which transcends all understanding" (Php 4.7).

Let' think about that higher perspective that brings peace. As a child, though I faced minimal conflict, I'd find peace and perspective by climbing up to the top of our big, old mesquite tree where I had a high, secret refuge—a place of satisfaction and warm contentment. That's what the peace of God is about; it's a peace that comes from a higher perspective, God's perspective.

Examples of conflict between the natural and spiritual today

First example of spiritual conflict today: Emiko (a fictitious name) faced a conflict when she was a student in my adult academic Bible Literature class in Petaluma, California. The reason she enrolled in my class was so that she could better understand those whom she sought to lead to Buddhism, for she was an Asian teacher of an Americanized version of Buddhism, whose followers have a militant zeal for spreading their message. (I had a chance to visit her Buddhist class.) Her Buddhist view offers *escape* from life's problems—in contrast to the biblical worldview, which offers redemption of self to *overcome* life's problems (Jn 16.33).

Emiko's conflict began after she bought a *Living Bible*, because every time she tried to read it, she got a headache. After repeated trials, she finally threw it away and dropped the class. Because of the spiritual conflict, she rejected exposure to God's worldview.

Second example of conflict today: Another conflict of worldviews arose when I taught English to college engineering students in Taiyuan, China in 1984-85. A student, to whom I'd loaned a Bible, was puzzled when he read the story about Jesus and a rich young ruler. Here's the incident. "Jesus looked at him [the ruler] and loved him. 'One thing you lack,' he said. 'Go, sell everything you have and give to the poor, and you will have treasure in heaven.*'" But since wealth had first place in the rich young ruler's heart, he was not willing to give it up. The story ends by saying "he went away sad" (Mk 10.17-22). * Afterwards, Jesus said that God rewards the faithful in eternity—the faithful, not the wealthy— and he added, "**Many who are first will be last, and the last first**" (Mk 10.31). God reverses the natural order.

In China, after reading this story, the student came to me, for he thought Americans—whom he believed to be Christians— seek and cherish wealth. When I said that Christian goals and worldly goals are not interchangeable, and that wealth is not the goal of Christianity, my student was disappointed, and he—like the rich, young ruler— "went away sad." At that time, China was going through a change and was beginning to view wealth as "beautiful," so the story from the Biblr disillusioned my student.

D. Applying God's higher spiritual perspective to life

Matthew was written for Jews to portray Jesus as Messiah and King (McGee 1983, Vol V, 4). It has three important discourses:

The Sermon on the Mount in Matthew 5-7 (in this chapter)
The Matthew 13 parables (chapters 20-23 in this book)
The Olivet Discourse in Matthew 24 and 25 (chapter 24 in this book)

---

* Jesus does not require this of all followers. In this case, wealth stood between this man and God.

A higher spiritual perspective in the Sermon on the Mount

In the Sermon on the Mount, Jesus presents the Lord's thoughts as being higher than the thoughts of human beings.

This chapter 16, which is about the Sermon on the Mount, presents a spiritual perspective too high for human beings to attain in their own power. In the sermon in Matthew 5-7, Jesus says that new covenant people are to forsake resentment, worry, and judgmentalism… to repent of unholy desires… to turn the other cheek in conflicts… to seek treasure in heaven, not seek treasure on earth… to love those who are enemies… to give for God's glory, not for self glory… to trust God… and to forgive as God forgives. And besides all that, Jesus speaks of the blessedness of those believers who are poor in spirit, mournful, meek, and persecuted—all of which are attributes that the world disdains.

The problem is that applying principles of the Sermon on the Mount to life brings challenges. Let me give an example. In college on holidays, I had to take a ten hour bus ride south from Austin, Texas to my hometown, Edinburg, with one bus change. In those days of gas rationing in World War II, this meant waiting in an impatient crowd, jostling to board. So I would say to myself, "All these people want to get home, so who am I to push myself ahead?" So I held back.

But what if I missed bus after bus, what then? In retrospect, I see that had there been a prolonged delay in my being able to get a seat on the bus, the dynamic would change in such a way that would necessitate recognition of my own need in the big picture. For as I have come to understand, self-interest in itself is not bad, but it must not be the ruling principle. I remember what Paul says: "Each of you should look not only to your own interests, but also to the interests of others" (Php 2.8). Since God cares about me, there are times when I must assert myself… but as he directs.

Here's another example. In the Northwest as a young married, I had occasion to apply Jesus' overarching principle of generosity. In days when our family finances were tight, one of my sisters-in-law borrowed my cashmere coat with a fur collar, which my father had given me. I thought my loan to her was for the evening, but day after day went by without her saying anything about my coat. Not wanting to push her, I waited before I asked about it. When I did inquire, she said she had no memory of the coat or its whereabouts, for on that night she had been drinking. So, because of our family's circumstances, I had to buy a cheap, cloth coat. Was I wise or foolish? Whatever the answer, God gave my husband and me his grace to accept the outcome.

Here's another example to think about. A grandson in college told me that in church one day, on an impulse, he emptied his pockets to put money in the collection plate, a lot of money in his young eyes. When he paused, I waited for him to tell me of the spiritual blessedness of his generosity, but instead he said, "As soon as I did it, I felt awful!" With that example, I can say, yes, the Sermon on the Mount does raise questions when a person applies what it says, but isn't God the one who says, "My ways are higher than your ways" (Is 55.9)?

In line with the general principles of the Sermon on the Mount, let's look at an experience in my husband's life—an incident that taught me to be more cautious about what I say about other people. As a preface, let me say that humor has its place in greasing abrasive contacts in life and in creating an atmosphere of goodwill, but humor can also be at the expense of others.

In the latter category of humor at the expense of others, an incident happened in World War II on a ship in the U.S. Navy. My husband George, Sr. as a teen-age sailor was good at story telling—in his timing and pacing and in this particular case in mimicking the speech of one of the sailors. This time the one he was mimicking happened to be a young sailor with a hairlip. So George acted out his story, and the sailors all laughed at his good impersonation, and the more they laughed, the more he got warmed up to exaggerate his mimicry. They were having a good time… until George turned around and there stood the young man with the hairlip. In telling this story, George expressed regret. You can imagine how he felt about what he had done. He apologized to the man, but there was nothing he could do to undo the hurt he had caused.

From this, I learned that when I'm talking about someone, I should imagine that the person I'm talking about is sitting in a room nearby and can overhear what I say. So I use that scenario to determine if what I'm saying would hurt the feelings of that person. I've also learned that what seems harmless and is given in a good spirit with no trace of malice—as in George's mimicry —can nevertheless do damage.

In all situations, what makes the difference is our motivation: Whose glory are we seeking? Our own glory or God's glory? Andrew Murray says, "Just as far as we enter into the world and please it, so we lose our power" (Murray 1990, 40), but if our aim is to please God, all things do work together for good (Ro 8.28 KJV).

The blessedness of living on a higher plane

If all this sounds too sensitive, too serious, and too far out of reach… it is. But remember. Christians, enjoy the *spiritual* blessings of the new covenant here and now. So, for God to work through people, all they have to do is to obey him in faith believing, and the end result will be supernatural blessing for themselves and others. Following Jesus and incorporating his thinking into the daily walk brings intimacy with him, a blessedness that cannot be produced through natural means. Remember also, if there were no too-high barriers to surmount, a person would be inclined to trust in his own ability instead of in the Lord, and in so doing, he'd miss the empowerment and transformation that only God can impart.

Finally, in seeking to elevate our perspective, let's consider how we should pray for someone in our life that is on a self-destructive path. Over time, I had to learn as a first step to identify with that one—to feel and think as he or she feels and thinks. Also, to truly empathize, I had to recognize a weakness of the flesh in myself, even though it may be different from that person's weakness.

But later I realized that in order to identify with God in the situation, I had to learn to take a second step; I had to learn to think as God thinks and to see as he sees. And with that step, I had to choose between lining up with the Lord on his side or lining up on the side of the erring person. After taking the first step—identifying with the person I'm praying for—this second step can be difficult because identifying with a person makes me not only sympathetic with the person I am praying for but also makes me inclined to excuse that person's bad behavior. Choosing God's side has become easier since I've realized that not to line up with the Lord is to play into Satan's agenda, and that thought sets me straight.

The following jingle reminds me of my dependence upon God. I've found that this verse reminds me that Jesus can accomplish in me what I cannot accomplish in myself. What a relief that is!

Here is a little poem that explains what I'm talking about:

Jesus says, "Follow me, and I will make you,
Make you what you cannot be;
Make you loving, trustful, godly,
Make you even like to me.*"

Let's close with a final thought about the natural and the spiritual: They are sometimes polar opposites. For example, natural hunger is overcome by eating, but spiritual hunger increases the more a person feeds on God's Word. A radio preacher verified what I've experienced—that the more I take in God's Word, the more my appetite for it increases.

So, when we Christians have no appetite for reading the Word, we can read it anyway to gain an appetite, for the more we take in his Word, the more our perspective becomes like his (Pr 23.7a HCSB). And the higher our perspective becomes, the more we are liberated to live as Christ would have us live.

This unit has been about the themes of the natural and the spiritual. The next unit presents the themes of grace and truth, the two most important biblical themes.

---

*Streams in the Desert. Page 90. Author L.S.P. Copyright 1996 by The Zondervan Corporation.

17 Grace and truth expressed by the unshakeable sovereign God

> Emotions are like the waves of the sea—spasmodic and turbulent. Trust in God is like the depths of the ocean—calm, steady, unshakeable, and unchanging.
> —The author

"Unshakeable!" That's how a good friend introduced me to a friend of hers. Of course, she knows I'm not unshakeable, but she knows that the Rock on which I stand is unshakeable. That Rock is the unshakeable, sovereign God.

God's expression of his grace and truth:

    A. *Jesus, the full expression of God's grace and truth*

    B. *Human beings, an expression of God's grace and truth*

    C. *Angels, even Satan, an expression of God's truth*

    D. *Prophetic literary devices as aids for presenting God's truth*

    E. *Comparing two parallel prophecies to confirm God's truth*

A. Jesus, the full expression of God's grace and truth

Only through the man Jesus has God the Father expressed his grace and truth fully: "The Word [Jesus] became flesh and lived for a while among us. We have seen his glory, the glory of the One and only Son, who came from the Father, full of grace and truth" (Jn 1.14).

These attributes of Christ—*grace and truth*—express the very heart of God. How amazing! So then to comprehend that the complex can be expressed so simply, consider the complex task of computer programming. Programmers can transmit information from complex programming languages to less complex "machine language" by breaking down all information to be expressed simply with *1* and *0*. So too, God expresses himself simply and fully through his *grace* and *truth* (Jn 1.14).

B. Human beings, an expression of God's s grace and truth

First, let's think about God's grace: We become so accustomed to hearing of God's *grace* that we become blasé about what it means for a person to become a Christian by God's grace. What happens in the new birth is that a person's spirit, which has been dead to God becomes alive to God. That person becomes born again! Such grace can be appreciated by realizing the uniqueness of that grace. For only to man—and to no other creature—does God grant the grace of his redeeming love through Jesus' death and resurrection. Jesus' entry into our world makes possible his sacrifice and our new birth.

Second, let's think about God's truth: Nineteenth century Horatius Bonar says that not only did God express his *grace* through the salvation offered through the cross, but he also expressed his *truth* there, for Jesus portrayed the torment that sinners experience in hell when separated from God.

Bonar says that Jesus' cry "I thirst!" expresses the bodily torment of the lost forever, and he adds, "O, what must hell be!… What must be the everlasting thirst! From above there came no answer. God was silent. From around there came derision. Man answered with laughter and with vinegar.*"

How great the agony! It's not customary for God to be silent in such times. Bonar writes, "He [God] feeds the young ravens when they cry. He regards the prayer of the needy. His ear is ever open to the cry of the destitute and the sorrowful, but at Calvary he answers not a word. No wonder that Christ should cry out, 'My God, my God, why hast thou forsaken me KJV? All heaven seems to stand aloof. Ah! this is the hour and the power of darkness. He has taken the sinner's place, and he must bear the sinner's anguish, both in soul and body. He must suffer the sinner's thirst, as well as the sinner's death. Love [grace] would have said, 'Oh, hear that cry and quench that thirst' but law [truth] would have said, 'Not so, else the sacrifice is… invalid.' Thus the Father kept silence… Justice took its course, and law [truth] was satisfied… Jesus said, 'It is finished,' and, bowing the head, he gave up the ghost" (Bonar 1977, 22-23, 128, 130, 131). Through the cross, Christ overcame "the devil's work;" through the cross, Christ was glorified; and through the cross, he saves people from God's judgment.

* A sponge soaked in vinegar was hoisted on a pole to Jesus on the cross to dull his pain, but he rejected it.

God loves the Jews and their Messiah, yet in his plan, God allowed Satan and his agents to vent their fury against Messiah's kinfolk, the Jews. God even allowed Satan to incite the Jews to cry for crucifixion of their Messiah. At the cross, God's perfect grace and truth came together when in prayer before the crucifixion, Jesus cried, "Now my heart is troubled, and what shall I say? 'Father, save me from this hour?' No, it was for this very reason I came to this hour. Father, glorify your name'" (Jn 12.27.)!

God also expresses his grace and truth through believers who in crisis say, "I'm in your hands, Father. Glorify your name!" No matter what happens, they can choose to say "Father, you're all I need," and they "count it all joy" (Ja 1.2 KJV). I for one can testify that to live for Jesus is to have an abiding joy. I can also say that this joy most abounds in times of deepest sorrow and greatest crisis, for in the face of catastrophe, surrender to the Lord brings joy indescribable. That's when God becomes most precious to me.[*]

The greatest crisis in my life came on July 19, 1969, the day before the first man landed on the moon. This happened before the oldest child in our family would return to college a second year, when the next three children would be in the last three years of high school, and when the youngest child would enter first grade.

On July 19, 1969, several in our family visited the hospital in Seattle and walked through the hall with George, Sr. while he pushed a walker with paraphernalia to which he was attached by tubes. Later, that evening, I got a phone call from the hospital. The voice on the line told me that George had hemorrhaged and died, He died of cancer of the esophagus, less than two weeks before his forty-fourth birthday.

I knew that this was too big for me to handle, and I knew that the unshakeable God wanted me to roll it over on him. So I did. And that's when the Lord did a miracle.[†] He lifted me up into his presence to a height of joy that was in the same measure as the sorrow would have been. Truly, the joy of the Lord was my strength.

---

[*] T. L. Holdcroft also speaks of a Christian's joy triumphing over sorrow and tragedy (1962, 191).

[†] The author was inspired by Catherine Marshall's experience after the death of her husband, as told in *A Man Called Peter*. In that account, the Lord blessed her through the funeral days, but the author believed God could extend that blessing through life beyond those early days of loss.

What I noticed in particular was how many problems other people around me had. Not only did the Lord carry me through the days of the funeral, but he has carried me and my family through all the days since that time. In my case, all that the Lord has asked of me has been that I not look back but look up, and he gave me the grace to do just that. My assignment has been to trust in the unshakeable Rock upon which I stand.

The blessedness God has given me in my life is not because I am anyone special but because of his grace and faithfulness. What I am saying is that as we step outside ourselves and live for God day by day, he will guide us, bless us, and carry us through any crisis that we face in life, whether great or small. His strength carries us through, for truly he is unshakeable.

And here's the most beautiful part about knowing God and his grace. Horatius Bonar says grace can be seen in the total unlikeness between the Lover and the Loved One: "Introduce one element of resemblance, one fragment or feature of loveableness, and grace is gone... God needed sin and death like ours for the display of his fulness... So it is sin that is our point of connection. Not our good, but our total want of good, nay our evil, our total evil... He saves the lost" (Bonar 1977, 22-23). Truly, Jesus is Redeemer of the lost.

C. Angels, even Satan, an expression of God's truth

Spiritual battles are real, Satan is real, and God is real. A person never fully comprehends just how real God is until Satan kicks up the dust of his temptations and distortions. The good news is that God reveals his glory in our dealings with Satan, this one who is the father of lies, this one who, as the highest of God's angels, later rebelled. Scripture calls Satan the adversary, the slanderer, the deceiver, and "the accuser of our brethren" (Re 12,10). But fortunately, God is victor not only over sin and death, but also over Satan.

Like people, angels have free will, but unlike people, they are spirit beings without physical bodies, and besides that, they receive what they deserve, the *truth* of God's justice. Through angels, God expresses two sides of truth. Innocent angels receive the blessedness of his truth, and rebellious angels receive the condemnation of his truth. This means that all angels receive exactly what they deserve—the *truth* of God's justice. This is in contrast to believers, who receive what they do *not* deserve, God's grace.

Scripture says before God created the world, he created Satan as the highest angel, and like all angels, Satan had free will to serve God or to rebel. He chose to rebel. Then, after challenging God's authority, he lost his high position and was expelled from heaven's inner circle. Later, in the Garden of Eden, Satan tempted Adam and Eve to sell out to him (Ge 3), and they did. They ceded to him the earthly authority God had given them. That's how Satan became "god of this age" (2Co 4.4), and "ruler of the kingdom of the air" (Eph 2.2). Today he rules over "spiritual forces of evil in the heavenly [atmospheric] realms" (Eph 6.12), and from there he wreaks his havoc.

But Satan's day of reckoning is coming. Scripture says that midway in the future tribulation, God will expel Satan even from the earth's atmosphere (Re 12.12, 13). Then, confined to earth, Satan will make a last-ditch stand by taking possession of the world's future ruler, Antichrist. Then, midway into the seven year tribulation, the Satan-possessed Antichrist will break his seven-year treaty with Israel, will end Judaic sacrifices, and will demand worship of an idol of himself (Da 9.27).

However, Antichrist's demand for idol worship will backfire on him, for Jews as a people have been delivered from idolatry ever since their Babylonian captivity. They know God hates idolatry. Therefore, during the tribulation when Antichrist demands worship of his idol, Jews as a people of that future generation of believers will turn away from the counterfeit Antichrist and will turn to the true Christ/Messiah. In those days of the tribulation, they will suffer Satan's persecution and God's testing as prophesied by Christ (Mt 24), and though they will suffer, yet afterwards as a people, they will look to their Savior and be welcomed into the messianic kingdom.

During that messianic kingdom, Satan will be held captive in a pit, and then after he is freed, he will enter his final conflict with God. He will lose that battle and will be cast into the lake of fire to be there forever with all unbelievers (Re 20.10).

D. Prophetic literary devices as aids for presenting God's truth

PROPHECY ABOUT THE LAST DAYS
Figure 26

Literary Device: *Allegory, from creation through earth's tribulation*

SATAN'S AGENDA IN TWO PARTS
Revelation 12.1-17. ---First half of Satan's Agenda
Revelation 20.1-15---Last half of Satan's Agenda

GOD'S FINAL TRIUMPH IN FOUR PARTS
Literary Devices: *Double Reference & Identity by Content*
Isaiah 14.1-17—a four-part passage about God's final triumph

SATAN'S AGENDA IN TWO PARTS
Allegory, a passage from creation through earth's tribulation
SATAN'S AGENDA—FIRST HALF OF ALLEGORY

Interpretation of the Allegory in Revelation 12.1-17. (Read in the Bible.)
In this allegory, God's highest angel, Satan the dragon, led a third of the angels to rebel, which caused God to expel them from heaven's inner circle (Lk 10.18). In this way, Satan lost his high authority in heaven and therefore had to set up his headquarters in "the heavenly [atmospheric] realms" (Eph 6.12). From there, in the present age, he seeks to usurp God's authority.

Satan the dragon knew that Messiah's birthplace was to be Bethlehem (Mi 5.2), so that's where he confronted Israel the woman, who was about to give birth; he wanted to devour her child, Israel's Messiah, but he did not succeed. Also, even though Satan the dragon prompted Herod the king to kill Jesus, Herod failed to destroy Messiah prematurely; therefore, Christ survived to fulfill his mission of salvation for mankind. By means of Identity by Content Meaning, Messiah is the one who will rule all nations "with an iron scepter," and he is the one "snatched up to God." These quotes refer to his reign and to his ascension to heaven respectively (Cf. Re 12.5 and Ac 1.9.).

In the atmospheric heavenlies (Da 9.27), Michael the Archangel will lead God's loyal angels in war against Satan and his rebel angels. Then, at midtribulation, Michael will hurl Satan to earth, which will cause Satan to lose access to God's throne where—in the past, he would accuse God's people. But until that yet future time when Satan is exiled to earth, he will continue to make accusations before God against God's people (Eze 28.17b; Is 14.12; Job 6).

After Satan is expelled from heaven at midtribulation, a loud voice in heaven will cry, "Rejoice, you heavens and you who dwell in them! But woe to the earth and the sea, because the devil has gone down to you! He is filled with fury, because he knows that his time is short" (Re 12.12). Now, forced to earth at midtribulation, Satan will lose his atmospheric headquarters and will then take possession of Antichrist to work through him to pursue Israel, the woman. Jews will flee and God will take care of them in the final half of the seven-year tribulation. This is called the "great tribulation." It lasts 1260 days, or three and a half years, and is also called "a time, times, and half a time."

In the great tribulation, Satan, enraged, will persecute the Jews and their sympathizers (Re 12.13-17a). He will spew water from his mouth like a river to sweep the woman away, but God will have the earth open its mouth to swallow the river. God will prevail.

SATAN'S AGENDA—LAST HALF OF THE ALLEGORY
Allegory, a passage about the messianic kingdom
---Revelation 20.1-15. Read this in your Bible---

Interpretation of the Allegory in Revelation 20.1-3:
When Christ returns, peace prevails, though sin and death are still present (Is 65.20). Satan the dragon cannot work there, for an angel will seize Satan, bind him, throw him into the Abyss, and seal it for the thousand years of the messianic kingdom.

Believers blessed and unbelievers indicted

Interpretation for the Allegory in Revelation 20.4-6:
At Christ's return, Christians, who will have been raptured to

232 • G. UNDERSTANDING THE THEMES OF GOD'S GRACE AND TRUTH

heaven before the tribulation, will return from heaven with Christ and will reign with him in the messianic kingdom. In addition, Jews—resurrected Israelites, resurrected tribulation martyrs, and surviving tribulation believers—will serve in places of authority (Re 20.4). But after the thousand-year messianic kingdom (Re 20.5a), unbelievers at Christ's return will be indicted for later sentencing before the great white throne. This will take place before eternity begins.

Consequences after Satan's attack on Jerusalem

Interpretation for the Allegory in Revelation 20.7-15:

After the kingdom, Satan gathers unbelievers to surround Jerusalem, but fire will strike from heaven. Satan will be thrown into the lake of fire to join Antichrist and the False Prophet there. This is "the second death"—separation from God forever—in contrast to death that is simply separation of soul and spirit from the body, as with believers. After death, Christians will live with God forever.

GOD'S FINAL TRIUMPH IN FOUR PARTS

GOD'S TRIUMPH---INTRODUCTION

----Isaiah 14.1-17. Read this in your Bible---

1) In Isaiah 14, introduction, verses 1-2
2) Double Reference to current king and future *Antichrist*, 3-11
3) Double Reference to current king and future *Satan*, 12-14
4) Double Reference to current king and future *Antichrist*, 15-17

The meaning and use of Double Reference

A Double Reference prophecy presents a near-future prophecy to foreshadow a far-future endtime prophecy. Prophecy about Babylon's king at times foreshadows Satan, and at times Antichrist. Identity by Content is the literary device used to identify the near prophecy and the far. Though prophets may not have understood that near-future and far-future prophecies would link kings of those eras, the Holy Spirit did have that in mind (Gray 1906, 58, 59).[*]

---

[*] Jesus said that often the prophets could not fully understand their own messages. He said, "I tell you that many prophets and kings desired to see what you see" (Lk 10.24).
  Peter also spoke of the grace that was to come. He said the prophets searched intently to find out the time and circumstances to which the Spirit in them was pointing when he (the Spirit) predicted Christ's sufferings (Is 53) and the glories that would follow (1Pe 1.10-12).

GOD'S TRIUMPH---FIRST PART
---Isaiah 14.1-2---
A PREVIEW OF PROPHECIES ON ISRAEL'S DESTINY
A short encouraging preview of Israel's final destiny

Text, Isaiah 14.1-2, is a straightforward message about Israel's future.
"The Lord will have compassion on Jacob; once again he will choose Israel and will settle them in their own land. Aliens will join them... And the house of Israel will possess the nations as menservants and maidservants in the Lord's land. They will make captives of their captors and rule over their oppressors." Israel will then enjoy peace and unity (Is 14.1-2. Cf. Re 12.5; Ps 2.9; Re 19.15).

GOD'S TRIUMPH---SECOND PART
---Isaiah 14.3-11---
Identity by Content and by Double Reference:
Defeat of a current king foreshadows the future Antichrist
Babylon's king in near future and Antichrist in far future, linked.

Text, Isaiah 14: 3-11, is about Israel's victory over Babylon's evil king:
"On the day the Lord gives you relief from suffering and turmoil and cruel bondage, you will take up this taunt against the king of Babylon: ... How his fury has ended! All the lands are at rest...; they break into singing. Even the pine trees and the cedars of Lebanon exult over you and say, 'Now that you have been laid low, no woodsman comes to cut us down.'

"The grave below is all astir to meet you at your coming; it rouses the spirits of the departed to greet you—all those who were leaders in the world; it makes them rise from their thrones... They will say to you [Babylon's king], 'You also have become weak, as we are; you have become like us.' All your pomp has been brought down to the grave, along with the noise of your harps; maggots are spread out beneath you and worms cover you."

Summary commentary on Isaiah 14: 3-11:

God says Israelites will taunt the oppressive king of Babylon. In the grave, the king joins other fallen leaders. The king's fall foreshadows Antichrist's far-future fall when he will be banished to the grave (Jamiesson, Fausset, Brown [JFB] 1866, Vol 2, Pt 1, 610).

The *near-future prophecy* was fulfilled in history when Isaiah's king of Babylon came to an ignominious end. The *far future prophecy* will be fulfilled when Satan's ruler, Antichrist, is vanquished. That's when the oppressed will rejoice (Re 19.).

GOD'S TRIUMPH---THIRD PART

---Isaiah 14.12-14---

Identity by Content and by Double Reference:
A current king foreshadows Satan himself in the future

Babylon's king in near future; Satan in far future (Double Reference)

Text, Isaiah 14.12-14, addresses Babylon's king as if he were Satan:
"How you have fallen from heaven, O morning star, son of the dawn! You have been cast down to the earth… You said in your heart, '*I will* ascend to heaven; '*I will* raise my throne above the stars of God; *I will* sit enthroned on the mount of assembly, on the utmost heights of the sacred mountain. *I will* ascend above the tops of the clouds; *I will* make myself like the Most High.'" Here, Identity by Content reveals *willful* Satan speaking of his power.

Satan "wanted to take to himself worship that belongs only to God" (Wiersbe 1993, 901, his commentary on Isaiah 14.12-15).

Commentary on Identity by Content in verses 12-14 in Isaiah 14:
Identity by Content indirectly identifies characters and time periods by clues in the content, without naming them. Also, if a passage is about a heavenly being, then that's the character's identity, even if, before or after, the text describes a human character.

Identity by Content shows that though God addresses a contemporary king (Is 14.3), his message is to Satan: "How you have fallen from heaven, O morning star, son of the dawn [Lucifer]. You have been cast down to the earth…" (Is 14.12). "Son of the dawn" identifies Satan as Lucifer (Light, a Hebrew transliteration).

GOD'S TRIUMPH---FOURTH PART
Isaiah 14.15-17---
Identity by Content and by Double Reference:
A current king foreshadows the future Antichrist

Babylon's king in near future and Antichrist in far future

Text, Isaiah 14.15-17, speaks to Babylon's contemporary king.

Babylon's king foreshadows the man, Antichrist: "But you are brought down to the grave, to the depths of the pit. Those who see you stare at you, they ponder your fate; 'Is this *the man* who shook the earth and made kingdoms tremble, *the man* who made the world a desert, who overthrew its cities and would not let his captives go home?'" ("The man" refers to a mortal man who dies, Antichrist, not to Satan, a spirit being, who does not die.)

Commentary on Isaiah 14: 15-17 :

Double Reference refers to Babylon's king in the near future and to Antichrist in the far future. At verse 15, when the story reverts back from Satan to a human being who dies, we see that according to the literary device of Identity by Content, this text points ahead to the future human Antichrist, for this cannot be about Satan, since Satan is a spirit, whose body cannot die. This refers to the ancient king of Babylon, who foreshadows the endtime Satan-possessed Antichrist, who will be a mortal being who can die. Isaiah prophesied that the king of Babylon would go down to his grave, defeated and powerless, like other heathen rulers.

Satan's final expulsion from the atmospheric realm will confine him to earth alone. There, Satan will take possession of Antichrist, who will then demand that Jews worship his idol in the temple.

After the messianic kingdom, Babylon's king—a foreshadowing of Antichrist—will be resurrected, judged, and cast into the lake of fire, where he'll suffer with Satan and all unbelievers.

—End of Section on Literary devices as aids—

---

* Re dates: John A. Martin says that Isaiah gives facts about Israel's society in c. 700 B.C." Charles H. Dyer writes about Ezekiel's prophetic activity as from 593-571 B.C. (Walvoord 1983, 2004).

A parallel literary pattern
for Isaiah 14 and Ezekiel 28

Compare the parallel prophecies of
Isaiah 14.3-17 and Ezekiel 28.1-19

Figure 27

Isaiah prophesied to the last four kings of Judah before the Babylonian captivity of the Jews, and Ezekiel prophesied later during the Babylonian captivity. Though far separated in time and space from each other, the messages and patterns of their prophecies are parallel and confirm the message of each and the other.

Parallel verses in numerical order

1. Double reference to the death of the king and of Antichrist

Babylon's king in near future and Antichrist in far future
Isaiah 14: Verses 3-11

Tyre's king in near future and Antichrist in far future
Ezekiel 28: Verses 1-10

-----

2. Double reference to the death of the king and to Satan's doom

Babylon king's death in near future and Satan's doom in far future
Isaiah 14: Verses 12-14

Tyre king's death in near future and Satan's doom in far future
Ezekiel 28: Verses 11-17

-----

3. Double reference to the death of the king and of Antichrist

Babylon's king in near future and Antichrist in far future
Isaiah 14: Verses 15-18

Tyre's king in near future and Antichrist in far future
Ezekiel 28: Verses 18-19

E. Comparing two parallel prophecies to confirm God's truth

Charles Lee Feinberg writes that the structure and message of Isaiah 14.1-17 and Ezekiel 28.1-19 "have distinct parallels" (Feinberg 1969, 158). What is amazing is that the passages are parallel even though they are about different kings in different countries and are presented by different prophets in different centuries. Isaiah ministered in Jerusalem under four Judaic kings; Ezekiel ministered later in Babylon after the Jews became captives there (Tidwell, no copyright date, seventeenth printing 1975, 112, 123). Biblical repetition through parallels shows the relatedness and significance of these prophecies by Isaiah and Ezekiel.

The two parallel passages in Isaiah 14 and Ezekiel 28 illustrate the role of Double Reference (Gray 1906, 58, 59), for both give a near-future prophecy to be fulfilled in the contemporary times of their respective kings and a far-future prophecy to be fulfilled in the end time. And both of these passages illustrate the role of Identity by Content, for in these prophecies, identities are determined from clues in the passages about Antichrist and Satan.

Figure 27, previous page, shows that the two parallel prophecies, Isaiah 14 and Ezekiel 28, follow the same literary pattern and give a common message—that in the last days, the sovereign God will bring an end to Satan and his man Antichrist and will bring victory to Israel. Isaiah's near-future prophecy about the contemporary king of Babylon is parallel to King Tyre's near-future prophecy in Ezekiel's prophecy.

Both passages end with the violent death of the contemporary kings, and both point to the future, final doom of the Satan-possessed Antichrist. These parallel passages use the poetic scriptural form of Double Reference to refer to near and future times. The passages present the fact that Antichrist will be Satan's tool to accomplish his purposes in the last days.

The parallel passages confirm the validity of the conclusions of one to the other. The next unit stresses the importance of context. The next chapter also presents the literary device of analogy, which can unify scripture and resolve paradoxes.

THINK JEWISH
to understand the Bible

h. UNDERSTANDING THE THEME OF THE UNITY OF SCRIPTURE

18. Analogy to cross biblical bounds and resolves issues
    A. *Analogy to cross bounds of Christian and Israelite worship*
    B. *Analogy to cross bounds of Old and New Testaments*
    C. *Analogy to cross bounds of the temporal and the eternal*
    D. *Analogy to cross bounds of Jewish and Gentile distinctions*
    E. *Analogy from life to resolve the paradox of grace and truth*
    F. *More analogies to resolve other biblical dilemmas*
    G. *Conclusions about analogies to resolve issues*

19. Whole Bible context to determine interpretation
    A. *The importance of context for understanding the Bible*
    B. *"King's Dream," a context aid on the times of the Gentiles*
    C. *"God's Clock," a context aid on the times of Israel*
    D. *The Old Testament, distinct but related to the New*
    E. *The benefits of reading the Bible as a unified whole*

18 Analogy to cross biblical bounds and to resolve issues

The great analogy is that Jesus entered my world so that I could enter his world. To see him is to see the Father and to follow him is to know the way, the truth, and the life.
—The author

In my years serving the Lord, I've discovered that I can gain understanding about what I face in life by finding a story in the Bible that can serve as an analogy of my situation. Most often I find a story in the Old Testament, for Hebrew scripture is a treasure house of stories about real people in real situations.

Other ways analogy can cross bounds and resolve paradoxes:

A. *Analogy to cross bounds of Christian and Israelite worship*
B. *Analogy to cross bounds of the Old and New Testaments*
C. *Analogy to cross bounds of the temporal and the eternal*
D. *Analogy to cross bounds of Jewish and Gentile distinctions*
E. *Analogy from life to resolve the paradox of grace and truth*
F. *Two analogies to resolve other biblical dilemmas*
G. **Conclusions about analogies that have resolved issues**

A. Analogy to cross bounds of Christian and Israelite worship

The illustrative analogy on the next two pages crosses the restrictive bounds of Christian and Israelite worship. This analogy compares the triunity of the Israelite desert temple with the triunity of the Christian temple of personhood. The original triunity is the three-in-one God—Father, Son, and Holy Spirit.—for we are made in his image.

In the diagrams on the next two pages, triunity is presented in the blueprint of the Jewish desert tabernacle, which is made up of "Courtyard, Holy Place, Most Holy Place"and also in the blueprint of the temple of the Christian believer, who is made up of "Body, Soul, Spirit." The Jewish temple was portable to accommodate Israelites in their past exodus on the way to the Promised Land. This portability is analogous of Christian worshippers in the future exodus through the present age on the way to eternity.

Figure 28 - The triunity of the Hebrew desert temple

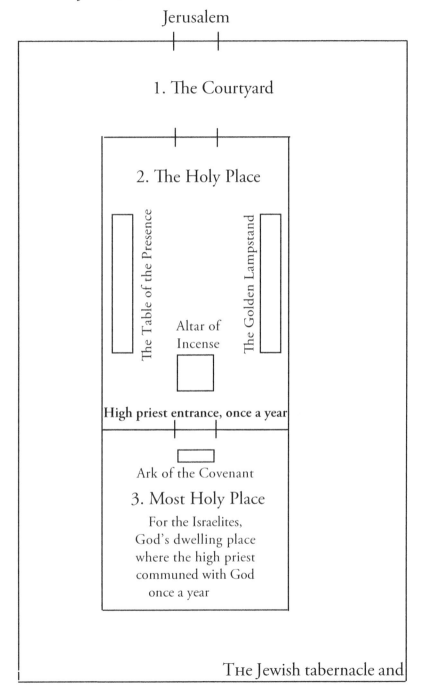

1. THE JEWISH TABERNACLE: A DESERT TEMPLE

Jerusalem

1. The Courtyard

2. The Holy Place

The Table of the Presence

The Golden Lampstand

Altar of Incense

High priest entrance, once a year

Ark of the Covenant

3. Most Holy Place

For the Israelites,
God's dwelling place
where the high priest
communed with God
once a year

The Jewish tabernacle and

Figure 29 - The triunity of Christian personhood

2. THE CHRISTIAN: TEMPLE OF THE HOLY SPIRIT

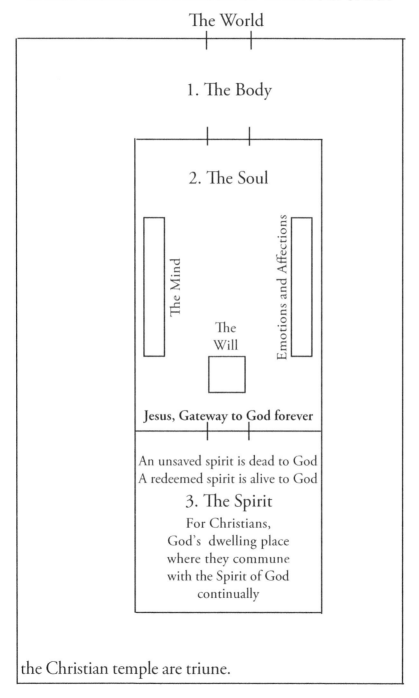

The World

1. The Body

2. The Soul

The Mind

Emotions and Affections

The Will

Jesus, Gateway to God forever

An unsaved spirit is dead to God
A redeemed spirit is alive to God

3. The Spirit

For Christians,
God's dwelling place
where they commune
with the Spirit of God
continually

the Christian temple are triune.

The Christian temple

Let's look at the makeup of a Christian's temple—body, soul, spirit:

A Christian's body is "The Courtyard," which encloses soul and spirit. Through the senses, a Christian connects with others.

A Christian's soul is *"The Holy Place"* for God's daily expression of himself to and through a believer. There God brings edification, enlightenment, and sanctification to the believer.

A Christian's Spirit is *"The Most Holy Place"* where he contacts God himself, the source of life. A Christian's Spirit is the place of restoration, refreshment, and communion with God. It is the place for God's continual guidance and glorification.

Let's look at details of the components of the human soul:

The soul is tripartite: Mind, Emotions-Affections, and Will.*

A Christian in his soul trains *"his mind"* by feeding on God's Word, the bread of life. As a priest for God, "he takes every thought captive to make it obedient to Christ" (2Co 10.5).

A Christian in his soul allows the Holy Spirit to flow from his spirit through *"his Emotions and Affections,"* thus enlightening and warming his heart and radiating outwardly to others.

A Christian in his soul by *"his will"* chooses whom to serve—God or the world. He can go through the gateway of his senses to live out his desires in the world, or he can go through the gateway of Jesus for communion with him. There in Christ, he finds guidance, fellowship, comfort, strength, and approval.

Let's look at the spirit, where a Christian meets with the Lord:

In Hebrew ministry, the high priest was to enter the Most Holy Place yearly to present incense ("prayers of the saints" [Re 5.8]) and sacrificial blood atonement. His goal was to restore the Israelites' relationship to God. *A Christian's goal, however, is to walk continually in the Spirit in fellowship with God.* This is a challenge for a Christian—to walk moment by moment in God's presence and to express his needs to him as they arise.

---

* This is the description of the body, soul, and spirit given by Brooks 1973, p 107 and by others.

Christian Priesthood

Let's look at a Christian as God's priest in the temple of his body:

James says this to the Christian, who is a priest for the Lord: "Anyone who chooses to be a friend of the world becomes an enemy of God" (Ja 4.4b), and God calls such unfaithfulness to the Lord adultery. This is a serious charge.

John says this to the Christian who is a priest for the Lord: "If anyone loves the world, the love of the Father is not in him." And he says this about what love for the world does: It creates sinful cravings, wrong focus, and pride (1Jn 2.16).

Jesus says that a Christian, as a priest for the Lord, cannot serve both God and the world, for he will hate one and love the other, or he will be devoted to one and despise the other (Mt 6.24).

Jesus in the book of Revelation intimates that a Christian, as a priest for the Lord, should keep the light burning in his spirit by continually renewing his first love for God. (Re 2.4,5).

Paul, in some translations, uses a two-word phrase to describe expression of love for the world and love for self. That phrase is "the flesh." He says, "To set the mind on "the flesh" is death, but to set the mind on the Spirit is life and peace" (Ro 8.6 ESV).*

Revivalist Charles Finney attested to the need for a Christian to be continually broken before God so that he is sensitive enough to hear the still, small voice that keeps his first love burning brightly. He said that without this kind of humble brokenness before the Lord, a Christian's heart can become hard and "crusted over" in a period of time.

Author's Application: "To set the mind on the flesh is death, but to set the mind on the Spirit is life and peace" (Ro. 8.6 ESV). I find that if I repeat that verse, I'm jolted back to reality, for the verse reminds me that truly, God is the one I love and the one whose praise I want to seek, not the world's approval and not my own craving. Repeating Romans 8.6 reframes the situation, makes my choice clear, quickens my soul, and brings victory.

B. *Analogy crosses the bounds of the Old and New Testaments*

Jesus often illustrates his teachings by analogy. He took the spiritual truth that God saves a sinner by "a look of faith," and he illustrates it with an analogy of the story of the brazen serpent (OT) and of the story of the cross (NT).

In the analogy during the Jewish wilderness exodus, the Israelites made accusations against Moses and God, saying, "Why have you brought us up out of Egypt to die in the desert? There is no bread! There is no water! And we detest this miserable food!" Then, since this attitude was displeasing to God, he brought judgment down upon them by allowing deadly snakes to bite them.

That changed their attitude. Their accusations changed to pleas for mercy, and though God heard their cry, he didn't remove the live snakes. Instead, he told Moses to put a bronze snake on a pole so that anyone bitten could look at the bronze snake and live. Those who looked, survived; those who refused, died (Nu 21.5-9).

By such Old Testament analogy, Jesus teaches the New Testament truth that a look of faith at Christ on the cross can save a sinner from hell. This analogy links the Old and New Testaments, for Jesus says, "Just as Moses lifted up the snake [on a pole] in the desert, so the Son of Man must be lifted up [on the cross], that everyone who believes in him may have eternal life" (Jn 3.14). In the exodus, when God's natural people, the Jews, looked at the bronze snake, a symbol of sin, they were healed physically. Today, when a sinner looks to the cross, he can be healed spiritually in body, soul, and spirit.

Spurgeon saved by a look of faith

Famed 1800s preacher Charles Spurgeon is one who by a look of faith traded his sins for God's righteousness. As a boy, he'd been troubled because he didn't know how to get right with God. He writes, "The secret of my distress was this: I did not know the gospel. I was in a Christian land; I had Christian parents. But I did not understand the freeness and simplicity of the gospel."

He says that one Sunday, he was forced by a snowstorm to stop at a little church with only a few people, and there he heard a sermon on an Old Testament text: "Look unto me, and be ye saved" (Is 45.22a KJV). He says that the preacher was "a poor man, a shoemaker, a tailor, or something of the sort" and that when he had managed to spin out ten minutes or so, he was "at the length of his tether." He looked at Spurgeon under the gallery and said, "Young man, you look very miserable… and you will always be miserable—miserable in life and miserable in death—if you do not obey my text. But if you obey, now, this moment, you will be saved."

Then he shouted, "Young man, LOOK to Jesus Christ; look NOW." Spurgeon says, "There and then, the cloud was gone; the darkness had rolled away, and that moment I saw the sun… Oh, that somebody had told me that before—'Trust Christ, and you will be saved'" (Spurgeon 1988, 219, 220).

By a look of faith at Jesus lifted high on the cross, Spurgeon was redeemed by God's grace! Jesus used analogy to connect the Old Testament with New Testament understanding.

C. Analogy to cross bounds between the temporal and the eternal

At the Last Supper Jesus presented a living analogy that is remarkable in two ways. First, when as a servant he washed his disciples' feet, he expressed *grace* to them at that moment. Second, by this act he was able to demonstrate the deeper meaning of the eternal *truth* of servanthood.

The difference between the eternal bath and daily washing

John tells us what happened at the Last Supper: "Jesus knew that the Father had put all things under his power, and that he had come from God and was returning to God, so he got up from the meal, took off his outer clothing, and wrapped a towel around his waist. After that, he poured water into a basin and began to wash his disciples' feet… 'No,' said Peter, 'you shall never wash my feet.' Jesus answered, 'Unless I wash you, you have no part with me.' 'Then, Lord,' Simon Peter replied, 'not just my feet but my hands and my head as well!' Jesus answered, 'A person who has had a bath needs only to wash his feet; his whole body is clean'" (Jn 13.3--10a). The eternal cleansing in the blood of the Lamb brings redemption and sonship; temporal cleansing in the daily walk sustains fellowship with the Lord. Both are needful.

In the above incident, Jesus told Peter, "Unless I wash you, you have no part with me." He said this because sin breaks *fellowship* with God and causes loss of intimacy with him, but this doesn't mean the person loses his *sonship*. Rather, sin brings a sense of alienation from God and other people, which then alerts the Christian of his need for cleansing. Scripture says, "If we confess our sins, he is faithful and just to forgive us our sins, and to cleanse us from all unrighteousness" (1Jn 1.9). To be continually restored by the Beloved is the miracle of the Christian walk.

Eternal forgiveness, God's purpose and man's privilege

Horatius Bonar writes, "Are all our sins, future as well as past, forgiven the moment we believe? In one sense they are; for from the time of our believing, we are treated by God as forgiven… [but] strictly speaking, no sin can be actually forgiven till it exists, just as no one can be raised up till he actually falls, and as we cannot wash off the soil from our feet until it is on them.

Bonar continues: "That God should treat his saints[*] as forgiven ones, and yet that he should be constantly forgiving, are two things quite compatible—and the 'bathing and washing' of our text (Jn 13.3-10) furnish an excellent illustration of their consistency… *Eternal forgiveness is God's purpose: Daily forgiveness is our enjoyment and privilege…* I simply take my worldliness, my coldness, my prayerlessness to God; I go and wash my feet as often as they need it" (Bonar 1977, 92, 93)!

Without this daily confession and cleansing, fellowship with God is interrupted, and if that interruption is allowed to continue, it hardens the heart, dishonors God, grieves his Spirit, leads to self-destruction, and turns others away from the Lord.

To those who receive him, God gives the right to be his children (Jn 1.12), and whether their walk honors or disgraces him, they never lose the freedom to make a choice each step they take, either for or against God. He leaves their response up to them. What a sacred responsibility for believers!

---

[*] "Saints" is the Bible's word for believers.

If Christians know the depths of God's love, they are motivated to serve him out of gratitude. At the end of Romans 8, Paul says that for Christians, nothing can separate them from the love of God in Christ. *In this we see that response to God's love is what distinguishes the motivation of Christians from the motivation of unbelievers.* Unbelievers try to win God's favor by their works. Christians live for God, not to earn his favor, but to express their fervent love and overflowing gratitude for what God has already done for them on the cross. Gratitude is the attitude of Christians.

D. Analogy to cross bounds of Jewish and Gentile distinctions

Although Jesus said he was sent only to the Jews, he nevertheless commended two Gentiles for their persistence in reaching out to him for their needs. Both of them spoke to him as though they were attorneys in a divine court. Each of them used the logic of analogy to break down what seemed to block their access to Christ the Healer. A Roman centurion based his petition for healing on Jesus' divine authority (*truth*), and a Canaanite woman persisted in her pleas because she counted on Jesus' mercy (*grace*).

A Gentile centurion's confidence in Jesus' authority (truth)

The Gentile Roman centurion petitioned Jesus, by building a case in terms of the chain of command in an army. As a man of earthly authority, he recognized Jesus as a man of spiritual authority. Therefore, in seeking his servant's healing, he sent elders to Jesus with a message: "Lord, don't trouble yourself, for I do not deserve to have you come under my roof. That is why I did not even consider myself worthy to come to you. But say the word, and my servant will be healed. For I myself am a man under authority, with soldiers under me. I tell this one, 'Go,' and he goes; and that one, 'Come,' and he comes. I say to my servant, 'Do this,' and he does it." When Jesus heard this, he told the crowd, "I tell you, I have not found such great faith even in Israel."

After the messengers went home, they found that the servant had been healed (Lk 7.6b-10). The centurion had trusted in Christ's authority (truth) and had therefore sought him with confidence.

A Gentile woman's confidence in Jesus' mercy (grace)

Another Gentile expressed faith through analogy and in so doing, she obliterated Jewish and Gentile distinctions, which otherwise would have denied her access to Jesus' ministry. The Bible says, "A Canaanite woman from that vicinity came to him, crying out, 'Lord, Son of David, have mercy on me! My daughter is suffering terribly from demon-possession.' Jesus did not answer a word. So his disciples came to him and urged him, 'Send her away, for she keeps crying out after us.' He answered, 'I was sent only to the lost sheep of Israel.' The woman… knelt before him. 'Lord, help me!' she said. He replied, 'It is not right to take the children's bread and toss it to their dogs. 'Yes, Lord,' she said, 'but even the dogs eat the crumbs that fall from their master's table.'"

"Then Jesus answered, 'Woman, you have great faith! Your request is granted.' And her daughter was healed from that very hour" (Mt 15.22-28). Jesus commended the faith by which she expressed confidence in his divine mercy (*grace*).

These two Gentiles expressed faith by the reasoning of analogy and broke through barriers that otherwise would have excluded non-Jews—the woman by her confidence in Jesus' mercy (*grace*), the centurion by his trust in Jesus' authority (*truth*). These Gentile outsiders recognized who Jesus is—God in the flesh—and through analogy, their faith transcended Jewish and Gentile distinctions.

E. Analogy from life to resolve the paradox of grace and truth

An analogy from an experience in my life reconciles for me the two dominant but seemingly contradictory themes of the Old and New Testaments—the theme of the *grace* of God's unconditional love and the *truth* of God's unchanging justice.

How a personal story began

The story of my analogy began when my father left me a modest trust fund that was to be administered by a small, independent, local bank in the Lower Rio Grande Valley of Texas. Over a period of more than thirty years, however, bank after bank swallowed up each previous bank until my father's small, local bank became absorbed into what became became one of the largest banks in the nation.

Meanwhile, the worth of the dollar dwindled, interest dropped, and administrative fees of the megabank threatened to wipe out my trust account; therefore, the best course of action for me was to request that the bank dissolve the trust and distribute the funds to my five children, who were to inherit the funds after my death anyway.

Problem defined and action taken

But there was a problem. A clause in the trust document prohibited breaking up the trust until after my death, and Texas law supported that clause. That meant that if the bank was to keep its legal integrity in its oversight of the trust, it would have to deny distribution of the funds to the beneficiaries before my death.

Nevertheless, I had to do what I could to save the inheritance from being wiped out, for I had a hope to which I clung, a hope that was based on what a bank officer had told me off-the-cuff twenty-five years earlier. He said that after my children became educated and of a certain age, I could get the bank to distribute the funds of the trust. That was the hope I needed. If I hadn't known that, I would have become discouraged after the trust came into financial jeopardy, for two local California attorneys had said I had little hope of success. Also, in my informal negotiating with the Texas bank, the spokesperson tried to discourage me in my pursuit. But because of my persistence, the bank came through. In the end, the spokesperson said if I sought counsel to represent me and paid court expenses, the bank would abide by the judge's ruling.

My day in court

Fortunately, the octogenarian Texas attorney that I chose from the internet found a 1969 Texas law that would permit termination of such a trust before my death, and this became the basis for his petition. In court he sought to convince the judge that he should allow distribution of the trust to the heirs in spite of the disturbing clause, but the judge was not convinced. He wanted to keep his integrity under the law by honoring the trust's terms.

Finally, before that day in court adjourned, the judge declared his ruling. He said he couldn't overrule the sovereignty of my father's orders in the trust. He said he was obligated to honor my father's desires just as they were expressed in the trust document. And therefore, because of his commitment to the terms of the trust, the judge said he would not mandate that the bank dissolve the trust. With that statement, my hope for resolution vanished.

But wait! That wasn't the end. The judge added that by applying the 1969 law my attorney found, he could *not mandate* that the bank dissolve the trust, but instead he would grant the bank the legal *option* to distribute the trust funds to the heirs. This ruling would maintain the sovereignty of the bank as guaranteed by the trust.

And though this ruling would not grant me the right to demand the bank to be forthcoming, it did allow me to wait patiently for the bank to keep its promise to me to distribute the funds according to the judge's ruling.

This "option" made possible legal distribution of the funds without jeopardizing the sovereignty of the bank. This option also guaranteed that it would be possible for the bank to keep its promise to me to abide by the judge's ruling. Therefore, the bank did grant me the *option* to accept the new terms, which, of course, I did. The irreconcilable became reconciled. The judge's ruling reconciled the truth of the trust's dictates and the grace of the bank in its willingness to abide by the judge's ruling.

F. More analogies to resolve other biblical dilemmas

The option of a new law to resolve a Persian king's dilemma

Later, I recognized that the dilemma that the Texas judge faced is analogous to a dilemma in scripture faced by a Persian king whose empire dominated the world. At that time, after the Jews' captivity under that Persian king, instead of returning to Israel with the other Jews, some of them had remained in Babylon. However, the lives of these exiles became threatened by the king when he came under the influence of an anti-Semitic courtier, Haman. And because of that influence, the king decreed that Jews were to be destroyed on the thirteenth of Adar. Then, much to his chagrin, the king discovered that his beloved Queen Esther was a Jew. And though she pleaded for the lives of her people, the king could not respond to her pleas because in that era of Persian supremacy, an official Persian decree could never be changed or rescinded.

Yet, the king found a way out. Although he could not change the irrevocable decree, he discovered that he could make a new law, and that's what he did. He decreed that he would give the threatened Jews the legal *option* to defend themselves against any who would attack them on the thirteenth of Adar. And that's what the forewarned Jews chose to do—to defend themselves and live. This solution is similar to that of the Texas judge who gave the bank the *option* to distribute the trust funds to my children.

The option of a new covenant to resolve "God's dilemma"

The dilemmas that my Texas judge and the Persian king faced are also analogous to what appears to be "God's dilemma"— the seeming conflict between God's expression of truth and his expression of grace. God's truth says "the wages of sin is death" (Ro 6.23a) and condemns to death and hell the sinners that he loves. So, since God's holiness requires the death of sinners and since he cannot break his Word, the question becomes, how can God save sinners whom he loves from the consequences of the truth that sin deserves death? And another question becomes, how can sinners be saved without God violating his own integrity?

Only a *new* covenant—one that is the law of life—could accomplish this. Actually, this was God's plan from the beginning. In that plan—as in the plan of the Persian king—the Lord would not go back on his decree that the penalty for sin is death. That decree could not be changed. But then through a *new* covenant, he could offer an *option*. Sinners would then be able to choose to accept God's new covenant, which offers the gift of "eternal life through Christ Jesus" (Ro 6.23b), for by the death of Jesus on the cross, the penalty that sinners deserve would be paid in full.

Paul writes, "There is therefore now no condemnation to those who are in Christ Jesus, who do not walk according to the flesh, but according to the Spirit. For the law of the Spirit of life in Christ Jesus has made me free from the law of sin and death. For what the law could not do in that it was weak through the flesh, God did by sending His own Son in the likeness of sinful flesh, on account of sin: He condemned sin in the flesh, that the righteous requirement of the law might be fulfilled in us who do not walk according to the flesh but according to the Spirit" (Ro 8.1-4. NKJV). Therefore, for all of us who are willing to accept the option of God's gift of life, his new covenant of grace swallows up the death and hell that we sinners deserve.

The new covenant of grace resolves God's dilemma.

G. Conclusions about these analogies that have resolved issues

In all three cases of these endangered persons—me in court, the Jews in Esther's day, and sinners in God's world—there is an advocate to appear before a sovereign, whether that sovereign be the king, the judge, or Christ. In my court case, I had an attorney as advocate, Jews had Esther, and sinners have Christ (1Jn 2.1). In each case, a sovereign faced the dilemma of how to honor an immutable edict yet save those endangered by it.

To resolve each of these three issues, the sovereign created a new order under a new law without changing or repealing the original, irrevocable one. In this way, disaster was averted and an *option* to choose deliverance was offered to those endangered.

In each of the cases, a new statute made it possible to save the day—for the judge to save my trust fund, for the king to save the Jewish people, and for God to save sinners.

After victory before the sovereign—I before the bank trustee, the Jews before the king, and sinners before God—we three could not make demands, because the successful outcome still rested in the sovereign's authority (*truth*) and mercy (*grace*). Yet even so, as petitioners, we had a part to play, for the final outcome depended on our acceptance of and submission to the sovereign's authority and mercy. In my case, after the judge's ruling, I could not force the bank to terminate the trust. Instead, the bank had the legal option to choose to distribute the trust funds. And I had the option to accept the bank's offer, which I gladly did. My part was to trust the bank to keep its promise to abide by the court's ruling. *Similarly, in the case involving salvation, God's hand cannot be forced; he always remains sovereign—but he offers a new covenant, an option of grace, to all who, in humble dependence come to him through faith in Jesus' sacrifice.* Therefore, "Let us then approach the throne of grace with confidence, so that we may receive mercy and find grace to help us in our time of need" (He 4.16).

Analogy drawn from experience can bring deeper truth into sharp focus. For me these analogies inspire worshipful submission to God and cause me to have reverence for his authority (*truth*). The end result is that I become more aware of and more appreciative of his mercy (*grace*), which I do not deserve.

Next, as we continue to examine the theme of the unity of scripture, let's look at whole Bible context to determine interpretation.

19 Whole Bible context to determine interpretation

Words are vehicles of thought, and context is largely what gives them meaning.
—Professor Martin Pickup

The challenge of reading the Bible is similar to the challenge of reading "The Great Books." Mortimer Adler says, "The enthusiasm with which people embark on a course of reading "The Great Books" often gives way, fairly soon, to a feeling of hopeless inadequacy… They think they should be able to understand the first book they pick up, without having read the others to which it is closely related…. [But] just as the whole book is the context for any of its parts, so related books provide an even larger context that helps you interpret the book you are reading…" (Adler and Van Doren 1940, 172-173). What Adler says about the interrelatedness of "the great books" applies to reading the books of the Bible. This is certainly applicable since the Bible itself claims God as the single author.

Whole-Bible context determines interpretation:
   A. *The importance of context for understanding the Bible*
   B. *"The King's Dream," a context aid about times of the Gentiles*
   C. *"God's Clock," a context aid about times and seasons of Israel*
   D. *The Old Testament, distinct but related to the New Testament*
   E. *The benefits of reading the Bible as a unified whole*

A. *The importance of context for understanding the Bible*

To place biblical events in perspective, we have to think broadly in a whole-Bible context. I learned about the importance of context when I taught English as a "foreign expert" at an engineering college in China in 1984-85. Besides teaching undergraduates and graduates, I taught English to college professors who taught English, and though they were proficient in the language, they had endless questions when reading American literature because they lacked knowledge about the context of Western culture. Later, however, when I brought back copies of Pearl Buck's *The Good Earth* from Hong Kong, they had no problem with that English text. In fact, they sailed right through it because it was about Chinese culture in the countryside, a social context with which they were familiar. The point of this book, *Think Jewish, to Understand the Bible,* is to give an overview of the Bible and its parts because familiarity with whole Bible context is necessary for fully understanding any part of the Bible.

The Bible presents prophecy frameworks of two types that have been helpful to me as context aids. One type focuses on context by giving a simple summary of biblical events, such as in Stephen's speech before he was stoned to death (Ac 7.1-51) and as in Paul's speeches about his conversion. Such simple summaries lay out clearly a short span of time, and they need no explanation.

A more complex context aid sets up a framework on which to hang historic and prophetic events in sequence over a long span of time (Figure 30, page 259 and Figure 31, page 263). This long sequence helps a reader of the Bible gain historical perspective. The following prophecy frameworks serve as context aid.

Context aids for *Times of the Gentiles* **and for** *Times of Israel*

Figure 30, page 259, a context aid about Times of the Gentiles
Times of the Gentiles began in 605 B.C. at the beginning of the Jews' Babylonian captivity. The Babylonian King's Dream (Da2) shows five successive Gentile empires, which reign before Christ returns to set up his messianic kingdom.

Figure 31, page 263, a context aid about Times and season of Israel: Times and Seasons of Israel began in 445 B.C. after Israel"s Babylonian captivity (Da 9:2427); It will last until Christ returns to rule in his messianic kingdom. God has "a clock" he turns on when he deals with *Jews as a people.* Today, he has turned his clock off, for he now deals with *Jews only as individuals* in need of a Savior, the way he now deals with everyone. Not until the tribulation will God again turn on his clock, for that's when he will again deal with *Jews as a people.*

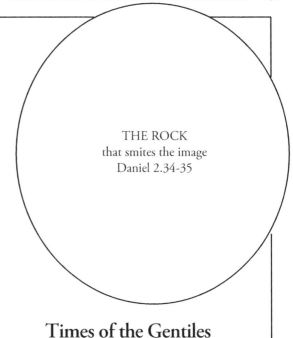

THE ROCK
that smites the image
Daniel 2.34-35

Times of the Gentiles

5 Successive Empires

BABYLONIAN	Head: Gold
MEDE-PERSIAN	Chest, arms: Silver
GREEK	Belly, thighs: Bronze
ROMAN	Legs: Iron
(Present Church Age	Ankles)
REVIVED ROMAN	Feet: Iron & Clay

Image in the king's dream

Figure 30

The Babylonian King's Dream
Gentile Empires from 605 B.C. to Christ's return
DANIEL 2

B. The King's Dream, a context aid about "Times of the Gentiles"

Figure 30, page 259, shows a diagram of the dream of King Nebuchadnezzar. This dream, which God interpreted for Daniel, predicts 5 successive Gentile ruling empires, of which the first 4 have already been fulfilled. God gave Daniel these prophecies about 5 Gentile empires while the Jews were in captivity under the first empire, Babylon. All this came centuries after Israel had enjoyed their own years of world prominence.*

Jesus says that when the idol worship of the tribulation begins, faithful Jews in Judea are to flee to the mountains (Mt 24.15,16) where God will take care of them (Re 12.6)—while he pours out his wrath on Satan's kingdom on earth. And since the first four empires have been fulfilled, we can be confident that this fifth future Revived Roman empire will also come to pass. And remember, the reason these empires have significance is because of their relationship to Israel, for as Walter K. Price says, God weaves the destiny of churches and nations around Israel's destiny (Price 1972).

Interestingly, in Daniel's time, Gentile rulers in the king's dream express the same spirit as that of the builders of the tower of Babel in scripture's earliest history (Ge 11.1-9). This heathen spirit, which centralizes and organizes opposition to God, will thread its way from the Tower of Babel through history until it peaks in earth's last days as the fifth world empire, which will be the Revived Roman empire under the endtime Antichrist. The book of Revelation, calls the revived Roman empire "Babylon," which is the same Hebrew name as for the Tower of Babel at earth's dawn (Re 17, 18). After that future revived Roman Empire, Babylon, Christ will return from heaven with this bride, the church (Re 19.9).

Returning now to the story of Daniel in ancient Babylon under Nebuchadnezzar, we enter the story of the Jews when they were captive slaves there. With Daniel were three young friends; Shadrach, Meshach, and Abednego (their Hebrew names); who were being groomed to be advisers to the King of Babylon. During that time, the

---

* When archeologists found no evidence that Israel was ever dominant in the world, skeptics derided scripture. But archeologist Thomas Levy—who lives in San Diego in the same block with the author's son—has been leading a team in Israel to restore Solomon's mines, as televised by *National Geographic,* This excavation shows Israel's wealth, prestige, and power in its golden era..

king became disturbed by a dream, which led him to make a demand. He told his advisers they would have to tell him the content and interpretation of a dream that he had forgotten. When they protested that no one could do that, he ordered that all of those advisers be slain.

In captivity, Daniel and his friends chose to be true to the God of Israel. Therefore, on hearing about the king's death decree, the young men prayed, and "during the night the mystery was revealed to Daniel." For this miracle, Daniel, filled with praise and thanksgiving, exclaimed, "Praise be to the name of God for ever… You have made known to us the dream of the king" (Da 2.19-23).

Figure 30, page 257 is about Times of the Gentiles.* The diagram of the king's dream shows the statue and the Rock (Christ) that will crush it. It also lists the five successive ruling Gentile empires that began in Daniel's time. History confirms the statue's sequence—Babylon as the head of gold, Mede-Persia as the silver breast and arms, Greece as bronze thighs, and Rome as legs of iron. The fifth empire, the future revived Roman empire, will be as the feet with ten toes, partly iron and partly clay. That empire will come to pass in the last days. In the dream the present church age is at the ankles in Figure 30, page 257—between ancient Rome and the future revived Roman Empire.

Daniel's interpretation of the king's dream

Text of Daniel 2.27-38, 44-45, 47: "No wise man, enchanter, magician or diviner can explain to the king the mystery he has asked about, but there is a God in heaven who reveals mysteries. He has shown King Nebuchadnezzar what will happen in days to come. Your dream and the visions that passed through your mind as you lay on your bed are these … O king, your mind turned to things to come, and the revealer of mysteries showed you what is going to happen…

"You looked, O king, and there before you stood a large statue—an enormous, dazzling statue, awesome in appearance [Figure 30, page 257]. The head of the statue was made of pure gold, its chest and arms of silver, its belly and thighs of bronze, its legs of iron, its feet partly of iron and partly of baked clay. While you were watching, a rock was cut out, but not by human hands. It struck the statue on its feet of iron and clay and smashed them. Then the iron, the clay, the bronze, the silver and the gold were broken to pieces at the same time and became like chaff on a threshing floor in the summer. The wind swept them away without leaving a trace. But the Rock that struck the statue became a huge mountain and filled the whole earth… Now we will interpret it to the king. You, O king, are the king of kings. The God of heaven has given you dominion and power and might and glory; in your hands he has placed mankind and the beasts of the field and the birds of the air. … You are that head of gold" (Da 2.27-38)…

"'In the time of those kings, the God of heaven will set up a kingdom that will never be destroyed, nor will it be left to another people. It will crush all those kingdoms and bring them to an end, but it will itself endure forever. This is the meaning of the vision of the rock cut out of a mountain, but not by human hands—a rock that broke the statue… . The great God has shown the king what will take place in the future…' The king said to Daniel, 'Surely your God is… a revealer of mysteries…'" (Da 2.44-45,47).

C. God's Clock," a context aid about Times and seasons of Israel

Times of Israel, Figure 31, page 263, is another context aid. Some scholars call this 490 year prophecy, God's Clock. When God's clock runs, it shows that God is dealing with the Jews either by discipline or by blessing during Israel's times of relating to him. However, in times when Israel is out of touch with God or in times of Jewish exile, the clock stops, and Jewish history pauses. For example, God's clock was stopped during Israel's enslavement in Babylon, and it is stopped now during the church age because of the Jews' present corporate unbelief. The church age years are not counted in Daniel's 490 year prophecy for Israel.

God's literary clock lays out a sequence of events. Daniel's prophecy of 490 years began in 445 B.C. when Artaxerxes in Babylon decreed that the Jews should return to their land to rebuild Jerusalem and its temple.

At the beginning of the future tribulation, the Jews will make a

Figure 31
Read left to right for progression of the 490 year prophecy.
Read down for facts about a period of time.
(Comments on the prophecies are in parentheses.)

ROUGH SKETCH OF TIMES AND SEASONS OF ISRAEL
God's Clock takes note of God's dealings with Israel for 490 years
Daniel 9.24-27

From c. 445 B.C. to the messianic kingdom: Seventy sevens = 490 years,
with those years of Israel's interim (the church age) not calculated in the 490 years

---

Clock runs··>Clock runs ····>   **(Clock stops)·· ->** Clock runs···> Clock runs···>

Artaxerxes' decree ··············>   **Church age·····>** Church in heaven··> Kingdom

---

Jews Rebuild··> Problems··>   **Israel's interim··>** Jacob's trouble···> Kingdom

7 sevens ····>   62 sevens····>   **Parenthetic·······>** One seven·········>Kingdom

(7 + 62 = 69 sevens)   **Church age length,** (70th seven)

(49 + 434 = 483 years·>)   **indeterminate->** 7 year tribulation-> Kingdom
  (483+7=490 years)

†

445 B.C . . .   c. 33 A.D.   Tribulation begins.   Then
 Date of "issuing of   **"Anointed One cut off"**   "Antichrist   the Rock
decree to rebuild"   (Messiah crucified)   will   smites
(From Artaxerxes'   confirm a   when
decree to Church Age =   **70 A.D.**   covenant…   Christ
69 sevens = 483 years)   **"Ruler (Titus)**   In the middle   returns
  who will come   of that 'seven'…
  will destroy the city   He will put an
  and the sanctuary.   end to sacrifice…
  (Titus did destroy   He will set up
  Jerusalem and   an abomination …"
  the temple.)   (At mid-tribulation, the
  Antichrist will end Jewish
  sacrifice and will seek to
  force worship of his image.)

TIMES OF THE GENTILES - A SUMMARY REVIEW
See the King's Dream in Figure 29, page 261
Daniel 2.36-45

From c. 605 B.C. in Babylon to the return of Christ to set up the Messianic kingdom = 5 Gentile empires:
BABYLON·>MEDE-PERSIA>GREECE·>ROME·>(Church age) REVIVED ROME·>(Jesus' return)

treaty with the endtime ruler, Antichrist (Da 9.27), who will guarantee them protection from their enemies. But something happens in the middle of that seven-year tribulation. Satan will be hurled from the heavenly atmosphere to earth by Michael the Archangel, and after Satan's banishment from the heavenlies to earth, Satan will take possession of the one called Antichrist, who will then break his treaty with Israel, will end Israel's temple sacrifices, will demand worship of his image, and will persecute the Jews.

But Antichrist overplays his hand. When he demands idol worship, the Jews will recognize him as a counterfeit Messiah, and fulfillment of God's promise to Israel is delayed. It says, "I will break the yoke off their necks and will tear off their bonds... No longer will foreigners enslave them..."[*] Jeremiah says this promise will be fulfilled when Jews serve the Lord their God and David their [resurrected] king (Je 3 0.8-9)). However, this will not happen until Christ returns and David is resurrected as king in the messianic kingdom (Je 30.8-9) (McGee 1981-83, Vol. 3, Je.30-31; JFB, Vol. 2, Part 2, 102).[*] According to these commentators and others, David will be king in Jerusalem under Christ, King of Kings.

Daniel's first prophetic endtime text and commentary

Daniel 9.24-27 (NIV)—Key to understanding biblical prophecy

"Seventy 'sevens' [490 years] are decreed for your people [Daniel's people the Jews] and your holy city [Jerusalem] to finish transgression, to put an end to sin, to atone for wickedness, to bring in everlasting righteousness, to seal up vision and prophecy, and to anoint the most holy [place]."

Commentary, Daniel 9.24-27—God's purpose for Israel for 490 years[*]:

1) to bring the rebellion to an end,

2) to put a stop to sin,

 3) to wipe away injustice,

4) to bring in everlasting righteousness,

5) to seal up [*to confirm* in NLT] vision and prophecy,

 6) to anoint the most holy place [temple in Jerusalem] (1-6, HCSB).

---

[*] God told Israel to submit to Babylon (Je 27.9-11). He promised he'd break the yoke of the Gentiles forever (Je 30.8,9). That will happen when Christ returns (Je 30.8, 9) (JFB, Vol 2 Pt 2, 102).

Daniel's second prophetic endtime text and commentary

Text for Daniel 9.25b-26a: "From the issuing of the decree [by Artaxerxes] to restore and rebuild Jerusalem until the Anointed One [Christ] comes, there will be seven 'sevens, [49 years]' and sixty-two 'sevens [434 years].' It will be rebuilt with streets and a trench, but in times of trouble. After the sixty-two 'sevens,' the Anointed One [Christ] will be cut off [crucified]... The people of the ruler who will come will destroy the city and the sanctuary [the temple]."

Commentary on Daniel 9.25b-26a:

City and temple rebuilding was fulfilled 49 years after 445 B.C. After 434 more years, Christ, the Anointed One, was "cut off [crucified]" (Culver 1954, 144, 148). The "ruler who will come" was fulfilled when Titus destroyed Jerusalem and its temple in A.D. 70. Christ will return after 490 years (This equals 49 years + 434 years + the 7 year tribulation in Figure 31, page 259[*]), but since the indeterminate years of the church age are excluded from Israel's 490 year calculation, we don't know when that happens.

Daniel's third prophetic endtime text and commentary

Text for Daniel 9.26b-27: "The end will come like a flood: War will continue until the end, and desolations have been decreed. He [the Antichrist] will confirm a covenant with many [Jews] for one 'seven.' In the middle [at mid-tribulation] he will put an end to sacrifice and offering. And on a wing he will set up an abomination that causes desolation, until the end..." [the abomination being an image of Antichrist to be worshiped in the Jewish temple]

Commentary on Daniel 9.26b-27:

At the bottom of Figure 31, page 259 is a summary of Times of the Gentiles. It is a prophecy about the revived Roman empire, which will bring war and misery like a flood until the end.

At the beginning of the tribulation, Israel will make a seven

---

[*] Jews had to go into captivity for 70 years, the number of sabbath years not observed for 490 years (70 x 7)—a period from rebuilding the temple until the yet future messianic kingdom begins, with the years of the church age not calculated therein. (A sabbath year came every seventh year.)

year peace treaty with Antichrist, but at midtribulation, Satan will be hurled to earth where he'll take possession of Antichrist, who will at that time stop Judaic sacrifice, will set up his image for worship, and will kill many Jews. But his mandatory idol worship will reveal to the Jews that he, Antichrist, is a fraud.

Now, let's get a look of what will happen to people involved during the messianic age. Antichrist and the false prophet will be thrown into the lake of fire, and Satan himself, during those thousand years of the kingdom, will be bound. Yet after the messianic kingdom, (Re 6) when Satan will be loosed by God, he will lead a rebellion, but he and his army will be defeated and cast into the lake of fire to be there forever.

D. The Old Testament, distinct but related to the New

As a person who thinks Jewish, I've discovered a Bible scholar who gives credence to my view of the Old Testament canon. Reviewer Stephen J. Andrews writes this about the view of theologian Christopher R. Seitz, who presents his view of the Old Testament canon in his book, *The Character of Christian Scripture: The Significance of a Two-Testament Bible*: Seitz disavows the tendency of modern scholars to value the Old Testament only when it is read in the light of the New Testament. Instead, Seitz writes that the Old Testament serves as a foundation for both testaments of scripture while at the same time still speaking in a separate but distinct and stable voice of its own. Seitz points out that Christian scripture has a unique two-testament character.

E. The benefits of reading the Bible as a unified whole

Since ancient scholars of Midrash saw Hebrew scripture as a unified whole, Martin Pickup asks, "'What if one regards the Old Testament books as the ancient Jews did—as the verbally inspired word of God? If every word of the Old Testament is truly the utterance of God, then a given statement in one Old Testament book would need to be considered not only within its own documentary context, but also in light of the broader context of the canon as a whole… They [ancient scholars] read the Old Testament not merely as a collection of different books written by different human authors… but as if it were all one book… the product of the mind of one author" (Pickup 2008, 359-360).

Take the challenge. Be willing to read the Bible as if it were a unified whole, whose author is the Lord. What a difference it makes! If you see God as the single author of the Bible, you receive life-giving faith (Ro 10.17). In my life as a youngster hearing stories about Daniel's loyalty to God, I envisioned the possibility of a desperate situation that would require knowledge or understanding I didn't have, and a conviction would arise within me that in such a moment, what I needed to know would come to me.

On the subject of inspired scripture, we can say that for Christians, the Bible's central directive is "God forbid that I should glory, save in the cross of our Lord Jesus Christ, by whom the world is crucified unto me, and I unto the world" (Ga 6.14 KJV). Simplified, that prayer is, "Lord, hide me behind the cross." For me, this is applicable whether I walk in victory, face defeat, or cannot see anything happening, for when I hide behind the cross, I cannot be puffed up by accomplishment, I cannot be crushed by disappointment, and I cannot be bored by everyday life. And since cut-and-dried formulas for living eventually fail, hiding behind the cross becomes the only reliable rule for life.

In Chapters 14 - 19, I have presented these themes:

The theme of the natural and spiritual (chapters 14-16)
The theme of God's grace and truth (Chapter 17)
The theme of the unity of scripture (chapters 18-19)

The next unit (Chapters 20-23) is about another biblical theme—the kingdom of heaven as presented in Jesus' parables.

Based upon the above information, it is possible to place the start of the captivity at 605 BC – since that is the very first time in which any Israelites were taken into captivity in Babylon.

Of course, even if 605 BC is used as the start of the captivity, there is still an apparent issue. Basically, the length of time between 605 BC and 537 BC is only 68 years – not 70 years.

THINK JEWISH
To understand the Bible

20 The kingdom of heaven in the parable of the sower

The parable of the sower shows that the people Jesus plants for the kingdom of heaven will either change their environment for God, or the environment will change them.

—The Author

All seven parables in Matthew 13 are significant because they inform Jesus' supporters and confound his enemies, but the parable of the sower is especially important because it discloses the meaning of the other six parables, for Jesus says, "Don't you understand this parable? How then will you understand any parable" (Mk 4.13)? So, I present the parable of the sower in chapters 20-22, but I present the other six parables of Matthew 13 only in chapter 23.

The kingdom of heaven in the parable of the sower (Mt 13.1-9):

 A. *Defining the kingdom of heaven: place, time, purpose*
 B. *Interpreting symbolism about the kingdom of heaven*
 C. *Contrasting two kinds of testimony in the kingdom of heaven*

A. Defining the kingdom of heaven: place, time, purpose

According to biblical scholars, the literal English translation of "the kingdom of heaven" from the original Greek is "the kingdom of the heavens." It is a phrase found only in Matthew, the gospel written with the Jewish people as the target audience; it is a phrase that signifies a place, a time, and a purpose.

As for the place element, the kingdom of heaven takes place in the "heavenlies"—that is, in the atmospheric realm where Satan set up his headquarters after losing his high position in heaven. It is a place of spiritual conflict. It is from there that Satan hijacked Adam's God-given authority in the earthly realm. He did this by enticing Adam to sin against God, who had given Adam authority over the earth. Satan wanted to accomplish this because earlier Satan, by his rebellion, had lost his authority in God's highest realm.

As for the time element, the proclamation of the kingdom of heaven began with Jesus' entry into his ministry. This was just as had been prophesied by ancient Judaic prophets and by John the Baptist in Jesus' day when he announced, "Behold the Lamb of God!" This was an announcement of Jesus' mission: He came to earth to die for you and me.

As for the purpose element in the kingdom of heaven, Jesus says this: "I will open my mouth in parables, [and] I will utter things hidden since the creation of the world" (Mt 13.35). For though there has been conflict between good and evil ever since Satan and his angels first rebelled, that battle came to a world-changing crisis at the time of Jesus' ministry on earth. And even though dark clouds were gathering, the Jews failed to understand the big change on the horizon. The movers and shakers of that day were concerned only with maintaining their political power and prestige, and the hometown folks in Nazareth were skeptical about this upstart named Jesus (Mt 13.53-58). These people, whether in high or lowly positions in society, were unaware that God himself had come to the planet for they were oblivious to the significance of what was about to happen—the blood sacrifice of the Lamb of God. There, on the cross, Jesus would win the victory for man. Yet even so, not until after Jesus' reign in the messianic kingdom will Satan's harassment of mankind end totally. Sin and death will be destroyed, and Satan will be cast into the lake of fire to be there forever.

A startling plan

In Matthew 13, Jesus tells of his world-changing plan in seven parables about the kingdom of heaven. In the first parable, which he himself names "the parable of the sower,"* he lays out God's plan. What he reveals is that he would reveal himself to the world by embedding his living Word in individuals scattered throughout the world—unlike in the past when he revealed himself through the nation, Israel, which was anchored in one place, as portrayed in Hebrew scripture. *Then from the testimony of these planted believers in the new day that was dawning, Jesus the sower was to reap a harvest of believers for the kingdom of heaven.*

---

* Some have called this Matthew 13 parable by the name of "the parable of the soils.," but Jesus calls this parable "the parable of the sower." The focus is on his world-changing ministry.

Differing responses to the gospel

Here's the text of the first parable of Matthew 13: "A farmer [sower] went out to sow his seed. As he was scattering the seed, some fell along the path, and the birds came and ate it up. Some fell on rocky places, where it did not have much soil. It sprang up quickly, because the soil was shallow. But when the sun came up, the plants were scorched, and they withered because they had no root. Other seed fell among thorns, which grew up and choked the plants. Still other seed fell on good soil, where it produced a crop—a hundred, sixty or thirty times what was sown. He who has ears, let him hear" (Mt 13.3b-9).

Note that Jesus speaks of the planted seeds as *people*. He says, "Listen then to what the parable of the sower means. When *anyone* hears the message about the kingdom and does not understand it, the evil one comes and snatches away what was sown in that person's heart. This is the seed sown along the path. What was sown on rocky places is the *man* who hears the word and at once receives it with joy. But since he has no root, he lasts only a short time. When trouble or persecution comes because of the word, he quickly falls away. What was sown among the thorns is the *man* who hears the word, but the worries of this life and the deceitfulness of wealth choke it, making it unfruitful. But what was sown on good soil is the *man* who hears the word and understands it. He produces a crop, yielding a hundred, sixty or thirty times what was sown" (Mt 13.18-23 NIV 1978. Italics added).

Preparation for soul winning ministry

This parable prepares Jesus' disciples for their future soul-winning ministry. They would learn that the people Jesus plants for the kingdom of heaven will either change their environment for God, or the environment will change them.

In this parable of the sower (Mt 13.1-9, 16-23), Jesus prepares his followers for entrance into a new covenant in the present age. Although good and evil will continue to exist, exemption from eternal damnation will come through God's eternal new covenant, ratified by the blood of the Lamb of God—not through God's old covenant, which was ratified by the temporary blood offerings of Israel's sacrificial animals. Jesus' sacrifice was to be the crisis point at which God begins his reversal of Satan's work in the world. Today, though good and evil continue in the kingdom of heaven, Christ on the cross has already won the victory for every believer.

The testimony of those who hear the gospel

Now let's look at the testimony of each person in the parable of the sower. As you read, pay attention to the part that understanding plays in the hearts of those persons who hear the message. The one planted beside the path in a hard place soon loses his testimony, for he has *no understanding.* Jesus says, "When anyone hears the message about the kingdom and does not understand it, the evil one comes and snatches away what was sown in his heart. This is the seed sown along the path" (Mt 13.19). This person of the first seed loses his testimony before he ever reaches out to tell others the good news, for it is snatched away by Satan's emissaries, the birds (Mt 13.19). This *first seed* has no understanding and no witness, in contrast to the *fourth seed,* which is about a man with understanding, who has a fruitful witness for God. About the fourth seed, Jesus says, "But what was sown on good soil is the man who hears the word and *understands it.* He produces a crop, yielding a hundred, sixty or thirty times what was sown" (Mt 13.23. Italics added).

And since the persons of the second and third seeds have some understanding, their testimony is fruitful, but not in full measure. The *second seed,* the one in rocky ground, is not rooted and grounded in love (Eph 3.17,18) and soon withers away under the heat of persecution or other troubles. This "is the *man* who hears the word and at once receives it with joy. But since he has no root, he lasts only a short time" before losing his testimony (Mt 13.20b,21. Italics added). The *third seed,* in spite of his good intentions, allows "the worries of this life and the deceitfulness of wealth" (Mt 13.22) to take his eyes off Jesus. He becomes unable to testify fully and freely.

But *ah, the fourth!* That believer is like the three year old who loves his mother and follows her everywhere she goes around the house, talking all the while. So too the Christian who loves Jesus follows him wherever he leads and communicates with him all through the day. That Christian understands who God is, what life is about, and draws others in his wake. With this kind of understanding, he seeks God's glory above all else, and he can stay on track by following the counsel of this verse:: "He that speaketh of himself seeketh his own glory: but he that seeketh his glory that sent him, the same is true, and no unrighteousness is in him" (Jn 7.17,18 KJV). This is a verse that helps me stay on course.

God's purpose is to reap a harvest of believers through whom he can reveal his grace and truth to the world so that others can enter the kingdom of heaven. Earlier in the history of the world—before Jesus came to earth—the lost had *to come to* Israel to be saved. Now Christians are told *to go out* into all the world to seek the lost (Mt 28.19,20) and to proclaim to them "the good news."

This scattering of believers in every part of the world is illustrated in the parable of the sower.

A divine encounter on an airplane flight

Earlier I told you about the adventures that a friend and I had when we presented the gospel with a tool called "the wordless book," a little booklet without pictures or words. Ever since using this tool to lead young people to the Lord at the county fair booth in Petaluma, California, I've used this little booklet to reach out to others when I have the opportunity.

Usually, I'm on the lookout for prospective Christians, but sometimes if I'm reluctant to speak up, the Lord sets me up anyway. That happened to me on an airplane flight. I was reading a serious Christian book, *Absolute Surrender,* by Andrew Murray, and ironically, I was hiding the title from view. The young man sitting next to me, probably in his early twenties, looked over and asked what I was reading. "Nonfiction," I said. I thought that would end the conversation, but he asked, "Is it interesting?" "Yes." He was persistent: "Oh? what's it about?" Finally, by this time, I saw that the Lord was setting me up to tell him the gospel.

He listened attentively, even commenting now and then. So,

after I finished the wordless book presentation, I asked my usual question: "Would you like to pray and ask Jesus to come into your heart?" What a reaction that invitation set off! He immediately boomed out for everyone on the airplane to hear: "In all my life, that's the most ridiculous thing I ever heard… and on an airplane flight!" His reaction was visceral, not necessarily from hostility but from dumbfounded astonishment.

But that outburst didn't stop our conversation. We even talked more about spiritual matters. As we conversed, I found out that his girlfriend, who didn't speak English, was sitting behind us and that he was learning her language. And as we talked, I learned that he was one of those boy wonders in the computer world. When he gave me his business card, he said he had a business with twenty employees and he hoped for it to "go public" before long. Then afterwards he said others had been talking to him about the Lord. Evidently, God had targeted him and had raised up people to talk to him.

Telling the gospel with the wordless book

Ordinarily, my initial approach to a person that I want to reach for the Lord is simple. While holding up the little wordless book, I ask, "Would you like to hear a story?" Then I tell the person that he can stop me after the first page if he doesn't want me to go on, but no one ever stops me. Then I hold up the gold page and explain that the gold page is about heaven. At that point, the listener can see where I'm going with the story. The beauty of the wordless book approach is that the presenter can make the story long or short and can quote however many verses are appropriate for the situation. Also, the listener can see that there's a beginning and an ending, which means that he doesn't have to start looking for a way to get himself our of the encounter gracefully.

Also, as in the above incident, ninety-nine percent of the time, I give a closing invitation for a person to receive the Lord then and there, even if I think the person may already be a Christian or if it seems that the person will probably say no. That way, if the person is a Christian, the invitation gives him a chance to testify, and if he's not a Christian and says no, then he has to live with his answer. The ones who say yes are the ones whom God has prepared for that moment. They are ones whom others have influenced, for many people plant seeds, but very few harvest.

Often God gives me a clue to show me that the person I'm talking with is someone I should invite into the kingdom. That happened, for example, on a long shuttle bus trip from Petaluma to the San Francisco airport. As we were riding along, some large black and white birds appeared in the sky, evidently in migration. A young woman sitting in front of me noticed the birds and turned around to talk to me about them, even though she was sitting with a friend, with whom she could have conversed. I saw that as an opportunity to converse with her, and I asked her if she would like to hear a story. It turned out that her heart was tender because she had just come back from a funeral for her nephew. So after I told her the story of the wordless book, she was ready to pray with me and ask the Lord to come into her heart.

Then I told her the green page—the page for growing. We grow by reading God's Word, by praying, and by doing what he wants us to do. And after a person receives the Lord, I hold up my hand with five fingers outstretched, and I quote what Jesus promises to those who belong to him. I point to each finger as I say these five words that Jesus spoke: "I-will-never-leave-you." And I often end by asking, "How long will Jesus live in your heart? That's when a person realizes that Christ will be in his heart forever.

B. Interpreting symbolism about the kingdom of heaven

Comparing scripture with scripture to unlock meaning

Note that symbolism sometimes carries over between parables, for symbolism can be interpreted by comparing scripture with scripture. For example, we can carry over the symbolism of birds from the parable of the sower to the parable of the mustard seed (Mt 13.31-32). Birds in the parable of the sower represent evil ones who destroy a believer's testimony. And since the parable of the mustard seed has parallels with the parable of the weeds, we can infer that the birds nesting in its tree are sons of the evil one, too. This parable of the mustard seed says, "The kingdom of heaven is like a mustard seed, which a man took and planted in his field. Though it is the smallest of all your seeds, yet when it grows, it is the largest of gar-den plants and becomes a tree, so that the birds of the air come and perch in its branches." The good news for a believer is that the evil birds are not an integral part of the tree and hence cannot become an actual part of the kingdom of heaven unless they themselves become believers in God.

Here, we see parallels between the parable of the weeds and the parable of the sower. "The one who sowed the good seed is the Son of Man." In both parables, the field is the world, and the good seeds are sons of the kingdom (Mr 13.37,38). Also, Jesus is the sower and the seeds are people in whom his Word dwells. Finally, the enemy is Satan that plants people in God's field.

The way of the cross in soul winning

In the parable of the sower, the symbolism of the seed is an apt choice, for we know that seeds must die in order to multiply and produce a crop. So too, Christians must die to self in order to fulfill their mission of bringing the lost into the kingdom of heaven. Esther Ahn Kim in her book, *If I Perish*, shows that she met a crisis by yielding to the way of the cross. She tells about her life in Korea during the occupation of Korea by Japan, in World War II. When Japanese occupiers commanded a crowd of students and teachers to bow in worship at a pagan shrine, she refused. There she stood, erect and alone. That's the day that Esther Kim marks as the day she died; she expected to be executed. Later, she was imprisoned under other charges, There, in the degradation of Japanese prisons and under threat of death, she lived out her testimony about God's faithfulness. In prison, she was used by God to win people to the Lord, and she became known far and wide for her witness—for the way of the cross is the way to winning souls for God. Figure 32 shows that one biblical passage can clarify the meaning of another.

Identity of the seed in the parable of the sower
Figure 32
The symbolism of the seed determined by biblical context

—In the parable of the weeds, "the good seed stands for the sons of the kingdom" (Mt 13.24). The seeds are *people*.

—In Luke's parable of the sower (Lk 8.11), *"the seed is the word of God."*

—In the gospel of John, the seed is *Jesus, the Word of God* (Jn 1.1-14).

—*Then,* by putting the above concepts together, we realize that *the seeds that are planted in the parable of the sower represent people in whom Jesus, the living Word, abides.*

C. Contrasting two kinds of testimony in the kingdom of heaven

I see two kinds of testimony in the kingdom of heaven—exemplar testimony and outreaching testimony. Matthew 13 illustrates outreaching fruitfulness in winning others to Christ, and John 15 illustrates exemplar fruitfulness that shines out from a person's character. I discovered this when I happened to look at the parable of the sower side by side with John 15.1-8, which is a word picture of a vine and its branches. In John 15, Jesus says, "I am the vine; you [believers] are the branches." When I read that, I realized that the sap, which imparts life, flows *directly* from Jesus the vine to the branches, the fruit-bearing Christians. In this symbolism, John shows that the Holy Spirit works within a believer to produce fruit of the Spirit—"love, joy, peace, patience, kindness, goodness, faithfulness, gentleness, and self control" (Ga 5.22). Here we see that the vine's fruitfulness results from God's presence in a person's personality and character. Exemplar testimony is about infusion of the fruit of the Spirit into his inner being where God dwells. On the other hand, fruitfulness in the parable of the sower is outreaching. It's about a person reaching out in testimony to bring others to Christ.

From my childhood experience, I can illustrate both kinds of testimony. When I was about eight or younger, I was impressed by a few words from our family's Baptist neighbor as she talked with our family at the funeral parlor after a car accident had killed her husband. Her words that day made a lasting impression on me. On that occasion, she revealed her trust in God by speaking in a familiar way about the Lord. The words she spoke that day are an example of how *words of testimony* can glorify God.

My mother, on the other hand, is an example of one whose *deeds and demeanor* throughout her life gave a powerful message. Though a college graduate—rare for women in those days—she had a beautiful, childlike trust in God. (Her graduating high school class in early Corpus Christi days had only a handful of students. Population today is 316,000.) She read Bible stories to us children, knelt every night to pray, gathered neighbor children to take to Sunday School, and was the one to jump up to serve our family at dinnertime when we needed something from the kitchen. And she was the embodiment of wisdom and love. Yet… I didn't hear my Presbyterian mother talk to others about the Lord in the familiar way that the Baptist neighbor did at the funeral parlor that day. What etched that moment in my memory was that I was surprised and touched by God through this neighbor's words, for to me as a small child, she had seemed somewhat distant and aloof. The choice, however, is not to live the life *or* talk the talk. Both are important.

The transforming power of the gospel

In my adult life, when I've observed others who testify, I've noticed that someone with a dramatic conversion can win others to the Lord by simply testifying to the change brought to their lives, I could see how they could win others to God, but I didn't have that kind of conversion. In my life, although I cannot testify to an overwhelming and dramatic life change, I do remember "joining the church" at the age of eight, at which time, the pastor spoke of stepping over the line from darkness into light.

Later after I was married and we had one child and another on the way, I witnessed the total transformation of my husband, who heard the gospel and responded. And though he walked with the Lord only six or eight weeks before he turned away from God's call, I became eager to learn more about reaching others for the Lord, for I saw firsthand how God's supernatural work can radically change a human being, and I saw how the simple gospel is the means to accomplish this supernatural work.

Still later, after our family moved to the Northwest, I faced the issue of what being born again is about. There, I visited with my elderly great Aunt Anna, a feisty redhead who was an enthusiastic fan of a Major League baseball team. Like most of my mother's relatives, she was a regular churchgoer. After I had visited her little country church one time, I decided that next time, if I was asked whether I was "saved," I would respond by saying, "Define your terms"… but no one asked me, and I didn't have to say anything.

Seeking witness opportunities

Now, I can see that having to set up my defense mechanism— "the define-your-terms plan"—made me aware that I had a fuzzy idea of what the gospel is about. At a later time, even though I was confident about my salvation, I took a little red gospel of John and signed the gospel invitation to receive the Lord and dated it. Nevertheless, I knew as a child that I belonged to the Lord. One of my earliest memories is of sitting on the curb with a little neighbor friend, Rose Mary Brasher talking with her about God.

If talk about winning souls is disquieting to Christians who have had no experience in evangelism, let me give you a word of encouragement about the kind of testimony that can be expressed by a Christian's life. The gospel is simple but powerful. In fact, the desire to evangelize is planted in the heart of the believer, and that desire can be fulfilled even before gaining knowledge about how to reach people for the Lord. For me, an opportunity arose while our family was living in a tiny house in the little town of Rainier, Oregon. This had been my husband's hometown since his family moved from Kentucky when he was about twelve. Rainier was where we lived when our third child was born.

In chapter 15, I described the primitive conditions and the difficulties that we faced when we first moved to that little house. That period of my life shows that no matter how limiting the circumstances nor how minimal the experience in winning others for the Lord, believers can nevertheless find opportunities to reach out tin faith to others to touch their lives for God, for there in that tiny house, such an opportunity arose for me. There I met someone who had been so abused by her husband, that she had allowed him to control her life to the extent that she became unable to make any move to free herself from physical harm, but when I met her, she had gotten out of that situation. Also, she had a condition that blocked sensation in her face, which meant she could suffer bodily harm, such as from a burn or other injury and not be aware of it. As I listened to her plight, my heart went out to her, and I was inspired to have faith to believe that with friendship and prayers, I could be helpful in pointing her to the Lord.

After she moved away, I heard that she had become a Christian, and I realized the Lord had used me in reaching out to her in spite of my lack of understanding about soul winning. For those of us who are Christians, let's encourage each other to reach out to others, no matter how limiting our circumstances, our knowledge, or our experience because God will teach us what we need to know to touch the lives of others if that is what we long for.

Let's close with an example of an ordinary kind of witness. This took place in Petaluma, California after my eight year old son Dave and I moved there. This was after my husband's death and after the other four children had left home.

One day after teaching my evening class in Bible Literature, I talked with the principal and the secretary. Then when the principal credited God for his deliverance from excessive drinking, the conversation turned to God, and at that point, the secretary began to ask questions about how to know God's will. This led me to tell them the story of the wordless book. While I was there, the night watchman, a Christian, came in and heard what we were talking about, and that became the beginning of my acquaintance with him. God so orders our lives that our paths cross the paths of others to accomplish his purpose in our lives.

In this unit on understanding the kingdom of heaven, this chapter is the first of three chapters about the parable of the sower.

21 The context for the parable of the sower

Let's encourage each other to reach out to others, no matter how limiting our circumstances, our knowledge, or our experience because God will teach us what we need to know to touch the lives of others if that is what we long for.

—The Author

When we "think Jewish," we find that the Matthew 13 parables are more than just stories that give tips on how to live. The first parable is the parable of the sower, which gives God's overall plan for the kingdom of heaven. Therefore, to understand God's plan, we will examine this parable in its kingdom of heaven context, in its immediate textual context, and in its modern context.

Understanding the parable of the sower in context:

A. The parable of the sower in its kingdom of heaven context
B. The parable of the sower in its immediate textual context
C. The parable of the sower in its modern context

A. The parable of the sower in its kingdom of heaven context
In the days of Jesus, John the Baptist electrified the people in Israel with this proclamation: "Repent, for the kingdom of heaven is near" (Mt 4.17). People went out to the wilderness to hear this Hebrew prophet, whose "clothes were made of camel's hair" and whose "food was locusts and wild honey" (Mt 3:4). And since Israel had not heard from a prophet of God for about four hundred years, John's message shook the nation of Israel to its core.

Jesus said no prophet was greater than John the Baptist, for he knew John was chosen ro come in the role of the Old Testament prophet Elijah (Ml 4.5). That is, John, was to proclaim the coming of Israel's promised Messiah. Therefore, at the end of Jesus' ministry when he was hanging on the cross helpless as a man, the people were disenchanted by the turn of events and cried out in mockery: "Let's see if Elijah comes to save him" (Mt 27.49).

Although the message of repentance and the message of the

imminent coming of the messianic kingdom captured the imagination of the Jewish people, they didn't understand the ramifica-
tions of what John proclaimed when he pointed at Jesus and said,
"Look, the Lamb of God who takes away the sin of the world" (Jn
1.29). And although Isaiah 53 and other scriptures prophesy of Jesus' crucifixion, neither the Jews nor John the Baptist understood
that Messiah had to die as a sacrifice to save his people from their
sins. Their expectation was simply that their Messiah would bring
victory and triumph to their nation. That will not happen, however, until the future when Jesus returns to earth with the church.

Since Jesus came to earth to present himself as the Messiah of
Israel, what brought about the delay of his kingdom? The situation
was that Israel's religious leaders envied Jesus' popularity. And because they feared the loss of their standing before the people and
before the ruling Roman government, they began to plot how to
bring about his death. So at that point, Jesus presented parables
to prepare his followers for "the delay" of his kingdom. He used
parables to avoid direct confrontation with religious leaders, and
though the tide was turning, the *major* crisis still lay ahead.

Although other gospels repeat the parables of Matthew 13,
they substitute the broader phrase, "the kingdom of God" instead
of the phrase, "the kingdom of heaven." But that doesn't mean
that both phrases mean the same all the time, says W. E. Vine. He
says, "With regard to… 'the kingdom of God' and the 'kingdom
of the heavens [literal Greek]' while they are often used interchangeably, it does not follow that in every case they mean exactly
the same and are quite identical" (Vine 1966, 295). Vine is saying
that though sometimes the two terms are interchangeable, sometimes they are not—for the kingdom of heaven is a period within
the overall kingdom of God.[*]

The seven Matthew 13 parables are about the kingdom of
heaven—the last six of which begin with specifics about that kingdom. Those six begin with "The kingdom of heaven is like…"
And though the first parable, the parable of the sower, does not
begin with that phrase, it fits in with the last six parables because

---

[*] Groups and subgroups are not always interchangeable: All lilies are flowers, but not all flowers are lilies.

it describes the beginning of the kingdom of heaven by showing Jesus planting his church on earth by embedding his living Word in people. The Matthew 13 parables begin with the planting of the church in the parable of the sower, and they end with the judgment of unbelievers at the great white throne in the parable of the Weeds and in the parable of the Net.

The kingdom of heaven is a phrase found only in Matthew, which was written specifically for Jews. So let's look at the time periods as though they were children's nested blocks, one within another. Within the kingdom of God is the kingdom of heaven, and within the kingdom of heaven are two people groups, Israel and the church, which pass through three time periods: the church age, the tribulation, and the messianic kingdom, as shown below.

Figure 33 below shows the church and Israel in the timeframe that Matthew calls "the kingdom of heaven."*

Figure 33
The church and Israel in the kingdom of heaven

THE CHURCH

The church age:	The tribulation:	The messianic Age:
It begins with Pentecost and ends with the rapture of the church.	It begins after the church is raptured to heaven and ends with the return of Christ to earth.	It begins with Christ's return and lasts a thousand years under Christ as King of Kings.

_____Eternity->

ISRAEL

Israel's Interim:	At midtribulation:	The messianic age:
Jews as a people reject Christ.	After severe testing, the Jews will reject Antichrist and will repent.	Christ will return. Israel will be redeemed and will be exalted on earth. under the reign of Christ.

* You may wonder why "the kingdom of heaven" has that title since it is about a time on *earth.*. The literal translation from Greek is "the kingdom of the heavens." According to a note in Vine's *Dictionary*, spiritual warfare takes place in the heavens during the time of "the kingdom of the heavens," and this atmospheric realm is a place of spiritual conflict between good and evil.

The kingdom of heaven, the subject of the Matthew 13 parables, includes the following:

1) the present church age of indeterminate length,

2) the seven year tribulation

3) the thousand-year messianic kingdom.

The kingdom of heaven began when Jesus began his ministry on earth and will end when eternity begins, for that's when conflict between good and evil will end.

Also within the time period of the kingdom of heaven lies the messianic kingdom, during which evil will be in abeyance and death will be rare, but immediately after the messianic kingdom, evil will be unbound until the time that Satan and his people are finally cast into the lake of fire where Antichrist and the false prophet will have been held throughout the thousand-year messianic kingdom. Only at eternity will evil in God's creation be abolished forever. Then after that cleansing, Christ will submit the kingdom to the Father for eternity.

Let's review. The kingdom of heaven includes the present church age, the tribulation, and the messianic kingdom.

Let's look more closely at the kingdom of heaven:

1) Let's look at Christ's glorified body in the kingdom of heaven.
2) Let's look at the church in the kingdom of heaven.
3) Let's look at Israel in the kingdom of heaven.
4) Let's look at unbelievers after the end of the kingdom of heaven.
5) Let's note when sin and death will be destroyed. (1Co 15.26b).

1) Let's look at Christ in his glorified body in the kingdom of heaven.
During and after the messianic kingdom, Jesus will reign in his glorified, resurrection body, which will forever bear the evidence of his crucifixion—the nail prints in his hands and feet, and a scar from the sword that pierced him in his side. Those scars are the ones Jesus showed to Thomas after his resurrection. He told him, "Reach out your hand and put it into my side. Stop doubting and believe." Those scars remain as a reminder of how great is God's love for humankind. I remember how amazed I was when I found

out that the Bible reveals that Jesus would always have a human body, though a glorified, immortal one. His glorified body will be the same kind of body Christians will receive (1 Co 15.52) in their rapture to heaven.

2) Let's look at the church in the kingdom of heaven.

The church exists on earth in the present church age, at which time human Christians enter the kingdom of heaven only *spiritually.* (Christians enter the kingdom by the same born-again experience by which future human Jewish survivors of the tribulation will enter the messianic kingdom when Christ returns [Pentecost 1958]). The church age lies between the Pentecostal birth of the church. and its rapture to heaven. In the last days, the church will return from heaven with Christ as his bride to reign with him in the messianic kingdom on earth.

3) Let's look at Israel in the kingdom of heaven.

The Bible reveals that for Jews as a people, the present church age is Israel's interim, a pause in God's program for them as a people. It's a time when they have no Judaic temple and no sacrifice for sin except for the sacrifice made by the Lord Jesus for all individual Jews and Gentiles who are willing to accept him as Savior.

The present church age comes after the tribulation period. During the tribulation, the church will be in heaven being purified to become Christ's bride, while at the same time, Jews as a people on earth will be tested to prove their faithfulness before their entry into the messianic kingdom. In the tribulation, under Antichrist's persecution, the Jews will repent, will turn to Christ, and will enter the thousand-year messianic kingdom, during which every knee will bow under the iron-scepter rule of Christ/Messiah (Ps 2.9; Rc 2.27). This will include both Jews and Gentiles. In that kingdom, though all the first ones who enter it will be redeemed by the new birth, some later descendants will reject Christ (Je 31.33-41) and will suffer the consequences.

4) Let's look at unbelievers after the end of the kingdom of heaven.

After the thousand-year messianic kingdom, Satan is released, and the kingdom's unbelievers are glad to join him in his last bid to usurp God's throne. These are the unbelievers in the messianic kingdom who, against their will, have been forced to bow down before Christ. After the thousand year kingdom, these rebels will join Satan's army and surround Jerusalem, but before they engage in battle, they will be consumed by fire from heaven (Re 20.9b). What this rebellion reveals is that in spite of a perfect environment under Christ and without Satan to tempt them during the messianic kingdom, there will still be some people in the kingdom who will nevertheless choose to go their own way; they will reject God no matter what happens. These are those who purport to seek utopia, a perfect society, but who in reality seek a world without God.

In the end, Satan will be cast into the lake of fire (Re 20.10) where Antichrist and his false Prophet will have existed during the thousand year messianic kingdom (Re 19.20). At the great white throne after Satan's downfall, wicked people—both the living and the resurrected dead—will be judged for their *deeds*. In other words, they will be judged by what they have done, not by what Christ has done for them. Therefore, before God the Father as Judge on the great white throne (Re 20.11-15), they will stand without Jesus as their Advocate and without Jesus as their Savior from sin. That means that by their own choice, they will stand condemned for their unforgiven sin.

5) Let's note when sin and death, will be destroyed. (1Co 15.26b).

At the end of time, Christ hands the kingdom over to his Father (1Co 15.24,28). That will be when sin and death are destroyed forever, and that's when eternity begins.

B. The parable of the sower in its immediate textual context

In the immediate textual context of Matthew 13, Jesus has reached a turning point in his ministry, for he knows his enemies are plotting his death. He stops proclaiming that the kingdom of heaven is near and instead begins to prepare believing Jews for an intervening era, the present church age. This knowledge will give the Jews patience to await the promised kingdom; it will prepare them to deal with the kingdom's delay.

In this immediate textual context when Jesus presents the Matthew 13 parables, he has become so popular with the common folk that he has to preach from a boat to protect himself from physical

harm when the surging crowd presses in too forcefully (Mt 13.1.2).
Yet at the same time, his popularity continues to enrage Jewish
leaders, who in their envy and hostility have already blasphemed
the Holy Spirit by accusing him of doing miracles through the
power of demons (Mt 12.24b). These are leaders who had hardened
their hearts when Jesus denounced their cities where he did most
of his miracles. Though the rebels conspire against Jesus (Mt 12.14),
they do not harm him at the time of his presentation of the Matthew 13 parables because they fear an uprising of the masses.

Also, in the immediate textual context, Jesus faces the unbelief
of his mother and brothers, who have heard that the crowds have
disrupted his life and robbed him of time to eat or rest, and they
worry about him (Mt 12.43-50), so they go to him to take charge of
him, for they say, "He is out of his mind" (Mk 3.20, 21). At this time,
they do not yet believe in him and would block him from his
ministry if they could.

When Jesus' family arrives where he is teaching, he responds
to their unbelief by refusing to leave his followers to see them.
Instead, he asks, "'Who are my mother and who are my brothers?'
Pointing to his disciples, he says, 'Here are my mother and my
brothers. For whoever does the will of my Father in heaven is my
brother and sister and mother'" (Mt 12.48-50). Jesus' response to his
family's unbelief epitomizes his willingness to accept rejection by
his larger family, the Jews.

Now the shadow of the cross looms before Jesus. He stops saying that "the kingdom of heaven is near" and prepares his Jewish
believers for a delay. His presentation of the Matthew 13 parables
comes at this pivotal moment in his life.

C. The parable of the sower in its modern context

What about living today in the mad rush of modern times? Is
reaching others with the good news of the gospel just another task
a Christians has to add to his to-do list? As it is, many Christians
already feel overwhelmed by the Bible's emphasis on witnessing
to others. I know the feeling. Years ago I used to read books about
witnessing and about the questions people ask, but when I tried
it, the other person never asked the right questions. But even if

the thought of witnessing isn't overwhelming, at least trying to do it may seem to be awkward or even fearsome. Therefore, for those of us who are Christians, let's encourage each other to reach out to others, no matter how limited our circumstances, our knowledge, or our experience because God will teach us what we need to know to touch the lives of others if that is what we long for.

Let me close this section on witnessing today in the modern context by telling about two experiences in my life when the Lord went before me to prepare the way. One of my first direct testimonies by words and scripture happened while our family lived with my husband's mother in Rainier, Oregon. This was during the time my husband was in the state hospital—a temporary interval when I fell heir to his side job—running our one-cab taxi service. The fares were mostly people from Rainier or from Longview across the river—townspeople or sailors and workers from the Longview port. This was before I had learned about the wordless book as a tool for evangelism.

One regular customer of our taxi—a little, elderly man—would go to town when he got his pension check and would spend that money but would save enough to take the cab home. Driving him home, I realized I would have a chance to lead this lonely man to the Lord. And so I stopped at a house on the road, left the man in the cab, and went in to ask Mrs. Fidler to tell this man about the way of salvation, but she turned down my request. She said that he was my assignment from the Lord, not hers. So as I drove further down the road to the man's home, I wondered what I was supposed to do. Once there, I went into his house with him to talk to him about the Lord. In my memory, it seems like the house had a dirt floor, but whether that was the case or not, it was a humble abode.

What made my task difficult is that I found when talking with him that he was hard of hearing. Nevertheless, armed with only one verse, I kept repeating it. I shouted, "If we confess our sins, he is faithful and just to forgive us our sins, and to cleanse us from all unrighteousness" (1Jn 1.9 KJV). I continued to shout the verse until he grasped not only the words I was saying but also their meaning.

This took some time… but finally, the light broke through, and he became a new creature in Christ. The Lord had set me up.

A second example of the Lord setting up the circumstances for my witness happened at a time, when I was in my late eighties and had been living in San Diego near my son John and his family for about a decade or more. In that experience, I learned that the simple statement, "Jesus died for *my* sins" can become a powerful statement, as you will see when I tell you the story.

Before the occasion of that testimony, I went to a neighboring complex to look for an elderly couple—strangers to whom I wanted to express my gratitude for a kind act they had done for one of my sons when he was visiting me. I knew the location of the building, but it had two condos.

I rang the doorbell of one of the condos, and a young woman answered the door. That was the wrong condo, I found out, but in conversing with the young woman about my search, I found her to be very friendly. She even introduced me to her mother sitting in the background, and she told me her name was Parisa (not her real name). So after that encounter, I realized that her friendliness was a clue for me that the Lord would give me an opportunity to witness to her later on. To take that opportunity, I had to overcome my reluctance, for this was going to be "a cold call."

Finally, one afternoon, I decided, "This is the day I'm going to ring Parisa's doorbell and talk to her." I would just ring the doorbell and tell Parisa the story of the wordless book. That was my mission. I rang the doorbell, but a man answered. "Is Parisa home?" I asked. "Yes," he said, and he called her. She arrived at the door and the man, who turned out to be her father, left. I reminded Parisa about my meeting her before and asked if I could tell her a story out of a little book that has no pictures or words. She was quite cordial and invited me to come in. She said her family had company but that we could talk, and she led me into the living room. The place, which was quite elegant, had a floor that looked like white marble.

I showed her the little wordless book with no pictures or words—only colored pages—and as I usually do, I told her I would tell her the first page and then if she wanted me to, I would stop. At one point in telling the story, she said, "I don't believe that," but she still showed interest in hearing more. To tell the story, I opened to the first page, the gold page, and said, "God is love, and he wants us to go to heaven to live with him forever. Then I quoted John 3.16: "God so loved the world that he sent his only Son…" Next I said, "Unfortunately we have done wrong things and have shut ourselves off from God's presence" and I turned to the dark page and quoted Romans 3.23: "All have sinned and fall short of the glory of God." With that statement, Parisa said that she knew that she had done wrong things.

Then I held up the booklet and held the middle pages together as if those pages were a wall between God on the gold page and the sinner on the dark page. I explained that God has a problem now because he loves us and wants to reach us but he cannot break down the wall because we have chosen to build that wall of sin. And since God is holy and we are sinners, that wall prevents us from connecting with him, for the Bible says, "The wages of sin is death" (Ro 6.23).

Then I gave Parisa time to think about how God's problem could be solved before I turned to the red page and said, "Fortunately, God is not only all-love; he is also all-wise, and he solved the problem by coming to earth as a man, Jesus. He paid the price for our sin by dying in our place so that we may live.

So, as I turned to the red page, I showed her that by opening that page, I eliminated the wall between the sinner's dark page and God's gold page. I showed her that the red page is about the blood of Jesus. Then with the wordless book, I showed that his blood removes the wall of sin, for it's Jesus' blood sacrifice that cleanses and makes us whole and breaks down the wall between us and God (1Jn 1.9). I quoted the verse that says, "If we confess our sins, he is faithful and just and will forgive us our sins and purify us from all unrighteousness" (1Jn 1.9).

Finally, for the white page, I explained that after being cleansed by the blood of Christ, we are new creatures in him. "Therefore if any man be in Christ, he is a new creature: old things are passed away; behold, all things are become new" (2Co 5.17 KJV)!

Then to tell Parisa how a person can receive the Lord, I went through the wordless book a second time. I said that to receive the Lord, you have to know that God loves you (gold page) and that you are a sinner (dark page). You have to know that Jesus is the only one who can save you. And you have to know that if you ask him to come into your heart, he will come in, and you will be born again (red page.) And then in a third time through the book, I told her the prayer to pray. I turned to the dark page and said, "I know I'm a sinner." I turned to the red page and said, "I know Jesus is the only one that can forgive me of my sins and save me." I turned to the page of light, the white page and said, "Lord, come into my heart and make me a new person. Thank you. Amen."

After the story, Parisa said, "Many men have died for humanity." And I paused and said very deliberately, "Yes… but Jesus died for *my* sins!"

That's when Parisa leaped to her feet and ran to the door. That's where her dog had been standing, waiting to be allowed to go outside. Obviously, what I said had hit home—that "Jesus died for *my* sins." She said, "Let's take him outside." I was expecting her to open the door and let the dog go out. So again she had to say, "Come on. Let's take him outside." I think she wanted to talk to me away from her parents and their guests in a nearby room. Surely, the Lord had set this up.

So as we continued to walk, I learned that Parisa's family was Muslim—that her mother prayed to Allah three times a day, but that was the extent of her Islamic participation. I also learned that Parisa was in her last term before college graduation and that she would be busy the next few weeks taking finals and that she'd be too busy to see anyone during that time.

After we were outside, I said, "Hey, why don't we go to my condo!" She agreed, Then after we crossed the street to my complex, she commented that she had never been over there before. It seemed that for both of us, this was like a great adventure. Then on our way through the complex, when the dog did his business, she had a kleenex for cleaning up after him and so we disposed of that when we got to my place. Everything was so normal.

She noticed the computerized pictures pasted on my furnace door, I played a little piece for her on the piano, and we talked some more. Best of all, she accepted the New Testament I gave her. Then I walked with her back to the traffic light. As we walked, she looked wistfully at her little dog and said, "I wish I could be like him. He doesn't have to think about more important things."

I gave her my home phone number because I didn't remember my cell phone number. She said she would rather text and would therefore need my cell number. Since I didn't know the number, she suggested that I write my cell phone number on a piece of paper and slip it under the front door. I'm sure Parisa didn't want me to knock on her door again and involve her parents. Much later, I did slide the paper with the cell phone number under the door, but I never heard from her. Later on, I rang the doorbell of the other couple in her building, but there was no answer. I was going to give her neighbors my cell phone number to pass along to Parisa since I didn't know if she'd received my note under the door. Parisa was about to graduate, so her family may have moved away. Since then I haven't seen lights on in the building in the evening. Parisa and her family were from Iran.

What I know is that God was in my meeting with Parisa, and what I also know is that in my Christian walk, there's never a dull moment.

In the next chapter about fruitful witness in the kingdom of heaven, we'll continues to look at the parable of the sower.

22 Fruitful witnessing in the parable of the sower

Our hearts have room for only one all-embracing devotion.
—On Bonhoeffer by Erwin Lutzer in *Hitler's Cross*, 185

When I taught English in China as a "foreign expert" in 1984-85, my expression of gratitude would often be brushed aside with, "I was doing my duty." Duty is honorable, and God does call us to be his witnesses, but the call of duty does not serve well as a motivation for witnessing, because effective testimony by a Christian springs from love for others and a passion for the Lord. Jesus explains that out of the overflow of the heart, the mouth speaks (Lk 6.45).

Fruitful witnessing in the parable of the sower

> A. *Understanding, the key to fruitful witnessing*
> B. *Guarding testimony, a necessity for fruitful witnessing*
> C. *Receiving empowerment for fruitful witnessing*
> D. *Reaping a harvest through the power of the gospel*

A. Understanding, the key to fruitful witnessing

Jesus' presentation of the parable of the sower (Mt 13..1-15) shows that the measure of fruitfulness in witnessing is in direct proportion to the receiver's understanding of the Word living within. The seeds planted in good ground are the people with the most understanding and the greatest fruitfulness. The seeds planted on hard ground are the people with the least understanding; they are ones who have no testimony. The implication is that the other seeds between those two poles are fruitful in proportion to the measure of their understanding.

But accepting this truth about the relatedness of understanding to fruitfulness can be disconcerting, as it was for a good friend of mine. When she read the parable of the sower, she had reservations about the necessity for a person to have understanding in order to have a fruitful witness. I think resistance to this truth about the relatedness of understanding to fruitfulness in witness arises from a misconception of the word *understanding*. Jesus here is not speaking of intellectual capacity on the part of the persons who hear the gospel, because this would mean that some persons would have an advantage over others simply by virtue of natural intellectual capacity.

The kind of understanding for fruitful witness

A moment of discovery showed me the kind of understanding fruitful witness requires. This discovery came when I saw a biblical reference in my concordance that says, "In that hour Jesus rejoiced in spirit." I wondered... hmm... What makes Jesus rejoice? Seeing the bread multiplied to feed five thousand? His victory over Satan's temptations? No. This is what I found: "In that hour Jesus rejoiced in spirit, and said, I thank thee, O Father, Lord of heaven and earth, that thou hast hid these things from the wise and prudent, and hast revealed them unto babes: even so, Father; for so it seemed good in thy sight" (Lk 10.21 KJV). Jesus also says that "unless you change and become like little children, you will never enter the kingdom of heaven" (Mt 18.2).

What do we know about babies and children? We know they have limited intellectual capacity, yet they recognize and respond to love. So too, sinners without God recognize and respond to the love of God in those who witnesses to them.

The phrase, "Jesus rejoiced," is found only once in the Bible, and according to the full statement, Jesus not only said his Father hid these things from the wise and prudent, he rejoiced in that truth, and we too can rejoice if we know that the Father denies understanding only to the proud and the unwilling and that he freely gives understanding to all the willing and needy. This means that we don't have to be "smart" enough, or be among the "in people," or become persons of high standing or persons of expertise. Jesus explains that "knowledge of the secrets of the kingdom of heaven has been given to you [common people], but not to them [his hardened enemies, the clever elite]" (Mt 13.11). God's standards are different from man's standards.

An illustration of God's standard for salvation

How important is this kind of understanding? Jesus reveals that right understanding results in a life that is rewarded now and in the hereafter. He told a story about Lazarus, a poor beggar covered with sores, who begged at a rich man's gate, where "the dogs came and licked his sores." Both the rich man and the poor man died.

Then, in the afterlife when the rich man was in torment, he cried out, "Father Abraham, have pity on me and send Lazarus to dip the tip of his finger in water and cool my tongue, because I am in agony in this fire (Lk 16.30)," for the rich man was in Hades* when he saw Lazarus by Abraham's side among the righteous dead. Abraham replied, "A great chasm has been fixed, so that those who want to go from here to you cannot, nor can anyone cross over from there to us" (Lk 16.26b). Then the rich man pleaded with Abraham to send Lazarus to his five brothers to warn them about this place of torment, but Abraham said, they have scripture to warn them and if they don't heed scripture, they won't believe even if someone were to come to them from the dead (Lk 16.19-31). The rich man's five brothers had hardened their hearts against the truth of the scripture that they already had, so they had no understanding upon which to build further. Since they did not respond to the light they had already been given, they would not then be able to respond even to a brother's message sent from the grave. They didn't believe because they didn't want to believe that there would be consequences to their unbelief. The five brothers had the witness of scripture, but they did not heed its message. Hence, the unbelieving brothers were not reconciled to God and had no testimony. They were like the seed that never germinated.

When Jesus states that a Christian's testimony is a result of his allowing God's light to shine through him, he is implying that this light-bearing is God's purpose for a Christian's life. Jesus

---

* Nestle Greek says "Hades." This is about the afterlife before Jesus' resurrection. Before Jesus' ascension to heaven, the dead descended into Sheol (the grave) which had two sections—*Paradise* for the righteous and *Hades* for the unrighteous. The apostle's creed says, "He [Jesus] descended into hell [Hades]." This explanation says that after death before ascending to heaven, Jesus descended to the grave (Sheol). From there, he took Paradise and its righteous ones to heaven (Eph 4.7-10). Jesus said that the thief on the cross beside him would be in heaven with him that day.

illustrates this truth in Mark 4 and Luke 8—the gospels that present the parable of the sower—by telling a parable about a lamp on a stand. Scripture, which says that the purpose of lighting a lamp on a stand is to give light, he also says, "No one lights a lamp and hides it in a jar or puts it under a bed. Instead, he puts it on a stand, so that those who come in can see the light... Therefore consider carefully how you listen. Whoever has [light, or understanding] will be given more; whoever does not have, even what he thinks he has will be taken from him" (Lk 8.16-18).

The purpose of a lamp on a stand is to give light, and the purpose of a Christian is to let God's light shine through him. He does this by walking with the Lord. "If we walk in the light, as he is in the light, we have fellowship with one another, and the blood of Jesus, his Son, purifies us from all sin" (Jn 1.7). I like to compare light generated by a Christian's walk with a certain kind of headlight that is generated by a cyclist pedaling his bike. So long as the cyclist pedals, the headlight and the taillight flash, and similarly, so long as the Christian goes forward with God, God's light shines through him to be a light for his path and to be a light for others.

Ever increasing understanding

This kind of understanding that brings light to others could be described as ever increasing understanding; that is, the believer gains more understanding as he lives out whatever understanding he already has, but he loses what understanding he has if he fails to live out what he understands. The faithful believer is the one who perseveres in expressing the measure of light he has (Lk 8.15), because the Christian life is dynamic, not static. For him, life either goes forward or backward; it does not stand still. This means that if a person's heart is not zealous for the Lord's presence, his heart can become a stagnant pool, a breeding ground for discord in the church and for misery in his personal life. The backslider— the one whose fervor for God is waning—is most miserable of all, for he doesn't fit in the church, and he doesn't fit in the world. He makes life miserable for himself and for everyone else that is in his life.

To whom does God give understanding?

In the parable of the sower—Matthew 13, Mark 4, and Luke 8—we see that understanding comes to hearts willing to be open to God. In Matthew, Jesus says this about those with hardened hearts: "You will be ever hearing but never understanding; you will be ever seeing but never perceiving. For this people's heart has become calloused; they hardly hear with their ears, and they have closed their eyes" (Mt 13.14,15a). Then Jesus adds something strange: "Otherwise they might see with their eyes, hear with their ears, understand with their hearts and turn, and I would *heal* them'" (Mt 13.15b; cp Is 6.9,10. Italics added). In Mark, Jesus gives the same truth about hardened hearts: "They may be ever seeing but never perceiving, and ever hearing but never understanding." And he adds something even stranger: "Otherwise they might turn and *be forgiven*" (Mark 4:12)! How odd that God says he doesn't *want* that person to understand because then he would heal him or forgive him!

One day I received light about this truth about the willingness of a person to hear from God. I learned this through an incident with our four children in Kelso, Washington after we moved across the river from Rainier, Oregon. (The fifth was born a couple of years after our move.) At that time, our four children were in grades two to six at Wallace school where I taught, and there in Kelso, my husband found a new job working as a logger in the woods.

Our family moved to a house with a huge, weed-filled backyard; it was right next to the railroad tracks,. So one day I put the four children to work pulling up weeds. At the outset, I didn't say anything about a reward for their efforts, and they had no reason to believe that a reward would be forthcoming because ordinarily they didn't receive rewards for their chores. Not surprisingly, they were halfhearted about their labor except for one, who put his heart into the job. Wanting to reward him, I called him aside, gave him a quarter—worth more in those days—told him not to tell the others, and sent him back to to work hard alongside the slackers, who didn't know that they too would get a quarter if they applied themselves to the task. The question is, wouldn't they all have pitched in if they had believed they would be rewarded—as opposed to working hard for the sake of obedience based on love?

This gives us something to think about—wouldn't everyone get in line with the Lord if they really, truly believed heaven and hell are a reality that has to be faced? God looks at how hearts respond in this life to his open invitation to be redeemed. The question is, will those persons go their own way, believing what they want to believe? Or will they believe the Lord when he tugs at their hearts by his love and convicts them of sin? (God doesn't force anyone to accept his gift of salvation.) The five brothers in Jesus' story refused to believe the truth that God had presented to them in scripture; therefore, neither would they be willing to receive a message, even if it came from someone in the grave.

B. Guarding testimony, a necessity for fruitful witnessing

What is meant by a person guarding his testimony?

Guarding testimony doesn't mean a Christian makes sure to be on his good behavior in front of the person he wants to lead to the Lord. It means that in *all* of his personal life,—alone or with others—he makes it top priority to stay close to the Lord, for this keeps him from losing his credibility as a witness for the Lord.

We can understand the need for this kind of super-vigilance by looking at the analogy of a witness in a courtroom scene. An attorney seeks to win a case by destroying the credibility of an opposing witness, for if he can do that, he can have that person's testimony thrown out of court. Similarly, when a Christian testifies on the Lord's behalf, Satan the adversary seeks to destroy that witness's credibility. Therefore, a Christian has to be willing to be vigilant in guarding his testimony by overcoming Satan's temptations and wiles. And what makes a Christian willing to stand guard over his testimony? His love for the one who redeemed him is what makes him treasure the opportunity to use his influence to be a witness.

Counsel about guarding testimony

Abraham, a man of faith, was vigilant about the influences under which he placed himself; in this way, he was vigilant in guarding the credibility of his influence. His nephew Lot, on the other hand, put himself under influences that compromised his faith, and he destroyed his testimony by his worldliness (2 Pe 2.4-10a).

G. Campbell Morgan, (1863-1945) uses this contrast to warn Christians about the danger of worldliness. He writes, "Lot was a good man… but he first pitched his tent towards Sodom. Then he went to live in Sodom. Finally he became so identified with Sodom that he lost all his influence. When the crisis came, there were not five men in the city whom he had influenced towards righteousness and God. That's why the Lord had to destroy the city. [But in contrast] Abraham stood under the terebinths in fellowship with God, and he was able to exert influence that nearly saved Sodom" (Morgan 1943, 64). Lot chose to please the world; Abraham chose to please God. What a difference that makes in a person's testimony for God!

Andrew Murray of the nineteenth century, a man of great stature, has written about the worth and desirability of guarding one's testimony. Murray says, "Just as far as we enter into the world and please it, so we lose our power. In the measure we are 'not of the world even as Christ was not of the world,' we shall be able to bless it [the world]… Every heresy, every neglect or denial of God's truth, weakens the spiritual life… But of all heresies the worst is the heresy of a worldly spirit. It dispossesses the Spirit of God and makes every truth powerless. It brings the church into subjection to the god of this world. If there is one prayer we need it is this: Lord, show us what thou meanest: 'not of this world'" (Murray 1990, 40, 41). To shun worldliness, a Christian has to be willing to suffer the consequences of being different.

When my friend Jean Maston and I took the gospel to the sidewalks in Petaluma, California for a number of years, the two of us had different worldly-spirit fears to overcome. She's the one who pushed me to get out there with her, but then after we were there and were ministering, she was the one who would worry about people looking at us suspiciously—not that we were doing anything wrong; we were simply engaged in free speech on public sidewalks. Later I'll describe the adventures we had in those days.

Resisting the temptation to allow a worldly spirit to dominate a life is the negative side for a Christian who guards the credibility of his testimony. Now let's look at two positive directives about treasuring and guarding testimony. One way to safeguard witness is for a Christian to love other Christians and to live in fellowship with them, for the Bible says that people can recognize Christians by their love for each other. Jesus says, "By this, all men will know that you are my disciples, if you love one another" (Jn 13.35). The other positive way to safeguard testimony is for a Christian to keep his inner, mental life under surveillance, "bringing into captivity every thought to the obedience of Christ" (2Co 10.5b).

Bringing every thought captive to make the inner life obedient to Christ (2Co 10.5) is necessary because a Christian's inner life is the very source of his outer witness. A Christian expresses outwardly and unconsciously what he believes in his heart. And though a Christian cannot have a spotless record, he can keep short accounts with the Lord by prompt confession and repentance. He can nip in the bud the hardening of his heart.

Again, on the positive side of treasuring and guarding testimony, the act of bold witness by a Christian inspires and enables holy living not only for testifying to others but also for a Christian's victory in his own personal life. Moishe Rosen, founder of "Jews for Jesus," says, "When I was driving a van with 'Jews for Jesus' lettering on it, I was much more careful to yield the right of way and to live up to the name that I was trying to exalt… Maybe all of us would keep ourselves a little cleaner and treat each other a little more kindly if others could see our 'Jesus' label'" (Rosen, Feb 2010). Here wee see that Moishe Rosen became painfully aware of his responsibility as a witness when he drove the van with its brazen message, *Jews for Jesus*, proudly displayed. He learned that bold witness makes a Christian stronger in his resistance to temptation.

Alas, we mortals do judge other Christians and our leaders instead of loving them, but it doesn't have to be that way, for Jesus says Christians can enter into the oneness of love that is enjoyed by the three persons of the godhead. Jesus says that a Christian can have a oneness of fellowship with other believers that is like the fellowship enjoyed by the Father, Son, and Holy Spirit. In fact, Jesus prays for unity between Christians and for those people who become Christians through their testimony. He says, "My prayer is not for them alone. I pray also for those who will believe in me through their message, that all of them may be one, Father, just as you are in me and I am in you. May they also be in us so that the world may believe you have sent me" (Jn 17.20-21a. Italics added).

As Christians, then, we draw others into God's orbit of love. This can make us one with them, even as Jesus and the Father are one. The job of a Christian is to do all he can to prevent the slightest strain in relationship with his brothers and sisters in Christ. For to be fruitful in ministry, a Christian must treasure and guard that fellowship.

Most importantly, to treasure and guard his testimony, a Christian does not need to try harder but to trust more. Jesus was asked, "What must we do to do the works God requires?" His answer was, "The work of God is this, to believe in the one he has sent" (Jn 6.28,29),

Let's review how a Christian guards his testimony…
> by treasuring and guarding it as his highest priority,
> by being willing to pay the price of being different from the world,
> by expressing his love for his brothers and sisters in Christ,
> by watching over his thought life,
> by keeping short accounts with the Lord,
> by seeking prayer for boldness in testimony, just as Paul asked,
> by trusting more, not by trying harder!

C. Receiving empowerment for fruitful witnessing

God does not send people out as witnesses without offering to equip them with power. Hear what he told his disciples before his ascension: "In a few days you will be baptized with the Holy Spirit[*]… You will receive power when the Holy Spirit comes on

---

[*] Disciples received the Holy Spirit in Jn 20.22 when they were born again, but they also needed the baptism in the Holy Spirit to work in them and to unite them as one body, the church.

The tongues of the baptism of the Spirit is a prayer language that remains with a Christian to exercise for his edification and for ministry to the body of Christ, but there are other gifts, too—the *gifts of tongues and interpretation,* which is a manifestation given to edify fellow Christians.

you; and you will be my *witnesses* in Jerusalem, and in all Judea and Samaria, to the ends of the earth" (Ac 1.8. Italics added). This promised experience was first fulfilled on the Day of Pentecost: "All of them were filled with the Holy Spirit and began to speak in other tongues as the Spirit enabled them" (Acts 2.4).

Empowerment for witness

The Bible says this Pentecostal experience empowers a person for witnessing (Ac 1.8) and builds him up spiritually (1Co 14.4)). Speaking in tongues may seem to be a strange way to receive God's empowerment, but consider how vicious the tongue can be. James says, "The tongue also is a fire, a world of evil…. It corrupts the whole person, sets the whole course of his life on fire, and is itself set on fire by hell" (Ja 3.6). James also says, "Behold also the ships, which though they be so great, and are driven of fierce winds, yet are they turned about with a very small helm… Even so the tongue is a little member, and boasteth great things." (Ja 3.4. KJV). Here we see the significance of a Christian allowing God to control his tongue.

As God empowers and edifies those who seek him, he does so in response to their thirst for knowing him better. This thirst, which comes with seeking the baptism in the Holy Spirit, is a thirst for the Lord; it is not a desire for tongues as an end in itself—just as people don't seek water baptism because they want their hair to get dripping wet. Getting wet is just what happens when a person is baptized in water, and speaking in tongues is just what happens as biblical evidence when a person is baptized in the Holy Spirit.

The baptism in the Holy Spirit

You can read about the baptism in the Spirit in the book of Acts, which describes occasions when people experienced the overflow of the Spirit as they spoke in tongues— by inference* in Acts 2.4,

---

* The inference in Acts 8.18 is that Simon the sorcerer heard people speak in tongues when the Spirit was given, for he must have witnessed such evidence. Acts 8.18 says, "When Simon saw that the Spirit was given at the laying on of the apostles' hands, he offered them money and said, "Give me also this ability so that everyone on whom I lay my hands may receive the Holy Spirit."" Incidentally, the disciples had to rebuke him for offering money.

Speaking in tongues is not referred to in all epistles—probably because the baptism in the Holy Spirit was commonly accepted and did not have to be addressed, except in Corinth, for in Corinth, Paul dealt with a problem that arose about tongues speaking.

10.46, and 19.6; also, Acts 8.18.

Earlier, before the Lord poured out his Spirit on Pentecost—after Jesus' resurrection and before his ascension—the disciples as individuals had been born again. This new birth happened when Jesus "breathed on them and said, 'Receive the Holy Spirit'" (Jn 20.21, 22). At that moment, they became Christians. But later, on the Day of Pentecost, those Christians were baptized in the Holy Spirit. They were filled to *overflowing*. In this outpouring, Jesus did these four things for them: He united them as a church body, gave them power for witness, gave them the heavenly language of tongues for continuing communication with him in prayer, and gave them spiritual gifts for ministry.

To understand the baptism of the Spirit, which is expressed through speaking in tongues, think of what Jesus says about any words we speak, good or evil. He says words are an *overflow* of what is in the heart (Lk 6.45). So here's what happens when the Spirit overflows from within a Christian where the Spirit already dwells: That person's words pour forth from the Spirit in a language that is not that person's own language. Jesus says, "If anyone is thirsty, let him come to me and drink. Whoever believes in me, as the scripture has said, streams of living water will flow from within him. By this he meant the Spirit, whom those who believed in him were later to receive [to overflowing]..." (Jn 7.37b-39).

Although speaking in tongues results from a release of the overflow of the Spirit within, no one becomes a better person than he was before or better than anyone else, because God's grace—ever and always—remains the only source of what is good in a Christian's life. Nor does God force his gifts on anyone. No, he looks for faith that seeks, receives, and trusts in him.

Testimony about receiving the baptism in the Holy Spirit

For four years I thirsted for God and sought his Holy Spirit empowerment; I was waiting for him to "zap" me, but nothing happened. Though he does at times come unexpectedly on people who know nothing about speaking in tongues, the Lord wants many like me to be willing to express faith by beginning to speak and vy trusting him for what is spoken. The truth of this statement is especially obvious in the NIV translation in Acts 2.4: "All of them were filled with the Holy Spirit and began to speak in other tongues as the Spirit *enabled* them" [italics added]. This enabling implies cooperation between the Christian who has faith and the God who bestows the gifts of the Spirit.

In 1963, when the late Father Dennis Bennett came to our town in Kelso, Washington for an all-city Pentecostal meeting, he gave us an analogy about a person receiving the Holy Spirit. That day, in a scenario that he set up, he said you need to get from point A to point B, but danger lurks ahead as in a minefield, and you don't know where the safe spots are. Father Bennett[*] said that you will never reach point B unless you begin to walk forward with trust in God to help you place your feet on safe ground.

After I learned I had to take a step of faith, I went forward in Father Bennett's meeting, confident that I would receive. I came ready to believe before, during, and after receiving because I knew this was my moment to receive. I also knew my faith would be tested, and it was. Fortunately, I had been warned about God's testing by my friend, Evangelist Rose Fidler. My experience was not emotional; in fact, I had a headache. But deep down, I had great joy, for God satisfied my soul by giving me what I wanted more than anything else—this new dimension in my life with the Lord. First came faith and later came an intensified sense of his power and presence. The consequence was that my prayer life and my witness were transformed.

I'm not saying you cannot be used by God to reach others for him before you are baptized in the Holy Spirit. Every child of God has the Spirit living within him and can walk in the Spirit and can give expression to the fruit of the Spirit in his walk, but the Pentecostal experience brings a new spiritual dimension of power in a person's ministry.

I can testify that there is now a difference in what I do for God. Before the experience, I obeyed his guidance out of strong

---

[*] Father Bennett, an Episcopalian priest, was greatly used of God in the charismatic movement across the nation. This book's author recommends his book, *Nine o'clock in the Morning.*

resolve—with a sense of "going out on a limb" for him. And at that time, the Lord honored my desire to please him; however, now after the overflow of the Spirit, I don't have to be so "brave," for I have an inner witness *at the time* I am doing what I do for the Lord.

Before this baptism, the Lord's presence was not upon me in the same measure of awareness. My sensitivity to God's presence has become enhanced—and communication with him and with others, more satisfying. I have become more effective in my witnessing and in my prayer life, and in other ways, too—even in my piano playing.

D. Reaping a harvest through the power of the gospel

Telling the good news is exciting. That's what I learned at a county fair in Petaluma, California in the 1970s and 1980s. There my good friend, Jean Maston, directed a booth manned by Christians from various denominations in the community. She used Child Evangelism's wordless book[*] to train workers to reach children for the Lord. See a mention of this in chapter 20.

At the fair on the wall behind us, we had a huge cloth with a chalk-drawn picture of Jesus on the seashore so that anyone who stopped to talk would know what they were getting into. Not only did parents bring their children and wait for them to hear the story, but also teens and adults would stop and listen to our story, and of all of those, many, if not most, would receive the Lord. Each year, there were so many redeemed in those few days that my head would be spinning after my turn in the booth. That was good training to prepare Jean and me for evangelism elsewhere.

Launching out for the Lord

Later, with that experience to bolster us, with a nudging from the Lord, and with the guidance of the Holy Spirit, we went out on the sidewalks to talk to youth. It had been so easy to talk at the fair when music played, loudspeakers blared, and people conversed

---

[*] This booklet from Child Evangelism has colored pages and is a nonthreatening, curiosity-arousing tool that lets a person present the gospel by applying scripture of his choice to each colored page. And since the presentation can be flexible, the one witnessing can disarm the listeners, who can see that the story has a beginning and an ending.

while they ate popcorn. At the fair, it was like being in a bubble because nobody paid attention to someone doing something so out-of-the-ordinary as talking about the Lord. Later, when Jean and I hit the sidewalks to reach the youth, I envisioned that we were taking that bubble with us, and in doing so, I had the same boldness and liberty for speaking that I had had at the fairground.

To give you a feel for how marvelously the Lord can work in chaotic situations, here is an account I wrote down on June 2, 1976; it gives you a snapshot of a day in the life of our sidewalk evangelism.

As Jean and I walked down my own street in Petaluma, Baker Street, I stopped to talk to three girls—high school, I think. (Jean had gone on ahead.) They listened eagerly to the story of the wordless book. I asked one girl if she would like to receive the Lord, and a different one said yes, and then the other one in the middle said she would like to, and finally the one that I had asked said yes. The work was so real. I talked to them about growing in the Lord since they were now Christians. Some might be skeptical about the simplicity of this presentation and the prayer to receive, but I've met people who as adult Christians say that they came to he Lord through a wordless-book presentation.

When I got to Western Avenue where Jean had gone ahead of me, I thought of going on the other side of where she was ministering because I saw some kids coming from that direction, but then when I saw a lone boy standing, staring at a sign on the little mom-pop grocery store window, I decided that he looked like someone with time on his hands. His name was Anthony, I found out afterwards. He was a seventh grader who had moved to Petaluma, California from New York three months before. He was small and had dark, wavy hair, and dark skin. He was serious, interested, and easy to talk with.

Just as I was ready to give the invitation to receive the Lord, his friend Mike came up. He said he'd heard the story at Sunday School, and I asked him to tell it to me. He remembered a lot about the blood of Jesus, and the rest. Then three or more boys walked up to listen. One of them said that someone *made* him listen to it at the fair—of course, no one *made* him listen—but he stayed with us and listened anyway. We went through the story again. (This is Anthony's third time through.) Then I asked Anthony if he would like to ask Jesus into his heart. He said yes. I asked each of the others. They didn't seem to think so. I suggested that we bow our heads together and those who wanted to could pray the prayer by following my lead. I started to pray and no one repeated after me. I was pretty sure I had made it clear that they were to pray aloud. After a long pause, I said they could pray silently. Then I thought, no, and looked up. Instead I asked Anthony to pray aloud with me since he's the one who had said "yes,"and then if any of the others wanted to pray with us, they could. Sure enough, Anthony prayed loud and clear for all to hear.

Afterwards one of them looked at Anthony and said, "What about him *now*?" I don't remember their exact words, but I know that all of us suddenly realized that now Anthony was on his way to heaven. The others were all staring at him, and he was standing there looking blessed by it all. One of the others suggested he had to go and said, "Come on." I thought possibly the others might have entertained the idea of being able to pray but they declined my invitation to stay longer.

Anthony had never even heard about Adam and Eve, but he said he'd gotten a Bible at a Sunday School in New York. I told him my son Dave was in seventh grade, too, and I invited him to come over some time—but he didn't. Speaking of Dave, once I'd talked on the sidewalk to a friend of his, Timothy, a boy on his A-basketball team. Later after Timothy, graduated from college and had a job, I heard he had died in a car accident. I was glad to know he was ready to meet his Master.

All of the above earlier incidents were happening in front of the tiny grocery store where kids were coming and going after school. Before I finished talking to Anthony, two girls came up and wanted to know what was going on. I found out one of them lives on my long block. She and her friend Pam were interested enough to stay to listen, even though the father of one of them came out of the store while we were talking. I think it must have been time for them to go. Anyway, it turned out that the father was willing to wait, and the girls also had to wait while I finished talking with Anthony. Then after I told the story to the two girls and gave the invitation, they wanted to know just what I meant, so I explained further. They readily received and went happily on their way with the patient father.

When I was talking to those girls, two other girls came up and said they had already talked with Jean, and when I asked if they had received, they said yes and looked very happy about it. They are the same two that came again the next Friday to speak to us. It was good to get that kind of feedback. There was also a boy on a bicycle who at one point went into the store, but who for a couple of moments sat on his bike taking in what was going on. So later at home, when Jean and I prayed for all those to whom we had spoken, we prayed for the boy on the bicycle, too.

For this kind of ministry, we had to have faith that God would work through us. The fact that kids would even talk with us amazed me. And we had to believe that God would direct the converted ones to carry through by attending a church. Usually we asked if they knew someone with a tie to a church, and most often they did know a friend or a family member. Afterwards, our follow-up was to pray in faith for those we had encountered.

The day I described was not unusual. We never went out without finding some young persons who responded to God's invitation after hearing "the good news." It's like Jesus said: "Open your eyes and look at the fields! They are ripe for harvest" (Jn 4:35). Lots of people plant seeds, but few harvest.

In the next chapter, the last six parables of Matthew 13 help us learn more about Israel and the church in the messianic kingdom, which is the future, final era in the kingdom of heaven before eternity.

23 The kingdom of heaven is like…

*The more original a discovery, the more obvious
it seems afterwards.*

--Arthur Koestler

"The kingdom of heaven is like…" That's the opening statement
of the last six parables in Matthew 13 and the first parable in Matthew 22.1-14. When Jesus talked to the Jews about the kingdom
of heaven, he was talking about Israel and the church, God's two
people groups—even though the church did not yet exist at that
time. With study, we learn is that the kingdom of heaven includes
the church age, the tribulation period, and the messianic kingdom.
And within this time period of the kingdom of heaven, there continues to be spiritual conflict between good and evil.

So let's look at those factors that enhance our understanding
of the kingdom of heaven in the parables. We'll look at the literary factor, historic/prophetic features, chronology, relationships,
man's view of the kingdom of heaven, and God's view of the kingdom of heaven.

Factors to consider in the study of the parables of Jesus:
  A. *The literary factor—parallelism in parable pairs*
  B. *The historic - prophetic factor in Matthew 22.1-14*
  C. *The chronological factor in the parables*
  D. *The relationship factor in the parables*
  E. *The love factor in the parables—God's view*

A.. *The literary factor—parallelism in parable pairs in Matthew 13*

Parallelism, a common literary form in the Hebrew Bible, is
used in Jesus' parables. It is used as a means for clarifying thought
through comparison and contrast. It is also an organizing principle that strengthens a reader's memory, besides appealing to his
aesthetic sensibility.

THREE PARALLEL PARABLE PAIRS IN MATTHEW 13

Figure 34

The literary factor of parallelism

Thinking Jewish, we see parallels between the church and Israel. In Matthew 13, six parables are numbered by their sequence.

Conflict of good and evil in the kingdom of heaven ends in judgment.

1) The weeds parable—about the church and unbelievers.

Jesus plants his people to make up the church, and Satan plants his unbelievers. Then unbelievers live alongside believers until the church's rapture to heaven before the tribulation. After the tribulation before the messianic kingdom begins, Christ will return to earth from heaven with the church, and at that time, unbelievers of all eras will be arraigned for final judgment at the great white throne, which will take place after the millennial kingdom ends.

6) The dragnet parable—about Israel and unbelievers.

On earth in the tribulation, Jews and their sympathizers are tested to see who enters the messianic kingdom. Meanwhile in heaven, the church is being prepared for marriage to Christ. When Christ returns to earth with the church as his bride, only believers enter the messianic kingdom. However, unbelievers arise during the messianic kingdom, and those unbelievers, led by Satan, will attack Jerusalem but will be killed by fire from heaven. These attackers and unbelievers of all eras will be resurrected to be judged at the great white throne, where they will be sentenced to the fiery furnace.

Man's perspective on the church and Israel: Man sees evil.

2) The mustard seed—on external evil in the spiritual church.

3) The leaven (yeast)—on internal evil in earthly Israel.

God's perspective on Israel and the church: God sees only his loved ones.

4) The treasure—on God's great redemptive plan for Israel.

5) The pearl—on God's great redemptive plan for the church.

CONFLICT OF GOOD AND EVIL
IN THE KINGDOM OF HEAVEN

1) The literary factor in the first parable pair in Matthew 13
The parallel weeds and dragnet parables in Matthew 13
A parable pair on the conflict of good and evil in the kingdom of heaven

The kingdom of heaven reveals conflict of good and evil between God and Satan. The parable of the weeds is about the church and unbelievers before the rapture of the church, and the parable of the dragnet is about Israel and unbelievers before the messianic kingdom begins.

In the kingdom of heaven, the weeds and dragnet parables portray believers caught in the conflict between good and evil—between God and Satan. For man, his struggle is "against the spiritual forces of evil in the heavenly realms" (Eph 6.12b). This conflict of good and evil will end in God's triumph at the end of time before the world enters eternity.

Text on the weeds parable in Matthew 13.24b-30:

"The kingdom of heaven is like a man who sowed good seed in his field. But while everyone was sleeping, his enemy came and sowed weeds among the wheat, and went away. When the wheat sprouted and formed heads, then the weeds also appeared. The owner's servants... said, 'Sir, didn't you sow good seed in your field? Where then did the weeds come from?' 'An enemy did this,' he replied. The servants asked him, 'Do you want us to go and pull them up?' 'No,' he answered, 'because while you are pulling the weeds, you may root up the wheat with them. Let both grow together until the harvest. At that time I will tell the harvesters: First collect the weeds and tie them in bundles to be burned; then gather the wheat and bring it into my barn.'"

Commentary by Jesus on the weeds parable

Jesus said this: "The one who sowed the good seed is the Son of Man. The field is the world, and the good seed stands for the sons of the kingdom [believers]. The weeds are sons of the evil one [unbelievers], and the enemy who sows them is the devil.

The harvest is the end of the age, and the harvesters are angels. As weeds are pulled up and burned in the fire, so it will be at the end of the age. The Son of Man will send out his angels and will weed out of his kingdom everything that causes sin and all who do evil. Angels will throw unbelievers into the fiery furnace, where there will be weeping and gnashing of teeth. Then the righteous will shine like the sun in the kingdom of their Father, He who has ears, let him hear" (Mt 13.37-43;a; cp Da 12.1-3).

Text on the parable of the dragnet for Matthew 13.47-50:

"Once again, the kingdom of heaven is like a dragnet that was let down into the lake and caught all kinds of fish. When it was full, the fishermen pulled it up on the shore. Then they sat down and collected the good fish in baskets, but threw the bad away. This is how it will be at the end of the age. The angels will come and separate the wicked from the righteous and will throw them [the wicked] into the fiery furnace, where there will be weeping and gnashing of teeth" (Mt 13.47-50).

Commentary on the dragnet parable:

The dragnet parable is about judgment of Israel and unbelievers after Christ returns. Judgment separates believers who enter the messianic kingdom from those unbelievers who are arraigned to appear later at the great white throne judgment before eternity.

Commentary on both the weeds and dragnet parables:

About the kingdom of heaven in the parallel parables of the weeds and the dragnet, good and evil develop simultaneously (Morgan 1943, 52). In the end, the righteous are rewarded forever and the unrighteous are punished.

MAN'S PERSPECTIVE ON GOOD AND EVIL
Man sees evil.

2) The literary factor in the second parable pair in Matthew 13 Parallel mustard seed and leaven parables in Matthew 13.

Text on the parable of the mustard seed in Matthew 13.31, 32:

"The kingdom of heaven is like a mustard seed, which a man took and planted in his field. Though it is the smallest of all your seeds, yet when it grows, it is the largest of garden plants and becomes a tree, so that the birds of the air come and perch in its branches" (Mt 13.32).

Commentary on the parable of the mustard seed:

In Matthew, Jesus says that the mustard seed parable symbolizes faith: "If you have faith as small as a mustard seed, you can say to this mountain, 'Move from here to there' and it will move…;'" (Mt 17.20)). In Luke, Jesus presents the same truth: "If you have faith as small as a mustard seed, you can say to this mulberry tree, 'Be uprooted and planted in the sea,' and it will obey you'" (Lk 17.6).

From such faith, the church has grown, for Jesus said he'd build his church on the faith Peter expressed when he said, "You are the Christ, the Son of the living God" (Mt 16.13-15). Jesus said, "Upon this rock [faith in Christ] I will build my church and the gates of hell shall not prevail against it" (Mt 16.18).

The meaning of the birds in the parable of the mustard seed is found in other Matthew 13 parables. In the parable of the weeds and in the parable of the sower, birds obviously symbolize evil. Applying that symbolism to the mustard seed parable, we can say that for the spiritual church today, we find good news and bad news. The bad news is that birds perch in the church's branches. The good news is that the birds cannot integrate into the *internal* life of the tree, for although evil influences surround earthly congregations, evil remains *external* to the living body of Christ. An unbeliever cannot be part of the living body of Christ unless he becomes born again himself. Therefore, evil cannot penetrate the universal church; it can only fly in and out of its external branches.

This parable of the mustard seed illustrates the birth and development of the church, which operates in the presence of *external* evil. The church is not just an organization; it is a living organism that has grown from the seed of faith. From a small beginning, it continues in its growth worldwide. When the ministry of the church began, there were only one hundred twenty people praying in the upper room and since then the church has grown exponentially. Jesus in this parable says that though the beginning of the church would be small and though Satan and his evil followers would oppose it, the church would survive and flourish (Eph 4.13-16). History reveals that this is what has come to pass.

Text on the parable of the leaven in Matthew 13.33 ESV: "The kingdom of heaven is like leaven [yeast] that a woman took and hid in three measures of flour, till it was all leavened."

Commentary on the parable of the leaven:

Though the kingdom of heaven is characterized by the presence of evil, the evil takes different forms in the church and in Israel. The mustard seed parable reveals that *external evil* cannot enter the spiritual body of the church, but the leaven parable reveals that for national Israel, *internal evil* passes from one generation to the next, just as leaven passes from one batch of dough to the next, The text of the parable of the leaven says, "The kingdom of heaven is like leaven [yeast] that a woman took and hid in three measures of flour, till it was all leavened" (Mt 13.33 ESV).

Biblically, leaven* consistently symbolizes evil, as in these examples:

Leaven is banned in Israelite sacrifices that typify Christ.

Jesus speaks of leaven as evil when he condemns the yeast of hypocrisy and legalism as exhibited by the Pharisees.

Jesus condemns the leaven that is the denial of the supernatural, as believed by the Saducees.

Jesus denounces the leaven of the material and political, as pursued by the Herodians (Mt 16.6,11; 1Co 5.7; Ga 5.9).

Paul to the church: "Get rid of the old yeast of malice and wickedness ... that you may be a *new* batch without yeast..." (1Co 5.7. Italics added). Christians counteract evil by walking in the light as *new* creatures in Christ (1Jn 1.7).

Internal evil (leaven) has triggered Israel's decline and God's judgments—first by Israel's division into two rival kingdoms, then by captivity in Babylon, later by lack of a prophet for four hundred years before Christ, then by Israel's rejection of their Messiah, and finally in 135

---

* Leaven is the Bible word for yeast and the Bible type for evil (Gray 1906, 196; Wight 1956, 77).

A.D. by the diaspora, when Jews as a people were expelled from Israel. A clue that the symbolism of leaven refers to Israel is seen in Jesus' use of Judaic phraseology in the parable of the leaven. He uses ancient Judaic phrases to describe Israel when he says, "The kingdom of heaven is like leaven [yeast] that a woman took and hid in *three measures of flour* [in Hebrew, literally 'three *seahs* of flour'], till it was all leavened." The Hebrew Bible uses the same phrase when Abraham entertained three mysterious, heavenly guests: "three *seahs* of flour [three measures of flour]" (Ge 18.6 ESV. Italics added). The same term, *measures of flour*, is also used about Judaic grain offerings that were presented in the temple.

Commentary on both the mustard seed and the leaven parables:

The parable of the mustard seed speaks of development of the church, and the parable of the leaven speaks of development of Israel. Both parables give *man's* view of evil. For the *spiritual church*, the mustard seed parable depicts evil as birds in the branches, remaining external to the true church. In contrast, for God's *earthly Israel*, leaven depicts evil as yeast, passing evil down internally through the generations... until the return of Israel's Savior.

GOD'S PERSPECTIVE ON GOOD AND EVIL
God sees his beloved people
3) The literary factor in the third parable pair in Matthew 13
Parallel treasure and pearl parables in Matthew 13

In Hollywood, when Richard Burton expressed his love for Elizabeth Taylor by giving her extravagantly expensive jewelry, he didn't agonize over the price that he had to pay for the gift. No, he gladly paid it because his gift expressed what was in his heart.

In the treasure and pearl parables, a man discovers something so valuable that he risks all he possesses to obtain it. There's no hint of pain in the sacrifice, only of great joy for gaining the beloved possession. Jesus "for the joy set before him endured the cross" (He 12.2); Jesus' joy is in his church, the pearl, and in Israel, his treasure. His perspective on the kingdom of heaven differs from man's perspective. *In the mustard seed and leaven parable pair, man focuses on the evil present in the church and Israel, but in this parable pair—the treasure and pearl parables—God focuses on his beloved people, the church and Israel.*

Text on the parable of the treasure in Matthew 13.44:

Jesus said, "The kingdom of heaven is like treasure hidden in a field. When a man found it, he hid it again (in the land), and then in his joy went and sold all he had and bought that field"(Mt 13.44).

Commentary on the parable of the treasure:

The Lord's treasure is Israel, for in the Bible, the Jewish people are known as "the people of the land [field]." It was to the land that God called Abraham, and according to Hebrew prophets, it is to the land that he will regather the Jews from throughout the world in the end time. Today, Jews as a people remain unbelieving and are therefore still "buried" in the land as God's treasure.

The Torah, the Jews' most sacred part of the Bible, speaks of Israel and its land as God's treasure. In the Torah, the Lord says, "Now if you obey me fully and keep my covenant, then out of all nations you will be my *treasured possession.* Although the whole earth is mine, you will be for me a kingdom of priests and a holy nation" (Ex 19.5,6. Italics added). Again in the Torah, God says to Israel, "You are a people holy to the LORD your God. Out of all the peoples on the face of the earth, the LORD has chosen you to be his *treasured possession*"(Dt 14.2. Italics added). Israel is God's treasure.

How beautiful Jesus' expression of his love for Israel, his treasure! For his people, he was willing to come to earth to sacrifice himself in order to buy that field. That was his joy: "Jesus, for the joy that was set before him, endured the cross…" (He 12 2). When Jesus paid the price on the cross, he bought the land and its future blessings. About Israel, Isaiah says, "Your days of sorrow will end. Then will all your people be righteous and they will possess the land forever. They are the shoot I have planted, the work of my hands, for the display of my *splendor* [*glory*]" (Is 60.20b-21. Italics added).

Text on the parable of the pearl in Matthew 13.45, 46:

Jesus says this about the church: "Again, the kingdom of heaven is like a merchant looking for fine pearls. When he found one of great value, he went away and sold everything he had and bought it."

Commentary on the parable of the pearl

A pearl is produced by an oyster in the sea. John Walvoord compares the formation of the church with the formation of the pearl when he says the pearl's "formation occurs because of an irritation in the tender side of an oyster... There is a sense in which the church was formed out of the wounds of Christ and has been made possible by his death and sacrifice" (Walvoord 1974, 105).

The symbolism of *the sea* has a negative connotation. "The wicked are like the tossing sea, which cannot rest, whose waves cast up mire and mud" (Is 57.20 OT). "They [the ungodly] are wild waves of *the sea*, foaming up their shame..." (NT Jd 13. Italics added). That's why the Man of Sin—the ungodly beast, the Antichrist—is shown rising out of *the sea* (Re 13.1), as John says. That's also why, in prophecy, there is no mention of *a sea* in the blessedness of eternity's new heaven and new earth (Re 21.1).

With these examples, *the sea* fits the parable because in the New Testament, the Greek word for church, *ecclesia*, means "called out ones." Like the pearl drawn out from the sea, Christians are called out from the sea of the ungodly to be God's people.

Commentary on both parables—treasure parable and pearl parable

The treasure and the pearl represent Israel and the church, respectively. At the end of Matthew 13, Jesus says, "Therefore every teacher of the law who has been instructed about the kingdom of heaven is like the owner of a house who brings out of his storeroom new treasures as well as old" (Mt 13.52). For Christ, national Israel is his treasure and the spiritual church is his joy. How can anyone not love the Savior who gave his all to bring salvation to his beloved people, Israel and the church!

B. *The historic - prophetic factor in Matthew 22.1-14*

Jesus' parable of the banquet in Matthew 22.1-14

Like the parables of Matthew 13, this parable in Matthew 22.1-14 begins with "The kingdom of heaven is like..." In this historic-prophetic story of the parable of the banquet, the king (God the Father) sends out invitations to his subjects (the Jews) to come to the wedding banquet of his Son (a feast in the messianic kingdom), but of those invited, some decline, some mistreat the messengers (prophets); and others kill the messengers, as they did with Jesus.

Continuing the parable of the banquet: When the king sees that the invited ones (Jews) refuse to come to the feast, he's enraged and sends his army to destroy them and to burn their city (Jerusalem in A.D. 70). Then, he sends his servants out to the street corners to invite anyone they can find —anyone in the present age, both Gentiles and Jews. This summary of the parable of the banquet has been fulfilled in history and is being fulfilled in the present.

But that's not the end of the parable. When the king opens the doors for the feast, he finds that one attendee has refused to put on the provided wedding garment (Christ's robe of righteousness). So, the king has him thrown out into the darkness, where there's "weeping and gnashing of teeth." All who have rejected Christ will suffer the consequence of that choice.

The parable of the banquet (Mt 22.1-14) reveals that since Jews as a people rejected Christ, God invites anyone (ones on the street corners) to enter the new covenant of the kingdom of heaven spiritually by putting on "Christ's robe of righteousness."

According to prophecy on the kingdom of heaven, God will deal with *Jews as a people* in the tribulation. They will repent, and turn away from Antichrist. Then when Christ returns to earth, they will receive him as Savior and enter the new covenant of the kingdom of heaven in the messianic kingdom. Scripture says, "Israel has experienced a hardening in part until the full number of the Gentiles has come in. And so all Israel will be saved" (Ro 11, 25b, 26a).

C. The chronological factor in the kingdom of heaven parables

In the present days of the new covenant, the door is open for all Jewish and Gentile Christians to enter the kingdom of heaven spiritually through Christ. Then when the age of the kingdom of heaven ends, Christ will turn over the messianic kingdom to the Father and will serve at his right hand throughout eternity (He 8.1).

Figure 35 shows that three judgments frame the chronology of the kingdom of heaven—judgment at the cross, judgment at Christ's return to earth, and judgment at the great white throne.

The chronology of the kingdom of heaven has three eras—

The chronological factor in kingdom of heaven parables (324-325)
Timing of the three judgments in the kingdom of heaven.

Figure 35

1. **The kingdom of heaven—judgment at the cross:**
Entry into the kingdom of heaven was made possible when the Lamb of God shed his blood on the cross.

The sins of Christians were judged at the cross forever, and their works will be rewarded in heaven at the future bema judgment seat of Christ for his glory. Works symbolized as silver, gold, and precious stones will bring eternal reward. Works symbolized as wood, hay, and stubble will be burned up (1Co 3.10-16), but all believers themselves will live forever.

2. **The kingdom of heaven—judgment after Jesus returns to earth:**
At that time, Christ judges who is to enter the messianic kingdom:
   a) Surviving tribulation believers enter the messianic kingdom.
   b) The resurrected dead—Old Testament saints and tribulation martyrs—enter the heavenly New Jerusalem.
   c) All unbelievers are arraigned for sentencing at the future great white throne after the messianic kingdom.

3. **End of conflict in the kingdom of heaven—final judgment:**
All unbelievers are to be judged at the great white throne. Then, Christ will turn the kingdom over to the Father.

The following text is in the past tense, but the passage is about the future judgment of unbelievers: "The dead were judged according to what they had done as recorded in the books {without Christ as their advocate!] The sea gave up the dead that were in it, and death and Hades gave up the dead that were in them... Then death and Hades were thrown into the lake of fire" (Re 20.13, 14). This is the judgment God has prepared for Satan and all who reject his Son.

church age, seven-year tribulation, messianic age. *On earth,* the tribulation is a time when God's people are prepared for the future through testing. *In heaven* after the rapture, Christians will have their earthly works tested by fire to determine rewards. In that cleansing by fire, what's been done for Christ will last; all else will be burned up (1Co 3.10-15). This testing purifies Christians to prepare them to become the bride of Christ to reign with him on earth.

Meanwhile, during that same tribulation period, Jews will be tested on earth and brought to repentance under God's wrath and under the persecution of Antichrist. They will be tested for their faithfulness in order to prepare them for entry into the messianic kingdom as subjects under the King of Kings.

After the messianic kingdom, unbelievers of all eras will be judged and sentenced at the great white throne, after which they will spend eternity in the lake of fire, according to their life's choice. About the status of God's people in eternity, Tim LaHaye quotes C. K. Barrett: "It is not the absorption of Christ and mankind, with consequent loss of distinct being into God, but rather the unchallenged reign of God alone in his pure goodness" (Barrett 1968, 361). Here, Barrett is saying that persons in eternity retain their individual identity. And LaHaye sums up God's purpose throughout eternity: "God receives the final glory because of the work of his Son on the cross" (LaHaye 2006, 414) (1Co 15.24-28).

D. The relationship factor in the parables

In the days of the Israelites before the age of the kingdom of heaven began, God related to two people groups—Jews and unbelievers. Now, to understand the period of time that Jesus calls the kingdom of heaven, let's look at the kingdom's relationship factor, according to Christ's relationship to three people groups today.

At Christ's return, God relates to three people groups:

> The purified church as Christ's bride, returning to earth with him
> Human Jews and sympathizers in the messianic kingdom on earth
> Resurrected Israelites / tribulation martyrs in New Jerusalem

In regard to the messianic kingdom, Revelation 21.24b says that human beings from earthly nations will be brought into the heavenly New Jerusalem to fellowship with the resurrected people there. And Revelation 21.26 says that people on earth will walk by the light of the New Jerusalem: "The nations will walk by its light, and the kings of the earth will bring their splendor into it [the New Jerusalem]. On no day will its gates ever be shut, for there will be no night there. The glory and honor of the nations [Gentiles] will be brought into it."

From this we see that in the messianic kingdom, human survivors and resurrected believers of all eras are distinct from each other and reside in different spheres, yet they relate interactively with each other (Re 21.24-27). Jesus says that "many [human beings] will come from the east and the west, and will take their places at the feast with [resurrected] Abraham, Isaac and Jacob" (Mt 8.11). About that feast, Jesus says to his disciples:, "I will not drink of this fruit of the vine from now on until that day when I drink it anew with you in my Father's kingdom" (Mt 26.29b).

E. The love factor in Jesus' parables (Mt 22.1-14)—God's view

As we read in the Word about God caring for the church and Israel, we see into God's great heart of love. This love factor in the kingdom of heaven parables gives us God's view of his people.

Therefore, a Christian, can see that just as the hand of God has led and blessed the church and Israel throughout the centuries, that same hand is extended to each individual Christian today to lead and bless each one throughout life and beyond into eternity.

Man's perspective is to focus on the presence of evil, but God's perspective is to focus on his love for his people.

A prayer with the right perspective— Author unknown

God grant me the serenity to accept the things I cannot change,
The courage to change the things I can,
And the wisdom to know the difference.

An example of God's love in guidance and blessing today

In my college days, since I was planning to major in music, I chose

324 • F. UNDERSTANDING THE KINGDOM OF HEAVEN IN MATTHEW 13

to travel far away to the University of Texas at Austin, a ten hour bus ride in those days. In the school of music, I had a good piano teacher, but she had a negative attitude that I had not had to deal with before, because I had grown up surrounded by praise. Therefore, I found myself dreading my piano lessons rather than looking forward to them.

I thought that maybe my teacher didn't see the problem from my point of view, so finally, I decided I had to act, but I was still puzzled about what step to take. I thought of sending my teacher a book—*How to Win Friends and Influence People*—but instead I decided to talk with her. So I did. I told her how I felt and went so far as to say that her other students reacted favorably to my performance. Anyway, thankfully, the Lord honored my desire to improve the situation. After that conversation, my teacher and I both enjoyed each other in our sessions together. It must have been the Lord that gave me eyes to see my alternatives, as well as giving me "the courage to change the things I can."

I was surprised when my teacher recommended me as a pupil of Dalies Frantz in the next semester, a rare privilege. His reputation was described as "Titan of the Keyboard" by the Denver Public Library in an internet posting on August 25, 2014—years after his death in 1965: "He {Frantz} was scheduled to record the piano soundtrack of a biopic about Frédéric Chopin, but the film *(A Song to Remember)* was postponed by the onset of World War II."

But that's not the end of the story. I was so in awe of having Dalies Frantz as my teacher that I practiced too hard, and as a result, I injured a finger and had to spend the rest of the semester playing left-hand piano pieces. Therefore, months later, at the end of my first year of college, since my finger had not yet healed, God gave me "the serenity to accept the things I cannot change": I knew I had to change my college major from music to English.

In this example, God showed me when to ask for courage to change the things I can.

About my finger—it didn't completely heal until decades later, but here I am, happily writing this book. God is good!

Next, we learn more about the messianic kingdom in prophecy.

THINK JEWISH
to understand the Bible:
Theology from my heart to your heart

J. UNDERSTANDING THE MESSIANIC KINGDOM IN PROPHECY

24. Christ's return, the focus of his Olivet sermon (Mt 24-25)
   A. *Christ's return, fulfillment of God's faithfulness to Israel*
   B. *Christ's return, the focus of the Olivet sermon*
   C. *Christ's return delayed—how responses differ*
   D. *Christ's return interpreted,—Think Jewish!*
   E. *Israel, trophy of God's faithfulness*

25. Perplexing theological issues of the messianic kingdom
   A. *The temple and animal sacrifice in the messianic kingdom*
   B. *Justification for animal sacrifice in the messianic kingdom*
   C. *Eternal human life for those on earth after the messianic kingdom*
   D. *The conclusion drawn from this study of the kingdom*

26. Understanding the true kingdom and its counterfeit
   A. *Israel's hope, the true kingdom*
   B. *The failure of counterfeit kingdoms*
   C. *The showdown after the true kingdom*
   D. *Redemption today and in the future*
   E. *What we know about eternity*
   F. *This book's final challenge*

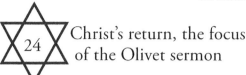

Christ's return, the focus of the Olivet sermon

Prophecy will bring us into an intimate
knowledge of the purpose of God.
—J. Dwight Pentecost in *Prophecy for* Today, 19

Christ's return, the focus of his Olivet Sermon (Mt 24-25):

A. Christ's return, fulfillment of God's promise to Israel
B. Christ's return, the focus of the Olivet sermon
C. Christ's return delayed—how responses differ
D. Christ's return interpreted—Think Jewish!
E. Israel, trophy of God's faithfulness

A. Christ's return, fulfillment of God's faithfulness to Israel

From Genesis to Revelation, God's faithfulness to Israel is central to the Bible's story. He covenanted with Abraham that the Jews would be his people forever, and he gave them the promise of an eternal kingdom, which will begin when Christ returns and will extend into the new heavens and the new earth of eternity. And although as a people, Jews have failed to be faithful to that covenant, God has been faithful to them throughout the generations. He has always redeemed a faithful Jewish remnant to carry forward his plan.

I think about God's faithfulness when I recall my parents' faithfulness. They would get me out of difficult situations I had created. One time in early grade school, we kids were to meet in front of the school as a group before being taken to the swimming pool, which was twelve miles away in another town—a very long distance in those times. Going to Cascade pool was a treat for all of us, and we looked forward to the fun. And with that kind of anticipation, I got ready and ran over to the school a couple of blocks away. I had my swimsuit, my swim cap, my towel, and some money—everything I needed. And I arrived there out of breath… only to find… I 'd been left behind! No one was there!

All hope was gone and there was nothing I could do about it except mourn my loss! And mourn I did, as I trudged back home to tell my mother the sad news. But presto! My mother flew into action, got the car out of the garage and rushed me to the pool. I was responsible for my tardiness, but my mother did not take that into account. She was just glad to save the day for me! Likewise, for me, what the Father takes into account about my life is that I am in his family through acceptance of his Son as my Savior.

All of us as human beings create situations from which only God can deliver us. Then when we face the problems that arise, we have to choose whether to stew over the consequences or to seek God's counsel. In my dilemma I looked to my mother and submitted to her guidance. So too, collectively under Christ in the messianic kingdom, citizens will have to choose whether to willingly submit to God's authority over them or to rebel. Some will choose to rebel even in the idyllic thousand-year kingdom during which Satan is bound. This means that during that kingdom, the rebels of later generations will be unredeemed, and Messiah will have to rule the world with an "iron scepter" (Re 12.5)—that is, by force. At the end of the thousand-year kingdom, a multitude of rebels will join Satan's army and surround Jerusalem… but Christ/Messiah will save the day. He will triumph over Satan and will sustain Israel as his people.

B. Christ's return, the focus of the Olivet sermon

Jesus' Olivet sermon, Matthew 24-25, is about the last days, which is the last part of a conflict that began with Adam and Eve's disobedience. When the first couple disobeyed, their disobedience resulted in God initiating redemption by killing an animal to clothe them with his righteousness, for by this first blood offering, God pointed ahead to mankind's redemption through his Son's blood sacrifice. In fact, all Judaic blood sacrifices point to the sacrifice of God's Son.

Also relevant in the creation story is that God barred Adam and Eve from the tree of life, lest they eat its fruit before the appointed time and live forever in their sinful condition. God will not allow anyone to eat of that fruit until after he lifts the earth's curse of sin and death (Re 22.2-3a). And though that curse will not be totally lifted until after the future thousand-year kingdom, Satan himself will be bound and imprisoned in a pit during the kingdom (Re 20.2-3). And while Christ rules in the messianic kingdom, every knee will bow and every tongue confess "that Christ is Lord" (Php 2.9-11). Ruling by force, Christ will begin fulfilling the Father's promise that Israel would have a land and a kingdom forever.

The messianic kingdom will be the climax of the Bible's story, for it marks the end of the times of the Gentiles and the beginning of Israel's prominence on the world stage. In that story, the red thread of blood-bought redemption weaves its way through the Bible—first through Israel's story, then through the church's story. Finally, the stories intersect in the earthly messianic kingdom of redeemed people, during which the resurrected church will be the bride of Christ and earthly Israel will be exalted among nations. But the story doesn't end there. It goes on into eternity, at which time all creation will have been redeemed for the glory of God.

The Bible's story steadfastly presses toward its final conclusion:
>from man's fall from grace,
>to rebellion of mankind at Babel,
>to God's promise to father Abraham,
>to God's proffered redemption at the cross,
>to the birth and life of the church on the earth,
>to the blessed society of Christ's messianic kingdom,
>to victory in conflict when Satan and his followers rebel,
>to God's ultimate goal of full expression of himself in eternity.

God will keep his promise to Israel about the messianic kingdom, but even so, not until *after* the messianic kingdom will he totally cleanse the earth of all evil, for not until then will he throw Satan, death, and Hades into the lake of fire (Re 20.10,14).

C. Christ's return delayed—how responses differ

At Christ/Messiah's coming, the Jews expected him to fulfill his role as Israel's deliverer, but the crucifixion "delayed" that deliverance; therefore, Christ had to prepare his followers for the delay, which has now lasted over two thousand years—and incidentally, response to this delay differs for Israel and the church, for each has its own unique calling.

In the Olivet sermon, Jesus tells his Jewish followers that in the tribulation, they'll be tested for their faithfulness. He tells them therefore to *watch* for his return at any moment, for at his return, the faithful will enter the kingdom, and unbelievers will be taken for judgment. The Bible says, "One [person] will be taken [to be judged] and the other left [to enter the kingdom] (Mt 24.40-41). *

Chronological response of people before and after Christ's return:

1) Response of Jewish and Gentile Christians today—Wait! (1 Th 1.9-10)
2) Response of Jews as a people in the tribulation—Watch! (Mt 24-25)
3) Response of unbelievers at Jesus' return—Shock and Panic! (Re 6.16-17)

1) Response of Jewish and Gentile Christians today—Wait! †

*I*n the kingdom of heaven, there is spiritual conflict between good and evil. However, on earth today, Jewish and Gentile Christians do not watch for impending judgment, for their sins were judged at the cross. Instead, they *wait* for Christ's return to rapture them to heaven before the tribulation begins. Paul describes the rapture: "The Lord himself will come down from heaven, with a loud command, with the voice of the archangel and with the trumpet call of God, and the dead in Christ will rise first. After that, we who are still alive and are left will be caught up together with them in the clouds to meet the Lord in the air. And so we will be with the Lord forever" (1Th 4.16-17).

Christians *await* their marriage to the Beloved. The wedding (Re 19.7) will take place in heaven during earth's tribulation, and the feast will take place on earth afterwards in the messianic kingdom.

2) Response of Jews as a people in the tribulation—Watch!

Jesus says that during the kingdom's delay, Jews as a people will face "the tribulation,"‡ a period of testing (Mt 24.21 KJV, ASV,

---

* J. Vernon McGee (1983, Vol 4, 122) says this passage shows the removing from earth by judgment those who will not enter the messianic kingdom, so this isn't about the church's rapture.
† L. S. Chafer (1948, 1976, Vol 4, 23) distinguishes Israel's *watching* from the church's *waiting*.
‡ In Mt 24.21, NIV says"distress." NET says "suffering." Most versions say "tribulation," which conforms with prophecy about the tribulation period when God pours out his wrath on earth.

ESV, NKJV). In those seven years, Antichrist will persecute Jews, and God will test their faithfulness, as he pours out his wrath on Satan's counterfeit, earthly kingdom under the Antichrist. Therefore, in the tribulation, believing Jews are to *watch* for Christ's return, for he will come at an hour when they don't expect him (Mt 24.44). When he comes, "one [person] will be taken [to be judged] and the other left [to enter the kingdom] (Mt 24.40-41).

During their suffering in the tribulation, Jews in their misery will repent of their rejection of Christ. Then when Christ returns, the tide will turn for them as a people. That's when they will be redeemed by God and exalted among nations, for in all generations, God has used a faithful Jewish remnant to advance the plan that he set up for Israel before he created the heavens and the earth.

Isaiah says God promises resurrection, triumph, and justice for Israel:
"But your dead will live; their bodies will rise. You who dwell in the dust, wake up and shout for joy. Your dew is like the dew of the morning; the earth will give birth to her dead... Hide yourselves for a little while until his [God's] wrath has passed by [until after the tribulation]..." (Is 26.19a,-20b).

"In that day [when Christ returns], the LORD Almighty will be a glorious crown, a beautiful wreath for the remnant of his people [the Jews]. He will be a spirit of justice to him who sits in judgment, a source of strength to those who turn back the battle at the gate [of Jerusalem]" (Is 28.5-6).

3) Response of unbelievers at Jesus' return—Shock and Panic!
Scripture uses the past tense to say that at Christ's return, unbelievers will suffer shock and panic, for they will face God's wrath: "Then the kings of the earth, the princes, the generals, the rich, the mighty, and every slave and every free man hid in caves and among the rocks of the mountains. They called to the mountains and the rocks, 'Fall on us and hide us from the face of him who sits on the throne and from the wrath of the Lamb! For the great day of their wrath has come and who can stand'" (Re 6.16-17)?

D. Christ's return interpreted, —Think Jewish!

To think Jewish about Jesus' Olivet sermon (Mt 24-25) affects its interpretation. For example, some interpreters believe that the church has replaced Jews in God's program. So, they apply the Olivet sermon to Christians. But interpreters who "think Jewish" recognize that in Matthew 24-25, Jesus is preparing his Jewish audience to be ready for the intense testing that lies ahead for a future generation of Jews during the tribulation. As we go through scripture, we see that God will use the testing of the seven-year tribulation period to draw the Jews as a people back to himself once again and to prepare them for entry into the messianic kingdom under Christ/Messiah.

As we think Jewish about the messianic kingdom, we'll examine the three passages of Matthew 25. They are about Christ's return after the tribulation, before the messianic kingdom begins.

Interpreting the three passages of Matthew 25 about the future:

1) *Parable of the ten virgins—about the need for the Jews during the tribulation to be watchful for Messiah's coming* (Mt 25.1-13)

2) *Parable of the talents—about the testing of the Jews' faithfulness during the tribulation* (Mt 25.14-30)

3) *Metaphor of the sheep and goats—about the judgment of Gentiles after the tribulation* (Mt 25.31-46)

1) *Parable of the ten virgins—about the need for the Jews during the tribulation to be watchful for Messiah's coming* (Mt 25.1-13)

The ten virgins (ten bridesmaids) *watch* for the Lamb's wedding procession, which they will join as they go together with them into the wedding feast. This parable is about a future generation of Jews who will be living during the tribulation on earth. They are instructed as a people to *watch* for Christ/Messiah's return, for when he comes the watchful ones will be ready to enter the wedding feast of the messianic kingdom.

The parable shows that the bridesmaids are to be like the five wise virgins who carried enough oil to last through a delay—not like the five foolish virgins, whose oil supply was insufficient. So when the bridegroom comes, the five foolish virgins, who have no oil, cannot go into the feast, for they have no time to buy more oil and cannot borrow from the five wise virgins. Therefore, only the faithful virgins,will enter the joy of the wedding feast. And that's how it will be for the Jews when Jesus returns to earth. Only the wise will be watchful throughout the kingdom's delay. Only they will enter into the joy of the Lord's messianic kingdom.

Similar ancient wedding customs in China still prevail. The day begins with the groom taking his betrothed from the bride's home to his father's compound and then to a nearby cafe for a banquet feast. During the school year that I taught in China, I used to see wedding parties dressed in red, the bridal color there, walking together on their way from the groom's father's home to the wedding banquet.

In the ten-virgins parable, oil symbolizes the Holy Spirit. Here we see that *all* Jews are called to be God's people, but not all respond. Those who respond will turn to Christ, will be forgiven, and will become born-again saints that will take part in the messianic wedding feast with Abraham, Isaac, and Jacob (Mt 8.11,12). The abundant oil that these wise virgins have in their lamps signifies the oil of the Spirit, which will dwell eternally within them after they've become redeemed believers of the messianic kingdom.

During the tribulation, God will open the eyes of the faithful Jews to recognize the Antichrist as a counterfeit. This will cause them to turn away from him to serve the true Christ/Messiah. Therefore, in the parable of the ten virgins, only these repentant, believing Jews will come prepared with enough oil in their lamps to last them through the delay of the coming of Christ in the wedding procession. In this parable of the ten bridesmaids, Jesus is speaking to a generation in the tribulation. He assures them that when they stay true to his covenant, he'll stay true to them; that is, he'll come to take them into the promised messianic feast.

Jews are the ones with whom God made his covenant of the promised kingdom, so that may be why they/re required to have faith to believe the promise throughout the trials of the tribulation. After those seven years, Gentiles sympathetic to Jews also enter covenant blessings but not by direct promise. So, for Jews as a people, the watchword during the tribulation is, "Be faithful!" As children of Abraham's covenant, they are to be faithful to the God of that covenant.

The parable of the ten virgins (ten bridesmaids) is not the only passage that uses a wedding feast symbol to refer to the time of the messianic kingdom. Another such biblical reference in John 3 gives words spoken by John the Baptist (Jn 3.22-30). As a representative of the Jews, he said, "A man can receive only what is given him from heaven. You yourselves can testify that I said, 'I am not the Christ but am sent ahead of him.' The bride [the church] belongs to the bridegroom [Christ]. The friend who attends the bridegroom [the Jews] waits and listens for him, and is full of joy when he hears the bridegroom's voice. That joy is mine, and it is now complete. He [Christ] must become greater; I must become less" (Jn 3.27-30).

This John 3 passage is about Jesus' wedding feast on earth during the messianic kingdom when Jews as a people will be guests at the wedding feast of the groom [Christ]. In fact, in this passage, Jews are called friends of the groom. Now from this example, we learn that "thinking Jewish" sheds new light on familiar passages.

2) Parable of the talents—about the testing of the Jews' faithfulness during the tribulation (Mt 25.14-30)

Scripture often refers to Jews as servants or stewards. In the parable of the talents, while the master (Christ) is away, the servants (Jews) are entrusted with talents (money) to invest. This means that when Christ as Master returns, Jews, who are stewards of the Abrahamic covenant, will be judged by the measure of their *faithfulness* to the God of that covenant.

Here we must differentiate between *Jews as a people* and *Jews as individuals*. In a future generation, Jews as a people, enter directly into the messianic kingdom as human beings. However, in the present age, Jews as individual believers enter the kingdom of heaven *spiritually* through the church (Eph 5.25-27; Re 19.7 mid). Matthew 24-25 addresses Jews as a people, who in a yet future generation will enter the messianic kingdom as human citizens. In the present age, Jewish Christians in the church become the bride of Christ and later will reign with him in the messianic kingdom.

For Jews as a people today, Judaic temple worship is not now available since the Islamic dome occupies the site that scripture designates as the place where Israel's messianic temple will stand. Today, the only option for Jewish reconciliation with God is for them to be willing to enter the new covenant through the blood of the Lord Jesus Christ, the Savior of Jews and Gentiles alike.

Let's summarize. Today God gives Jews as individuals an opportunity to accept Jesus as Messiah and to become part of the church; later they will reign with him as his bride. But for Jews as a people in a future generation, Messiah will bring that generation of Jews directly into his messianic kingdom as born-again human citizens.

3) Metaphor of the sheep and goats—about the judgment of Gentiles after the tribulation (Mt 25.31-46)

This third passage, Matthew 25.31-46, is not a parable. It is about Gentiles who survive the future tribulation. Jesus says he'll judge them by how they treated the Jews. To describe believing and unbelieving Gentile survivors of the tribulation respectively, Jesus speaks metaphorically about sheep and goats. In the passage, he speaks of the reality of a future time of judgment on earth by saying, "When the Son of Man comes in his glory, and all the angels with him, he will sit on his throne in heavenly glory. All the nations (Gentiles) will be gathered before him, and he will separate the people one from another as a shepherd separates sheep from goats" (Mt 25.31-34).

This passage in Matthew 25.31-46 is about the shepherd separating believing Gentiles from unbelieving Gentiles. Jesus says that when he comes in glory, he'll gather the nations (Gentiles) and say to the sheep (believing Gentiles), "Come... take your inheritance... For I was hungry and you gave me something to eat, I was thirsty and you gave me something to drink, I was a stranger and you invited me in, I needed clothes and you clothed me, I was sick and you looked after me, I was in prison and you came to visit me." Then the righteous will ask when they did those things and he'll reply, "Whatever you did for one of the least of these brothers of mine [the Jews], you did for me." Therefore, these redeemed sheep, the Gentile sympathizers of the Jews, will enter the messianic kingdom, along with the redeemed Jews of Israel.

But as for the unbelieving Gentiles, the goats, Christ says, "Whatever you did not do for one of the least of these [Jews], you did not do for me" (Mt 25.45). Therefore, Christ will destroy the mortal life of those unbelieving Gentile survivors of the tribulation. Then, from other passages, we know that he arraigns these unbelievers for resurrection and for judgment at the great white throne at the end of time before eternity begins This sorting of sheep and goats in this Gentile judgment will take place in fulfillment of God's promise to Abraham, for he promised that he will bless or curse those who bless or curse Israel (Ge 12.3).

E. Israel, trophy of God's faithfulness

When a person wends his way through a maze, he doesn't know where a turn will take him, for he faces a nonsensical situation. In Matthew 25, Jesus prepares the *Jews as a people* for a future time that without his counsel would otherwise seem to be senseless. He assures them that in spite of Antichrist's antisemitic persecution and the execution of Jewish believers during the tribulation period, God's hand will still be upon that generation of faithful Jews. In the Olivet sermon, Jesus prepares a future generation of Jews for the dark period of the tribulation, which today is still future.

When Jesus returns to earth after the marriage takes place in heaven, the church as his bride will return to earth with him, at which time Christ will judge the tribulation survivors. Of these human survivors, only the redeemed Jews and Gentiles will enter the kingdom where John the Baptist and countless others of the redeemed Hebrew saints will sit down with Abraham, Isaac, and Jacob. This will take place at the wedding feast to celebrate the marriage of the Lamb to the church, his bride. What a joyous time!

Every year during the kingdom, the Jews will celebrate the feast of Tabernacles to remind them of their triumphant entry into the messianic kingdom. This final journey is an exodus through the thousand-year messianic kingdom on the way to eternity. And it will be in fulfillment of the "type" that is described as the first exodus from Egypt to the promised land.

In this final exodus, the Israelis will sing the song of Moses, which says, "You will bring them [the Jews] in and plant them on the mountain of your inheritance... The Lord [Jesus] will reign for ever and ever" (Ex 15.17,18). He will reign first in the messianic kingdom and then in eternity in submission to the Father. In the messianic kingdom, the Jews will remember God's promise as given to Israel in the book of Isaiah, which says, "For the LORD will take delight in you, and your land will be married." This marriage metaphor says that the land of Israel will forever belong to Israel and their God (Is 62.4).

The prophet Jeremiah warned the Jews to remain faithful in serving God. He writes, "Cursed is the one who trusts in man, who depends on flesh for his strength and whose heart turns away from the LORD. The heart is deceitful above all things and beyond cure... I the LORD search the heart and examine the mind, to reward a man... according to what his deeds deserve" (Je 17.5-10. Italics).

Since Israel is God's covenant nation, he therefore tests their faithfulness to their covenant with him. But unfortunately we have seen that in the past *as a people* they have failed. They failed in their response to the prophets, when they killed them. They failed when they crucified their Messiah. And when they had opportunity for repentance on the day of Pentecost, they rejected that offer, and roughly forty years later, their temple was destroyed in A.D. 70. Yet, because the Jews now have no temple and no priesthood, the church age has become a time of prolonged opportunity for them to be reconciled to God by recognizing Jesus as their High Priest and Savior. In the present age, those Jews who carry forward God's plan are those who become Jewish Christians.

In the future kingdom, God will express his glory through his people—through the church as Jesus' bride and through Israel as a nation exalted above all the other nations of the world. Through the ages in each generation, a faithful Jewish remnant has always survived, and that remnant has flowed relentlessly through history in the same way that the warm waters of the Gulf Stream flow forcefully through cold water by means of one of the strongest known currents. That natural stream by its strength pushes aside all else in order to go where it wills. This description of the Gulf Stream illustrates the strength and persistence of God in bringing the Jews to repentance and in bringing them to acceptance of their Messiah.

In the end, the Jews will be a trophy of God's faithfulness—his trophy of truth—for he expresses his glory through the faithful remnant of Israel when he keeps his promises to them. In fact, when John in a vision in Revelation sees Jesus in heaven returning to earth to deliver the Jewish people, he identifies Jesus as the one who is "Faithful and True" (Re 19.11).

Let's close with a scene of the blessedness of the messianic kingdom, as prophesied by Isaiah:

> "He will strike the earth with the rod of his mouth;
>   with the breath of his lips he will slay the wicked.
> Righteousness will be his belt
>   and faithfulness the sash around his waist.
> The wolf will live with the lamb,
>   the leopard will lie down with the goat,
> the calf and the lion and the yearling together;
>   and a little child will lead them…
> They will neither harm nor destroy
>   on all my holy mountain,
> for the earth will be full of the knowledge of the LORD
>   as the waters cover the sea" (Is 11.4b-9).

In the next chapter we'll face issues concerning the future messianic kingdom, for though we read about the peace and joy of that earthly paradise, we still have to resolve perplexing issues about that future time.

Perplexing theological issues of God's messianic kingdom

25

> Take the blood from the body, and you have nothing left but a corpse. Take the blood of Calvary from Christianity, and you have lifeless creed instead of living faith.
> —Arthur M. Barnett

Before we tackle issues, let's get a glimpse into God's thousand year messianic kingdom where he promises *joy*, *wholeness*, and his *steadfast love:*
> "The ransomed of the LORD shall return,
>   and come to Zion with songs and
>   everlasting *joy* upon their heads:
> they shall obtain joy and gladness,
>   and sorrow and sighing shall flee away" (Is 35.10).

In that era of *wholeness*, Isaiah predicts youthful buoyancy:
> "Never again will there be in it
>   an infant who lives but a few days,
>   or an old man who does not live out his years;
> he who dies at a hundred
>   will be thought a mere youth;
> he who fails to reach a hundred
>   will be considered accursed" (Is 65.20).

God promises *his steadfast love for Israel:*
> "To me this is like the days of Noah,
>   when I swore that the waters of Noah
>   would never again cover the earth.
> So now I have sworn not to be angry with you,
>   never to rebuke you again.
>   Though the mountains be shaken
>   and the hills be removed,
> yet my unfailing love for you will not be shaken
>   nor my covenant of peace be removed,"
>   says the LORD, who has compassion on you" (Is 54..9-10).

Perplexing theological issues of the messianic kingdom:

A. *The temple and animal sacrifice in the messianic kingdom*
B. *Justification for animal sacrifice in the messianic kingdom*
C. *Eternal human life for those on earth after the messianic kingdom*
D. *The conclusion drawn from this study of the kingdom*

A. *The temple and animal sacrifice in the messianic kingdom*

Issues about the temple in the messianic kingdom

Ezekiel 40-48 is about the temple in Israel's messianic kingdom. There we see details of an architectural plan for a temple that is different from all previous Hebrew temples. Also the ordinances, rituals, and priesthood of that temple differ somewhat from those described in the Torah. This discrepancy leads us to believe that Ezekiel 40-48 is about a future Judaic temple. Moreover, the abundance of minutiae about the temple leads us to conclude that this temple of the future messianic kingdom will indeed be a real stone-and-mortar temple, not just a symbolic representation.

The Judaic temple exists for offering blood sacrifice to bring reconciliation between God and man. Scripture explains this: "For the life of a creature is in its blood, and I have given it to you to make atonement[*] for yourselves on the altar; it is the blood that makes atonement for one's life" (Le 17.11). As described in this verse from the Torah, we see that God states that the shedding of blood is necessary for atonement.[*] God who is holy cannot tolerate sin.

All Judaic animal sacrifice points to Christ's sacrifice, as a substitute death for sinners. Christ's blood sacrifice has met God's requirement for holiness, and his blood sacrifice fully satisfies man's need for forgiveness and restores him to fellowship with the Lord. In fact, blood sacrifice is central to both Judaism and Christianity. Arthur M. Barrett says, "Take the blood from the body, and you have nothing left but a corpse. Take the blood of Calvary from Christianity, and you have lifeless creed instead of living faith."

Through this atonement by the blood sacrifice of Jesus, believers exchange their old life for his new life. To explain how

---

[*] One way to aid understanding and remembrance for the word *atonement* is to think, "at-one-ment."

this exchange has been made possible, Paul says, "Sin entered the world through one man [Adam], and death through sin, and in this way death came to all men, because all sinned" (Ro 5.12). Then Paul explains, "But the gift is not like the trespass. For if the many died by the trespass of the one man [Adam], how much more did God's grace… overflow to the many!" (Ro 5.15).

Simply stated, man fell from grace because of the sin of one man, Adam, and man is redeemed by the blood sacrifice of one man, Jesus.

The message of animal sacrifice

The necessity for animal sacrifice can best be understood from mankind's history—from the time of animal sacrifice by Adam's sons. Cain offered "some of the fruits of the soil" and was not accepted by God. Abel offered a blood sacrifice from "the firstborn of his flock" and was accepted by God (Ge 4.1-7). The message of blood sacrifice is that God is holy, sin is unacceptable, and man needs a blood substitute to be reconciled with the Lord.

Christ/Messiah is that substitute Savior. Born of the heavenly Father and a virgin mother, he's the only one without sin, so he's the only one who can make reconciliation possible. And though we cannot fully understand God's love expressed through his Son on the cross, what we do understand is that sin separates from God and that sinners deserve death, as symbolized by the blood.

What makes animal sacrifice in the messianic kingdom a perplexing issue is that Jesus has already made his one and only perfect blood sacrifice for man's salvation. So the question is, *why* is animal sacrifice required in Israel's future temple of the kingdom?

B. Justification for animal sacrifice in the messianic kingdom

Six factors supporting justification for sacrifice in the kingdom:

1) Justification for Judaic animal sacrifice—a topic of debate
2) Type of sacrifice—dictated by the identities of Israel and the church
3) Purpose of Judaic animal sacrifice—renewed fellowship with God
4) Acceptability of sacrifice—determined by motivation
5) Significance of animal sacrifice—in Israel's past and future
6) Animal sacrifice demystified—distinguishing sonship and fellowship

1) Justification for Judaic animal sacrifice—a topic of debate

How do today's biblical scholars defend the legitimacy of animal sacrifice in the future messianic kingdom? Many say that messianic animal sacrifice is simply a *memorial* that points back to Jesus' sacrifice on the cross, just as Old Testament sacrifice is a *type* that points ahead to his sacrifice on the cross. The people with this view argue that animal sacrifice in the past was *not efficacious* by reason of the fact that the offerings in themselves do not take away sin; they only point to Christ's sacrifice. Others say that *atonement* in the book of Hebrews (NT) and in Leviticus (OT) means "a covering," in which case Old Testament animal sacrifice would only cover sin until Christ's sacrifice would become a reality.

Though these explanations are reasonable, they minimize the importance the Israelites themselves placed on what God ordained for them. The Israelites did not see their sacrifices as types, symbols, or expendable rituals. They thought in terms of obedience that would please God: They confessed real sins and sacrificed live animals for those sins. Therefore, their offering was *adequate* when given in love for God and in obedience to him. What I am saying is that for David and other Israelites who truly loved the Lord, their sacrifices were more than the exercise of formal ritual.

In a debate about the role of animal sacrifice, John Whitcomb counters the types-memorial view by saying that though the death of God's Son "has always been and always will be the final basis of spiritual salvation," animal sacrifice under the levitical order did possess "an outward efficacy for the removal of *ceremonial* pollution" (Whitcomb 1985. Italics added). Jerry M. Hullinger also refers to the animal sacrifices as atonement to remove ceremonial uncleanness. He says the sacrifices would be necessary in the messianic kingdom because of the glorious presence of Jehovah dwelling once again in the Jewish temple on earth (Hullinger 1995). These interpreters that address ceremonial pollution, claim greater efficacy for God's ordained offerings than interpreters already presented here, but in my estimation, their interpretation still falls short.

I didn't come to a satisfactory conclusion about animal sacri-

343. PERPLEXING THEOLOGICAL ISSUES OF THE MESSIANIC KINGDOM • 343

fice in the future messianic kingdom until I pondered this fact—
that atonement reconciles sinners with God. As I contemplated this
truth, the fog began to lift. I thought, God himself commanded
animal sacrifice; therefore, when Israelites of old and Israelis of the
future (Eze 40-48) by faith obey his command to offer animal sacrifice, he brings to pass what he intends—their restored fellowship
with himself. Therefore, we can conclude that the Judaic way for
renewing fellowship with God is through animal sacrifice. And
we can conclude that the Judaic mode accomplishes for the Jews
what God intends—restoration of fellowship with himself.

And since we see that reconciliation is God's purpose and that
he delights in the future messianic offerings, we can therefore attribute full efficacy to those sacrifices commanded by God.

2) Type of sacrifice—dictated by the identities of Jews and Christians
Sometimes recognizing Israel's identity as God's earthly people
and recognizing the church's identity as God's spiritual people
resolves biblical issues, and here is an example of that fact.

Since Jews as a people are identified as God's earthly people,
their sacrifice is *earthly animal sacrifice* in both their past temple
and in their future messianic temple. Christians, however, who
are identified as his spiritual people, offer *spiritual sacrifice* (He 13.15)
by responding to God spiritually through faith (He 13.15). And these
offerings by both Israel and the church are honored by God.

3) Purpose of Judaic animal sacrifice—renewed fellowship with God
In both Christianity and Judaism, believers become reconciled
with God by the blood of the sacrifice that they offer—for Christians by the blood of Christ and for Jews by the blood of an animal. Scripture also reveals the symbolism—that animal sacrifice
points to the blood that Christ would shed for his brothers.

Jewish believers and Christian believers also need a way to
express the depth of their devotion to God, and for that too, God
provides appropriate sacrifice for Israel and the church. Burnt sacrifice is the animal sacrifice for expressing Judaic dedication to
God, and spiritual sacrifice is the offering for expressing Christian
dedication to God.

In Romans 12.1-2, Paul describes Christian dedication by

saying that the surrender of the will by Christians is their burnt sacrifice, figuratively speaking. He writes, "Therefore, I urge you, brothers, in view of God's mercy, to offer your bodies as living sacrifices, holy and pleasing to God—this is your *spiritual* act of worship. Do not conform any longer to the pattern of this world, but be transformed by the renewing of your mind. Then you will be able to test and approve what God's will is—his good, pleasing and perfect will" (Ro 12.1-2. Italics added).

4) Acceptability of sacrifice—determined by motivation

In our search for those factors that justify animal sacrifice, we find an important one in the New Testament book of Hebrews, which was written to Hebrew Christians. (Remember that all Christians were Jewish in the early days of the church, for Christianity was a sect within Judaism.) These early-church Christians who are addressed in the book of Hebrews were wavering in their Christian faith because they faced the temptation to return to the practice of animal sacrifice in order to escape persecution from Jewish leaders.

To these wavering Christians, the author of Hebrews says that Christ's sacrifice is unique, for it is the one and only sacrifice that transforms the human heart. Keep in mind that these Jewish Christians had already been transformed by the new birth; therefore, to return to animal sacrifice would have been to reject the Lord's sacrifice on the cross. Theirs was a problem of the heart. They had to see that there could be no turning back. Peter understood this, for during Jesus' lifetime when many began to abandon him, Jesus asked Peter if he too was going to stop following him. Peter responded by saying, "To whom shall we go? You have the words of eternal life" (Jn 6.68).

Then years later, we see into Paul's heart, in a decision he made to take part in a Jewish purification rite. Here's what happened. When Paul reported to the Christian leaders in Jerusalem about his ministry to the Gentiles, they gave him advice. They told him that since he taught that Gentile Christians are not required to be circumcised, he should reassure the Jewish Christians that he still honors the Torah. Therefore, those leaders advised him to take part in a Judaic purification rite that required animal sacrifice, for by so doing, he would demonstrate to Jews and to fellow Christians that he still lived according to the law (Ac 21.20-24).

Paul remembered Jesus' words about the law: "Do not think that I have come to abolish the Law or the Prophets; I have not come to abolish them but to fulfill them. I tell you the truth, until heaven and earth disappear, not the smallest letter, not the least stroke of a pen, will by any means disappear from the Law until everything is accomplished" (Mt 5.17-18).

Paul knew that he could agree to participate in that Jewish purification rite without being disloyal to Christ, for he knew that as a Christian, he wasn't circumscribed by the law. He referred to scripture to prove his point: "'Everything is permissible for me'—but not everything is beneficial. 'Everything is permissible for me'—but I will not be mastered by anything" (1Co 6.12). Therefore, Paul chose to follow the counsel of the Jewish leaders; he agreed to present the blood offering of the Judaic purification rite.

Paul knew he would be scripturally correct in making the animal sacrifice, for he knew that since he would accomplish a beneficial purpose in offering his sacrifice, he wouldn't be disloyal to Christ. The beneficial purpose was that he would demonstrate that Christianity does not abolish the law; instead, it fulfills the law.

However, Paul was prevented from offering that sacrifice because a riot erupted. This uprising happened because the crowd thought Paul had brought a Gentile into the temple and that he had thereby desecrated it. That perception, though false, caused him to be arrested, and his arrest by authorities then made it impossible for him to carry through on the blood-sacrifice ritual.

Nevertheless, the record reveals that Paul had no objection to making the blood sacrifice. But how can that be? Didn't he upbraid the Galatians because they punctiliously observed Hebrew traditions? Didn't he say, "I fear for you, that somehow I have wasted my efforts on you" (Ga 4.10)? And didn't he say that "all who rely on observing the law are under a curse if they do not continue to do everything written in the Book of the Law" (Ga 3,10)?

The answer to all the above is yes. Yet nevertheless, since Paul knew that Christianity is the fulfillment of the law—not the abolishment of the law—he was free to participate in the Judaic rite. Therefore, Paul's willingness to participate confirms the legitimacy of animal sacrifice offered since Jesus' crucifixion (Ac 24.16-18).

Also, besides knowing the legitimacy of animal sacrifice since the crucifixion, Paul knew that as with any Judaic or Christian ritual, *what matters to God is the motivation of the offerer.* King David understood this, for he loved God's law, and the prophets understood this, too, for they taught that God is offended by an offering made from a wrong motive.

What we can say confidently is that Paul's participation in the purification rite was simply his Judaic expression of devotion to the Lord. His willingness to offer animal sacrifice was not, and should not be construed to be, a compromise of his loyalty to the Lord Jesus, for in Judaism as in Christianity, the attitude of the heart is the ground for God's judgment of people's actions.

In Paul's case, he deemed his return to animal sacrifice to be a sincere expression of his devotion to the Lord, but on the other hand, the motivation of the wavering Christians addressed in the book of Hebrews was different. Their animal sacrifice would have been inspired by the motivation of escaping the persecution that Christians had to face in that day. For them to offer animal sacrifice would have meant a cowardly rejection of the sacrifice made by their Savior (He 6.4-6) by returning to Judaism.

5) Significance of animal sacrifice—in Israel's past and future

In my pursuit for answers about blood sacrifice, I found what Hobart E. Freeman writes in the *Grace Journal*—that too often interpreters fail to look at sacrifice from the Hebraic view. Freeman says Israelites did not see their sacrifices as types but as acts of significance, for only in hindsight do people call them types. He says that "sacrifice to the pious Jew was not simply a perfunctory ritual but was an important element in his moral obedience to the revealed will of God." Freeman says sacrifice was "by its nature intensely personal, ethical, moral, and spiritual, for *it was intended to reflect the attitude of the heart and will toward God.*" (*Grace Journal*, Winter 1963). Freeman adds that when a person diminishes the sacredness and effectiveness of Hebrew animal sacrifice, he minimizes what God commands in the Torah. Also, note that what applies to animal sacrifice in ancient Israel applies to their animal sacrifices in the messianic era (Eze 40-48).

Freeman's view addresses animal sacrifice in reference to the Old Testament, but what he says also helps us understand animal sacrifice in the future messianic kingdom. For if we apply Freeman's view of messianic kingdom sacrifices, and if we then take into account what he says about God's purpose for all animal sacrifices—"to reflect the offerer's attitude of the heart and will toward God"—we conclude that the Judaic practice of animal sacrifice in the messianic kingdom will be more than just memorials or types or ceremonial cleansers. They accomplish for Jews what God intends.

Having said that, the New Testament book of Hebrews nevertheless *appears* to rule out the legitimacy of animal sacrifice after Jesus' crucifixion. The author of Hebrews says, "It is impossible for the blood of bulls and goats to take away sins (He 10.4)… Where these [sins] have been forgiven [by the blood of Jesus], there is no longer any [other] sacrifice for sin" (He 10.4 , 18). That's the apparent perception, but the reality is that Hebrew scripture does say that God will reinstitute the animal sacrifice of the future messianic kingdom (Is 56:6-8; Zch 14:16; Je 33:15-19.).

6) Animal sacrifice demystified—distinguishing sonship and fellowship

That a believer in the messianic age is reborn as God's child forever, is pointed out by J. Dwight Pentecost, who quotes John F. Walvoord as saying, "All believers will be indwelt by the Holy Spirit in the Millennium [messianic kingdom], even as they are in the present age" (J. Dwight Pentecost 1958, 486) (Eze 36.27; 37.14; cf Je 31.33). We know this to be true, for we know that believers, both today and in the future messianic kingdom, live under the new covenant, and under that covenant, God's Holy Spirit indwells those who accept Christ as Redeemer.

The key to understanding offerings under the new covenant in the church today and in Israel in the future is to recognize the distinction between sonship and fellowship. We can understand the difference in a human relationship, for we know that sonship begins with a child's birth, and fellowship takes place as the child progresses through life. The distinction is that *sonship* endures even when *fellowship* is temporarily interrupted or broken.

Now let me explain how such a distinction between sonship and fellowship applies to Jews and their sympathizers in the messianic kingdom. In spite of their relationship to God as his redeemed people, Jews during the messianic kingdom will need frequent forgiveness and cleansing, for although the sonship of those future believers will have been forever established, their fellowship with God will be interrupted when their feet get dirty as they walk on the earth. Therefore, just like born-again Christians in the present age, those messianic believers will be mortal beings in need of continued renewal of fellowship in their walk with God, and animal sacrifice is the means whereby Jews connect with God to fulfill that renewal in their lives.

For Jews in the messianic kingdom, renewed fellowship with God is celebrated in the Judaic mode of animal sacrifice in temple worship. For Jewish and Gentile Christians today, renewed fellowship with God is observed by faith expressed through confession, prayer, and praise. For Christians, the spiritual ritual for remembrance of such renewal is celebrated in the communion service. How I appreciate my security in the Father's steadfast love! In my nineties, what a delightful journey I've enjoyed in knowing I'm secure in my relationship to God as his child and also in knowing that I can walk in uninterrupted fellowship with him —so long as I keep my eyes focused on him.

C. Eternal human life for those on earth after the messianic kingdom

Another issue about the last days poses this question: How can redeemed human beings who have natural bodies—not resurrected bodies—continue to live on the new earth throughout eternity? The question about humans on earth after the messianic kingdom is a question that I used to ponder. Then one day while I wondered about this, I saw the Bible on my desk opened at just the right place: "Blessed are those who wash their robes, that they may have the right to *the tree of life* and may go through the gates into the city [the New Jerusalem]" (Re 22.14).

That's when I knew that I had the answer. Let me explain. In the creation story, Adam and Eve were denied access to the tree of life so that they would not live forever in their sinful condition, but in eternity after the messianic kingdom, earthly believers will have access to the tree of life and will eat its fruit and will drink from the spring of the water of life (Re 21.6b). Eating that blessed food and drinking that living water will keep them alive on earth with God forevermore (Hoyt 1969, 230, 231). That tree of life and that water of life must represent God's sustenance throughout eternity for the surviving earthly human beings.

In Genesis, when God looked at the creation he had finished, he saw that it was good. From his eternal vantage point, he could see the beginning and the end, and he knew that it was good. The book of Revelation confirms this eternal truth.

D. The conclusion drawn from this study of the kingdom

With all this intellectual interpretation of perplexing issues that we have considered, what is most striking to me is the simplicity of the Christian life that God offers to every believer. My conclusion is that all that matters is that believers in their daily lives can have a close walk with the Lord.

This walk with God is not limited by intellectual capacity or by any other human capacity or lack thereof. Case in point: My intellectual capacity as a child was limited, but I had a personal relationship with Jesus as my Lord and Savior; which stood me in good stead as I grew older. If I lost something, I asked the Lord to help me find it. If I had a problem that I felt I couldn't talk to others about, I'd go to the Lord. If I felt like it, I would dance in the Spirit at night in the dark on our front sidewalk, free as a bird. Every Sunday I was in Sunday School learning more about God.

All in all in my childhood, I was anchored in the Lord, and that's what matters more than anything else. Didn't Jesus say, "I tell you the truth, unless you change and become like little children, you will never enter the kingdom of heaven (Mt 18.3)?

In the next chapter, let's look at God's true kingdom and its counterfeit, utopia.

26 God's true kingdom and its counterfeit

> The experience of the twentieth century shows emphatically
> that utopianism is never far from gangsterism.
> —Paul Johnson, *Modern Times*

Israel's *hope* is the future messianic kingdom under Christ's rule. Paul speaks of the certainty of Israel's hope when he says, "Hope does not disappoint us" (Ro 5.5, 9). This sacred hope is not like secular hope, which is just a wish or a desire. In fact, the only similarity between secular and sacred hope is that both are about the future.

Israel's hope defined by comparing it timewise to faith and love:
1) Faith is *now*: Faith believes before evidence appears.
2) Israel's hope is *future*: Hope awaits Christ's return.
3) Love is *eternal*: "Love never ends" (1Co 13.8 NET).

Israel's hope, secure in God's promise to Abraham:
1) With *faith*, Abraham believed God's promises in Genesis:
   A people forever,
   A land forever,
   A kingdom forever,
   And blessing for all the peoples of the earth.

2) Then with *Israel's hope*, Abraham focused on the certainty of the future that God promises Israel (Ge 12, 13, 15, 17).

Understanding the true kingdom, and its counterfeit:
   A. *Israel's hope, the true kingdom*
   B. *The failure of counterfeit kingdoms*
   C. *The showdown after the true kingdom*
   D. *Redemption today and in the future kingdom*
   E. *What we know about eternity*
   F. *This book's challenge*

351

A. Israel's hope, the true kingdom

Let's review. With his call from the Lord, Abraham broke free from the cyclical worldview of the lost people in the ancient world. He broke free from a circular view that goes nowhere, for it always ends up where it began. Abraham abandoned that hopeless path to follow a straight-arrow path that leads to a future in God's's kingdom (Ge 13.15). Abraham's message to the world is the Torah's *Shema*, Judaism's statement of faith—that Jehovah is the true God, that he is the only God, and that he alone is worthy to be worshiped. The first line of the Shema says, "Hear O Israel, the Lord is our God, the Lord is One," (Dt 6.4). Standing on this truth has been Israel's holy calling. And it's this truth on which the church also stands—that there is only *one* triune God.

The ancient prophets reminded the people of Israel of the hope that they have in the coming of their conquering Messiah, and this message still encourages them. Without that hope, the Jews would be tempted to despair during the darkness of the persecution of the yet future tribulation period when many will be killed.

Hebrew prophet Zechariah says Christ/Messiah at his return will descend to earth on the Mount of Olives at the very same place where Jesus' disciples saw him ascend to heaven. Zechariah writes of the cataclysm that takes place at his return: "On that day his [Christ's] feet will stand on the Mount of Olives, east of Jerusalem, and the Mount of Olives will be split in two from east to west, forming a great valley, with half of the mountain moving north and half moving south" (Zch 14.4).

Hebrew prophet Micah says the towering elevation of that mountain will make it "chief among the mountains," and peoples will stream into the temple there to honor the Lord of Israel during the ensuing messianic kingdom of the last days (Mi 4.1).

Hebrew prophet Isaiah also encourages Israel by presenting Israel's hope, the coming of Christ/Messiah. God tells them, "Say to those with fearful hearts, 'Be strong, do not fear; your God will come, he will come with vengeance; with divine retribution he will come to save you'" (Is 35.4). Zechariah, Micah, Isaiah and other prophets all speak with authority about Israel's hope, and in so doing, they tell of the grandeur and joy of the future kingdom.

Isaiah also describes a spiritual awakening in the world after Israel's hope is fulfilled by the coming of the Messiah as king of Israel and as King of Kings. Isaiah says, "Many peoples will come and say, 'Come, let us go up to the mountain of the LORD, to the house of the God of Jacob. He will teach us his ways, so that we may walk in his paths.' The law will go out from Zion, the word of the LORD from Jerusalem. He [Christ/Messiah] will judge between the nations and will settle disputes for many peoples. They will beat their swords into plowshares and their spears into pruning hooks. Nation will not take up sword against nation, nor will they train for war anymore" (Is 2.3-4).

And again, Isaiah writes about the blessed transformation that brings the people of the kingdom into good health and that will restore nature itself. He says, "Then will the eyes of the blind be opened and the ears of the deaf unstopped. Then will the lame leap like a deer, and the mute tongue shout for joy. Water will gush forth in the wilderness and streams in the desert" (Is 35.5,6).

What a blessed hope for Israel and the world under the future rule of Christ/Messiah! As stated earlier, the ensuing journey through this thousand-year messianic kingdom will be the final exodus into eternity for the Jews. And just as ancient Israel was delivered from slavery when they made their first exodus to the promised land, so too Israel in a future generation will be delivered from the enslaving tyranny of Antichrist by their exodus through the thousand-year messianic kingdom. Then they will be with God forever.

B. The failure of counterfeit kingdoms

Though the messianic kingdom is promised by God, sinful men continue to seek utopia, a counterfeit kingdom of man's own making. Though their efforts always fail, the dream never dies. Such fantasy seekers fail the test of truth that President Abraham Lincoln presented when he asked, "If you call a tail a leg, how many legs does a dog have?" "Five," utopianists would say, but they're wrong. Calling a tail a leg does not make it a leg. And though Lincoln warns against building on a false premise, people nevertheless continue to fall for the utopian lie that man can build the ideal, lasting state without God. And because the lie is repeated so often, it's difficult for anyone to set the record straight, for in spite of the dismal historical record, radicals continue to stay the course. They persevere to assuage their sense of guilt, which is caused by sin, and they express these rebellious feelings through the building of a fantasy state. Others, in the pursuit of this dream, pride themselves on the seeming nobility of their cause and get a sense of satisfaction in looking down on those who oppose their views. Most people however, probably just get swept along by the popularity of the concept and the promise of "a free lunch."

Therefore, the recurrence of this lie—that man can build a lasting utopia—has been passed down through generations, no matter how often the seeking of that dream ends in disaster. This fantasy is the lie, upon which twentieth century utopian fascism and utopian communism were built, both of which led to the greatest mass human destruction the world has ever seen. In observation of this misguidedness, historian Paul Johnson writes, "Utopianism is never far from gangsterism" (Johnson 1983, 708).

God's world program for the earth and Satan's program for the earth have been in conflict ever since man first tried to build the tower of Babel; that was long before the time of Abraham, father of Israel (Ge 11). Satan's motivation has always been the same—to institute a perfect plan without God. At Babel the people wanted to unite the world to make a name for themselves. That sounds innocent enough; it sounds as innocent as what Peter said when he protested that Jesus would not die. In Peter's case, Jesus rebuked Satan for expressing himself through Peter, for Satan's desire was to derail God's plan of redemption through Christ's death at the appointed time. In each case—for people at Babel and for Peter—the Lord had to abort those manmade plans that Satan inspired.

As with the tower-building project of Babel and with other cases, what man sees as a noble project, God sees as an act of rebellion, for he'll not allow man's utopian ideal to come into full fruition until the end of time under Antichrist. Alfred Edersheim says, "The gathering of all material forces into one common center [at Babel] would have led to universal despotism and to universal idolatry—in short, to the full development of what… is reserved for the judgment of the last days" (Edersheim, undated, 25).

Utopian seekers believe what they want to believe. Motivated by pride and greed, they fall for Satan's lies. Scripture says, "They perish because they refused to love the truth and so be saved. For this reason, God sends them a powerful delusion so that they will believe the lie and so that all will be condemned who have not believed the truth but have delighted in wickedness" (2Th 2.10b,11).

At the beginning of the tribulation, even the Jews will believe in Antichrist, but later God will open their eyes to recognize the future Antichrist to be a counterfeit messiah, and this will bring them to repentance and faith in Christ/Messiah. In the present age, however, faith in utopianism continues and will do so until the seven-year tribulation. At that time God will give the future counterfeit Babylonian kingdom a cup "filled with the wine of the fury of his wrath" (Re 16.19b). Yet, meanwhile, even during the tribulation, God will continue to prepare believers for his kingdom.

In the book of Revelation, John tells about his vision of Babylon during the tribulation when that city-state will become the world's ruling government and the fulfillment of the utopian dream. The intrigue of that heyday will be intense, yet for believers, their victory is certain. because in the end, the Lord's defeat of his enemies will be final, and victory for his people will be joyous.

The future day of Satan's counterfeit kingdom is described in Revelation 17.3-5: "Then the angel carried me away in the Spirit into a desert. There I saw a woman [religious Babylon] sitting on a scarlet beast [Antichrist] that was covered with blasphemous names and had seven heads and ten horns [ten kingdoms]. The woman was dressed in purple and scarlet, and was glittering with gold, precious stones and pearls. In her hand, she held a golden cup, filled with abominable things and the filth of her adulteries. This title was written on her forehead (Re 17.3-5):

'MYSTERY BABYLON THE GREAT
THE MOTHER OF PROSTITUTES AND
OF THE ABOMINATIONS OF THE EARTH'"

In Revelation 17 and 18, the plot thickens when John writes on the subject of religion, politics, and commerce in the counterfeit kingdom in the last days. Religious Babylon is represented by *the prostitute,* political Babylon is represented by *the kings,* and commercial Babylon is represented by *the merchants.*

About religious Babylon, John writes, "I saw that the woman was drunk with the blood of the saints, the blood of those who bore testimony to Jesus" (Re 17.6). What a revolting but accurate portrait of the apostate church in the last days!

About the people of political and commercial Babylon, John cites their relationship to religion (the prostitute): "All the nations have drunk the maddening wine of her [the prostitute's] adulteries. The kings of the earth committed adultery with her, and the merchants of the earth grew rich from her excessive luxuries" (Re 18.3). This describes the future people of the apostasy.

And John also tells more about his vision of political Babylon: "The ten horns you saw are ten kings who have not yet received a kingdom, but who for one hour will receive authority as kings along with the beast [Antichrist]. They have one purpose and will give their power and authority to the beast [Antichrist]. They will make war against the Lamb [Christ], but the Lamb will overcome them because he is Lord of Lords and King of kings—and with him will be his called, chosen and faithful followers" (Re 17.12-14).

The following excerpt from Revelation tells of Satan's uprising and of his final defeat: "Then the angel said to me [John], 'The waters you saw, where the prostitute [the counterfeit church] sits, are peoples, multitudes, nations and languages. The beast [Antichrist] and the ten horns [ten kings] you saw will hate the prostitute. They will bring her to ruin and leave her naked; they will eat her flesh and burn her with fire. For God has put it into their hearts to accomplish his purpose by agreeing to give the beast [Antichrist] power to rule—until God's words are fulfilled. The woman you saw is the great city [Babylon] that rules over the kings of the earth'" (Re 17.15-18) .

Though Isaiah gave a near prophecy on Babylon approximately 2700 years ago, he also gave a far prophecy about the empire's disastrous future final end—the end that is portrayed in Revelation.

Hebrew prophet Isaiah (OT) says this to the king of Babylon:
"Go down, sit in the dust, *Virgin Daughter of Babylon*…
    Lift up your skirts, bare your legs,
        and wade through the streams.
    Your nakedness will be exposed
        and your shame uncovered.
    I will take vengeance; I will spare no one."
    Our Redeemer—the LORD Almighty is his name—
        is the Holy One of Israel" (Is 47.1-4)….
      "I was angry with my people
        and desecrated my inheritance;
    I gave them into your [Babylon's] hand,
        and you showed them no mercy' (Is 47.6a)…
    You have trusted in your wickedness
        and have said, 'No one sees me'…
    Disaster will come upon you,
        and you will not know how to conjure it away" (Is 47.10-11).

According to John in the book of Revelation, this fall of Babylon will come at the end of the tribulation after God pours out his seventh bowl of wrath. About that future fall of Satan's kingdom of Babylon. John speaks in the past tense: "The great city [Babylon] split into three parts, and the cities of the nations collapsed. God remembered Babylon the Great and gave her the cup filled with the wine of the fury of his wrath" (Re 16.19). Afterward, an angel shouted, "Fallen! Fallen is Babylon the Great! She has become a home for demons and a haunt for every evil spirit, a haunt for every unclean and detestable bird" (Re 18.2). Also, "Terrified at her torment, they [kings, merchants, people] will stand far off and cry: 'Woe! Woe, O great city, O Babylon, city of power! In one hour your doom has come'" (Re 18.10)! In postmodernity with a world economy sometimes on the brink of disaster, this scene of panic is not difficult to imagine.

"Babylon, the mother of prostitutes," has to be obliterated from the face of the earth before the world is ready for Christ to reign with his virgin bride the church. So, when Babylon falls, this will mark the end of the times of the Gentiles and will open the door for the dawn of the millennial glory of Christ's kingdom. At that time, the scene of degradation and mayhem will give way to God's people rejoicing. This will be victory for those resurrected ones in the holy city of New Jerusalem and for God's earthly people the Jews, whom God will vindicate and exalt during the thousand-year messianic kingdom.

C. The showdown after the true kingdom

In the future when the counterfeit kingdom of Babylon falls, secular man's counterfeit dream will go up in smoke and will be replaced by the glorious fulfillment of the promised messianic kingdom for Israel and the church. In the true kingdom, the church dwells in the *New* Jerusalem and shares that home with all the resurrected Israelites and tribulation saints. In the messianic kingdom, Christ's bride, the church, reigns with him over the redeemed people on earth, who, though human, will have new hearts and new minds under the new covenant (Je 31.31-33).

This ideal, earthly, millennial kingdom will be the fulfillment of what God says about his creation in Genesis: "God saw all that he had made, and it was very good… (Genesis 1.31)."

Having grown up in an earlier time in America's Bible belt, I had at least a small taste of what living in a stable and harmonious society can be like. In Edinburg, a small town in the Rio Grande Valley of Texas, almost everyone went to church or had ties to a church. Even as late as in 1950, after my husband and I moved to Mercedes in the Valley for two years, a Christian woman knocked on our door to invite us newcomers to church. Going to church was the thing to do, and living by a high moral standard was upheld by public opinion.

So, was everyone a role model for living in that small town? No, though many were. But, let's take a closer look. The doctor who successfully operated on my mother's cancer was a man who earlier had murdered his wife when he discovered her in an adulterous affair. The justice of peace with whom my father had casual contact in professional circles murdered his son-in-law and had no regrets because he felt that the victim deserved to die. Our lifetime neighbor friend murdered a man in a dispute over money. I think the court deemed all these men to be temporarily insane.

Though I learned about these things, the incidents didn't penetrate the innocence of my childhood world, for none of them involved our small church or my school or my everyday activities— for as a child, I was not well acquainted with the perpetrators of the crimes; I just knew who they were. However, I did know the children of the men who killed. In fact, for a short time, I took tap dancing lessons with the doctor's daughter and was in a dance recital with her. And the son of our lifelong neighbor was like a third brother to my brothers and me. His father was the one who committed murder over a money dispute and later died in a car accident. In spite of their fathers' criminality, their children grew up to be good citizens.

What did influence me was that public opinion was on the side of law, order, courtesy, and respectability even though from time to time, there was this dark undercurrent breaking out from below the surface of society. In Christ's thousand-year kingdom, however, that undercurrent finds no outlet until the end of the period when Satan will be unshackled and will lead a rebellion. Until that time, all the people of the messianic kingdom will outwardly conform, and stability and harmony will prevail.

It's hard to imagine anyone in that glorious future kingdom rebelling, so let's think about this. In this ideal environment where the Lord himself rules and the temple is filled with his Shekinah glory, some refuse to accept the Savior as their own, and as time goes by in future generations, unbelievers will multiply. In those thousand years, although every knee will bow to the King of Kings and blessings will abound, the curse of sin and death will not yet be totally lifted, for man will still have free will governed by a heart that wants its own way; therefore, though all in the first generation of the kingdom enter as believers, many in later generations will fail to receive Christ/Messiah as Savior. Therefore, under Messiah's iron rule, these rebels will worship side by side with the redeemed and will enjoy the prosperity, peace, and endless blessings of this ideal environment. Yet, nevertheless, they want their own way and cannot have it, so they harden their hearts against God.

That rebels will grudgingly comply in the messianic kingdom reminds me of a similar response after the 9-11 bombing of America's World Trade Center. After that tragedy, members of Congress spontaneously gathered on the capitol steps to sing "God Bless America." They united in an expression of faith, and in that crisis, no one dared to complain about separation of church and state though I'm sure many did not approve of that display of devotion to God. At that interval of time, public opinion would not allow expression of dissent against the song that was sung. However, at the first opportunity, anti-God sentiment began to be expressed. So too on the world's endtime scene, rebels will rise up to confront God, even though throughout the messianic kingdom, Satan will have been bound and gagged for the thousand years! Such is the intransigence of man about religious fervor. The defiance of rebels flares up because self-centeredness will express itself if given the opportunity.

The author of the Bible's book of James writes, "What causes fights and quarrels among you? Don't they come from your desires that battle within you? You want something but don't get it. You kill and covet, but you cannot have what you want. You quarrel and fight. You do not have, because you do not ask God. When you ask, you do not receive, because you ask with wrong motives, that you may spend what you get on your pleasures. You adulterous people…" (Ja 4.1-4). Therefore, during the kingdom, as generations pass from the stage, fewer will accept Christ as Savior. By the last generation of the kingdom, a multitude in the world will think Satan can lead them in victory against Messiah, but they're wrong. When their armies, led by Satan, surround Jerusalem, fire will come down from heaven and consume them.

To see evidence of society's tendency toward complacent drifting and unbelief, look at how the seeds of destruction have been at work in Europe as it has grown older. There you see an abandonment of church attendance and of Christian morality, disregard for God's Word, loss of a work ethic, and an increase in antisemitism. In America you see a drift in the same direction, which will continue, at least until God sends a mighty revival. So, the Bible's message is believable—that at the end of the thousand years of the kingdom, a multitude will follow Satan and will surround Jerusalem to defeat the Messiah they hate. And the rest of the Bible's message is also believable,… that God will take care of his own and will send fire from heaven to consume those enemies.

Reading Revelation 18 through 22 gives the full impact of the drama and the glory of the last days and gives us pause to consider how important the faith of one person can be when he enters into God's calling for his life. Through the faith of one man, Abraham, the Lord changed the world. None of our glorious future would come to pass if Abraham had failed to believe. By his faith and obedience, he staked his life on God's promises about Israel's hope. About Abraham's faith, the Bible says, "Against all hope, Abraham in hope believed and so became the father of many nations… Without weakening in his faith, he faced the fact that his body was as good as dead—since he was about a hundred years old—and that Sarah's womb was also dead. Yet he did not waver through unbelief regarding the promise of God, but was strengthened in his faith and gave glory to God" (Ro 4.18-20 NT).

Besides Abraham's faith in earthly Israel's future, Abraham also believed in the future heavenly New Jerusalem, which God promised. Scripture says, "By faith he [Abraham] made his home in the promised land like a stranger in a foreign country; he lived in tents, as did Isaac and Jacob, who were heirs with him of the same promise. For he was looking forward to the city with foundations, whose architect and builder is God" (He 11.9-10. Italics added). This is the New Jerusalem.

D. Redemption today and in the future (Jn 3.16-17)

Today God promises redemption for all who believe: "For God so loved the world that he gave his only begotten Son, that whosoever believeth in him should not perish, but have everlasting life. For God sent not his Son into the world to condemn the world; but that the world through him might be saved" (Jn 3.16-17 KJV).

In the future messianic kingdom, Israel's hope will be fulfilled.

Israel's hope, the *true* earthly kingdom under Christ/Messiah, is the world's only hope. To see the future through the eyes of God is to gain a higher perspective. On my daily walks, I sometimes see a crow scanning the sky from the highest twig on the tallest tree as it looks for signs of danger, and from there it warns other crows about approaching enemies with its "Caw, caw, caw!" So too, from the Word's higher perspective, the believer can see beyond the present into the future.

Isaiah describes the empowerment of a higher perspective:
"Those who *hope* in the Lord
   will renew their strength.
They will soar on wings like eagles;
   they will walk and not be faint" (Is 40.31. Italics added).

E. What we know about eternity

In creation, the messianic kingdom is the climax of God's expression of himself, but in that kingdom, sin and death will still exist; they will not be eliminated until eternity begins.

What's different in eternity is this—that noble attributes will be defined differently. In this present world, attributes are defined by their opposites. For example, without darkness, we wouldn't recognize light. Without hate, we wouldn't recognize love. And without these opposites, we wouldn't comprehend God's expression of himself. Also, during the tribulation, Israelis *as a people* will not recognize the Christ called "Faithful and True" until after they have encountered Antichrist, the "Unfaithful and Counterfeit."

In eternity, by contrast, God's attributes will need no counterpart. There will be no night to define the day, no death to define life, no evil to define righteousness, no temple in the New Jerusalem because "the Lord God Almighty and the Lamb are its temple (Re 21.22). Yet, though all eternity will be swallowed up in God, believers nevertheless will recognize God's attributes and will retain their personhood. Isn't this a miracle—that Abraham has kept his identity in eternity (Lk 16.25), even as do all other people. Finally, in eternity Jesus,will forever share the throne with his Father.

F. This book's challenge

Think about this challenge: Jesus says if you want to be his disciple—that is, if you are a Christian and want to learn from the Lord—you must surrender all. He says, "If anyone comes to me and does not hate his father and mother, his wife and children, his brothers and sisters—yes, even his own life—he cannot be my disciple" (Luke 14:26). God wants to be all in all in our hearts. For the rich, young ruler, *his* surrender would have required that he give up his riches to follow Jesus, and since he was unwilling to do that, he went away sad.

The author of Hebrews gives us a picture of what is required: "And so Jesus also suffered outside the city gate to make the people holy through his own blood. Let us, then, go to him outside the camp, bearing the disgrace he bore. For here we do not have an enduring city, but *we are looking for the city that is to come*" (He 13.12-14. Italics added).

Is God asking you to surrender all to him?

Today, Jesus' invitation to be reconciled with his Father is open to all. There is, however, a caveat that Jesus attaches to his invitation to become a disciple. He warns that there is a cost to being his disciple: "Suppose one of you wants to build a tower. Will he not first sit down and estimate the cost to see if he has enough money to complete it? For if he lays the foundation and is not able to finish it, everyone who sees it will ridicule him, saying, this fellow began to build and was not able to finish… In the same way, if any of you who does not give up everything he has cannot be my disciple" (Lk 14.28, 29, 33).

Will you say yes to God's invitation, or will you go away sad?

THINK JEWISH
to understand the Bible

K. UNDERSTANDING THE AUTHOR
27.A tribute to the late Dr. DeWitt Reddick, University of Texas

27 A tribute to the late Dr. Dewitt Reddick at the University of Texas, Austin

And now these three remain: faith, hope and love.
But the greatest of these is love..
—The apostle Paul in 1Corinthians 13.13

"Sister's going to cry! Sister's going to cry!" And sure enough Sister would begin to cry.

My oldest brother knew how to push my buttons to get the response he wanted... until I finally caught on about how to stop the tormenting. I learned that if I didn't cry, it took the fun out of his teasing. I didn't fully understand, however, until I wrote about the matter in a creative writing exercise in college. That was when I realized the importance of expressing love through forgiveness—not that I consciously harbored a grudge, however.

And as a side note on family dynamics, when later in life I spoke to my father about what used to happen with my brother, he said, "Yes, you were a sensitive child". THe surprise there was that I didn't know that he'd even noticed. He was a wonderful father, with whom I had delightful conversations as an adult and with whom I did things as a child, but in our family's daily life, I wasn't aware that he was cognizant of what was going on behind the scenes.

Imagine my surprise when in my seventies, I spoke to that brother about the childhood teasing! He didn't remember anything about it. Incidentally, he's a good guy; he turned out well.

Yes, human interaction and influence is a fascinating dynamic. In the first chapter of this book, I wrote that in my early adult life, I was influenced by Carl Zimmerman in a Bible study group. Encountering his wisdom inspired me to seek wisdom through study of God's Word, and that pursuit has been a beacon on my life's journey. Paul calls wisdom one of the gifts of the Spirit (1Co 12.8), and he says to "eagerly desire the greater gifts," but then he adds "and now I will show you the most excellent way" (1Co 12.31). That "most excellent" way is love. And that is what Professor DeWitt

Reddick taught me and others by example and by his teaching in the Century Class at University Presbyterian in Austin, Texas.

Now, in this final chapter of my book, I want to acknowledge what a great influence Dr. Reddick had on my life when he taught our Sunday School class.

I would often go home to my dormitory room and tell my Episcopalian roommate what DeWitt had said. I remember how impressed she was with his teaching. For example, he challenged us students to try new things, even something as simple as taking a different route home from school The idea was that we can live creatively by throwing aside shackles of habit that may bind us.

He would tell us stories about students that sought his counsel and how those students learned to work things out. What was amazing to me was that when he told about people with problems—maybe even about misfits or undesirables—his love shone through in such a way that you could get an accurate picture but without condemnation. When I heard those stories, I wanted to be one of those people that got his personal advice, but after learning from him, I found that I didn't need to go to him because I could figure out what he would have told me if I had gone to him. That's how much he influenced me.

In his Century Class, we were divided into "Scottish clans"—a tribute to our Presbyterian Scottish heritage—and once in a great while, we met with DeWitt in one of the small groups for an informal social time. (We called him by his first name—not so common in that time.) I think I learned as much about him at a wiener roast with our small group as I did under his talks, though I needed both. In a small group setting, I saw his love lived out in a life situation. I saw how his heart went out to each of us. His teeth-protruding smile was infectious and God glorifying. He knew how to set everyone at ease, for he would draw out those people who would tend to withdraw in a social situation.

His reputation for caring and friendliness went beyond our Sunday School class. Noted in his field as a journalism professor, he was repeatedly voted the most popular professor on campus.

Recently, I looked up Dr. DeWitt Reddick on the web browser Google and came across Judith Powers, who in 1968 wrote about her favorite memory from her days at the University of Texas, Austin. (I knew him in the late 1940s.) She wrote that her journalism professor, Dr. DeWitt Reddick "was one of the kindest people I have ever known." How many people are there who knew him—that would more than two decades later in life—say the same thing, putting him in the category of "one of the kindest people I have ever known"? There would be more people than we could count, I'm sure.

In closing I want to pay tribute to two other people in my life to whom I failed to express my appreciation fully in their lifetime. First, I want to pay tribute to my late devoted piano teacher, Irma Frisby, who taught me from age four to the time I left home to go to college. She poured her life into her piano students, and I was privileged to be one of them. From her, I learned the blessedness of having total heartfelt support.

And finally, I want to pay tribute to Pamphylia, our family's faithful Mexican servant since before my birth until my graduation from high school. She spoke no English, and though uneducated, she had quaint ways of describing people that she met in our home. For example, she called a friend of my oldest brother "four eyes" in Spanish because he wore glasses. She cared for our family and cared about us children. This is just a nudge for us to take notice of those for whom we should express our appreciation while we still have a chance to do so.

I'm glad that I can make this the last chapter of my book so that my readers and I will be reminded to be conscious of how we influence others and how others influence us, often without realizing it.

The Bible says this about faith, hope, and love: It says the greatest of these is LOVE (1 Co 13)!

abeyance—temporary suspension; e,g, during Christ's 1000 year reign and before the last battle, conflict will be in abeyance

abrogate—revoke; overturn

Abyss—a bottomless pit for the demonic

admonitions—gentle but earnest warnings

advent—the first coming or the second coming of Christ to earth

advocacy of Christ—the Savior's confirmation of a person's salvation through his blood sacrifice

allegory—a story that expresses truths or generalizations by means of symbolic figures

ambiguity—the state of being open to more than one interpretation

amillennial—a belief that there will be no literal millennium. See premillennial and postmillennial

anathema—abhorrent; hateful; despicable

anointed—in a special sense, to be anointed by God is to be chosen and empowered by him

Antichrist—lit. against Christ; a great world leader of the last days, a counterfeit who will set himself up as the Messiah, or Christ, to be worshiped

anti-Semite—one who is hostile toward Jews (or Arabs)

antitype—biblically, the fulfillment, or spiritual reality, of a type

apocalyptic—describing or prophesying the end times

apostle—A NT term: literally, "sent ones." One of a group made up especially of the twelve disciples and Paul, chosen by Jesus to preach the gospel.

Arabs—Semites descended from Abraham through his son Ishmael

ark of the covenant—the only furniture in the Most Holy Place, where the high priest presented the blood of the Lamb for forgiveness of Israel's sins in the past year.

ascension—the event of Jesus rising into heaven after his resurrection

atonement—"at-one-ment." Reconciliation between God and people; biblically by blood sacrifice.

backslider—one who has known the Lord and has strayed from following him

bema judgment seat—the judgment seat of Christ in heaven where the works of Christians will be rewarded

birthright—a right of possession or privilege from birth, especially as eldest child

Canaan—the promised land to which Abraham migrated

canon—the books of the Bible officially accepted as holy Scripture

celestial—heavenly; divine

censer—a handheld vessel that priests used to carry live coals for offering incense before the Lord

charismatic—a modern term meaning Pentecostal, usually referring to Spirit-baptized Christians in mainline churches

Christ—"the anointed one," the same meaning for Christ and Messiah— Christ, a Greek NT word and Messiah, a Hebrew OT word

christendom—the professing church, in contrast to the living church, is made up of believers and unbelievers

circa—approximately, roughly

circumcision—cut off the male foreskin

communion—fellowship; shared intimacy, esp. mental or spiritual; in churches, a ritual of bread and wine, also called Eucharist

concordance—Alphabetical list of words in biblical text with citations of where they are to be found

convocation—a large formal assembly of people

crucible—a vessel for melting a substance at a high degree of heat; hence, a severe test

deconstruction—a method of critical analysis that emphasizes the relational quality of meaning and the assumptions implicit

covenant—a binding agreement between

two or more parties; God's covenant with Abraham was about relationship

deconstruction—Deconstruction focuses on a text itself rather than seeing it as an expression of the author's intention. It stresses the limitlessness (or impossibility) of interpretation and rejects the Western philosophical tradition of seeking certainty through reasoning

deductive method—in Bible study is to move from
1. God to evidences
2. whole to parts
3. universal to particular
4. infinite to finite
5. truth to human experience
6. cause to effects
(Morey 1996, 6); opposite of inductive

deity—In Christianity, the creator and supreme being

diaspora—Jews in exile from Israel since their Babylonian captivity

dichotomy—contrast between two things that are entirely different

disciples—followers of Jesus, especially, Jesus twelve disciples

DNA—A nucleic acid that carries the genetic information in the cell and is capable of self-replication

doctrine—theologically, a set or system of beliefs taught by a group

double reference—s literary device used in a prophecy to point to both contemporary and endtime events or characters

dualism—a biblical view of reality's dual distinctions - heavenly/earthly, good/evil, etc.. God is seen as transcendent and distinct from the universe. Differs from monism

edify—build up

efficacy—power to produce an effect; efficacious, the adjectival form

elect—the redeemed ones, used sometimes of Jews, sometimes of Christians

Ephraim—younger son of Joseph. In the divided kingdom of N. Israel and S. Judah, Israel is sometimes called

Ephraim

epistemology—the investigation of that which distinguishes justified belief from opinion

epistles—the letters that became books in the NT. All the books in the NT are letters to congregations or individuals except for the four gospels, Acts, and Revelation

eschatology—a branch of theology concerned with the end times

eternal—forever, everlasting; for God, without beginning or end; for man, never ending life

ethnoreligious—an ethnic group whose members are also unified by a common religious background (Jews).

Eucharist—communion service, memorial service of Jesus' "last supper" with his disciples; also called a mass by Catholics

evangelical, an—a Christian who believes in a born again experience and reaches out to others with the good news. exegesis—an interpretation of a text. In Mt 13, for example, the author takes into account biblical context and cultural and literary factors. In this way, she seeks to find God's intent

exodus—a going out; in the Bible, the departure of the Israelites from Egypt and slavery

expiatory—capable of paying the penalty for guilt or sin

exposition—explanation; a setting forth of meaning or purpose

feasts or festivals of Israel—(Gray 43 Scofield 186) See Table Two

flesh or "in the flesh"—a term that refers to the natural, physical, or earthly. Sometimes translated, "sinful nature."

foreshadow; to prefigure—to present a person, place, event, or thing in current time as a type of a future reality.

Gentiles—non-Jewish people; sometimes referred to as "Greeks" or "nations." In the OT, Gentiles were unbelievers with "no hope and without God." In the NT, Gentile and Jewish individu-

als can become Christian believers, but the Jewish people remain a distinct people group

gleaning—grain that is gathered after a harvest; Jews were commanded to leave the gleaning—the corners of the fields—for the poor to gather.

glorify—to elevate to celestial glory. "Not yet glorified" says that Jesus had not yet ascended into heaven

godhead—Father, Son, and Holy Spirit

Good Friday—the commemoration of Jesus' crucifixion, three days before his resurrection on Easter

gospel—literally, "good news." It's the proclamation of the redemption preached by Jesus and the Apostles, which is the central content of Christian revelation. Also refers to the books about the life of Christ: Matthew, Mark, Luke, and John

grace—mercy; undeserved favor

Hades—In NT, the holding place for the unbelieving dead

heavenlies, the—the atmospheric realm where spiritual conflict takes place

Hebrew—refers to the Jewish people or their language

Hebrew Bible—the Tanach; the same in content as the OT part of the Protestant Bible. Order differs and verse and chapter numbers differ slightly

Hebrews—Jewish people; also a book in the NT written to the Jewish people

hermeneutic—interpretation for contemporary purposes; rooted in exegesis

hiatus—a biblical literary device: a pause or gap in a sequence, series, or process

Holy Ghost—same as Holy Spirit

hyperbole—poetic overstatement not meant to be taken literally

identity by content—a biblical literary device in prophecy to identify contemporary and endtime events or characters by inference in the content

imminent return—a phrase that means Jesus could come at any time

immutable—unchanging over time

implode—collapse violently inward

incarnate—God in the flesh

inductive method—the inferring of general laws from particular instances; opposite of deductive method

iniquity—A grossly immoral act; sin

intercessory prayer—prayer for others

intifadah—an uprising by Palestinian Arabs (in both the Gaza Strip and the West Bank)

Islam—the religion of Muslims; founded by Muhammed

Israelis—modern name for citizens of Israel

Israelites—name for ancient Jews

Jehovah—the name God used in his covenant relationship with the Jewish people; means I AM; also called Yahweh. To the Jews, the name Jehovah was so sacred they chose to substitute the word Lord (also in caps in Protestant OT)

Jews—God's covenant people; Semites descended from Abraham through his son Isaac. Also called Hebrews, Israelites, Israelis. Name derived from Judah, which is one of the twelve tribes of Israel, the heads of which were sons of Jacob, later called Israel

Jews, American—*Orthodox* Jews are the strictest observers of the law; *Conservative* Jews are more moderate; Reformed Jews are more liberal

Judaic—of or relating to Judaism

Judaism—the religion of the Jewish people, based on the Torah of the Hebrew Bible

justify—In theology, to free of the guilt and penalty attached to sin

king—In the days of the Israelites, those kings chosen by God were anointed

Lamb of God—the name of the Christ as sacrifice: to redeem from sin and to reconcile man to God the Father

Last Supper—the time of the institution

of communion as a church ritual on the evening of Judas's betrayal of Jesus

legalism—an attitude of self-glorification by strict adherence to an external code

leaven—yeast; symbol of evil

legalist—one who depends on moral law rather than on personal faith

licentiousness—lacking legal or moral restraints

LORD—(with small caps) the substitute title used out of reverence for writing the sacred name of Jehovah, the covenant God of Israel

Lord—NT title by which the disciples honored Jesus

Lord's Day—the first day of the week for Christian rest and devotion; celebrates the resurrection of the Lord and spiritual deliverance from the slavery of sin (Mt 28.1,7; 1Co 16.2; Acts 20.7)

mediator—one who acts as a go-between for two parties. Also biblically, under the new covenant, a mediator establishes a new relationship

Messiah—"the anointed one," the same meaning for Messiah and Christ. Messiah, a Hebrew OT word and Christ, a Greek NT word

messianic—related to Messiah; used interchangeably with millennial age

Midrash—an ancient commentary on part of the Hebrew scriptures; attached to the biblical text

millennium—lit., a thousand years. It's another name for messianic kingdom. Biblically, it's a period of God's kingdom on earth before eternity begins.

monism—views reality as a single whole outside of which nothing exists; differs from dualism

monotheism—belief in one God

Mosaic—pertaining to the law of Moses

mundane—lacking interest or excitement; dull. Also, of this earthly world rather than a heavenly one

Muslims—believers in Islam; alternative name, Moslems. Many Arabs are Muslims

mystery—in some biblical translations a transliteration of the Greek word *mysterion*; a secret hidden in the past but now revealed

narrative—a story form of connected events

NT—abbreviation for New Testament

objective truth—truth based on universal absolutes; opposite of subjective truth

Old Testament—the first of two parts of the Protestant Bible. Except for order and differences in division of verses and chapters, the OT is the same in content as the Hebrew Bible

Olivet sermon—Jesus' sermon on the Mount of Olives (Matthew 24, 25)

omnipotent—all powerful

omniscient—all knowing

OT—abbreviation for Old Testament

paganism—polytheistic, monistic religion

Palestine—Israel, which was renamed by the Romans, who occupied it

parable—a simple story with moral or spiritual implications; a form used by Jesus

patriarchs—biblically, Abraham, Isaac, and Jacob and Jacobs sons, the heads of the twelve tribes of Israel

Paul—NT apostle, converted after Jesus' ascension

Pentateuch—the first five books of the Bible; also known as the "Torah," "the law," "the Books of Moses"

Peter—NT apostle, one of the twelve

Pharaoh—the generic title for the kings of ancient Egypt

polytheism—belief in more than one god

postmillennial—a theology that the world will become progressively better with the ultimate triumph of the gospel. Christ will return after the millennial period. This belief was most popular in the 19th century. See also amillennial and premillennial

prefigures—see foreshadows

preincarnate—OT appearances of Christ before he took on human flesh. He's often referred to as the angel of the Lord

priest—one who ministers for the people before God

premillennial—a theology that Christ will take the church out of the world before the tribulation period. See also amillennial and postmillennial

pretribulation—a theology which says that Christ raptures the church to heaven before the tribulation begins

prodigal—spending money or resources freely and recklessly

progenitor—forefather

prophet—one who speaks for God to the people

proselytize—to try to convert someone to another religion or belief

Protestant—a denomination - or member thereof - that denies the universal authority of the Pope and affirms the Reformation principles of justification by faith alone, the priesthood of all believers, and the primacy of the Bible as the only source of revealed truth

rapture—in last days, the church's ascent into heaven to be with Jesus forever

redeem—To set free; rescue, or ransom; to save from a state of sinfulness and its consequences

redemption—a substitutionary act of saving people from sin through Jesus' blood sacrifice

redemptive—of, relating to, or bringing about redemption

regeneration—the rebirth of the believer; the experience of being born again; entry into the new covenant

remnant—biblically, a small surviving group of faithful Jews from one generation to the next

replacement theology—an interpretation that says the church has replaced Israel

sabbath—the seventh day rest given to set the Jewish people apart as the people of God; celebrates creation and physical deliverance from slavery (Ex 20.8-11; Dt 5.12-15)

saint—a person redeemed by the blood of the Lamb of God, Jesus the Savior

salvation—deliverance from the power and penalty of sin; restoration to wholeness

sanctification/sanctifying—the process for Christian growth, as one dedicated to and set apart for God

Sanhedrin—the highest judicial and ecclesiastical council of ancient Israel, composed of from 70 to 72 members.

Seder meal—Passover meal

Semites—descendants of Shem, son of Noah; includes Jews and Arabs

Shema—Dt 6.4-9 is the central statement of faith for Judaism: "Hear, O Israel: the Lord our God, the Lord, is one"

sin—that which displeases God

Shofar—a ram's horn trumpet used as a battle alert, now sounded on the Jewish new year and on the Day of Atonement

Son of Man—name designation for Messiah. In NT he is God incarnate and agent of divine judgment

sovereignty—supremacy of authority or rule

spirit—that part of man in whom the Holy Spirit can dwell

Spirit—the Holy Spirit, third person of the trinity

spiritualize—to reject usual literary rules for understanding in order to manipulate the text to make it fit an interpretation, an agenda, or conventional wisdom

subjective truth—a viewpoint based on individual outlook, not on a universal precept; opposite of objective truth

symbiotic—Of or about a relationship of mutual benefit or dependence.

synagogue—a Judaic congregation or their meeting place

synoptic gospels—Matthew, Mark, Luke.

tabernacle—a fixed or movable habitation of light construction, such as a tent or booth

Talmud—body of Jewish civil and ceremonial law

Tanach—the entire Hebrew Bible. The Ptotestant OT is the same but in a different order

testator—one who makes a last will and testament

the elect—the redeemed ones, used sometimes of Jews, sometimes of Christians

theism—used in this text as belief in a personal God as creator and ruler of the world

temple in Jerusalem—in biblical times, the name of the building on Mount Moriah for Judaic animal sacrifice and worship. The last such temple was destroyed in a.d. 70. Since then synagogues, which originated during Babylonian captivity, are the places that local Jewish congregations worship; sometimes called temples

testament—a will; also a covenant

theocracy—a nation under the direct rule of God

theology—the study of the nature of God and religious truth

theophany—appearance of preincarnate Christ in OT times as "the angel of the Lord" or in some other guise

tithe—an Old Testament injunction requiring the Israelites to give one tenth of their wealth to God

thou and thee—Elizabethan English for you; used in King James Bible

Torah—the first five books of the Hebrew Bible: Genesis, Exodus, Leviticus, Numbers, Deuteronomy. Also called the Pentateuch, the law, the Book of Moses. It is the touchstone, or criterion, by which something is judged or recognized as biblical

transcendent—greater than, surpassing; used of the deity as being above and independent of the material universe

transgression—violation of a law, duty, or command

transliteration—a letter or word written in the closest corresponding letters of a different language

tribulation——biblically, the seven years before Christ returns to earth; a period of intense distress for the Jews and the world under the antichrist

trinity—the foundational doctrine of biblical Christianity: one eternal God is three persons: Father, Son, and Holy Spirit

triune/triunity—three parts in one; description of the Godhead and of personhood.

transgression—violation of a law, duty, or command

truth—Jesus says, "I am the way, *the truth*, and the life" (Jn 14.6)

triunity—the state of a three-in-one being

type—a foreshadowing. A person, place, event, or thing, which acts as a figure, representation, or symbol of what is to come. such as the OT ritual of Passover, which points to the NT reality of Christ's sacrifice to deliver from the slavery of sin. A type is earthly; its fulfillment can be earthly or heavenly but with spiritual significance

typology—the study of types and antitypes

unregenerate—nor redeemed

unilaterally—an action by only one party without the agreement of another

utopia—man's ideal of a perfect society

Yahweh—a name for God, whose meaning is I AM and whose pronunciation is approximated by modern scholars because ancient Hebrew characters had no consonants. "Jehovah" in some translations

Zion—the Jewish people; the hill of Jerusalem; Israel

Zionist—a person in a movement that supports the establishment and survival of Israel as a nation. Established 1897

Zionism—a national movement for the return of the Jewish people to their homeland and for the resumption of Jewish sovereignty in Israel

Bibliography

Abraham, Ken, compiler. *God Keeps His Promises.* Urichsville, Ohio: Barour and Company, Inc.

Abrams, Elliott. *Faith or Fear: How Jews Can Survive in a Christian America.* New York: The Free Press, 1997.

Accordance 7.4.1 software. Oaktree Software, Inc.: 2007 www.accordancebible.com

Adler, Mortimer J. and Charles Van Doren. *How to Read a Book.* New York: Simon & Schuster, Inc.

Adler, Mortimer J. and Peter Wolff. *A General Introduction to the Great Books and to a Liberal Education*, Volume One in the series. Chicago: Encyclopedia Britannica, 1959.

Allison, Gregg R. "The Kingdom and the Church" in *The Kingdom of God.* edited by Christopher W. Morgan and Robert A. Peterson. Wheaton, IL: Crossway 2012.

American-Israeli Cooperative Enterprise. *Jewish Virtual Library* re Golan Heights. Internet 2006.
http://www.jewishvirtuallibrary.org/jsource/Peace/golan_hts.html

American Jewish Committee. *American Jewish Year Book.* Storrs, CT: Jewish Publication Society of America, 2003, 160.
http://www.jewishdatabank.org/AJYB/AJY-2003.pdf

Anders, Max. *Bible Prophecy in 12 Lessons.* Nashville, TN: Thomas Nelson, Inc., 1997.

Andrews, Stephen J., reviewer of *The Character of Christian Scripture: The Significance of a Two-Testament Bible* by Christopher R. Seitz. Grand Rapid: Baker Academic, 2011. Review in *SBL Review of Biblical Literature,* 20 March 2015.

Arendt, Hannah. *Totalitarianism: Part Three of the Origins of Totalitarianism.* New York: Harcourt, Brace, and Jovanovich, 1968.

Armstrong, Karen. *A History of God: The 4000-year quest of Judaism, Christianity and Islam.* New York: Alfred A. Knopf, 1994, 361.

Bailey, Keith M. *Christ's Coming and His Kingdom: A study in Bible prophecy.* Harrisburg, PA: Christian Publications, Inc., 1981.

Barnett, Arthur M. Quoted by Irving L. Jensen in *Leviticus: A self study guide,* p 50. Chicago: Moody Bible Institute, 1967.

Barrett, C. K. *First Epistle to the Corinthians.* New York: Harper & Row 1968

Bartleman, Frank. *Another Wave Rolls In!* Voice Christian Publications, Inc., 1962. Whitaker Books, printed 1971. Original - Bartleman 1925.

Bartlett, John. *Familiar Quotations.* Boston: Little, Brown, 1937.

Baughman, Ray E. *The Kingdom of God Visualized.* Chicago: Moody Press, 1972.

BBC News. "Gaza crisis: key maps and timeline" ©MMIX: 1/6/09.
http://news.bbc.co.uk/2/hi/middle_east/5122404.stm

Beacham, Roy E. "Kingdom, Parables of" in *Dictionary of Premillennial Theology*, ed. Mal Couch. Grand Rapids, MI: Kregel Publications, 1996.

Beck, William F. *The New Testament in the Language of Today: an American translation.* St. Louis, MO: Concordia Publishing House, 1963.

Beechick, Allen. *The Pre-Tribulation Rapture.* Denver: Accent Books, 1980.

Bennett, Dennis. *Nine O'clock in the Morning.* South Plainfield, NJ: Bridge Publishing, Inc, 1970.

Bierderwolf, William E. *The Second Coming Bible.* Grand Rapids, MI: Baker Book House. Reprinted original *The Millennium Bible*, 1972.

Blaising, Craig and Darrell L. Bock. *Progressive Dispensationalism.* Grand Rapids, MI: Baker Books, 1993.

Bloomfield, Arthur E. *Before the Last Battle - Armageddon.* Minneapolis: Bethany Fellowship, 1971.

_____. *The End of the Days.* Minneapolis: Bethany Fellowship, 1961.

Bonar, Horatius. *Christ the Healer.* Reprint of original in *Fifty-two Sermons.* Grand Rapids, MI: Baker Book House, 1977.

Bosworth, F. F., *Christ the Healer,* 7th edition. Grand Rapids: Fleming H. Revell, 1973, 2000.

Bowman, Rick. "Abrahamic Covenant" in *Dictionary of Premillennial Theology,* ed. Mal Couch. Grand Rapids: Kregel Publications, 1996.

Bright, John. *The Kingdom of God: The biblical concept and its meaning for the church.* Nashville: Abingdon Press, 1953

Britannica Encyclopedia. Chicago: Encyclpedia Brittanica Publications, 1997.

Broadman and Holman Reference. *The Concise Holman Bible Dictionary.* Nashville: Broadman & Holman Publishers, 1997.

Brooks, Keith L. *Matthew: The gospel of God's king.* Chicago: The Moody Bible Institute, 1963.

Brook, Pat. Understanding Your Spiritual Authority. Monroeville, PA 1973

_____.*Revelation: The Future Foretold.* Chicago: Moody Press, 1962.

_____. *Great Prophetic Themes.* Chicago: Moody Institute, 1962.

Brother Lawrence. *The Practice of the Presence of God with Spiritual Maxims.* Grand Rapids, MI: Spire Books, 1958.

Bruce, F. F. *The Time Is Fulfilled: Five aspects of the fulfillment of the Old Testament in the New.* Grand Rapids: Eerdmans, 1978.

Cahill, Thomas. *The Gifts of the Jews: How a tribe of desert nomads changed the way everyone thinks and feels.* New York: Doubleday, 1998.

Campbell, Donald K. and Jeffrey L. Townsend. *The Coming Millennial Kingdom: A case for premillennial interpretation.* Grand Rapids: Kregel, 1997.

Cargal, Timothy B. and twelve other contributors to commentary. *The Life & Times Historical Reference Bible: A chronological journey through the Bible, culture, and history.* Nashville: Thomas Nelson, 1997.

Carson, D.A. *The Gagging of God: Christianity confronts pluralism.* Grand Rapids: Zondervan, 1996.

Central Intelligence Agency (CIA). *The World Factbook.* Internet 2006. http://odci.gov/cia/publications/factbook/geos/gz.html (Gaza) http://odci.gov/cia/publications/factbook/geos/we.html (West Bank)

Chafer, Lewis Sperry. *Systematic Theology, Vols 1-8.* Grand Rapids, MI: Kregel Publications, 1948.

Cohen, Gary. *Understanding Revelation.* Chicago: Moody Press, 1968.

Comay, Joan and Ronald Brownrigg. *Who's Who in the Bible: Two volumes in one.* New York: Barnes & Noble Books,1971.

Congdon, Robert. "Art Thou He That Should Come?" in *Israel My Glory.* Westville, NJ: Friends of Israel Gospel Ministry, Jan/Feb 2002, p 13.

Couch, Mal, ed. *Dictionary of Premillennial Theology.* Grand Rapids: Kregel, 1996.

Cruden, Alexander. *Cruden's Complete Concordance to the Old and New Testaments.* Grand Rapids: Zondervan, 1968.

Culver, Robert D. *Daniel and the Latter Days: A study in millennialism.* Chicago: Moody Press, 1954.

Dabbah, Ezra. "Letter" from Brooklyn, New York in *Newsweek,* April 29, 2002.

Dailey, Timothy. *The Gathering Storm.* Grand Rapids: Chosen Books, 1992.

Davidson, *Elishua. Islam Israel and the Last Days.* Eugene, OR: Harvest House Publishers, 1991.

D'Elia, John A. *A Place at the Table: George Eldon Ladd and the rehabilitation of evangelical scholarship in America.* New York: Oxford University Press, 2008.

DeHaan, M.R., *Revelation.* Grand Rapids:, MI: Zondervan, 1946.

DeLoach, Charles. *Seeds of Conflict.* Plainfield,NJ: Logos International, 1974.

Dockery, David S. and Timothy George. *The Great Tradition of Christian Thinking.* Wheaton IL: Crossway 2012.

Doron, Reuven. *One New Man.* Cedar Rapids, IA: Embrace Israel Ministries, 1999.

Dorries, David W. "The making of Smith Wigglesworth, Parts 1 and 2." from Assemblies of God *Heritage, Vol. 12, Nos. 3 and 4,* Fall 1992, pp 4-32 and 20-29. Springfield, MO: General Council of the Assemblies of God, 1992.

Dorsett, Lyle W. *A Passion for Souls: The Life of D. L. Moody.* Chicago: Moody Publishers, 1997.

Douglas, J. D. *The New International Dictionary of the Christian Church.* Grand Rapids: Zondervan, 1974.

du Plessis, David J. *The Spirit bade me go.* Plainfield NJ: Logos International,1970.

Dummelow, J. R., ed. *A Commentary on the Holy Bible: by various writers.* New York: Macmillan, 1936.

Eaton, Harriet. *Leviticus: Book of Sanctification: The Priest's Guide Book: Chapters One to Seven.* No publisher or date listed.

Eckstein, Yechiel, Rabbi. *Ask the Rabbi: Selected transcripts from Rabbi Yechiel Eckstein's radio program.* Chicago: The Fellowship of Christians and Jews, 1990.

_____. *How Firm a Foundation: A gift of Jewish wisdom for Christians and Jews.* Brewster, MA: Paraclete Press, 1997.

Edersheim, Alfred. *Old Testament Bible History.* Wilmington, DE: Associate Publishers and Authors, no date.

Eliade, Mircea. *The Myth of the Eternal Return: Or, cosmos and history.* Princeton, NJ: Princeton University Press, 1954.

Ellisen, Stanley A. *Biography of a Great Planet.* Wheaton, IL: Tyndale House, 1975.

Encyclopedia Brittanica, Fifteenth Edition, Macromedia—Knowledge in Depth. "Israel," Book 22:144-147. Chicago: Encyclopedia Brittanica Publications, 1997.

Engber, Daniel and Ron Stoddardt. "Are Snowflakes Really Different?" in *Slate* magazine. Washington Post. Newsweek Interactive Co. LLC: Explainer Dept. July 20, 2006. http://www.slate.com/id/2146238/

Enns, Paul. *The Moody Handbook of Theology.* Chicago: Moody Press, 1989.

Erickson, Millard J. A *Basic Guide to Eschatology: Making sense of the millennium.* Grand Rapids: Baker Books, 1998.

Esses, Michael. *Next Visitor to Planet Earth.* Plainfield, NJ: Logos International, 1975.

Evans, Pearl. *Marx or Jesus: Two Men—Two Plans.* San Diego: Small Helm Press, 1989.

Evans, Tony. *The Best Is Yet to Come: Bible prophecies through the ages.* Chicago: Moody Press, 2000.

Feder, Don. "Passover offers hope to each generation" in townhall.com. Boston: Creators Syndicate, Inc., March 27, 2002.

Fee, Gordon and Douglas Stuart. *How to Read the Bible for all its worth.* Grand Rapids, MI: Zondervan. 2003.

Feinberg, Charles Lee, ed. *Prophecy and the Seventies.* Chicago: Moody Press, 1971.

_____. "Where is the Modern Church Going?" in *Prophecy and the Seventies*. Charles Lee Feinberg, ed. Chicago: Moody Press, 1971.

_____. "Why Must Christ Return?" in *Prophecy and the Seventies*, Charles Lee Feinberg, ed. Chicago: Moody Press, 1971.

_____. *The Prophecy of Ezekiel*. Chicago: Moody Press, 1969.

_____. "Does the historical partial fulfillment permit a literal interpretation?" in Millennial Series: Part 17: The kingdom promises to David. *Bibliotheca Sacra* 110:438 (Apr 53) p 97.

Millennial Series: Part 18: The New Covenant with Israel. *Bibliotheca Sacra* 110:439 (Jul 53) p193.

Feis, Herbert. *The Birth of Israel: The tousled diplomatic bed*. New York: W.W. Norton, 1969.

Feltman, Melbourne I., Executive Director, *The Holy Scriptures: According to the Masoretic text*. Chicago: The Menorah Press, 1957.

Fields, Suzanne. "When God is in the Details" in Townhall.com. April 10, 2001.

Finney, Charles G. *Power from on High*. Clapman Crescent, London, S.W. 4: Victory Press

Fishbane, Michael, ed. *The Jewish Study Bible* with glossary from Accordance software. Oxford England: Oxford University Press.

Forbes.com from AP. May 10, 2006.
http://www.forbes.com/technology/feeds/ap/2006/05/10/ap2734504.html

Freeman, Hobart E. "The Problem of the efficacy of the Old Testament sacrifices" in Grace Journal 4:1 Winter 63 p 21-28. Grace Seminary: Grace Journal.

Fruchtenbaum, Arnold G. *Israelology*, excerpt from *Dictionary of Premillennial Theology*. Tustin, CA: Ariel Ministries, 1989.

Gaebelein, Arno. Quotation from article, "Arno Gaebelein" by Mal Couch in *Dictionary of Premillennial Theology*, ed. Mal Couch. Grand Rapids: Kregel Publications, 1996.

Gaebelein, Frank E., ed. *The Expositor's Bible Commentary for Macintosh*. Grand Rapids, MI: Zondervan Interactive, Accordance software 7.4.1, 2007.

Gannett, Alden. "Where Is the Promise of His Coming?" in *Prophecy and the Seventies*. Charles Lee Feinberg, ed. Chicago: Moody Press, 1971.

Gentry, Peter J. and Stephen J. Wellum. *God's Kingdom through God's Covenants: A concise biblical theology*. Wheaton, IL: Crossway, 2015.

Ger, Stephen C. "Zechariah: Minor prophet with a major message" in The *Conservative Theological Journal,* April 1999, p 89.

Ghazali, Said and Tim Butcher. "Night withdrawal from Gaza ends 38-year occupation" in *Telegraph.co.uk*, 7/25/06. Great Britain: Telegraph Group Limited 2006.
http://www.telegraph.co.uk/news/main.jhtml?xml=/news/2005/09/12/wmid12.xml

Golan Residence Committee. "The Story of the Golan" on the web: Web Golan, English edition, site visited April 23, 2002.
http://english.golan.org.il/ts.exe?tsurl=0.166.1189.0.0

Gray, James M. *Christian Workers' Commentary on the Whole Bible*. Old Tappan, NJ: Spire Books by Fleming H. Revell, 1971.

_____. *Synthetic Bible Studies*. NY: Fleming H. Revell, 1906.

Greenberg, Paul. "The Search: We leave Egypt tonight." Washington, D.C.: Heritage Foundation, March 26, 2002.
http://www.townhall.com/columnists/paulgreenberg/printpg20020326.shtml

Gross, Neil and Solon Simmons. "How Religious are America's College and University Professors?" Brooklyn, NY: Social Science Research Council (SSRC), Feb 6, 2007.
http://religion.ssrc.org/reforum/Gross_Simmons.pdf

Grun, Bernard. *The Timetables of History: A horizontal linkage of people and events*, 3rd ed. New York: Simon & Schuster/Touchstone, 1991.

Halley, Henry H. *Bible Handbook*. Chicago, Illinois: No publisher given, 1955, 1927.

Ham, Mary Katherine. "The Last Stand of the West" in *Townhall*, Magazine. Nashville, TN: Townhall, June 2008, p 42.

Hammond, Inc. *Historical World Atlas: Volume Two*. Newsweek, 1991.

Hanh, Thich Nhat. *Living Buddha, Living Christ*. New York: Riverhead Books/Putnam's Sons, 1995.

Harkabi, Yehoshafat. *Israel's Fateful Hour*. New York: Harper & Row,1988.

Hart, Benjamin. *Radical Islam vs. America*. Ottawa, IL: Green Hill Pulishers, 2003.

Hartman, Fred. *Zechariah: Israel's Messenger of the Messiah's Triumph*. Bellmawr, NJ: The Friends of Israel, 1994.

Heilman Samuel C. and Steven M. Cohen. *Cosmopolitans and Parochials: Modern Orthodox Jews in America*. Chicago: University of Chicago Press, 1989.

Henry, Matthew, Thomas Scott, et al. *The Pocket Bible Commentary, Volume 6: Lamentations—Malachi*. Chicago: Moody Press. No copyright.

Hertzberg, Arthur. "The Tragedy of Victory" in *A Middle East Reader*, eds. Robert B. Silvers and Barbara Epstein. New York: New York Review of Books, 1995.

Herzig, Steve. "How Many Gods?" in *Israel My Glory*. Westville, NJ: The Friends of Israel Gospel Ministry Jan/Feb 2009.

_____.*Jewish Culture and Customs: A sampler of Jewish life*. Bellmawr, NJ: Friends of Israel Ministry, 1997.

Hiebert, Paul G. "Conversion and Worldview Transformation" in *International Journal of Frontier Missions*. Eds. Ralph Winter and Rory Clark. Pasadena, CA: *Vol 14.2 Apr-June 1997.*

Hoehner, Harold W. "Evidence from Revelation 20" in *The Coming Millennial Kingdom*. Eds. Donald Campblell and Jeffrey Townsend. Grand Rapids, MI: Kregel Publications, 1997.

Holahan, David. April 27, 2008 article, "'History of the first Arab-Israeli War' Gives Thorough Overview of Israeli-Palestine Relations" in *The Hartford Courant*. Hartford, CT: The Hartford Courant. 2008.
http://www.courant.com/features/booksmags/hc-israel0427.artapr27,0,1135119.story

Holdcroft, L. Thomas. *The Doctrine of God*. Oakland, CA 94612: Western Book Company, 1978.

_____. *The Holy Spirit: A Pentecostal interpretation*. Abbotsford, Canada: CeeTeC Publishing., 1962, 1971, 1999.

Hooker, Richard. World Civilizations: European Middle Ages. "The Byzantine Empire: An Overview." Washington State University Online, ©1996.
http://www.wsu.edu.8080/~dee/MA/BYZ.HTM.

Hoyt, Herman A. *The End Times*. Winona Lake, IN: BMH Books, 1969.

Hunt, Dave. *The Cult Explosion*. Eugene, OR: Harvest House, 1980.

Hullinger, Jerry M. "The Problem of Animal Sacrifices in Ezekiel 40-48." in *The Theological Journal Library*. Dallas: *Bibliotheca Sacra* 152:607, July 1995, 279-289.

Hutchins, Noah W. *Infoplease website from Columbia Electronic Encyclopedia*. "Arab-

Israeli Wars." NY: Columbia University Press, 2007
http://www.infoplease.com/ce6/history/A0856666.html

_____. "Arafat and the Abomination of Desolation" from map in *Prophetic Observer*, Oklahoma City: March 1995.

_____. *Rapture and Resurrection*. Oklahoma City: Hearthstone Publishing, Ltd., 1992.

Ibach, Robert D. Review of "The Sabbatical/Jubilee Cycle and the Seven-Year Famine in Egypt" by Calum Carmichael, 1999, Biblica 80: 224-39. Ibach review in *Bibliotheca Sacra* 157:625 Jan 2000.

Ironside, H. A. *Isaiah*. Neptune, NJ: Loizeaux Brothers, 1952

_____. *Daniel the Prophet*. Neptune, NJ: Loizeaux Brothers, 1920.

_____. *Revelation: An Ironside Expository Commentary*, Grand Rapids, MI: Kregel, 1920, 2004.

_____. *Not Wrath But Rapture: Or, will the church participate in the great tribulation?* Neptune, NJ: Loizeaux Brothers, No copyright listed.

Jacobsen, Henry. *The War We Can't Lose*. Wheaton, IL: Victor Books, division of SP Publications.

James, William T. *Prophecy at Ground Zero: From today's Mideast madness to the second coming of Christ.* Lancaster, PA: Starburst Publishers, 2002.

Jamieson, Robert and A. R. Fausset and David Brown. Bible Commentary, Vols. 1-3. Peabody, MA.: Hendrickson Publishers, Inc., pubic domain, fourth printing, March 2008.

Jelinek, A. "Why be moral? The contradiction of postmodern morality in America" in *Apologetics of Theological Journals Library* (Accordance 6.7) [JCA 1:1]. Summer 1997.

Jensen. Irving L. *Leviticus: A self-study guide*. Chicago: Moody Bible Institute, 1967.

_____. Minor Prophets of Judah: A self-study guide. Chicago: Moody Bible Institute, 1975.

Jeremiah, David with C. C. Carlson. *The Handwriting on the Wall*. Dallas: Word, 1992.

Jewish Agency for Israel. Article under *Israel and Zionism* by Sergio della Pergola: "World Jewish Population." Jerusalem, Israel, 2002.
http://www.jafi.org.il/education/100/concepts/demography/demjpop.html

Jews for Jesus Newsletter. Unidentified author. "From Passover to Pentecost," Volume 10:5766, p 4. San Francisco: Jews for Jesus: June 2006.

Jews for Jesus:. *Stories of Jews for Jesus*: Ed.: Matt Sieger. A Story by Richard and Monica Harvey. San Francisco: Purple Pomegranate Productions, 2010.

Jones, Peter. *Spirit Wars: Pagan revival in Christian America*. Mulkiteo, Washington: WinePress; Escondido, CA: Main Entry Editions, 1997.

Jordan, Joe and Tom Davis. *Countdown to Armageddon*. Eugene, OR: Harvest House, 1999. XX

Josephus, Flavius. *The Works of Flavius Josephus, the Learned and Authentic Jewish Historian:* Antiquities Book XVIII, Chapter III, #3, p 392. Halifax: Milner and Sowerby, 1864.

Appendix, Dissertation I: "The testimonies of Josephus concerning Jesus Christ, John the Baptist, and James the Just, vindicated," pp 665-673. Halifax: Milner and Sowerby, 1864.

Kaiser, Walter C., Jr. *The Messiah in the Old Testament: Studies in Old Testament biblical theology*. Grand Rapids: Zondervan, 1955.

Keil, C. F. and Franz Delitzsch. *Commentary on the Old Testament* in Accordance Jewish Collection 4. Accordance Bible Software, 2005.

Kim, Esther Ahn. *If I Perish*. Chicago: Moody Bible Institute, 1977. (Reprinted by Moody Publishers).

Kincheloe, Raymond McFarland. *A Personal Adventure in Prophecy: Understanding Revelation*. Wheaton, IL: Tyndale House, 1974.

Knapp, Christopher. *The Kings of Judah and Israel*. Neptune, NJ: Loizeaux Brothers, First edition, 1909.

Kohlenberger III, John R. *The Interlinear NIV Hebrew-English Old Testament*. Grand Rapids: Zondervan, 1987.

Kopecky, Donald W. "Salvation in the tribulation Part 1" in Bibliotheca Sacra 109:435 (Jul 52) p 266.

Kreloff, Steven A. *God's Plan for Israel: A study of Romans 9-11*. Neptune, NJ: Loizeaux, 1995.

Kuhlman, Paul and John I. Paton. *Outline Studies of Prophetic Truths*. Lincoln, Nebraska: Back to the Bible Broadcast, 1959.

Ladd, George Eldon. *The Last Things: An eschatology for laymen*. Grand Rapids: Eerdmans, 1978.

_____. *The Blessed Hope*. Grand Rapids, MI: W. E. Eerdmans, 1956, pp 19-60.

LaHaye, Tim and Ed Hindson. *The Popular Bible Prophecy Commentary: Understanding the meaning of every prophetic passage*. Eugene, OR: Harvest House 2006.

_____. *The Beginning of the End*. Wheaton, IL: Tyndale House, 1972.

Lander, Eric S. Use of DNA in identification" at the "Winding Your Way through DNA" symposium, 1992 by Access Excellence at the National Health Museum. San Francisco: University of California San Francisco. Access Excellence: ©1994-2007. http://www.accessexcellence.org/MTC/copyright.html

Larkin, Clarence. *The Book of Revelation*. Philadelphia: Rev. Clarence Larkin Estate, 1919.

_____. *The Second Coming of Christ*. Glenside, PA Rev. Clarence Larkin Estate, 1918-1922.

LaSor, William Sanford. *Israel: A biblical view*. Grand Rapids: Eerdmans, 1976.

Levine, Meyer and Toby Kurzband. *The Story of the Synagogue* from the Jewish Heritage Series. New York: Behrman House, 1957.

Levitt, Zola. *Broken Branches: Has the church replaced Israel?* Dallas: Zola Levitt Ministries, 1995.

Levy, David. "Marriage Supper of the Lamb, Revelation 19:1-10" in *Israel My Glory* magazine. Bellmawr, NJ: Friends of Israel Ministry, June/July 1998.

_____, *Guarding the Gospel of Grace*. Bellmawr, NJ: *The Friends of Israel*, 1997.

_____. *Malachi: Messenger of rebuke and renewal*. New Jersey: Friends of Israel Ministry, 1992.

_____. *Joel: The Day of the Lord*. Bellmawr, NJ: The Friends of Israel Ministry, 1987.

Levy, David I. *Gray Matter: A neurosurgeon discovers the power of prayer… one patient at a time*. Carol Stream, IL: Tyndale House Publishers, 2011.

Lewis, C. S. *Mere Christianity*. New York: MacMillan Company, 1952.

Library of Congress Country Studies. *Country Studies/Area Handbook Program*. Washington, D.C.: Federal Research Division of Library of Congress, 1998.

Liebman, Charles. *The Ambivalent American Jew*. Philadelphia: Jewish Publication

Society, 1973 quoted in Samuel Heilm and and Steven Cohen, *Cosmopolitans and Parochials: Modern Orthodox Jews in America*. Chicago: University of Chicago Press, 1989.

Linsted, Rob and Emil Gaverluk. *Why the Church Will Not Go through the Tribulation*. Oklahoma City: Southwest Radio Church, 1982.

Lippman, Thomas W. *Understanding Islam: An introduction to the Muslim World*, Revised edition. New York: Penguin Mentor Book, 1990.

Lipset, Seymour Martin and Earl Raab. *Jews and the New American Scene*. Cambridge: Harvard University Press, 1995.

Lowith, Karl. *Meaning in History*. Chicago: Phoenix Books of The University of Chicago Press, 1949.

Ludwigson, R. *A Survey of Bible Prophecy*. Grand Rapids: Zondervan, 1975.

Lutzer, Erwin W. *Hitler's Cross*. Chicago: Moody Press, 1995.

MacArthur, Jack. *Expositional Commentary on Revelation*. Eugene, OR: Certajn Sound, 1973.

MacPherson, Dave. *The Incredible Cover-Up: The true story of the pre-trib rapture*. Plainfield, NJ: Logos International, 1975.

Mackintosh, C. H. *Notes on the Book of Genesis*. New York: Loizeaux Brothers, 1880.
_____. *Notes on the Book of Leviticus*. Neptune, NJ: Loizeaux Brothers, 1880.

Marshall, Alfred. *The Interlinear Greek-English New Testament*. Grand Rapids: Zondervan, 1959.

Martin, Alfred and John Martin. *Isaiah: The glory of the Messiah*. Chicago: Moody Press, 1983.

Mason, Clarence E., Jr. "The Names of Christ in Revelation" in *Prophecy and the Seventies*, Charles Lee Feinberg, ed. Chicago: Moody Press, 1971.

Mason, Clarence E., Jr. "The Believer's Resurrection Body" in *Prophecy and the Seventies*, Charles Lee Feinberg, ed. Chicago: Moody Press, 1971.

Maxcy, Karen. "The Middle East: Religion, Politics and Peace: A conversation with Professor Carla Klausner, Department of History" in *Perspectives*. Kansas City: University of Missouri, Spring 2002.

Mazour, Anatole G. *A World History: Men and nations*. New York: Harcourt Brace & World, 1968.

McClain, Alva J. *Daniel's Prophecy of the Seventy Weeks*. Grand Rapids: Zondervan, 1940.

McGee, J. Vernon. *The Prophet Ezekiel*. Nashville, TN: Thomas Nelson, 1991.
_____. *Thru the Bible with J. Vernon McGee, Volumes I-V*. Nashville: Thomas Nelson, 1981-83.
_____. *Delving Through Daniel*. Pasadena, CA: Through the Bible Books, Fourth Edition: 1971, no copyright date.

McQuaid, Elwood. *Zvi: The miraculous story of triumph over the Holocaust*. Bellmawr, NJ: Friends of Israel Gospel Ministry, 2000.

Mears, Henriettta C. *What the Bible is All About*. Glendale, CA: Regal Books, a Division of G/L Publications, 1966.

Medved, Michael. "Why They Fight: The story of the Arab/Israeli conflict" on the Michael Medved Show. 2 CD's, Product MMX1N-011/012. Seattle: Tree Farm Communications Inc., Nov. 23, 2001.

Menkus, Belden, ed. assisted by Rabbi Arthur Gilbert. *Meet the American Jew*. Nashville: Broadman Press, 1963.

Meyer, Lawrence. *Israel Now: Portrait of a troubled land*. New York: Delacorte Press,

1982.

MidEast Web and Ami Isseroff. "Population of Palestine Prior to 1948." Publisher: Mideast Web and Ami Isseroff, 2002-07.

Missler, Charles W. "Pentecost, the Feast of" in *Dictionary of Premillennial Theology*. Grand Rapids: Kregel Publications, 1996.

Montgomery, John Warwick. *The Suicide of Christian Theology*. Minneapolis: Bethany Fellowship, 1970.

Morey, Robert. *The Trinity: Evidence and issues*. Grand Rapids: World, 1996.

Morgan, G. Campbell. *The Parables and Metaphors of our Lord*. Old Tappan, NJ: Fleming H. Revell Co., 1943.

Morris, Tom. *Philosophy for Dummies*. Foster City, CA: IDG Books, 1999.

Murray, Andrew. *The Holiest of All: An exposition of the epistle to the Hebrews*. Grand Rapids: Fleming H. Revell, 1993.

_____. *Revival*. Minneapolis: Bethany House, 1990.

_____. *Absolute Surrender*. Chicago: Moody Press, No copyright date.

Nault, William H., ed. *The World Book Encyclopedia*. Chicago: Field Enterprises Educational Coporation, 1974.

Nave, Orville J., Compiler. *Nave's Topical Bible*. Nashville: The Southwestern Company, 1962.

Nee, Watchman. *Sit, Walk, Stand*. Fort Washington, PA: Christian Literature Crusade, 1957.

_____. *Twelve Baskets Full*, Vol 1. Christian Literature Crusade. 1966.

Neff, vid. "Beyond Self-Help Chatter." *Christianity Today*. October 23, 2000: . pp. 86,87.

NET Bible Notes (New English Translation). Biblical Studies Press, L.L.C. In *Accordance, Jewish Collection 4*. Accordance software v7.4, 1996-2005. www.netbible,com

Newell, William R. *The Book of the Revelation*. Chicago: Moody Press, 1935.

New York International Bible Society. *The Holy Bible: New International Version of* (NIV). Grand Rapids: Zondervan Bible Publishers. Software, *Accordance* 3.6.

Olford, Stephen F. "The Judgment Seat of Christ" in *Prophecy and the Seventies*, Charles Lee Feinberg, ed. Chicago: Moody Press, 1971.

Pagels, Heinz. *The Dreams of Reason*. New York: Simon and Schuster, 1988.

Palestine Facts. "British Mandate: British Mandate Overview," Palestine Facts 2007. http://www.palestinefacts.org/pf_early_palestine_name_origin.php

------. "Early History, Palestine Origin," Palestine Facts 2006.

Penn-Lewis, Jessie. *The Centrality of the Cross*. Fort Washington, PA: Christian Literature Crusade. No date; in the public domain.

Penrose, Roger. *The Emperor's New Mind: Concerning computers, minds, and the laws of physics*. New York: Oxford University Press, 1989.

Pentecost, J. Dwight. *Thy Kingdom Come: Tracing God's kingdom program and covenant promises throughout history*. Grand Rapids: Kregel, 1995.

_____. *Prophecy for Today: The Middle East crisis and the future of the world*. Grand Rapids, MI: Zondervan, 1961.

_____. *Things to Come*. Grand Rapids: Zondervan, 1958.

Peres, Shimon. Speech on "Combating terrorism." before American Israeli Public Affairs Committee (AIPAC), April 21, 2002.

Peters, George N. H. *The Theocratic Kingdom*. Grand Rapids: Kregel, 1952.

Pick, Aaron. *Dictionary of Old Testament Words for English Readers*. Grand Rapids:

Kregel, 1845.

Pickup, Martin. "New Testament Interpretation of the Old Testament: The theological rationale of Midrashic exegesis" in *The Journal of the Evangelical Theological Society*. Lynchburg, VA: The Evangelical Theological Society, June 2008.

Poythress, Vern S. *Understanding Dispensationalists*. Grand Rapids: Zondervan, 1987,

Price, Randall. *Unholy War*. Eugene, OR: Harvest House, 2001.

Price, Stanley E. "The Church in Revelation" in *The Gospel Truth*. Oklahoma City: Southwest Radio Church. June 1989.

Price, Walter K. *Jesus' Prophetic Sermon: The Olivet key to Israel, the church, and the nations*. Chicago: Moody Press, 1972.

Queens College Hillel. "30% of Nobel Prize Winners in Medicine are Jews." Flushing, NY: IsraelWire 3/16/year unknown. http://www.qchillel.org/news/031699.htm

Reisman, Judith. *Kinsey: Crimes and Consequences*. Crestwood KY: First Principles Press, 1998, 2000.

Riskin, Rabbi Shlomo. "Timeless Message: Dealing with Present by Understanding the Past," *JUF News*, May 1993, p. 51 in *The Feasts of Israel* by Bruce Scott. Bellmawr, NJ: The Friends of Israel Gospel Ministry, 1997.

Rogers, Adrian. *Unveiling the End Times in Our Time: The Triumph of the Lamb in Revelation*. Nashville, TN: B&H Publishing Group, 2004.

Rose, Tom. "Legacy of a Terrorist." *Israel My Glory.*. Bellmawr, NJ: The Friends of Israel Gospel Ministry: Sept/Oct 2002, p 16.

Rosen, Moishe. "Moishe's Musings... on Labels" in Jews for Jesus newsletter, San Francisco, CA: Jews for Jesus, February 2010.

_____. "Moishe's Musings" in Jews for Jesus newsletter. San Francisco, CA: Jews for Jesus, June 2007.

_____. Rosen, Moishe. "A Message from Moishe" in Jews for Jesus newsletter. San Francisco, California: Jews for Jesus, January 2003.

Rosen, Moishe and William Proctor. *Stories of Jews for Jesus*. Old Tappan, NJ: Fleming H. Revell, 1973,1978, 1984.

Rosenberg, Joel C. *Inside the Revolution: How the Followers of Jihad, Jefferson & Jesus Are Battling to Dominate the Middle East and Transform the World*. Carol Stream, IL: Tyndale House Publishers, Inc., 1960... 1995.

Russell, D.S. *The Method and Message of Jewish Apocalyptic*. Philadelphia: Westminster, 1964.

Ryrie, Charles and Joe Jordan and Tom Davis, eds. *Countdown to Armageddon: The Final Battle and Beyond*. Eugene, OR: Harvest House, 1999.

Sarna, Nahum M. *Exploring Exodus: The heritage of biblical Israel*. New York: Schocken Books, 1986.

Saucy, Robert L. *The Case for Progressive Dispensationalism*. E-book. Grand Rapids, MI: Zondervan, 1993.

Schreiner, Thomas R. "Some Reflections on *Sola Fide*." Ed, Andreas Kostenburger, Wake Forest, N.C.: JETS, Journal of the Evangelical Theological Society. Volume 58 No. 1, March, 2015.

Scofield, C. I. *The New Scofield Study Bible* (KJV). New York: Oxford University Press, 1998.

Scott, Bruce. *The Feasts of Israel: Seasons of the Messiah*. Bellmawr, NJ: The Friends of Israel Gospel Ministry, 1997.

Seitz, Christopher R. and Craig Bartholomew. *The Character of Christian Scripture:*

The Significance of a Two-Testament Bible. Ada, MI: Baker Publishing Group 49301, October 2011.

Sheridan, Susan Rich. *Drawing/Writing and the new illiteracy: Where verbal meets visual.* Amherst, MA: *Drawing/Writing Publications*, 1997, "Holographs" in Appendix.

Showers, Renald E. *There Really Is a Difference! A comparison of covenant and dispensational theology.* Bellmawr, NJ: The Friends of Israel Gospel Ministry, 1990.

_____. *The Most High God: A commentary on the book of Daniel.* Bellmawr, NJ: The Friends of Israel, 1982.

Sieger, Matt, ed. *Stories of Jews for Jesus.* San Francisco: Purple Pomegranate Productions. 2010.

Silvers, Robert B. and Barbara Epstein, eds. *A Middle East Reader: Selected Essays on the Middle East from the New York Review of Books.* New York: The New York Review of Books, 1991.

Simpson, James. "Trail: The Arab-Israeli Conflict: Resolution remains elusive in the tinderbox of the Middle East" in Time-Europe Web Exclusive, online April 24, 2002.
http://www.time.com/time/europe/timetrails/israel/

Smith, Dinitia. "Philosopher Gamely In Defense Of His Ideas," New York: ©New York Times, May 30, 1998, sect. B., p. 7.

Smith, Hannah Whitall. *The Christian's Secret of a Happy Life.* Westwood, NJ; Fleming H. Revel, 1952.

Smith, Jerome H., ed. *The New Treasury of Scripture Knowledge.* Nashville: Thomas Nelson, 1992.

Smith, Wilbur. *You Can Know the Future.* Glendale, CA: Regal Books Division, G/L Publications, 1971.

Spangler, Ann and Lois Tverberg. *Sitting at the Feet of Rabbi Jesus: How the Jewishness of Jesus can transform your faith.* Grand Rapids:: Zondervan, 2009.

Spencer, William David. "An Evangelical Statement on the Trinity" in *Man, Woman, and the Triune God.* Minneapolis, MN: A special edition journal of Christians for Biblical Equality, published for Evangelical Theological Society members, 2011.

Spurgeon, C. H. *Faith's Checkbook.* Pearl Evans, ed.. San Diego: Small Helm Press, 1988.

_____. *All of Grace.* Ebook in public domain: www.philmorgan.org.

Stallard, Mike. "Progressive Dispensationalism." Clarks Summit, PA: Baptist Bible Seminary, no date.

Stedman, Ray C. *Authentic Christianity:* "To Jew and Gentile," Revelation 7.1-17 in Revelation Series." Mount Hermon, CA: Ray Stedman Ministries, 2010.
http://www.raystedman.org/new-testament/revelation/to-jew-and-gentile

Steinberger, G. *In the Footprints of the Lamb.* Minneapolis: Bethany Fellowship, 1936.

Stern, David H. *Jewish New Testament Commentary.* Clarksville, MD: Jewish New Testament Publications, 1996.

Stevens, Charles H. "The Church of Christ and the Kingdom of Christ in Contrast" in *Prophecy and the Seventies*, Charles Lee Feinberg, ed. Chicago: Moody Press, 1971.

_____. "Is God Through with the Jew?" in *Prophecy and the Seventies*, Charles Lee Feinberg, ed. Chicago: Moody Press, 1971.

Stormont, George. *A Man Who Walked with God.* Tulsa, OK: Harrison House, 1989.

Strong, James. *Strong's Exhaustive Concordance of the Bible.* Grand Rapids: World, 1986.

Tan, Paul Lee. *The Interpretation of Prophecy.* Dallas: Bible Communications, 1974.

Tatford, Frederick A. *God's Program of the Ages.* Grand Rapids: Kregel, 1967.

Telchin, Stan. *Betrayed!* Grand Rapids: Chosen Books, 1981.

The American Jewish Year Book 2003, p160. Philadelphia, Jerusalem: Jewish publication Society of America. Made available by the North American Jewish Data Bank with permission of the American Jewish Committee and the editors of the American Jewish Yearbook.
>   http://www.jewishdatabank.org/AJYB/AJY-2003.pdf
>   http://www.jewishdatabank.org

The Jewish Agency for Israel. "Global Overview" under "Israel and Zionism, "in "World Jewish Population (2002)" by Sergio DellaPergola. New York: *American Jewish Year Book 2002,* 102.
>   http://www.jafi.org.il/education/100/concepts/demography/demjpop.html

Thomson, Clive A. "The necessity of blood sacrifices in Ezekiel's temple" in Bibliotheca Sacra 123;491 p 237. Dallas, Texas: Dallas Theological Seminary July 1966.

Tidwell, J. B. *The Bible Book by Book.* Michigan: Eerdmans, 17th printing 1975.

Tinder, Glenn. *Political Thinking: The perennial questions.* New York: HarperCollins, 1991.

Todd, Paul Lewis, General Editor. *Men and Nations: A World Hisotry.* New York: Harcourt, Brace, and World, 1968.

U.S. State Department. "The Story of the Golan" on the web: Golan Residence Committee, Web Golan, English edition.

U.S. State Department Background Notes 1998. "Israel." Internet: WorldRover, 1998.
>   http://www.worldrover.com/history/israel_history.html

Vine, W. E. *An Expository Dictionary of New Testament Words.* Old Tappan, NJ: Fleming H. Revell, 1966.

Waller, Douglas. "The Peace Breakdown: The White House plays a risky game at Camp David - and loses. Yet peace hopes stay alive" in *Time*: Camp David, August 7, 2000.
>   http://www.time.com/time/europe/timetrails/israel/is000807.html

Walvoord, John F.

_____. *Armageddon, Oil and the Middle East Crisis.* Grand Rapids: Zondervan, 1984.

_____. *Matthew: Thy Kingdom Come.* Chicago: Moody Press,1974.

_____. *Daniel, The Key to Prophetic Revelation"A commentary.* Chicago: Moody Press, 1971.

_____.*The Millennial Kingdom.* Grand Rapids, MI: Zondervan, 1959.

Walvoord, John F. and Roy B. Zuck, eds. and writers. *The Bible Knowledge Commentary / New Testament / Old Testament: An Exposition of the Scriptures by Dallas Seminary Faculty.* Colorado Springs, CO: Victor, Cook Communications Ministries, 1983, 2004.

Wells, David F. *No Place for Truth: Or whatever happened to evangelical theology?* Grand Rapids: William B. Eerdmans, 1993.

Whitcomb, John C. "Christ's Atonement and Animal Sacrifices in Israel." Winona Lake, IN: *Grace Theological Journal* 6.2 (A985): 201-217, Fall 1985. The Theological Journal Library. Dallas: Accordance program, 2005.

Wiersbe, Warren W. *The Essential Everyday Bible Commentary.* Nashville: Thomas Nelson Publishers, 1993.

Wigglesworth, Smith. *Greater Works: Experiencing God's Power.* New Kensington, Pennsylvania: Whitaker House, 1998/99.

Wight, Fred H. *Devotional Studies of Old Testament Types.* Chicago: Moody Press, 1956.

Williams, Gary J. "Penal Substitution: A Response to Recent Criticisms." Andreas J. Kostenberger, ed., *Journal of Evangelical Theological Society,* Volume 50, No. 1, Lynchburg, VA: JETS, March 2007.

Willmington, H. L. *The King is Coming: An outline study of the last days.* Wheaton, IL: Tyndale House, 1973..

Wood, Leon J. *The Bible and Future Events: An introductory survey of Last Day events.* Grand Rapids: Academie Books of Zondervan, 1973.

Woodward, Kenneth L. "Overcoming Sin," 36, 37 in *Newsweek,* May 21, 2001.

World book Encyclopedia. Chicago: Field Enterprises Educational Corporation, 1974.

Wright, N.T. Book Review of *How God Became King: The Forgotten Story of the Gospels.* NY: HarperOne, 2012, xvii + 282 pp. Review is in JETS, Vol 56, No 1, May 2013.

Vine, W. E. *An Expository Dictionary of New Testament Words.* Old Tappan, NJ: Fleming H. Revell, 1940.

Young, Edward J. *The Book of Isaiah, Volumes 1-3.* Grand Rapids: William B. Eerdmans, 1972.

Young, Robert. *Young's Literal Translation of the Bible.* Grand Rapids: Baker Book House, 1898.

Zacharias, Ravi. *Deliver Us from Evil: Restoring the soul in a disintegrating culture.* Nashville: Thomas Nelson, 1998.

63256762R00215

Made in the USA
Middletown, DE
25 August 2019